HUTCHINSON

Dictionary of
20th Century
World History

Titles in this series

Dictionary of Abbreviations
Dictionary of Biology
Dictionary of Chemistry
Dictionary of Classical Music
Dictionary of Computing and Multimedia
Guide to Countries of the World
Dictionary of Geography
Dictionary of Mathematics
Dictionary of Physics
Dictionary of Science
Dictionary of World War I
Dictionary of World War II
Dictionary of 20th Century World History
Dictionary of Battles
On This Day
Chronology of World Events

Family Encyclopedia

HUTCHINSON

Dictionary of
20th Century
World History

BROCKHAMPTON PRESS
LONDON

Helicon Publishing Ltd
42 Hythe Bridge Street
Oxford OX1 2EP

Printed and bound in Great Britain by
Mackays of Chatham Plc,
Chatham, Kent

This edition published 1997 by
Brockhampton Press Ltd
20 Bloomsbury Street
London WC1B 3QA
(*a member of the Hodder Headline PLC Group*)

ISBN 1-86019-578-4

British Cataloguing in Publication Data

A catalogue record for this book is available
from the British Library

A

Abbas II Hilmi 1874–1944. Last ◊khedive (viceroy) of Egypt, 1892–1914. On the outbreak of war between Britain and Turkey in 1914, he sided with Turkey and was deposed following the establishment of a British protectorate over Egypt.

Abd el-Krim el-Khettabi 1881–1963. Moroccan chief known as the 'Wolf of the Rif' as many of the Arabs came from the Rif Mountains. With his brother Muhammad, he led the *Rif revolt* against the French and Spanish invaders, inflicting disastrous defeat on the Spanish at Anual in 1921, but surrendered to a large French army under Pétain in 1926. Banished to the island of Réunion, he was released in 1947 and died in voluntary exile in Cairo.

abdication crisis in British history, the constitutional upheaval of the period 16 Nov 1936 to 10 Dec 1936, brought about by the English king Edward VIII's decision to marry Wallis Simpson, an American divorcee. The marriage of the 'Supreme Governor' of the Church of England to a divorced person was considered unsuitable and the king was finally forced to abdicate on 10 Dec and left for voluntary exile in France. He was created Duke of Windsor and married Mrs Simpson on 3 June 1937.

Abdul-Hamid II 1842–1918. Last sultan of Turkey 1876–1909. In 1908 the ◊Young Turks under Enver Pasha forced Abdul-Hamid to restore the constitution of 1876 and in 1909 insisted on his deposition. He died in confinement. For his part in the ◊Armenian massacres suppressing the revolt of 1894–96 he was known as 'the Great Assassin'; his actions still motivate Armenian violence against the Turks.

Abdullah ibn Hussein 1882–1951. King of Jordan from 1946. He worked with the British guerrilla leader T E ◊Lawrence in the Arab revolt of World War I. Abdullah became king of Transjordan 1946; on the incorporation of Arab Palestine (after the 1948–49 Arab–Israeli War) he renamed the country the Hashemite Kingdom of Jordan. He was assassinated.

Abdullah Sheik Muhammad 1905–1982. Indian politician, known as the 'Lion of Kashmir'. He headed the struggle for constitutional government against the Maharajah of Kashmir, and in 1948, following a coup, became prime minister. He agreed to the accession of the state to India, but was dismissed and imprisoned from 1953 (with brief intervals) until 1966, when he called for Kashmiri self- determination. He became chief minister of Jammu and Kashmir 1975, accepting the sovereignty of India.

Abkhazia autonomous republic in Georgia, situated on the Black Sea. The region has been the scene of secessionist activity on the part of the minority Muslim Abkhazi community since 1989, culminating in the republic's declaration of independence 1992. Georgian troops invaded and took control Aug 1992, but secessionist guerrillas subsequently gained control of the northern half of the republic.

Acheson Dean (Gooderham) 1893–1971. US politician. As undersecretary of state 1945–47 in ◊Truman's Democratic administration, he was associated with George C Marshall in preparing the ◊Marshall Plan, and succeeded him as secretary of state 1949–53.

Action Française French extreme nationalist political movement founded 1899, first led by Charles Maurras (1868–1952). It stressed the essential unity of all French people in contrast to the socialist doctrines of class warfare. Its influence peaked in the 1920s.

Adams Gerry (Gerard) 1948– . Northern Ireland politician, president of Provisional Sinn Féin (the political wing of the IRA) from 1978. He was elected member of Parliament for Belfast West 1983 but declined to take up his Westminster seat, stating that he did not believe in the British government. He has been criticized for failing to denounce IRA violence. He was interned in the 1970s because of his connections with the IRA, and later released.

Addams Jane 1860–1935. US sociologist and campaigner for women's rights. In 1889 she founded and led the social settlement of Hull House, Chicago, one of the earliest community centres. She was vice president of the National American Women Suffrage Alliance 1911–14, and in 1915 led the Women's Peace Party and the first Women's Peace Congress. She shared the Nobel Peace Prize 1931.

Adenauer Konrad 1876–1967. German Christian Democrat politician, chancellor of West Germany 1949–63. With the French president de Gaulle he achieved the postwar reconciliation of France and Germany and strongly supported all measures designed to strengthen the Western bloc in Europe.

Aehrenthal Count Aloys von 1854–1912. Foreign minister of Austria–Hungary during the ◊Bosnian Crisis of 1908.

aerial bombardment another name for ◊Blitzkrieg.

affirmative action government policy of positive discrimination that favours members of minority ethnic groups and women in such areas as employment and education, designed to counter the effects of long-term discrimination against them. In Europe, Sweden, Belgium, the Netherlands, and Italy actively promote affirmative action through legal and financial incentives.

Afghanistan mountainous, landlocked country in S central Asia, bounded N by Tajikistan, Turkmenistan, and Uzbekistan, W by Iran, and S and E by Pakistan and China.

chronology
1747 Afghanistan became an independent emirate.
1839–42 and 1878–80 Afghan Wars instigated by Britain to counter the threat to British India from expanding Russian influence in Afghanistan.
1919 Afghanistan recovered full independence following Third Afghan War.
1953 Lt-Gen Daud Khan became prime minister and introduced reform programme.
1963 Daud Khan forced to resign and constitutional monarchy established.
1973 Monarchy overthrown in coup by Daud Khan.
1978 Daud Khan ousted by Taraki and the Democratic Party of Afghanistan (PDPA).
1979 Taraki replaced by Hafizullah Amin; Soviet Union entered country to prop up government; they installed Babrak Karmal in power. Amin executed.
1986 Replacement of Karmal as leader by Dr ◊Najibullah Ahmadzai. Partial Soviet troop withdrawal.
1988 New non-Marxist constitution adopted.
1989 Complete withdrawal of Soviet troops; state of emergency imposed in response to intensification of civil war.
1990 PDPA renamed the Homeland Party; President Najibullah elected its president.

1991 UN peace plan accepted by President Najibullah but rejected by the ◊mujaheddin. US and Soviet military aid withdrawn. Mujaheddin began talks with Russians and Kabul government.

1992 April: Najibullah regime overthrown. June: after a succession of short-term presidents, Burhanuddin Rabbani named interim head of state; Islamic law introduced. Sept: Hezb-i-Islami barred from government participation after shell attacks on Kabul. Dec: Rabbani elected president for two-year term by constituent assembly.

1993 Jan: renewed bombardment of Kabul by Hezb-i-Islami and other rebel forces. Interim parliament appointed by constituent assembly. March: peace agreement signed between Rabbani and dissident mujaheddin leader Gulbuddin Hekmatyar, under which Hekmatyar to become prime minister.

African National Congress (ANC) multiracial nationalist organization formed in South Africa 1912 to extend the franchise to the whole population and end all racial discrimination there. Its president is Nelson ◊Mandela. Although originally nonviolent, the ANC was banned by the government from 1960 to Jan 1990, and in exile in Mozambique developed a military wing, *Umkhonto we Sizwe*, which engaged in sabotage and guerrilla training. The armed struggle was suspended Aug 1990 after the organization's headquarters were moved from Zambia to Johannesburg. Talks between the ANC and the South African government have taken place intermittently since Dec 1991, with the proposed aim of creating a nonracial constitution. In Oct 1992, accusations of inhumane treatment of prisoners held in ANC camps outside South Africa led Mandela to institute an inquiry and promise an end to such abuses.

African nationalism political movement for the unification of Africa. African nationalism has its roots among the educated elite (mainly 'returned' Americans of African descent and freed slaves or their descendants) in W Africa in the 19th century. Christian mission-educated, many challenged overseas mission control and founded independent churches. These were often involved in anticolonial rebellions, for example in Natal 1906 and Nyasaland 1915. The Kitwala (Watchtower Movement) and Kimbanguist churches provided strong support for the nationalist cause in the 1950s. Early African political organizations included the Aborigines Rights Protection Society in the Gold Coast 1897, the ◊African National Congress in South Africa 1912, and the National Congress of West Africa 1920.

After World War I nationalists fostered moves for self-determination. The ◊Fourteen Points encouraged such demands in Tunisia, and delegates to London 1919 from the Native National Congress in South Africa stressed the contribution to the war effort by the South African Native Labour Corps. Most nationalist groups functioned within the territorial boundaries of single colonies, for example the Tanganyika African Association and the Rhodesian Bantu Voters Association. One or two groups, including the National Congress of British West Africa, had wider pan-African visions. The first pan-African Congress was held in London 1900 and others followed after 1919.

Pan-African sentiment in Africa and the Americas was intensified with the Italian invasion of ◊Ethiopia in 1935. By 1939 African nationalist groups existed in nearly every territory of the continent. Africa's direct involvement in World War II, the weakening of the principal colonial powers, increasing anticolonialism from America (the ◊Atlantic Charter 1941 encouraged self-government), and Soviet criticism of imperialism inspired African nationalists.

Since 1958 pan-Africanism has become partially absorbed into wider Third World movements. In May 1963 it was decided to establish the ◊Organization of African Unity (OAU).

Afrika Korps German army in the western desert of North Africa 1941–43 during World War II, commanded by Field Marshal Erwin ◊Rommel. They were driven out of N Africa by May 1943.

Agadir Incident or the *Second Moroccan Crisis* international crisis provoked by Kaiser Wilhelm II of Germany, July–Nov 1911. By sending the gunboat *Panther* to demand territorial concessions from the French, he hoped to drive a wedge into the Anglo-French entente. In fact, German aggression during the second Moroccan crisis merely served to reinforce Anglo-French fears of Germany's intentions. The crisis gave rise to the term 'gunboat diplomacy'.

Aga Khan IV 1936–   . Spiritual head (*imam*) of the *Ismaili* Muslim sect. He succeeded his grandfather 1957.

agitprop Soviet government bureau established Sept 1920 in charge of Communist agitation and propaganda. The idea was developed by later left-wing groups in the West for the use of theatre and other entertainment to convey political messages.

Agnew Spiro 1918–   . US vice president 1969–73. A Republican, he was governor of Maryland 1966–69, and vice president under ◊Nixon. He took the lead in a campaign against the press and opponents of the ◊Vietnam War. Although he was one of the few administration officials not to be implicated in the ◊Watergate affair, he resigned 1973, shortly before pleading 'no contest' to a charge of income-tax evasion.

Ahmadiyya Islamic religious movement founded by Mirza Ghulam Ahmad (1839–1908). His followers reject the doctrine that Muhammad was the last of the prophets and accept Ahmad's claim to be the Mahdi and Promised Messiah. In 1974 the Ahmadis were denounced as non-Muslims by other Muslims.

air raid aerial attack, usually on a civilian target such as a factory, railway line, or communications centre. In World War II (1939–45), raids were usually made by bomber aircraft, but many thousands were killed in London 1944 by German V1 and V2 rockets. The air raids on Britain 1940–41 became known as *the Blitz*. The Allies made retaliatory raids over European cities 1942–45.

Alanbrooke Alan Francis Brooke, 1st Viscount Alanbrooke 1883–1963. British army officer, Chief of Staff in World War II and largely responsible for the strategy that led to the German defeat.

Albania country in SE Europe, bounded N and E by Yugoslavia, SE by Greece, and W and SW by the Adriatic Sea.

chronology
1912 Independence achieved from Turkey.
1925 Republic proclaimed.
1928–39 Monarchy of King ◊Zog.
1939–44 Under Italian and then German rule.
1946 Communist republic proclaimed under the leadership of Enver ◊Hoxha.
1949 Admitted into ◊Comecon.
1961 Break with Khrushchev's USSR.
1967 Albania declared itself the 'first atheist state in the world'.
1978 Break with 'revisionist' China.
1985 Death of Hoxha.
1987 Normal diplomatic relations restored with Canada, Greece, and West Germany.

1988 Attendance of conference of Balkan states for the first time since the 1930s.

1990 One-party system abandoned; first opposition party formed.

1991 April: Party of Labour of Albania (PLA) won first multiparty elections; Ramiz ◊Alia re-elected president; three successive governments formed. PLA renamed Socialist Party of Albania (PSS).

1992 Former communist officials arrested on corruption charges. Presidential elections won by Democratic Party of Albania (DP); Sali Berisha elected president. Alia charged with corruption and abuse of power; totalitarian and communist parties banned.

1993 Jan: Nexhmije Hoxha, widow of Enver Hoxha, sentenced to nine years' imprisonment for misuse of government funds 1985–90.

Albert I 1875–1934. King of the Belgians from 1909, the younger son of Philip, Count of Flanders, and the nephew of Leopold II. In 1900 he married Duchess Elisabeth of Bavaria. In World War I he commanded the Allied army that retook the Belgian coast in 1918.

Alcock John William 1892–1919. British aviator. On 14 June 1919, he and Arthur Whitten Brown (1886–1948) made the first nonstop transatlantic flight, from Newfoundland to Ireland.

Alessandri Palma Arturo 1868–1950. Chilean president 1920–25, 1932–37. Reforms proposed in his first presidential term were blocked by an opposition-controlled Congress. Forced into exile, he returned to achieve a measure of economic recovery at the expense of the repression of opponents, a policy which made him a controversial figure in Chilean history.

Alexander I Karageorgevich 1888–1934. Regent of Serbia 1912–21 and king of Yugoslavia 1921–34, as dictator from 1929. Second son of ◊Peter I, King of Serbia, he was declared regent for his father 1912 and on his father's death became king of the state of South Slavs—Yugoslavia—that had come into being 1918.

Alexander Obrenovich 1876–1903. King of Serbia from 1889 while still a minor, on the abdication of his father, King Milan. He took power into his own hands 1893 and in 1900 married a widow, Draga Mashin. In 1903 Alexander and his queen were murdered, and ◊Peter I Karageorgevich was placed on the throne.

Alexandra 1872–1918. Last tsarina of Russia 1894-1917. She was the former Princess Alix of Hessen and granddaughter of Britain's Queen

Victoria. She married ◊Nicholas II and, from 1907, fell under the spell of ◊Rasputin, a 'holy man' brought to the palace to try to cure her son of haemophilia. She was shot with the rest of her family by the ◊Bolsheviks in the Russian Revolution.

Alfaro Eloy 1842–1912. Ecuadorian general and politician, president 1895–1901, 1906–11. He was involved in various revolts before over-throwing President Luis Cordero 1895, backed by the military. Despite his liberal support, he was unable to avoid political conflict or run an orderly government.

Alfonsín Foulkes Raúl Ricardo 1927–   . Argentine politician, president 1983–89, leader of the moderate Radical Union Party (UCR). As president from the country's return to civilian government, he set up an investigation of the army's human-rights violations. Economic problems caused him to seek help from the International Monetary Fund and introduce austerity measures.

Alfonso XIII 1886–1941. King of Spain 1886–1931. He assumed power 1906 and married Princess Ena, granddaughter of Queen Victoria of the United Kingdom, in the same year. He abdicated 1931 soon after the fall of the Primo de Rivera dictatorship 1923–30 (which he supported), and Spain became a republic. His assassination was attempted several times.

Algeciras Conference international conference held Jan–April 1906 when France, Germany, Britain, Russia, and Austria–Hungary, together with the USA, Spain, the Low Countries, Portugal, and Sweden, met to settle the question of Morocco. The conference was prompted by increased German demands in what had traditionally been seen as a French area of influence, but it resulted in a reassertion of Anglo-French friendship and the increased isolation of Germany. France and Spain gained control of Morocco.

Algeria country in N Africa, bounded E by Tunisia and Libya, SE by Niger, SW by Mali and Mauritania, NW by Morocco, and N by the Mediterranean Sea.

chronology
1962 Independence achieved from France. Republic declared. Ahmed ◊Ben Bella elected prime minister.
1963 Ben Bella elected Algeria's first president.
1965 Ben Bella deposed by military, led by Colonel Houari ◊Boumédienne.

1976 New constitution approved.
1978 Death of Boumédienne.
1979 Benjedid ◊Chadli elected president. Ben Bella released from house arrest. National Liberation Front (FLN) adopted new party structure.
1981 Algeria helped secure release of US prisoners in Iran.
1983 Chadli re-elected.
1988 Riots in protest at government policies; 170 killed. Reform programme introduced. Diplomatic relations with Egypt restored.
1989 Constitutional changes proposed, leading to limited political pluralism.
1990 Fundamentalist Islamic Salvation Front (FIS) won Algerian municipal and provincial elections.
1991 Dec: FIS won first round of multiparty elections.
1992 Jan: Chadli resigned; military took control of government; Mohamed Boudiaf became president; FIS leaders detained. Feb: state of emergency declared. March: FIS ordered to disband. June: Boudiaf assassinated; Ali Kafi chosen as new head of state and Belnid Absessalem as prime minister.

Algiers, Battle of bitter conflict in Algiers 1954–62 between the Algerian nationalist population and the French colonial army and French settlers. The conflict ended with Algerian independence 1962.

Alia Ramiz 1925– . Albanian communist politician, head of state 1982–92. He gradually relaxed the isolationist policies of his predecessor Enver Hoxha and following public unrest introduced political and economic reforms, including free elections 1991, when he was elected executive president.

Aliens Act in the UK, an act of Parliament passed by the Conservative government 1905 to restrict the immigration of 'undesirable persons' into Britain; it was aimed at restricting Jewish immigration.

Allenby Henry Hynman, 1st Viscount Allenby 1861–1936. English field marshal. In World War I he served in France before taking command 1917–19 of the British forces in the Middle East. His defeat of the Turkish forces at Megiddo in Palestine in Sept 1918 was followed almost at once by the capitulation of Turkey. He was high commissioner in Egypt 1919–35.

Allende (Gossens) Salvador 1908–1973. Chilean left-wing politician. Elected president 1970 as the candidate of the Popular Front alliance, Allende never succeeded in keeping the electoral alliance together in government. His failure to solve the country's economic problems or to deal with political subversion allowed the army, backed by the CIA, to stage the 1973 coup which brought about the death of Allende and many of his supporters.

Alliance, the in UK politics, a loose union 1981–87 formed by the ◊Liberal Party and Social Democratic Party (SDP) for electoral purposes.

Alliance for Progress programme of US assistance to Latin American countries, initiated by President Kennedy 1961 under the auspices of the ◊Organization of American States.

Allies, the in World War I, the 23 countries allied against the Central Powers (Germany, Austria-Hungary, Turkey, and Bulgaria), including France, Italy, Russia, the UK, Australia and other Commonwealth nations, and, in the latter part of the war, the USA; and in World War II, the 49 countries allied against the ◊Axis powers (Germany, Italy, and Japan), including France, the UK, Australia and other Commonwealth nations, the USA, and the USSR.

Amal radical Lebanese Shi'ite military force, established by Musa Sadr in the 1970s; its headquarters are in Borj al-Barajneh. The movement split into extremist and moderate groups 1982, but both sides agreed on the aim of increasing Shi'ite political representation in Lebanon.

Amanullah Khan 1892–1960. Emir (ruler) of Afghanistan 1919–29. Third son of Habibullah Khan, he seized the throne on his father's assassination and concluded a treaty with the British, but his policy of westernization led to rebellion 1928. Amanullah had to flee, abdicated 1929, and settled in Rome, Italy.

American Federation of Labor and Congress of Industrial Organizations (AFL–CIO) federation of North American trade unions, representing (1992) about 20% of the workforce in North America.

American Legion community organization in the USA, originally for ex-servicemen of World War I, founded 1919. It has approximately 2.7 million members, and has admitted veterans of World War II, the Korean War, and the Vietnam War.

Amery Leo(pold Stennett) 1873–1955. English Conservative politician, First Lord of the Admiralty 1922–24, secretary for the colonies 1924–29, secretary for the dominions 1925–29, and secretary of state for India and Burma (now Myanmar) 1940–45.

Amethyst Incident UK–China episode arising when on 20 April 1949 a British frigate, HMS *Amethyst*, sailing on the Chang Jiang (Yangtze) River, was fired at by communist Chinese forces. The ship was trapped for 14 weeks before breaking free and completing the journey to the sea. The temporary detention of this British vessel has been interpreted as an attempt by the Chinese to assert their sovereignty over what had been considered an international waterway.

Amin (Dada) Idi 1926–   . Ugandan politician, president 1971–79. He led the coup that deposed Milton ◊Obote 1971, expelled the Asian community 1972, and exercised a reign of terror over his people. He fled to Libya when insurgent Ugandan and Tanzanian troops invaded the country 1979.

Amritsar Massacre also called *Jallianwallah Bagh massacre* the killing of 379 Indians (and wounding of 1,200) in Amritsar, at the site of a Sikh religious shrine in the Punjab 1919. British troops under General Edward Dyer (1864–1927) opened fire without warning on a crowd of some 10,000, assembled to protest against the arrest of two Indian National Congress leaders.

anarchism political belief that society should have no government, laws, police, or other authority, but should be a free association of all its members. It does not mean 'without order'; most theories of anarchism imply an order of a very strict and symmetrical kind, but they maintain that such order can be achieved by cooperation. Anarchism must not be confused with nihilism (a purely negative and destructive activity directed against society); anarchism is essentially a pacifist movement.

Anastasia 1901–1918. Russian Grand Duchess, youngest daughter of ◊Nicholas II. During the Russian Revolution she was presumed shot with her parents by the ◊Bolsheviks after the Revolution of 1917, but it has been alleged that Anastasia escaped.

Andean Group (Spanish *Grupo Andino*) South American organization aimed at economic and social cooperation between member states. It was established under the Treaty of Cartagena 1969, by Bolivia, Chile, Colombia, Ecuador, and Peru; Venezuela joined 1973, but Chile withdrew 1976. The organization is based in Lima, Peru.

Anderson Elizabeth Garrett 1836–1917. The first English woman to qualify in medicine. Refused entry into medical school, Anderson studied privately and was licensed by the Society of Apothecaries in London 1865.

She was physician to the Marylebone Dispensary for Women and Children (later renamed the Elizabeth Garrett Anderson Hospital), a London hospital now staffed by women and serving women patients.

Andorra land-locked country in the E Pyrenees, bounded N by France and S by Spain.

chronology

1970 Extension of franchise to third-generation female and second-generation male Andorrans.

1976 First political organization (Democratic Party of Andorra) formed.

1977 Franchise extended to first-generation Andorrans.

1981 First prime minister appointed by General Council.

1982 With the appointment of an Executive Council, executive and legislative powers were separated.

1991 Andorra's first constitution planned; links with European Community (EC) formalized.

1993 First constitution approved in a referendum.

Andreotti Giulio 1919– . Italian Christian Democrat politician. He headed six post-war governments: 1972-73, 1976–79 (four successive terms), and 1989–92. In addition he was defence minister eight times, and foreign minister five times. He was a fervent European.

Andropov Yuri 1914–1984. Soviet communist politician, president of the USSR 1983–84. As chief of the ◊KGB 1967–82, he established a reputation for efficiently suppressing dissent.

Angell Norman 1874–1967. British writer on politics and economics. In 1910 he acquired an international reputation with his book *The Great Illusion*, which maintained that any war must prove ruinous to the victors as well as to the vanquished. Nobel Peace Prize 1933.

Anglo-Irish Agreement or *Hillsborough Agreement* concord reached 1985 between the UK premier Margaret Thatcher and Irish premier Garret FitzGerald. One sign of the improved relations between the two countries was increased cooperation between police and security forces across the border with Northern Ireland. The pact also gave the Irish Republic a greater voice in the conduct of Northern Ireland's affairs. However, the agreement was rejected by Northern Ireland Unionists as a step towards renunciation of British sovereignty. In March 1988 talks led to further strengthening of the agreement.

Angola country in SW Africa, bounded W by the Atlantic Ocean, N and NE by Zaire, E by Zambia, and S by Namibia. The Cabinda enclave, a district of Angola, is bounded W by the Atlantic Ocean, N by the river Congo, and E and S by Zaire.

chronology

1951 Angola became an overseas territory of Portugal.

1956 First independence movement formed, the People's Movement for the Liberation of Angola (MPLA).

1961 Unsuccessful independence rebellion.

1962 Second nationalist movement formed, the National Front for the Liberation of Angola (FNLA).

1966 Third nationalist movement formed, the National Union for the Total Independence of Angola (◊UNITA).

1975 Independence achieved from Portugal. Transitional government of independence formed from representatives of MPLA, FNLA, UNITA, and Portuguese government. MPLA proclaimed People's Republic of Angola under the presidency of Dr Agostinho Neto. FNLA and UNITA proclaimed People's Democratic Republic of Angola.

1976 MPLA gained control of most of the country. South African troops withdrawn, but Cuban units remained.

1977 MPLA restructured to become the People's Movement for the Liberation of Angola–Workers' Party (MPLA–PT).

1979 Death of Neto; succeeded by José1 Eduardo dos Santos.

1980 Constitution amended to provide for an elected people's assembly. UNITA guerrillas, aided by South Africa, continued raids against the Luanda government and bases of the South West Africa People's Organization (◊SWAPO) in Angola.

1984 South Africa promised to withdraw its forces if the Luanda government guaranteed that areas they vacated would not be filled by Cuban or SWAPO units (they Lusaka Agreement).

1985 South African forces officially withdrawn.

1986 Further South African raids into Angola. UNITA continuing to receive South African support.

1988 Peace treaty, providing for the withdrawal of all foreign troops, signed with South Africa and Cuba.

1989 Cease-fire agreed with UNITA broke down and guerrilla activity restarted.

1990 Peace offer by rebels. Return to multiparty politics promised.

1991 Peace agreement signed, civil war between MPLA–PT and UNITA officially ended. Amnesty for all political prisoners.

1992 MPLA's general-election victory fiercely disputed by UNITA, plunging the country into renewed civil war. UNITA offered, and eventually accepted, seats in the new government, but fighting continued.

1993 Continued fighting posed the threat of return to civil war.

Annales school or *total history* group of historians formed in France in 1929, and centred around the journal *Annales d'histoire économique et sociale* which pioneered new methods of historical enquiry. Its leading members included Fernand Braudel, who coined the term total history, and Marc ◊Bloch. Their view was that to arrive at worthwhile conclusions on broad historical debates, all aspects of a society had to be considered. Thus they widened the scope of research away from political history to include social and economic factors as well.

Anschluss (German 'union') the annexation of Austria with Germany, accomplished by the German chancellor Adolf Hitler 12 March 1938.

Anti-Comintern Pact (Anti-Communist Pact) agreement signed between Germany and Japan 25 Nov 1936, opposing communism as a menace to peace and order. The pact was signed by Italy 1937 and by Hungary, Spain, and the Japanese puppet state of ◊Manchukuo in 1939. While directed against the USSR, the agreement also had the effect of giving international recognition to Japanese rule in Manchuria.

anticommunism fierce antagonism towards communism linked particularly with right-wing politician Joseph ◊McCarthy's activities in the USA during the 1950s. He made numerous unsubstantiated claims that the State Department had been infiltrated by Communist activity, thus triggering a wave of anticommunist hysteria. He did not succeed in identifying any Communists employed by the government.

Antigua and Barbuda country comprising three islands in the E Caribbean (Antigua, Barbuda, and uninhabited Redonda).

chronology

1871–1956 Antigua and Barbuda administered by Britain as part of the Leeward Islands federation.

1967 Antigua and Barbuda became an associated state within the Commonwealth, with full internal independence.

1971 Progressive Labour Movement (PLM) won the general election by defeating the Antigua Labour Movement (ALP).
1976 PLM called for early independence, but ALP urged caution. ALP won the general election.
1981 Independence from Britain achieved.
1983 Assisted US invasion of Grenada.
1984 ALP won a decisive victory in the general election.
1985 ALP re-elected.
1989 Another sweeping general election victory for the ALP under Vere Bird.
1991 Bird remained in power despite calls for his resignation.

anti-Semitism literally, prejudice against Semitic people, but in practice it has meant prejudice or discrimination against, and persecution of, the Jews as an ethnic group. Historically this was practised for almost 2,000 years by European Christians. Anti-Semitism was a tenet of Hitler's Germany (the '◊final solution'), and in the ◊Holocaust 1933–45 about 6 million Jews died in concentration camps and in local extermination ◊pogroms, such as the siege of the Warsaw ghetto. In eastern Europe, as well as in Islamic nations, anti-Semitism exists and is promulgated by neofascist groups. It is a form of racism.

Antonescu Ion 1882–1946. Romanian general and politician who headed a pro-German government during World War II and was executed for war crimes 1946.

ANZAC (acronym for *A*ustralian and *N*ew *Z*ealand *A*rmy *C*orps) general term for all troops of both countries serving in World War I and to some extent those in World War II.

Anzam Treaty (*A*ustralia, *N*ew *Z*ealand, *a*nd *M*alaya) arrangement to coordinate service planning in defending air and sea communications in the region 1948. Cover was extended to the defence of Malaya 1954–55, but this was incorporated into the Anglo-Malayan Defence Agreement shortly after Malayan independence 1957.

Anzio, Battle of in World War II, the beachhead invasion of Italy 22 Jan–23 May 1944 by Allied troops; failure to use information gained by deciphering German codes led to Allied troops being stranded temporarily after German attacks.

ANZUS acronym for Australia, New Zealand, and the United States (Pacific Security Treaty), a military alliance established 1951. It was replaced 1954 by the ◊Southeast Asia Treaty Organization, (SEATO).

Aoun Michel 1935– . Lebanese soldier and Maronite Christian politician, president 1988–90. As commander of the Lebanese army, he was made president without Muslim support, his appointment precipitating a civil war between Christians and Muslims. His unwillingness to accept a 1989 Arab League-sponsored peace agreement increased his isolation until the following year when he surrendered to military pressure. He left the country 1991 and was pardoned by the new government the same year.

apartheid racial-segregation policy of the government of South Africa, which was legislated 1948, when the Afrikaner National Party gained power. Nonwhites (Bantu, coloured or mixed, or Indian) do not share full rights of citizenship with the 4.5 million whites (for example, the 23 million black people cannot vote in parliamentary elections), and many public facilities and institutions were until 1990 (and in some cases remain) restricted to the use of one race only; the establishment of ◊Black National States is another manifestation of apartheid. In 1991 President de Klerk repealed the key elements of apartheid legislation.

Apollo project US space project to land a person on the Moon, announced 1961 by President Kennedy and achieved 20 July 1969, when Neil Armstrong was the first to set foot there. He was accompanied on the Moon's surface by Col Edwin E Aldrin Jr; Michael Collins remained in the orbiting command module.

apparatchik in a communist political system, an employee of the *apparat*, or state bureaucracy; that is, a full-time, senior party official.

appeasement historically, the conciliatory policy adopted by the British government, in particular under Neville Chamberlain, towards the Nazi and Fascist dictators in Europe in the 1930s in an effort to maintain peace. It was strongly opposed by Winston Churchill, but the ◊Munich Agreement 1938 was almost universally hailed as its justification. Appeasement ended when Germany occupied Bohemia–Moravia March 1939.

Aquino (Maria) Corazon (born Cojuangco) 1933– . President of the Philippines 1986–92. She was instrumental in the nonviolent overthrow of President Ferdinand Marcos 1986. As president, she sought to rule in a conciliatory manner, but encountered opposition from left (communist guerrillas) and right (army coup attempts), and her land reforms were seen as inadequate.

Arab-Israeli Wars series of wars between Israel and various Arab states in the Middle East since the founding of the state of Israel 1948.

First Arab-Israeli War 15 May 1948–13 Jan/24 March 1949. As soon as the independent state of Israel had been proclaimed by the Jews, it was invaded by combined Arab forces. The Israelis defeated them and went on to annex territory until they controlled 75% of what had been Palestine under British mandate.

Second Arab-Israeli War 29 Oct–4 Nov 1956. After Egypt had taken control of the Suez Canal and blockaded the Straits of Tiran, Israel, with British and French support, invaded and captured Sinai and the Gaza Strip, from which it withdrew under heavy US pressure after the entry of a United Nations force.

Third Arab-Israeli War 5–10 June 1967, the *Six-Day War*. It resulted in the Israeli capture of the Golan Heights from Syria; the eastern half of Jerusalem and the West Bank from Jordan; and, in the south, the Gaza Strip and Sinai peninsula as far as the Suez Canal.

Fourth Arab-Israeli War 6-24 Oct 1973, the 'October War' or *Yom Kippur War*, so called because the Israeli forces were taken by surprise on the Day of Atonement. It started with the recrossing of the Suez Canal by Egyptian forces who made initial gains, though there was some later loss of ground by the Syrians in the north.

Fifth Arab-Israeli War From 1978 the presence of Palestinian guerrillas in Lebanon led to Arab raids on Israel and Israeli retaliatory incursions, but on 6 June 1982 Israel launched a full-scale invasion. By 14 June Beirut was encircled, and ◊Palestine Liberation Organization (PLO) and Syrian forces were evacuated (mainly to Syria) 21–31 Aug, but in Feb 1985 there was a unilateral Israeli withdrawal from the country without any gain or losses incurred. Israel maintains a 'security zone' in S Lebanon and supports the South Lebanese Army militia as a buffer against Palestinian guerrilla incursions.

Arab League organization of Arab states established in Cairo 1945 to promote Arab unity, primarily in opposition to Israel. The original members were Egypt, Syria, Iraq, Lebanon, Transjordan (Jordan 1949), Saudi Arabia, and Yemen. In 1979 Egypt was suspended and the league's headquarters transferred to Tunis in protest against the Egypt-Israeli peace, but

Egypt was readmitted as a full member May 1989, and in March 1990 its headquarters returned to Cairo.

Arafat Yassir 1929– . Palestinian nationalist politician, cofounder of al-◊Fatah 1956 and president of the ◊Palestine Liberation Organization (PLO) from 1969. His support for Saddam Hussein after Iraq's invasion of Kuwait 1990 weakened his international standing, but he has since been influential in Middle East peace talks.

Arbenz Guzmán Jácobo 1913–1971. Guatemalan social democratic politician and president from 1951 until his overthrow 1954 by rebels operating with the help of the US ◊Central Intelligence Agency.

Arendt Hannah 1906–1975. German-born US scholar and political scientist. With the rise of the Nazis, she moved to Paris and emigrated to the USA 1940. Her works include *The Origins of Modern Totalitarianism* 1951, *The Human Condition* 1958, *On Revolution* 1963, *Eichmann in Jerusalem* 1963, and *On Violence* 1972.

Arevalo Bermejo Juan José 1904–1990. Guatemalan president 1945-51, elected to head a civilian government after a popular revolt ended a 14-year period of military rule. However, many of his liberal reforms were later undone by subsequent military rulers.

Argentina country in South America, bounded W and S by Chile, N by Bolivia, and E by Paraguay, Brazil, Uruguay, and the Atlantic Ocean.

chronology

1946 Juan ◊Perón elected president, supported by his wife 'Evita'.

1952 'Evita' ◊Perón died.

1955 Perón overthrown and civilian administration restored.

1966 Coup brought back military rule.

1973 A Peronist party won the presidential and congressional elections. Perón returned from exile in Spain as president, with his third wife, Isabel (◊Perón), as vice president.

1974 Perón died, succeeded by Isabel.

1976 Coup resulted in rule by a military junta led by Lt-Gen Jorge Videla. Congress dissolved, and hundreds of people, including Isabel Perón, were detained.

1976–83 Ferocious campaign against left-wing elements, the 'dirty war'.

1978 Videla retired. Succeeded by General Roberto Viola, who promised a return to democracy.

1981 Viola died suddenly. Replaced by General Leopoldo ◊Galtieri.

1982 With a deteriorating economy, Galtieri sought popular support by ordering an invasion of the British-held Falkland Islands. After losing the short war (◊Falklands War), Galtieri was removed and replaced by General Reynaldo Bignone.

1983 Amnesty law passed and democratic constitution of 1853 revived. General elections won by Raúl Alfonsín and his party. Armed forces under scrutiny.

1984 National Commission on the Disappearance of Persons (CONADEP) reported on over 8,000 people who had disappeared during the 'dirty war' of 1976–83.

1985 A deteriorating economy forced Alfonsín to seek help from the International Monetary Fund and introduce an austerity programme.

1986 Unsuccessful attempt on Alfonsín's life.

1988 Unsuccessful army coup.

1989 Carlos ◊Menem, of the Justicialist Party, elected president.

1990 Full diplomatic relations with the UK restored. Menem elected Justicialist Party leader. Revolt by army officers thwarted.

1992 New currency introduced.

Arias Sanchez Oscar 1940– . Costa Rican politician, president 1986–90, secretary general of the left-wing National Liberation Party (PLN) from 1979. He advocated a neutralist policy and in 1987 was the leading promoter of the Central American Peace Plan (see ◊Nicaragua). He lost the presidency to Rafael Angel Caldéron 1990. He was awarded the Nobel Peace Prize 1987.

arielism set of ideas rejecting North American materialism, inspired by Uruguayan writer José Enrique Rodó (1871–1917) in his short essay *Ariel* 1900.

Aristide Jean-Bertrand 1953– . President of Haiti Dec 1990–Oct 1991. A left-wing Catholic priest opposed to the right-wing regime of the Duvalier family, he campaigned for the National Front for Change and Democracy, representing a loose coalition of peasants, trade unionists, and clerics, and won 70% of the vote. He was deposed by the military Sept 1991.

Armenia country in W Asia, bounded E by Azerbaijan, N by Georgia, W by Turkey, and S by Iran.

chronology

1918 Became an independent republic.

1920 Occupied by the Red Army.

1936 Became a constituent republic of the USSR.

1988 Feb: demonstrations in Yerevan called for transfer of Nagorno-Karabakh from Azerbaijan to Armenian control. Dec: earthquake claimed around 25,000 lives and caused extensive damage.

1989 Jan–Nov: strife-torn Nagorno-Karabakh placed under 'temporary' direct rule from Moscow. Pro-autonomy Armenian National Movement founded. Nov: civil war erupted with Azerbaijan over Nagorno-Karabakh.

1990 March: Armenia boycotted USSR constitutional referendum. Aug: nationalists secured control of Armenian supreme soviet; former dissident Levon Ter-Petrossian indirectly elected president; independence declared. Nakhichevan republic affected by Nagorno-Karabakh dispute.

1991 March: overwhelming support for independence in referendum. Dec: Armenia joined new Commonwealth of Independent States (CIS); Nagorno-Karabakh declared its independence; Armenia granted diplomatic recognition by USA.

1992 Jan: admitted into Conference on Security and Cooperation in Europe (CSCE). March: joined United Nations (UN). Conflict over Nagorno-Karabakh worsened.

Armenian member of the largest ethnic group inhabiting Armenia. There are Armenian minorities in Azerbaijan, as well as in Turkey and Iran. Christianity was introduced to the ancient Armenian kingdom in the 3rd century. There are 4–5 million speakers of Armenian, which belongs to the Indo-European family of languages.

Armenian massacres series of massacres of Armenians by Turkish soldiers between 1895 and 1915. Reforms promised to Armenian Christians by Turkish rulers never materialized; unrest broke out and there were massacres by Turkish troops 1895. Again in 1909 and 1915, the Turks massacred altogether more than a million Armenians and deported others into the N Syrian desert, where they died of starvation; those who could, fled to Russia or Persia. Only some 100,000 were left.

armistice cessation of hostilities while awaiting a peace settlement. 'The Armistice' refers specifically to the end of World War I between Germany and the Allies 11 Nov 1918. On 22 June 1940 French representatives signed an armistice with Germany in the same railway carriage at Compiègne as in

1918. No armistice was signed with either Germany or Japan 1945; both nations surrendered and there was no provision for the suspension of fighting. The Korean armistice, signed at Panmunjom 27 July 1953, terminated the ◊Korean War 1950-53.

arms control attempts to limit the arms race between the superpowers by reaching agreements to restrict the production of certain weapons; see ◊disarmament.

Armstrong Robert, Baron Armstrong of Ilminster 1927–   . British civil servant, cabinet secretary in Margaret Thatcher's government. He achieved notoriety as a key witness in the *Spycatcher* trial in Australia 1987. Defending the British Government's attempts to prevent Peter Wright's book alleging 'dirty tricks' from being published, he admitted to having sometimes been 'economical with the truth'. He retired 1988 and was made a life peer.

Arnhem, Battle of in World War II, airborne operation by the Allies, 17–26 Sept 1944, to secure a bridgehead over the Rhine, thereby opening the way for a thrust towards the Ruhr and a possible early end to the war. It was only partially successful, with 7,600 casualties. Arnhem is a city in the Netherlands, on the Rhine SE of Utrecht; population (1991) 131,700. It produces salt, chemicals, and pharmaceuticals.

Arras, Battle of battle of World War I, April–May 1917. It was an effective but costly British attack on German forces in support of a French offensive, which was only partially successful, on the ◊Siegfried Line. British casualties totalled 84,000 as compared to 75,000 German casualties.

ASEAN acronym for ◊Association of South East Asian Nations.

Ashdown Paddy (Jeremy John Durham) 1941–   . English politician, leader of the merged Social and Liberal Democrats from 1988. He served in the Royal Marines as a commando, leading a Special Boat Section in Borneo, and was a member of the Diplomatic Service 1971–76. He became a Liberal member of Parliament 1983. His constituency is Yeovil, Somerset.

Asquith Herbert Henry, 1st Earl of Oxford and Asquith 1852–1928. British Liberal politician, prime minister 1908–16. As chancellor of the Exchequer he introduced old-age pensions 1908. He limited the powers of the House of Lords and attempted to give Ireland Home Rule.

Assad Hafez al 1930–   . Syrian Ba'athist politician, president from 1971. He became prime minister after a bloodless military coup 1970, and the following year was the first president to be elected by popular vote. Having suppressed dissent, he was re-elected 1978 and 1985. He is a Shia (Alawite) Muslim.

Association of South East Asian Nations (ASEAN) regional alliance formed in Bangkok 1967; it took over the nonmilitary role of the ◊Southeast Asia Treaty Organization 1975. Its members are Indonesia, Malaysia, the Philippines, Singapore, Thailand, and (from 1984) Brunei; its headquarters are in Jakarta, Indonesia.

Astor prominent US and British family. *John Jacob Astor* (1763–1848) was a US millionaire. His great-grandson *Waldorf Astor*, 2nd Viscount Astor (1879–1952), was Conservative member of Parliament for Plymouth 1910–19, when he succeeded to the peerage. He was chief proprietor of the British *Observer* newspaper. His US-born wife Nancy Witcher Langhorne (1879–1964), *Lady Astor*, was the first woman member of Parliament to take a seat in the House of Commons 1919, when she succeeded her husband for the constituency of Plymouth. Government policy was said to be decided at Cliveden, their country home.

Atatürk Kemal. Name assumed 1934 by Mustafa Kemal Pasha 1881–1938. (Atatürk 'Father of the Turks') Turkish politician and general, first president of Turkey from 1923. After World War I he established a provisional rebel government and in 1921–22 the Turkish armies under his leadership expelled the Greeks who were occupying Turkey. He was the founder of the modern republic, which he ruled as virtual dictator, with a policy of consistent and radical westernization.

Atlantic, Battle of the continuous battle fought in the Atlantic Ocean during World War II by the sea and air forces of the Allies and Germany, to control the supply routes to the UK. The number of U-boats destroyed by the Allies during the war was nearly 800. At least 2,200 convoys of 75,000 merchant ships crossed the Atlantic, protected by US naval forces. Before the US entry into the war 1941, destroyers were supplied to the British under the ◊Lend-Lease Act 1941.

Atlantic, Battle of the German campaign during World War I to prevent merchant shipping from delivering food supplies from the USA to the Allies, chiefly the UK. By 1917, some 875,000 tons of shipping had been lost. The odds were only turned by the belated use of naval *convoys* and *depth charges* to deter submarine attack.

Atlantic Charter declaration issued during World War II by the British prime minister Churchill and the US president Roosevelt after meetings Aug 1941. It stressed their countries' broad strategy and war aims and was largely a propaganda exercise to demonstrate public solidarity between the Allies.

atom bomb bomb deriving its explosive force from nuclear fission (see ◊nuclear warfare) as a result of a neutron chain reaction, developed in the 1940s in the USA into a usable weapon.

Attlee Clement (Richard), 1st Earl 1883–1967. British Labour politician. In the coalition government during World War II he was Lord Privy Seal 1940-42, dominions secretary 1942-43, and Lord President of the Council 1943-45, as well as deputy prime minister from 1942. As prime minister 1945-51 he introduced a sweeping programme of nationalization and a whole new system of social services.

Auchinleck Sir Claude John Eyre 1884–1981. British commander in World War II. He won the First Battle of El ◊Alamein 1942 in N Egypt. In 1943 he became commander in chief in India and founded the modern Indian and Pakistani armies. In 1946 he was promoted to field marshal; he retired 1947.

Aung San 1916–1947. Burmese (Myanmar) politician. He was a founder and leader of the Anti-Fascist People's Freedom League, which led Burma's fight for independence from Great Britain.During World War II he collaborated first with Japan and then with the UK. In 1947 he became head of Burma's provisional government but was assassinated the same year by political opponents. His daughter Suu Kyi (1961–   ) spearheaded a nonviolent prodemocracy movement in Myanmar (formerly Burma) from 1988.

Auriol Vincent 1884–1966. French Socialist politician. He was president of the two Constituent Assemblies of 1946 and first president of the ◊Fourth Republic 1947–54.

Auschwitz (Polish *Oswiecim*) town near Kraków in Poland, the site of a notorious ◊concentration camp used by the Nazis in World War II to exterminate Jews and other political and social minorities, as part of the ◊'final solution'. Each of the four gas chambers could hold 6,000 people.

Ausgleich compromise between Austria and Hungary 8 Feb 1867 that established the Austro–Hungarian Dual Monarchy under Habsburg rule. It endured until the collapse of Austria-Hungary 1918.

Australia country occupying all of the Earth's smallest continent, situated S of Indonesia, between the Pacific and Indian oceans.

chronology
1942 Statute of Westminster Adoption Act gave Australia autonomy from UK in internal and external affairs.
1944 Liberal Party founded by Robert ◊Menzies.
1951 Australia joined New Zealand and the USA as a signatory to the ◊ANZUS Pacific security treaty.
1966 Menzies resigned after being Liberal prime minister for 17 years, and was succeeded by Harold ◊Holt.
1967 A referendum was passed giving Aborigines full citizenship rights.
1968 John ◊Gorton became prime minister after Holt's death.
1971 Gorton succeeded by William McMahon, heading a Liberal–Country Party coalition.
1972 Gough ◊Whitlam became prime minister, leading a Labor government.
1975 Senate blocked the government's financial legislation; Whitlam dismissed by the governor general, who invited Malcolm ◊Fraser to form a Liberal–Country Party caretaker government. The action of the governor general, John ◊Kerr, was widely criticized.
1977 Kerr resigned.
1978 Northern Territory attained self-government.
1983 Australian Labor Party, returned to power under Bob Hawke, convened meeting of employers and unions to seek consensus on economic policy to deal with growing unemployment.
1986 Australia Act passed by UK government, eliminating last vestiges of British legal authority in Australia.
1988 Labor foreign minister Bill Hayden appointed governor general designate. Free-trade agreement with New Zealand signed.
1990 Hawke won record fourth election victory, defeating Liberal Party by small majority.
1991 Paul ◊Keating became new Labor Party leader and prime minister.
1992 Keating's popularity declined as economic problems continued. Oath of allegiance to British Crown abandoned.
1993 Labor Party won general election, entering fifth term of office.

Austria landlocked country in central Europe, bounded E by Hungary, S by Slovenia and Italy, W by Switzerland and Liechtenstein, NW by Germany, and N by the Czech and Slovak republics.

chronology

1867 Emperor Franz Josef established dual monarchy of Austria–Hungary.

1914 Archduke Franz Ferdinand assassinated by a Serbian nationalist; Austria–Hungary invaded Serbia, precipitating World War I.

1918 Habsburg empire ended; republic proclaimed.

1938 Austria incorporated into German Third Reich by Hitler (the ◊*Anschluss*).

1945 Under Allied occupation, constitution of 1920 reinstated and coalition government formed by the Socialist Party of Austria (SPÖ) and the Austrian People's Party (ÖVP).

1955 Allied occupation ended, and the independence of Austria formally recognized.

1966 ÖVP in power with Josef Klaus as chancellor.

1970 SPÖ formed a minority government, with Dr Bruno Kreisky as chancellor.

1983 Kreisky resigned and was replaced by Dr Fred Sinowatz, leading a coalition.

1986 Dr Kurt ◊Waldheim elected president. Sinowatz resigned, succeeded by Franz ◊Vranitzky. No party won an overall majority; Vranitzky formed a coalition of the SPÖ and the ÖVP, with ÖVP leader, Dr Alois Mock, as vice chancellor.

1989 Austria sought European Community membership.

1990 Vranitzky re-elected.

1991 Bid for EC membership endorsed by the Community.

1992 Thomas Klestil elected president, replacing Waldheim.

Austro-Hungarian Empire the Dual Monarchy established by the Habsburg Franz Joseph 1867 between his empire of Austria and his kingdom of Hungary (including territory that became Czechoslovakia as well as parts of Poland, the Ukraine, Romania, Yugoslavia, and Italy). It collapsed autumn 1918 with the end of World War I. Only two king-emperors ruled: Franz Joseph 1867–1916 and Charles 1916–18.

Autonomisti semiclandestine amalgam of Marxist student organizations in W Europe, linked with guerrilla groups and such acts as the kidnapping and murder of Italian former premier Aldo Moro by the Red Brigades 1978.

Axis alliance of Nazi Germany and Fascist Italy before and during World War II. The *Rome–Berlin Axis* was formed 1936, when Italy was being threatened with sanctions because of its invasion of Ethiopia (Abyssinia). It became a full military and political alliance May 1939. A ten-year alliance between Germany, Italy, and Japan (*Rome–Berlin–Tokyo Axis*) was signed Sept 1940 and was subsequently joined by Hungary, Bulgaria, Romania, and the puppet states of Slovakia and Croatia. The Axis collapsed with the fall of Mussolini and the surrender of Italy 1943 and Germany and Japan 1945.

Ayub Khan Muhammad 1907–1974. Pakistani soldier and president from 1958 to 1969. He served in the Burma Campaign 1942–45, and was commander in chief of the Pakistan army 1951. In 1958 Ayub Khan assumed power after a bloodless army coup. He won the presidential elections 1960 and 1965, and established a stable economy and achieved limited land reforms. His militaristic form of government was unpopular, particularly with the Bengalis. He resigned 1969 after widespread opposition and civil disorder, notably in Kashmir.

Azaña Manuel 1880–1940. Spanish politician and first prime minister 1931–33 of the second Spanish republic. He was last president of the republic during the Civil War 1936–39, before the establishment of a dictatorship under Franco.

Azerbaijan country in W Asia, bounded S by Iran, E by the Caspian Sea, W by Armenia and Georgia, and N by Russia.

chronology
1917–18 A member of the anti-Bolshevik Transcaucasian Federation.
1918 Became an independent republic.
1920 Occupied by the Red Army.
1922–36 Formed part of the Transcaucasian Federal Republic with Georgia and Armenia.
1936 Became a constituent republic of the USSR.
1988 Riots followed Nagorno-Karabakh's request for transfer to Armenia.
1989 Jan–Nov: strife-torn Nagorno-Karabakh placed under 'temporary' direct rule from Moscow. Azerbaijan Popular Front established. Nov: civil war erupted with Armenia.
1990 Jan: Soviet troops dispatched to Baku to restore order. Aug: communists won parliamentary elections. Nakhichevan republic affected by Nagorno-Karabakh dispute.

1991 Aug: Azeri leadership supported attempted anti-Gorbachev coup in Moscow; independence declared. Sept: former communist Ayaz Mutalibov elected president. Dec: joined new Commonwealth of Independent States (CIS); Nagorno-Karabakh declared independence.

1992 Jan: admitted into Conference on Security and Cooperation in Europe (CSCE); March: Mutalibov resigned; Azerbaijan became a member of the United Nations (UN); accorded diplomatic recognition by the USA. June: Albulfaz Elchibey, leader of the Popular Front, elected president; renewed campaign against Armenia in the fight for Nagorno-Karabakh.

1993 Prime Minister Rakham Guseinov resigned over differences with President Elchibey.

B

Baader-Meinhof gang popular name for the West German left-wing guerrilla group the *Rote Armee Fraktion* (Red Army Faction), active from 1968 against what it perceived as US imperialism. The three main founding members were Andreas Baader (1943–77), Gudrun Ensslin, and Ulrike Meinhof (1934–76).

Ba'ath Party ruling political party in Iraq and Syria. Despite public support of pan-Arab unity and its foundations 1943 as a party of Arab nationalism, its ideology has been so vague that it has fostered widely differing (and often opposing) parties in Syria and Iraq.

Babangida Ibrahim 1941– . Nigerian politician and soldier, president from 1985. He became head of the Nigerian army in 1983 and in 1985 led a coup against President Buhari, assuming the presidency himself. He has promised a return to civilian rule.

Babi Yar ravine near Kiev, Ukraine, where more than 100,000 people (80,000 Jews; the others were Poles, Russians, and Ukrainians) were killed by the Nazis 1941. The site was ignored until the Soviet poet Yevtushenko wrote a poem called 'Babi Yar' 1961 in protest at plans for a sports centre on the site.

Baden-Powell Robert Stephenson Smyth, 1st Baron Baden-Powell 1857–1941. British general, founder of the Scout Association. He fought in defence of Mafeking (now Mafikeng) during the Second South African War. After 1907 he devoted his time to developing the Scout movement, which rapidly spread throughout the world. He was created a peer in 1929.

Badoglio Pietro 1871–1956. Italian soldier and Fascist politician. A veteran of campaigns against the peoples of Tripoli and Cyrenaica, in 1935 he became commander in chief in Ethiopia, adopting ruthless measures to break patriot resistance. He was created viceroy of Ethiopia and duke of Addis Ababa in 1936. He resigned during the disastrous campaign into

Greece 1940 and succeeded Mussolini as prime minister of Italy from July 1943 to June 1944, negotiating the armistice with the Allies.

Baghdad Pact military treaty of 1955 concluded by the UK, Iran, Iraq, Pakistan, and Turkey, with the USA cooperating; it was replaced by the ◊Central Treaty Organization (CENTO) when Iraq withdrew in 1958.

Bahamas country comprising a group of about 700 islands and about 2,400 uninhabited islets and cays in the Caribbean, 80 km/50 mi from the SE coast of Florida. They extend for about 1,223 km/760 mi from NW to SE, but only 22 of the islands are inhabited.

chronology
1964 Independence achieved from Britain.
1967 First national assembly elections; Lynden ◊Pindling became first prime minister.
1972 Constitutional conference to discuss full independence.
1973 Full independence achieved.
1983 Allegations of drug trafficking by government ministers.
1984 Deputy prime minister and two cabinet ministers resigned. Pindling denied any personal involvement and was endorsed as party leader.
1987 Pindling re-elected despite claims of frauds.
1992 Free National Movement (FNM) led by Hubert Ingraham won absolute majority in assembly elections.

Bahrain country comprising a group of islands in the Persian Gulf, between Saudi Arabia and Iran.

chronology
1861 Became British protectorate.
1968 Britain announced its intention to withdraw its forces. Bahrain formed, with Qatar and the Trucial States, the Federation of Arab Emirates.
1971 Qatar and the Trucial States withdrew from the federation and Bahrain became an independent state.
1973 New constitution adopted, with an elected national assembly.
1975 Prime minister resigned and national assembly dissolved. Emir and his family assumed virtually absolute power.
1986 Gulf University established in Bahrain. A causeway was opened linking the island with Saudi Arabia.
1988 Bahrain recognized Afghan rebel government.
1991 Bahrain joined United Nations coalition that ousted Iraq from its occupation of Kuwait.

Baker James (Addison), III 1930– . US Republican politician. Under President Reagan, he was White House chief of staff 1981–85 and Treasury secretary 1985-88. After managing George Bush's successful presidential campaign 1988, Baker was appointed secretary of state 1989 and played a prominent role in the 1990-91 Gulf crisis, and the subsequent search for a lasting Middle East peace settlement. In 1992 he left the State Department to become White House chief of staff and to oversee Bush's re-election campaign.

Baker Kenneth (Wilfrid) 1934– . British Conservative politician, home secretary 1990-92. He was environment secretary 1985–86, education secretary 1986–89, and chair of the Conservative Party 1989–90, retaining his cabinet seat, before becoming home secretary in John Major's government.

Baldwin Stanley, 1st Earl Baldwin of Bewdley 1867–1947. British Conservative politician, prime minister 1923-24, 1924-29, and 1935-37; he weathered the general strike 1926, secured complete adult suffrage 1928, and handled the ◊abdication crisis of Edward VIII 1936, but failed to prepare Britain for World War II.

Balewa alternative title of Nigerian politician ◊Tafawa Balewa.

Balfour Arthur James, 1st Earl of ◊Balfour 1848–1930. British Conservative politician, prime minister 1902-05 and foreign secretary 1916-19, when he issued the Balfour Declaration 1917 and was involved in peace negotiations after World War I, signing the Treaty of Versailles.

Balfour Declaration letter, dated 2 Nov 1917, from the British foreign secretary A J Balfour to Lord Rothschild (chair, British Zionist Federation) stating: 'HM government view with favour the establishment in Palestine of a national home for the Jewish people.' It led to the foundation of Israel 1948.

Balkans peninsula of SE Europe, stretching into the Mediterranean Sea between the Adriatic and Aegean seas, comprising Albania, Bosnia-Herzegovina, Bulgaria, Croatia, Greece, Romania, Slovenia, the part of Turkey in Europe, and Yugoslavia. The great ethnic diversity resulting from successive waves of invasion has made the Balkans a byword for political dissension. The Balkans' economy developed comparatively slowly until after World War II, largely because of the predominantly mountainous terrain. Political differences have remained strong, for example, the confrontation of Greece and Turkey over Cyprus, and the differing types of communism that prevailed until the early 1990s in the rest. More recently, ethnic interfighting has dominated the peninsula as first Slovenia and Croatia, and then Bosnia-Herzegovina, have battled to win independence from the Serb-dominated Yugoslav federation. Despite international recognition being awarded to all three republics early 1992, fierce fighting between Serb, Croat, and Muslim factions in Bosnia-Herzegovina continued. To '*Balkanize*' is to divide into small warring states.

Baltic States collective name for the states of ◊Estonia, ◊Latvia, and ◊Lithuania, former constituent republics of the USSR (from 1940). They regained independence Sept 1991.

Balkan Wars two wars 1912–13 and 1913 (preceding World War I) which resulted in the expulsion by the Balkan states of Ottoman Turkey from Europe, except for a small area around Istanbul.

Banda Hastings Kamuzu 1902–   . Malawi politician, president from 1966. He led his country's independence movement and was prime minister of Nyasaland (the former name of Malawi) from 1963. He became Malawi's first president 1966 and 1971 was named president for life; his rule has been authoritarian. Despite civil unrest during 1992, he has resisted calls for free, multiparty elections. In 1993 Banda ignored the outcome of a referendum in favour of multiparty elections.

Bandaranaike Sirimavo (born Ratwatte) 1916–   . Sri Lankan politician who succeeded her husband Solomon Bandaranaike to become the world's first female prime minister, 1960–65 and 1970–77, but was expelled from parliament 1980 for abuse of her powers while in office.

Bandaranaike Solomon West Ridgeway Dias 1899–1959. Sri Lankan nationalist politician. In 1952 he founded the Sri Lanka Freedom party and in 1956 became prime minister, pledged to a socialist programme and a neutral foreign policy. He failed to satisfy extremists and was assassinated by a Buddhist monk.

Bandung Conference first conference 1955 of the Afro-Asian nations, proclaiming anticolonialism and neutrality between East and West.

Bangladesh (formerly *East Pakistan*) country in southern Asia, bounded N, W, and E by India, SE by Myanmar, and S by the Bay of Bengal.

chronology
1947 Formed into eastern province of Pakistan on partition of British India.

1970 Half a million killed in flood.

1971 Bangladesh emerged as independent nation, under leadership of Sheik Mujibur ◊Rahman, after civil war.

1975 Mujibur Rahman assassinated. Martial law imposed.

1976–77 Maj-Gen Zia ur-Rahman assumed power.

1978–79 Elections held and civilian rule restored.

1981 Assassination of Maj-Gen Zia.

1982 Lt-Gen ◊Ershad assumed power in army coup. Martial law reimposed.

1986 Elections held but disputed. Martial law ended.

1987 State of emergency declared in response to opposition demonstrations.

1988 Assembly elections boycotted by main opposition parties. State of emergency lifted. Islam made state religion. Monsoon floods left 30 million homeless and thousands dead.

1989 Power devolved to Chittagong Hill Tracts to end 14-year conflict between local people and army-protected settlers.

1990 Following mass antigovernment protests, President Ershad resigned; Shahabuddin Ahmad became interim president.

1991 Feb: elections resulted in coalition government with Bangladesh Nationalist Party (BNP) dominant. April: cyclone killed around 139,000 and left up to 10 million homeless. Sept: parliamentary government restored; Abdur Rahman Biswas elected president.

Bantustan or *homeland* name until 1978 for a ◊Black National State in the Republic of South Africa.

Barbados island country in the Caribbean, one of the Lesser Antilles. It is about 483 km/300 mi N of Venezuela.

chronology

1951 Universal adult suffrage introduced. Barbados Labour Party (BLP) won general election.

1954 Ministerial government established.

1961 Independence achieved from Britain. Democratic Labour Party (DLP), led by Errol Barrow, in power.

1966 Barbados achieved full independence within Commonwealth. Barrow became the new nation's first prime minister.

1972 Diplomatic relations with Cuba established.

1976 BLP, led by Tom Adams, returned to power.

1983 Barbados supported US invasion of Grenada.

1985 Adams died; Bernard St John became prime minister.

1986 DLP, led by Barrow, returned to power.

1987 Barrow died; Erskine Lloyd Sandiford became prime minister.

1989 New National Democratic Party (NDP) opposition formed.

1991 DLP, under Erskine Sandiford, won general election.

Barbarossa, operation German code name for the plans to invade the USSR in 1941 during World War II.

Barbie Klaus 1913–1991. German Nazi, a member of the φSS from 1936. During World War II he was involved in the deportation of Jews from the occupied Netherlands 1940–42 and in tracking down Jews and Resistance workers in France 1942–45. He was arrested 1983 and convicted of crimes against humanity in France 1987.

Barre Raymond 1924–   . French politician, member of the centre-right Union pour la Démocratie Française; prime minister 1976–81, when he also held the Finance Ministry portfolio and gained a reputation as a tough and determined budget-cutter.

Barton Edmund 1849–1920. Australian politician. He was leader of the federation movement from 1896 and first prime minister of Australia 1901–03.

Baruch Bernard (Mannes) 1870–1965. US financier. He was a friend of British prime minister Churchill and a self-appointed, unpaid adviser to US presidents Wilson, F D Roosevelt, and Truman. He strongly advocated international control of nuclear energy.

Barzun Jacques Martin 1907–   . French-born US historian and educator whose speciality was 19th-century European intellectual life. His book *The Modern Researcher* 1970 is recognized as a classic study of historical method. Among his many historical works is *Romanticism and the Modern Ego* 1943.

Bataan peninsula in Luzon, the Philippines, which was defended against the Japanese in World War II by US and Filipino troops under General MacArthur 1 Jan–9 April 1942. MacArthur was evacuated, but some 67,000 Allied prisoners died on the *Bataan Death March* to camps in the interior.

Batista Fulgencio 1901–1973. Cuban dictator 1933–44, when he stood down, and again 1952–59, after seizing power in a coup. His authoritarian methods enabled him to jail his opponents and amass a large personal fortune. He was overthrown by rebel forces led by Fidel ◊Castro 1959.

Baudouin 1930– . King of the Belgians from 1951. In 1950 his father, ◊Leopold III, abdicated and Baudouin was known until his succession July 1951 as *Le Prince Royal*. In 1960 he married Fabiola de Mora y Aragón (1928–), member of a Spanish noble family.

Bay of Pigs inlet on the S coast of Cuba about 145 km/90 mi SW of Havana. It was the site of an unsuccessful invasion attempt by 1,500 US-sponsored Cuban exiles 17–20 April 1961; 1,173 were taken prisoner.

Beard Charles Austin 1874–1948. US historian and a leader of the Progressive movement, active in promoting political and social reform. As a chief exponent of critical economic history, he published *An Economic Interpretation of the Constitution of the United States* 1913 and *The Economic Origins of Jeffersonian Democracy* 1915. With his wife, Mary, he wrote *A Basic History of the United States* 1944, long a standard textbook in the USA.

Beaverbrook (William) Max(well) Aitken, 1st Baron Beaverbrook 1879–1964. British financier, newspaper proprietor, and politician, born in Canada. He bought a majority interest in the *Daily Express* 1919, founded the *Sunday Express* 1921, and bought the London *Evening Standard* 1929. He served in Lloyd George's World War I cabinet and Churchill's World War II cabinet.

Bebel August 1840–1913. German socialist. In 1869, with Wilhelm Liebknecht, he was a founding member of the Verband deutsche Arbeitervereine (League of German Workers' Clubs), and became its leading speaker in the Reichstag. Also known as the Eisenach Party, it was based in Saxony and SW Germany before being incorporated into the SPD (Sozialdemokratische Partei Deutschlands/German Social Democratic Party) 1875.

Beer-hall Putsch un successful uprising led by Adolf Hitler, attempting to overthrow the government of Bavaria in Nov 1923. More than 2,000 Nazi demonstrators were met by armed police, who opened fire, killing 16 of Hitler's supporters. At the subsequent trial for treason, General Ludendorff, who had supported Hitler, was acquitted. Hitler was sentenced to prison, where he wrote ◊*Mein Kampf*.

Begin Menachem 1913–1992. Israeli politician. He was leader of the extremist ◊Irgun Zvai Leumi organization in Palestine from 1942, and prime minister of Israel 1977–83, as head of the right-wing Likud party. In 1978 Begin shared a Nobel Peace Prize with President Sadat of Egypt for work on the ◊Camp David Agreements for a Middle East peace settlement.

Beirut or *Beyrouth* capital and port of ◊Lebanon, devastated by civil war in the 1970s and 1980s, when it was occupied by armies of neighbouring countries.

Belarus or *Byelorussia* or *Belorussia* country in E central Europe, bounded S by Ukraine, E by Russia, W by Poland, and N by Latvia and Lithuania.

chronology
1918–19 Briefly independent from Russia.
1937–41 More than 100,000 people were shot in mass executions ordered by Stalin.
1941–44 Occupied by Nazi Germany.
1945 Became a founding member of the United Nations.
1986 April: fallout from the Chernobyl nuclear reactor in Ukraine contaminated a large area.
1989 Byelorussian Popular Front established as well as a more extreme nationalist organization, the Tolaka group.
1990 Sept: Byelorussian established as state language and republican sovereignty declared.
1991 April: Minsk hit by nationalist-backed general strike, calling for disbandment of Communist Party (CP) workplace cells. Aug: declared independence from Soviet Union in wake of failed anti-Gorbachev coup; CP suspended. Sept: Shushkevich elected president. Dec: Commonwealth of Independent States (CIS) formed in Minsk; Belarus accorded diplomatic recognition by USA.
1992 Jan: admitted into Conference on Security and Cooperation in Europe (CSCE). May: protocols signed with USA agreeing to honour START disarmament treaty.

Belaúnde Terry Fernando 1913–   . President of Peru from 1963 to 1968 and from 1980 to 1985. He championed land reform and the construction of roads to open up the Amazon valley. He fled to the USA 1968 after being deposed by a military junta. After his return, his second term in office was marked by rampant inflation, enormous foreign debts, terrorism, mass killings, and human-rights violations by the armed forces.

Belgium country in W Europe, bounded N by the Netherlands, NW by the North Sea, S and W by France, E by Luxembourg and Germany.

chronology

1914 Invaded by Germany.

1940 Again invaded by Germany.

1948 Belgium became founding member of Benelux Customs Union.

1949 Belgium became founding member of Council of Europe and NATO.

1951 ◊Leopold III abdicated in favour of his son ◊Baudouin.

1952 Belgium became founding member of European Coal and Steel Community.

1957 Belgium became founding member of the European Economic Community.

1971 Steps towards regional autonomy taken.

1972 German-speaking members included in the cabinet for the first time.

1973 Linguistic parity achieved in government appointments.

1974 Leo Tindemans became prime minister. Separate regional councils and ministerial committees established.

1978 Wilfried ◊Martens succeeded Tindemans as prime minister.

1980 Open violence over language divisions. Regional assemblies for Flanders and Wallonia and a three-member executive for Brussels created.

1981 Short-lived coalition led by Mark Eyskens was followed by the return of Martens.

1987 Martens head of caretaker government after break-up of coalition.

1988 Following a general election, Martens formed a new coalition between the Flemish Christian Social Party (CVP), French Socialist Party (PS), Flemish Socialist Party (SP), French Social Christian Party (PSC), and the Flemish People's Party (VU).

1992 Martens-led coalition collapsed; Jean-Luc Dehaene formed a new CVP-led coalition. It was announced that a federal system would be introduced.

Belize (formerly *British Honduras*) country in Central America, bounded N by Mexico, W and S by Guatemala, and E by the Caribbean Sea.

chronology

1862 Belize became a British colony.

1954 Constitution adopted, providing for limited internal self-government. General election won by George Price.

1964 Self-government achieved from the UK (universal adult suffrage introduced).

1965 Two-chamber national assembly introduced, with Price as prime minister.

1970 Capital moved from Belize City to Belmopan.

1973 British Honduras became Belize.

1975 British troops sent to defend the disputed frontier with Guatemala.

1977 Negotiations undertaken with Guatemala but no agreement reached.

1980 United Nations called for full independence.

1981 Full independence achieved. Price became prime minister.

1984 Price defeated in general election. Manuel Esquivel formed the government. The UK reaffirmed its undertaking to defend the frontier.

1989 Price and the People's United Party (PUP) won the general election.

1991 Diplomatic relations with Guatemala established.

Belsen site of a Nazi ◊concentration camp in Lower Saxony, Germany.

Ben Ali Zine el Abidine 1936– . Tunisian politician, president from 1987. After training in France and the USA, he returned to Tunisia and became director-general of national security. He was made minister of the interior and then prime minister under the ageing president for life, Habib ◊Bourguiba, whom he deposed 1987 by a bloodless coup with the aid of ministerial colleagues. He ended the personality cult established by Bourguiba and moved toward a pluralist political system.

Ben Barka Mehdi 1920–1965. Moroccan politician. He became president of the National Consultative Assembly 1956 on the country's independence from France. He was assassinated by Moroccan agents with the aid of the French secret service.

Ben Bella Ahmed 1916– . Algerian politician. He was leader of the National Liberation Front (FLN) from 1952, the first prime minister of independent Algeria 1962–63, and its first president 1963–65. In 1965 Ben Bella was overthrown by Col Houari ◊Boumédienne and detained until 1979. In 1985 he founded a new party, Mouvement pour la Démocratie en Algérie, and returned to Algeria 1990 after nine years in exile.

Benelux (acronym from *Be*lgium, the *Ne*therlands, and *Lux*embourg) customs union agreed by Belgium, the Netherlands, and Luxembourg 1948, fully effective 1960. It was the precursor of the European Community.

Beneš Eduard 1884–1948. Czechoslovak politician. He worked with Tomáš ◊Masaryk towards Czechoslovak nationalism from 1918 and was foreign minister and representative at the League of Nations. He was president of the republic from 1935 until forced to resign by the Germans; he headed a government in exile in London during World War II. He returned home as president 1945 but resigned again after the Communist coup 1948.

Ben-Gurion David. Adopted name of David Gruen 1886–1973. Israeli statesman and socialist politician, one of the founders of the state of Israel, the country's first prime minister 1948–53, and again 1955–63.

Benin country in W Africa, bounded E by Nigeria, N by Niger and Burkina Faso, W by Togo, and S by the Gulf of Guinea.

chronology
1851 Under French control.
1958 Became self-governing dominion within the French Community.
1960 Independence achieved from France.
1960–72 Acute political instability, with switches from civilian to military rule.
1972 Military regime established by General Mathieu ◊Kerekou.
1974 Kerekou announced that the country would follow a path of 'scientific socialism'.
1975 Name of country changed from Dahomey to Benin.
1977 Return to civilian rule under a new constitution.
1980 Kerekou formally elected president by the national revolutionary assembly.
1989 Marxist-Leninism dropped as official ideology. Strikes and protests against Kerekou's rule mounted; demonstrations banned and army deployed against protesters.
1990 Referendum support for multiparty politics.
1991 Multiparty elections held. Kerekou defeated in presidential elections by Nicéphore Soglo.

Benn Tony (Anthony Wedgwood) 1925– . British Labour politician, formerly the leading figure on the party's left wing. He was minister of technology 1966–70 and of industry 1974–75, but his campaign against entry to the European Community led to his transfer to the Department of Energy 1975–79. A skilled parliamentary orator, he unsuccessfully contested the Labour Party leadership 1988.

Ben Zvi Izhak 1884–1963. Israeli politician, president 1952–63. He was born in Poltava, Russia, and became active in the Zionist movement in Ukraine. In 1907 he went to Palestine but was deported 1915 with ◊Ben-Gurion. They served in the Jewish Legion under Field Marshal Allenby, who commanded the British forces in the Middle East.

Berchtesgaden village in SE Bavaria, Germany, site of Hitler's country residence, the Berghof, which was captured by US troops 4 May 1945 and destroyed.

Berchtold Count Leopold von 1863–1942. Prime minister and foreign minister of Austria–Hungary 1912–15 and a crucial figure in the events that led to World War I, because his indecisive stance caused tension with Serbia.

Bérégovoy Pierre 1925–93 . French socialist politician, prime minister from 1992. A close ally of François ◊Mitterrand, he was named Chief of Staff 1981 after managing the successful presidential campaign. He was social affairs minister 1982–84 and finance minister 1984–86 and 1988–92.

Beria Lavrenti 1899–1953. Soviet politician who in 1938 became minister of the interior and head of the Soviet police force that imprisoned, liquidated, and transported millions of Soviet citizens. On Stalin's death 1953, he attempted to seize power but was foiled and shot after a secret trial. Apologists for Stalin have blamed Beria for the atrocities committed by Soviet police during Stalin's dictatorship.

Berlin blockade in June 1948, the closing of entry to Berlin from the west by Soviet forces. It was an attempt to prevent the other Allies (the USA, France, and the UK) unifying the western part of Germany. The British and US forces responded by sending supplies to the city by air for over a year (the *Berlin airlift*). In May 1949 the blockade was lifted; the airlift continued until Sept. The blockade marked the formal division of the city into Eastern and Western sectors.

Berlinguer Enrico 1922–1984. Italian Communist who freed the party from Soviet influence. Secretary general of the Italian Communist Party, by 1976 he was near to the premiership, but the murder of Aldo Moro, the prime minister, by Red Brigade guerrillas, prompted a move toward support for the socialists.

Berlin Wall dividing barrier between East and West Berlin 1961–89, erected by East Germany to prevent East Germans from leaving for West Germany. Escapers were shot on sight.

Bernadotte Count Folke 1895–1948. Swedish diplomat and president of the Swedish Red Cross. In 1945 he conveyed Nazi commander Himmler's offer of capitulation to the British and US governments, and in 1948 was United Nations mediator in Palestine, where he was assassinated by Israeli ◊Stern Gang guerrillas. He was a nephew of Gustaf VI of Sweden.

Bernhard Prince of the Netherlands 1911– . Formerly Prince Bernhard of Lippe-Biesterfeld, he married Princess Juliana in 1937. When Germany invaded the Netherlands in 1940, he escaped to England and became liaison officer for the Dutch and British forces, playing a part in the organization of the Dutch Resistance.

Bernstein Edouard 1850–1932. German socialist thinker, journalist, and politician. He was elected to the Reichstag 1902. He was a proponent of reformist rather than revolutionary socialism, whereby a socialist society could be achieved within an existing parliamentary structure merely by workers' parties obtaining a majority.

Berri Nabih 1939– . Lebanese politician and soldier, leader of Amal ('Hope'), the Syrian-backed Shi'ite nationalist movement. He became minister of justice in the government of President ◊Gemayel 1984. In 1988 Amal was disbanded after defeat by the Iranian-backed Hezbollah ('Children of God') during the Lebanese civil wars, and Berri joined the cabinet of Selim Hoss 1989. In Dec 1990 Berri was made minister of state in the newly formed Karami cabinet, and in 1992 retained the same post in the cabinet of Rashid al-Sohl.

Berrigan Daniel 1921– . and Philip 1924– . US Roman Catholic priests. The brothers, opponents of the Vietnam War, broke into the draft-records offices at Catonsville, Maryland, to burn the files with napalm. They were sentenced in 1968 to three and six years' imprisonment respectively, but went underground. Subsequently Philip Berrigan was tried with others in 1972 for allegedly conspiring to kidnap President Nixon's adviser Henry Kissinger and blow up government offices in Washington DC; he was then sentenced to two years' imprisonment.

Besant Annie 1847–1933. English socialist and feminist activist. Separated from her clerical husband in 1873 because of her freethinking views, she was associated with the radical atheist Charles Bradlaugh and the socialist Fabian Society. She and Bradlaugh published a treatise advocating birth control and were prosecuted; as a result she lost custody of her daughter. In 1889 she became a disciple of Madame Blavatsky. She thereafter preached theosophy and went to India. As a supporter of Indian independence, she founded the Central Hindu College 1898 and the Indian Home Rule League 1916, and became president of the Indian National Congress in 1917. Her *Theosophy and the New Psychology* was published 1904.

Bessmertnykh Aleksandr 1934– . Soviet politician, foreign minister Jan–Aug 1991. He began as a diplomat and worked mostly in the USA, at the United Nations headquarters in New York and the Soviet embassy in Washington DC. He succeeded Edvard Shevardnadze as foreign minister in Jan 1991, but was dismissed in August of the same year for exhibiting 'passivity' during the failed anti-Gorbachev coup.

Betancourt Rómulo 1908–1981. Venezuelan president 1959–64 whose rule was plagued by guerrilla violence and economic and political division. He expanded welfare programmes, increased expenditure on education, encouraged foreign investment, and tried to diversify the Venezuelan economy to decrease its dependence on oil exports.

Bethmann Hollweg Theobald von 1856–1921. German politician, imperial chancellor 1909–17, largely responsible for engineering popular support for World War I in Germany, but his power was overthrown by a military dictatorship under ◊Ludendorff and ◊Hindenburg.

Bevan Aneurin (Nye) 1897–1960. British Labour politician. Son of a Welsh miner, and himself a miner at 13, he became member of Parliament for Ebbw Vale 1929-60. As minister of health 1945-51, he inaugurated the National Health Service (NHS); he was minister of labour Jan–April 1951, when he resigned (with Harold Wilson) on the introduction of NHS charges and led a Bevanite faction against the government. In 1956 he became chief Labour spokesperson on foreign affairs, and deputy leader of the Labour party 1959. He was an outstanding speaker.

Beveridge William Henry, 1st Baron Beveridge 1879–1963. British economist. A civil servant, he acted as Lloyd George's lieutenant in the social legislation of the Liberal government before World War I. The ◊*Beveridge Report* 1942 formed the basis of the welfare state in Britain.

Beveridge Report, the popular name of *Social Insurance and Allied Services*, a report written by William Beveridge 1942 that formed the basis for the social reform legislation of the Labour Government of 1945–50.

Bevin Ernest 1881–1951. British Labour politician. Chief creator of the Transport and General Workers' Union, he was its general secretary from 1921 to 1940, when he entered the war cabinet as minister of labour and national service. He organized the 'Bevin boys', chosen by ballot to work in the coal mines as war service, and was foreign secretary in the Labour government 1945–51.

Bhindranwale Sant Jarnail Singh 1947–1984. Indian Sikh fundamentalist leader who campaigned for the creation of a separate state of Khalistan during the early 1980s, precipitating a bloody Hindu–Sikh conflict in the Punjab. Having taken refuge in the Golden Temple complex in Amritsar and built up an arms cache for guerrilla activities, Bhindranwale, along with around 500 followers, died at the hands of Indian security forces who stormed the temple in 'Operation Blue Star' June 1984.

Bhumibol Adulyadej 1927–   . King of Thailand from 1946. Born in the USA and educated in Bangkok and Switzerland, he succeeded to the throne on the assassination of his brother. In 1973 he was active, with popular support, in overthrowing the military government of Marshal Thanom Kittikachorn and thus ended a sequence of army-dominated regimes in power from 1932.

Bhutan mountainous, landlocked country in the eastern Himalayas (SE Asia), bounded N and W by Tibet (China) and to the S and E by India.

chronology

1907 First hereditary monarch installed.

1910 Anglo-Bhutanese Treaty signed.

1949 Indo-Bhutan Treaty of Friendship signed.

1952 King Jigme Dorji Wangchuk installed.

1953 National assembly established.

1959 4,000 Tibetan refugees given asylum.

1968 King established first cabinet.

1972 King died and was succeeded by his son Jigme Singye Wangchuk.

1979 Tibetan refugees told to take Bhutanese citizenship or leave; most stayed.

1983 Bhutan became a founding member of the South Asian Regional Association for Cooperation (SAARC).

1988 King imposed 'code of conduct' suppressing Nepalese customs.

1990 Hundreds of people allegedly killed during prodemocracy demonstrations.

Bhutto Benazir 1953–   . Pakistani politician, leader of the Pakistan People's Party (PPP) from 1984 (in exile until 1986), and prime minister of Pakistan 1988–90, when the opposition manoeuvred her from office and charged her with corruption. In May 1991 new charges were brought against her. She was the first female leader of a Muslim state.

Bhutto Zulfikar Ali 1928–1979. Pakistani politician, president 1971–73; prime minister from 1973 until the 1977 military coup led by General ◊Zia ul-Haq. In 1978 Bhutto was sentenced to death for conspiring to murder a political opponent and was hanged the following year. He was the father of Benazir Bhutto.

Biafra, Republic of African state proclaimed in 1967 when fears that Nigerian central government was increasingly in the hands of the rival Hausa tribe led the predominantly Ibo Eastern Region of Nigeria to secede under Lt Col Odumegwu Ojukwu. On the proclamation of Biafra, civil war ensued with the rest of the federation. In a bitterly fought campaign federal forces confined the Biafrans to a shrinking area of the interior by 1968, and by 1970 Biafra ceased to exist.

Bidault Georges 1899–1983. French politician, prime minister 1946, 1949-50. He was a leader of the French resistance during World War II and foreign minister and president in de Gaulle's provisional government. He left the Gaullists over Algerian independence an in 1962 he became head of the ◊Organisation de l'Armée Secrète (OAS), formed 1961 by French settlers devoted to perpetuating their own rule in Algeria. He was charged with treason in 1963 and left the country, but was allowed to return in 1968.

Biffen (William) John 1930–   . British Conservative politician. In 1971 he was elected to Parliament for a Shropshire seat. Despite being to the left of Margaret Thatcher, he held key positions in government from 1979, including leader of the House of Commons from 1982, but was dropped after the general election of 1987.

Big Bertha any of three large German howitzer guns that were mounted on railway wagons during World War I.

Bikini atoll in the ◊Marshall Islands, W Pacific, where the USA carried out 23 atomic- and hydrogen- bomb tests (some underwater) 1946–58.

Biko Steve (Stephen) 1946–1977. South African civil-rights leader. An active opponent of ◊apartheid, he was arrested in Sept 1977; he died in detention six days later. Since his death in the custody of South African police, he has been a symbol of the anti-apartheid movement.

Birch John M 1918–1945. American Baptist missionary, commissioned by the US Air Force to carry out intelligence work behind the Chinese lines where he was killed by the communists; the US extreme right-wing *John Birch Society* 1958 is named after him.

Birendra Bir Bikram Shah Dev 1945–   . King of Nepal from 1972, when he succeeded his father Mahendra; he was formally crowned 1975. King Birendra has overseen Nepal's return to multiparty politics and introduced a new constitution 1990.

Birkenhead Frederick Edwin Smith, 1st Earl of Birkenhead 1872–1930. British Conservative politician. A flamboyant character, known as 'FE', he joined with Edward Carson in organizing armed resistance in Ulster to Irish Home Rule. He was Lord Chancellor 1919-22 and a much criticized secretary for India 1924-28.

Bizonia name given to the unified US and British occupied zones of Germany after 1 Jan 1947. This unification was brought about largely by increasing East–West tensions and the need for integrated economic planning. Bizonia became Tri-zone in April 1948 with the inclusion of the French zone.

Bjelke-Petersen Joh(annes) 1911–   . Australian right-wing politician, leader of the Queensland National Party (QNP) and premier of Queensland 1968–87.

Black and Tans nickname of a special auxiliary force of the Royal Irish Constabulary employed by the British 1920–21 to combat the Sinn Féiners (Irish nationalists) in Ireland; the name derives from the colours of the uniforms, khaki with black hats and belts.

Black Muslim member of a religious group founded 1929 in the USA and led, from 1934, by Elijah Muhammad (then Elijah Poole) (1897–1975) after he had a vision of Allah. Its growth from 1946 as a black separatist organization was due to Malcolm X (1926–1965), the son of a Baptist minister who, in 1964, broke away and founded his own Organization for Afro-American Unity, preaching 'active self-defence'. Under the leadership of Louis Farrakhan, the movement underwent a recent revival.

black nationalism movement towards black separatism in the USA during the 1960s; see ◊Black Power.

Black National State area in the Republic of South Africa set aside for development towards self-government by black Africans in accordance with ◊apartheid. Before 1980 these areas were known as *black homelands* or *bantustans*. They make up less than 14% of the country and tend to be in arid areas (though some have mineral wealth), and may be in scattered blocks. Those that achieved nominal independence are Transkei 1976, Bophuthatswana 1977, Venda 1979, and Ciskei 1981. They are not recognized outside South Africa because of their racial basis.

Black Power movement towards black separatism in the USA during the 1960s, embodied in the *Black Panther Party* founded 1966 by Huey Newton and Bobby Seale. Its declared aim was the establishment of a separate black state in the USA established by a black plebiscite under the aegis of the United Nations. Following a National Black Political Convention 1972, a National Black Assembly was established to exercise pressure on the Democratic and Republican parties.

Black September guerrilla splinter group of the ◊Palestine Liberation Organization formed 1970. Operating from bases in Syria and Lebanon, it was responsible for the kidnappings at the Munich Olympics 1972 that led to the deaths of 11 Israelis, and more recent hijack and bomb attempts. The group is named after the month in which Palestinian guerrillas were expelled from Jordan by King Hussein.

Blackshirts term widely used to describe fascist paramilitary organizations. Originating with Mussolini's fascist Squadristi in the 1920s, it was also applied to the Nazi SS (*Schutzstaffel*) and to the followers of Oswald Mosley's British Union of Fascists.

Black Thursday day of the Wall Street stock market crash 29 Oct 1929, which precipitated the ◊Depression in the USA and throughout the world.

Blake George 1922– . British double agent who worked for MI6 and also for the USSR. Blake was unmasked by a Polish defector 1960 and imprisoned, but escaped to the Eastern bloc 1966. He is said to have betrayed at least 42 British agents to the Soviet side.

Blamey Thomas Albert 1884–1951. Australian field marshal. Born in New South Wales, he served at Gallipoli, Turkey, and on the Western Front in World War I. In World War II he was commander in chief, under MacArthur, of the Allied Land Forces in the SW Pacific 1942–45.

Blériot Louis 1872–1936. French aviator who made the first flight across the English Channel on 25 July 1909.

Blitzkrieg (German 'lightning war') swift military campaign, as used by Germany at the beginning of World War II 1939–41. The abbreviated *Blitz* was applied to the attempted saturation bombing of London by the German air force between Sept 1940 and May 1941.

Bloch Marc 1886–1944. French historian, leading member of the ◊Annales school. Professor of economic history at the Sorbonne from 1936, he undertook most of his research in medieval European history, exploring the relationship between freedom and servitude in his thesis *Kings and Serfs* 1920 and *Feudal Society* 1939-40. He held that economic structures and systems of belief were just as important to the study of history as legal norms and institutional practices, and pioneered the use of comparative history.

Blomberg Werner von 1878–1946. German general and Nazi politician, minister of defence 1933–35, minister of war, and head of the *Wehrmacht* (army) 1935–38 under Hitler's chancellorship. He was discredited by his marriage to a prostitute and dismissed in Jan 1938, enabling Hitler to exercise more direct control over the armed forces. In spite of his removal from office, Blomberg was interrogated about war crimes by the Nuremberg tribunal. He died during the trial and was never in the dock.

Blue Division Spanish volunteers who fought with the German army against the USSR during World War II.

Blum Léon 1872–1950. French politician. He was converted to socialism by the ◊Dreyfus affair 1899 and in 1936 became the first socialist prime minister of France. He was again premier for a few weeks 1938. Imprisoned under the ◊Vichy government 1942 as a danger to French security, he was released by the Allies 1945. He again became premier for a few weeks 1946.

Blunt Anthony 1907–1983. British art historian and double agent. As a Cambridge lecturer, he recruited for the Soviet secret service and, as a member of the British Secret Service 1940–45, passed information to the USSR. In 1951 he assisted the defection to the USSR of the British agents Guy ◊Burgess and Donald Maclean (1913–1983). He was the author of many respected works on French and Italian art. Unmasked 1964, he was given immunity after his confession.

Boateng Paul 1951–   . British Labour politician and broadcaster. Elected member of Parliament for Brent South 1987, he was appointed to Labour's Treasury team in 1989, the first black appointee to a front-bench post. He has served on numerous committees on crime and race relations.

Bohlen Charles 'Chip' 1904–1974. US diplomat. Educated at Harvard, he entered the foreign service 1929. Interpreter and adviser to presidents Roosevelt at ◊Tehran and ◊Yalta, and Truman at ◊Potsdam, he served as ambassador to the USSR 1953–57.

Bokassa Jean-Bédel 1921–   . President of the Central African Republic 1966–79 and later self-proclaimed emperor 1977–79. Commander in chief from 1963, in Dec 1965 he led the military coup that gave him the presidency. On 4 Dec 1976 he proclaimed the Central African Empire and one year later crowned himself as emperor for life.

His regime was characterized by arbitrary state violence and cruelty. Overthrown in 1979, Bokassa was in exile until 1986.

Upon his return he was sentenced to death, but this was commuted to life imprisonment 1988.

Bolger Jim (James) Brendan 1935–   . New Zealand politician and prime minister from 1990. A successful sheep and cattle farmer, Bolger was elected to Parliament 1972. He held a variety of cabinet posts under Robert Muldoon's leadership 1977–84, and was an effective, if uncharismatic, leader of the opposition from March 1986, taking the National Party to electoral victory Oct 1990. His subsequent failure to honour election pledges, leading to cuts in welfare provision, led to a sharp fall in his popularity.

Bolivia landlocked country in central Andes mountains in South America, bounded N and E by Brazil, SE by Paraguay, S by Argentina, and W by Chile and Peru.

chronology
1825 Liberated from Spanish rule by Simón Bolívar; independence achieved (formerly known as Upper Peru).
1952 Dr Víctor Paz Estenssoro elected president.
1956 Dr Hernán Siles Zuazo became president.
1960 Estenssoro returned to power.
1964 Army coup led by vice president, General René Barrientos.
1966 Barrientos became president.

1967 Uprising, led by 'Che' ◊Guevara, put down with US help.

1969 Barrientos killed in plane crash, replaced by Vice President Siles Salinas. Army coup deposed him.

1970 Army coup put General Juan Torres González in power.

1971 Torres replaced by Col Hugo Banzer Suárez.

1973 Banzer promised a return to democratic government.

1974 Attempted coup prompted Banzer to postpone elections and ban political and trade-union activity.

1978 Elections declared invalid after allegations of fraud.

1980 More inconclusive elections followed by another coup, led by General Luis García. Allegations of corruption and drug trafficking led to cancellation of US and EC aid.

1981 García forced to resign. Replaced by General Celso Torrelio Villa.

1982 Torrelio resigned. Replaced by military junta led by General Guido Vildoso. Because of worsening economy, Vildoso asked congress to install a civilian administration. Dr Siles Zuazo chosen as president.

1983 Economic aid from USA and Europe resumed.

1984 New coalition government formed by Siles. Abduction of president by right-wing officers. The president undertook a five-day hunger strike as an example to the nation.

1985 President Siles resigned. Election result inconclusive; Dr Paz Estenssoro, at the age of 77, chosen by congress as president.

1989 Jaime Paz Zamora, Movement of the Revolutionary Left (MIR) elected president in power-sharing arrangement with Hugo Banzer Suárez, pledged to maintain fiscal and monetary discipline and preserve free-market policies.

1992 The new Solidarity Civil Union (UCS) party gained support.

Bolkiah Hassanal 1946– . Sultan of Brunei from 1967, following the abdication of his father, Omar Ali Saifuddin (1916–1986). As absolute ruler, Bolkiah also assumed the posts of prime minister and defence minister on independence 1984.

Bolshevik member of the majority of the Russian Social Democratic Party who split from the ◊Mensheviks 1903. The Bolsheviks, under ◊Lenin, advocated the destruction of capitalist political and economic institutions, and the setting-up of a socialist state with power in the hands of the workers. The Bolsheviks set the ◊Russian Revolution 1917 in motion. They changed their name to the Russian Communist Party 1918.

Bonar Law British Conservative politician; see ◊Law, Andrew Bonar.

Bondfield Margaret Grace 1873–1953. British socialist who became a trade-union organizer to improve working conditions for women. She was a Labour member of Parliament 1923-24 and 1926-31, and was the first woman to enter the cabinet—as minister of labour 1929–31.

Bonham-Carter Violet, Lady Asquith of Yarnbury 1887–1969. British peeress, president of the Liberal party 1945–47.

Bonhoeffer Dietrich 1906–1945. German Lutheran theologian and opponent of Nazism. Involved in a plot against Hitler, he was executed by the Nazis in Flossenburg concentration camp. His *Letters and Papers from Prison* 1953 became the textbook of modern radical theology, advocating the idea of a 'religionless' Christianity.

Bonner Yelena 1923–   . Soviet human-rights campaigner. Disillusioned by the Soviet invasion of Czechoslovakia 1968, she resigned from the Communist Party after marrying her second husband, Andrei ◊Sakharov 1971, and became active in the dissident movement.

Bonus Army or *Bonus Expeditionary Force* in US history, a march on Washington DC by unemployed ex-servicemen during the great Depression to lobby Congress for immediate cash payment of a promised war veterans' bonus.

Boothby Robert John Graham, Baron Boothby 1900–1986. Scottish politician. He became a Unionist member of Parliament 1924 and was parliamentary private secretary to Churchill 1926–29. He advocated Britain's entry into the European Community, and was a powerful speaker.

bootlegging illegal manufacture, distribution, or sale of a product. The term originated in the USA, when the sale of alcohol to American Indians was illegal and bottles were hidden for sale in the legs of the jackboots of unscrupulous traders. The term was later used for all illegal liquor sales during the period of ◊Prohibition in the USA 1920–33, and is often applied to unauthorized commercial tape recordings and the copying of computer software.

Borah William Edgar 1865–1940. US Republican politician. Born in Illinois, he was a senator for Idaho from 1906. An archisolationist, he was chiefly responsible for the USA's repudiation of the League of Nations following World War I.

Boris III 1894–1943. Tsar of Bulgaria from 1918, when he succeeded his father, Ferdinand I. From 1934 he was virtual dictator until his sudden and mysterious death following a visit to Hitler. His son Simeon II was tsar until deposed 1946.

Bormann Martin 1900–1945. German Nazi leader. He took part in the abortive Munich ◊putsch (uprising) 1923 and rose to high positions in the Nazi (National Socialist) Party, becoming deputy party leader May 1941.

Bosch Juan 1909– . President of the Dominican Republic 1963. His left-wing Partido Revolucionario Dominicano won a landslide victory in the 1962 elections. In office, he attempted agrarian reform and labour legislation. He was opposed by the USA, and overthrown by the army. His achievement was to establish a democratic political party after three decades of dictatorship.

Bosnia-Herzegovina Serbo-Croatian *Bosna-Hercegovina* country in central Europe, bounded N and W by Croatia, E by the Yugoslavian republic of Serbia, and E and S by the Yugoslavian republic of Montenegro.

chronology
1918 Incorporated in the future Yugoslavia.
1941 Occupied by Nazi Germany.
1945 Became republic within Yugoslav Socialist Federation.
1980 Upsurge in Islamic nationalism.
1990 Ethnic violence erupted between Muslims and Serbs. Nov–Dec: communists defeated in multiparty elections; coalition formed by Serb, Muslim, and Croatian parties.
1991 May: Serbia–Croatia conflict spread disorder into Bosnia-Herzegovina. Aug: Serbia revealed plans to annex the SE part of the republic. Sept: Serbian enclaves established by force. Oct: 'sovereignty' declared. Nov: plebiscite by Serbs favoured remaining within Yugoslavia; Serbs and Croats established autonomous communities.
1992 Feb–March: Muslims and Croats voted overwhelmingly in favour of independence; referendum boycotted by Serbs. April: USA and EC recognized Bosnian independence. Ethnic hostilities escalated, with Serb forces occupying E and Croatian forces much of W; state of emergency declared; all-out civil war ensued. May: admitted to United Nations. June: Canadian–French UN forces drafted into Sarajevo to break three-month siege of city by Serbs. July: Canadian forces replaced by French, Egyptians, and

Ukrainians. Official cease-fire broken intermittently by both sides; UN and EC mediators vainly sought truce. Fighting continued, with accusations of 'ethnic cleansing' being practised, particularly by Serbs. Oct: UN Security Council voted to create a war crimes commission and imposed ban on military flights over Bosnia-Herzegovina. First British troops deployed.

1993 Jan: UN–EC peace plan, proposing to divide country into 10 autonomous, ethnically-controlled provinces, accepted in principle by Serbs and Croats but fighting continued. March: USA began airdrops of food and medical supplies.

Bosnian Crisis period of international tension 1908 when Austria attempted to capitalize on Turkish weakness after the ◊Young Turk revolt by annexing the provinces of Bosnia and Herzegovina. Austria obtained Russian approval in exchange for conceding Russian access to the Bosporus straits.

Botha Louis 1862–1919. South African soldier and politician, a commander in the Second South African War (Boer War). In 1907 Botha became premier of the Transvaal and in 1910 of the first Union South African government. On the outbreak of World War I 1914 he rallied South Africa to the Commonwealth, suppressed a Boer revolt, and conquered German South West Africa.

Botha P(ieter) W(illem) 1916– . South African politician, prime minister from 1978. Botha initiated a modification of ◊apartheid, which later slowed in the face of Afrikaner (Boer) opposition. In 1984 he became the first executive state president. In 1989 he unwillingly resigned both party leadership and presidency after suffering a stroke, and was succeeded by F W de Klerk.

Botswana landlocked country in central southern Africa, bounded S and SE by South Africa, W and N by Namibia, and NE by Zimbabwe.

chronology
1885 Became a British protectorate.
1960 New constitution created a legislative council.
1963 End of rule by High Commission.
1965 Capital transferred from Mafeking to Gaborone. Internal self-government achieved. Sir Seretse ◊Khama elected head of government.
1966 Independence achieved from Britain. New constitution came into effect; name changed from Bechuanaland to Botswana; Seretse Khama elected president.

1980 Seretse Khama died; succeeded by Vice President Quett ◊Masire.
1984 Masire re-elected.
1985 South African raid on Gaborone.
1987 Joint permanent commission with Mozambique established, to improve relations.
1989 The Botswana Democratic Party (BDP) and Masire re-elected.

Bottomley Virginia 1948– . British Conservative politician, health secretary from April 1992, member of Parliament for Surrey Southwest from 1984.

Boumédienne Houari. Adopted name of Mohammed Boukharouba 1925–1978. Algerian politician who brought the nationalist leader Ben Bella to power by a revolt 1962, and superseded him as president in 1965 by a further coup.

Bourgeois Léon Victor Auguste 1851–1925. French politician. Entering politics as a Radical, he was prime minister in 1895, and later served in many cabinets. He was one of the pioneer advocates of the League of Nations. He was awarded the Nobel Peace Prize 1920.

Bourguiba Habib ben Ali 1903– . Tunisian politician, first president of Tunisia 1957–87. Educated at the University of Paris, he became a journalist and was frequently imprisoned by the French for his nationalist aims as leader of the Néo-Destour party. He became prime minister 1956, president (for life from 1974) and prime minister of the Tunisian republic 1957; he was overthrown in a bloodless coup 1987.

Boutros-Ghali Boutros 1922– . Egyptian diplomat and politician, deputy prime minister 1991–92. He worked towards peace in the Middle East in the foreign ministry posts he held 1977–91. He became secretary general of the United Nations Jan 1992, and during his first year of office had to deal with the war in Bosnia-Herzegovina and famine in Somalia.

Boxer member of the *I ho ch'üan* ('Righteous Harmonious Fists'), a society of Chinese nationalists dedicated to fighting European influence. The *Boxer Rebellion* or *Uprising* 1900 was instigated by the empress Zi Xi. European and US legations in Beijing were besieged and thousands of Chinese Christian converts and missionaries murdered. An international punitive force was dispatched, Beijing was captured 14 Aug 1900, and China agreed to pay a large indemnity.

Bradley Omar Nelson 1893–1981. US general in World War II. In 1943 he commanded the 2nd US Corps in their victories in Tunisia and Sicily, leading to the surrender of 250,000 Axis troops, and in 1944 led the US troops in the invasion of France. His command, as the 12th Army Group, grew to 1.3 million troops, the largest US force ever assembled.

Brain Trust nickname of an informal group of experts who advised US president Franklin D Roosevelt on his ◊New Deal policy.

Brandt Willy. Adopted name of Karl Herbert Frahm 1913–1992. German socialist politician, federal chancellor (premier) of West Germany 1969–74. He played a key role in the remoulding of the Social Democratic Party (SPD) as a moderate socialist force (leader 1964–87). As mayor of West Berlin 1957–66, Brandt became internationally known during the Berlin Wall crisis 1961. Nobel Peace Prize 1971.

Brandt Commission officially the Independent Commission on International Development Issues, established 1977 and chaired by the former West German chancellor Willy ◊Brandt. Consisting of 18 eminent persons acting independently of governments, the commission examined the problems of developing countries and sought to identify corrective measures that would command international support. It was disbanded 1983.

Brauchitsch Walther von 1881–1948. German field marshal. A staff officer in World War I, he became in 1938 commander in chief of the army and a member of Hitler's secret cabinet council. He was dismissed after his failure to invade Moscow 1941. Captured in 1945, he died before being tried in the ◊Nuremburg trials.

Braun Eva 1910–1945. German mistress of Adolf Hitler. Secretary to Hitler's photographer and personal friend, Heinrich Hoffmann, she became Hitler's mistress in the 1930s and married him in the air-raid shelter of the Chancellery in Berlin on 29 April 1945. The next day they committed suicide together.

Brazil largest country in South America (almost half the continent), bounded SW by Uruguay, Argentina, Paraguay and Bolivia; W by Peru and Colombia; N by Venezuela, Guyana, Surinam, and French Guiana; and NE and SE by the Atlantic Ocean.

chronology
1930 Dr Getúlio ◊Vargas became president.
1945 Vargas deposed by the military.

1946 New constitution adopted.

1951 Vargas returned to office.

1954 Vargas committed suicide.

1956 Juscelino ◊Kubitschek became president.

1960 Capital moved to Brasília.

1961 João Goulart became president.

1964 Bloodless coup made General Castelo Branco president; he assumed dictatorial powers, abolishing free political parties.

1967 New constitution adopted. Branco succeeded by Marshal da Costa e Silva.

1969 Da Costa e Silva resigned and a military junta took over.

1974 General Ernesto Geisel became president.

1978 General Baptista de Figueiredo became president.

1979 Political parties legalized again.

1984 Mass calls for a return to fully democratic government.

1985 Tancredo Neves became first civilian president in 21 years. Neves died and was succeeded by the vice president, José Sarney.

1988 New constitution approved, transferring power from the president to the congress. Measures announced to halt large-scale burning of Amazonian rainforest for cattle grazing.

1989 Forest Protection Service and Ministry for Land Reform abolished. International concern over how much of the Amazon has been burned. Fernando ◊Collor, National Reconstruction Party (PRN), elected president, pledging free- market economic policies.

1990 Government won the general election, offset by mass abstentions.

1992 June: Earth Summit, global conference on the environment, held in Rio de Janeiro. Sept: Collor charged with corruption and stripped of his powers. Replaced by vice president, Itamar Franco. Dec: Collor banned from public office.

Brest-Litovsk, Treaty of bilateral treaty signed 3 March 1918 between Russia and Germany, Austria–Hungary, and their allies. Under its terms, Russia agreed to recognize the independence of Georgia, Ukraine, Poland and the Baltic States, and pay heavy compensation. Under the Nov 1918 Armistice that ended World War I, it was annulled, since Russia was one of the winning allies.

Bretton Woods township in New Hampshire, USA, where the United Nations Monetary and Financial Conference was held in 1944 to discuss postwar international payments problems. The agreements reached on financial assistance and measures to stabilize exchange rates led to the creation of the International Bank for Reconstruction and Development in 1945 and the International Monetary Fund (IMF).

Brezhnev Leonid Ilyich 1906–1982. Soviet leader. A protégé of Stalin and Khrushchev, he came to power (after he and ◊Kosygin forced Khrushchev to resign) as general secretary of the Soviet Communist Party (CPSU) 1964–82 and was president 1977–82. Domestically he was conservative; abroad the USSR was established as a military and political uperpower during the Brezhnev era, extending its influence in Africa and Asia.

Brezhnev Doctrine Soviet doctrine 1968 designed to justify the invasion of Czechoslovakia. It laid down for the USSR as a duty the direct maintenance of 'correct' socialism in countries within the Soviet sphere of influence. In 1979 it was extended, by the invasion of Afghanistan, to the direct establishment of 'correct' socialism in countries not already within its sphere. The doctrine was renounced by Mikhail ◊Gorbachev in 1989. Soviet troops were withdrawn from Afghanistan and the satellite states of E Europe were allowed to decide their own forms of government, with non-communist and 'reform communist' governments being established from Sept 1989.

Briand Aristide 1862–1932. French radical socialist politician. He was prime minister 1909–11, 1913, 1915–17, 1921–22, 1925-26 and 1929, and foreign minister 1925–32. In 1925 he concluded the ◊Locarno Pact (settling Germany's western frontier) and in 1928 the ◊Kellogg–Briand Pact renouncing war; in 1930 he outlined a scheme for a United States of Europe.

Bridges Harry 1901–1990. Australian-born US labour leader. In 1931 he formed a trade union of clockworkers and in 1934, after police opened fire on a picket line and killed two strikers, he organized a successful general strike. He was head of the International Longshoremen's and Warehousemen's Union for many years.

Britain, Battle of World War II air battle between German and British air forces over Britain lasting 10 July–31 Oct 1940.

British Empire various territories all over the world conquered or colonized by Britain from about 1600, most now independent or ruled by other powers; the British Empire was at its largest at the end of World War I, with over 25% of the world's population and area. The ◊Commonwealth is composed of former and remaining territories of the British Empire.

British Expeditionary Force (BEF) British army serving in France in World War I 1914–18. Also the 1939–40 army in Europe in World War II, which was evacuated from Dunkirk, France.

Brittan Leon 1939– . British Conservative politician and lawyer. Chief secretary to the Treasury 1981-83, home secretary 1983-85, secretary for trade and industry 1985-86 (resigned over his part in the Westland affair) and senior European Commissioner from 1988.

Broadmoor special hospital (established 1863) in Crowthorne, Berkshire, England, for those formerly described as 'criminally insane'. Patients are admitted if considered by a psychiatrist to be both mentally disordered and potentially dangerous. The average length of stay is eight years; in 1991 patients numbered 515.

Broederbond white South African secret society formed after the Boer War to protect Afrikaner interests. Its exact membership and power remains uncertain, but it was rumoured to have been highly influential during the governments of Hendrik Verwoerd and B J Vorster.

Brooke Peter Leonard 1934– . British Conservative politician, a member of Parliament from 1977. He was appointed chair of the Conservative Party by Margaret Thatcher 1987, and was Northern Ireland secretary 1989–April 1992. In Sept 1992 he was chosen to succeed David Mellor as National Heritage secretary.

Brookeborough Basil Brooke, Viscount Brookeborough 1888–1973. Unionist politician of Northern Ireland. He entered Parliament in 1929, held ministerial posts 1933–45, and was prime minister of Northern Ireland 1943–63. He was a staunch advocate of strong links with Britain.

Brown (James) Gordon 1951– . British Labour politician. He entered Parliament in 1983, rising quickly to the opposition front bench, with a reputation as an outstanding debater.

Brown George, Baron George-Brown 1914–1985. British Labour politician. He entered Parliament in 1945, was briefly minister of works 1951, and contested the leadership of the party on the death of Gaitskell, but was defeated by Harold Wilson. He was secretary for economic affairs 1964–66 and foreign secretary 1966–68. He was created a life peer 1970.

Brownshirts the SA (*Sturmabteilung*), or Storm Troops, the private army of the German Nazi party, who derived their name from the colour of their uniform.

Bruce Stanley Melbourne, 1st Viscount Bruce of Melbourne 1883–1967. Australian National Party politician, prime minister 1923–29. He was elected to parliament in 1918. As prime minister he introduced a number of social welfare measures.

Brundtland Gro Harlem 1939–   . Norwegian Labour politician. Environment minister 1974–76, she briefly took over as prime minister 1981, and was elected prime minister 1986 and again 1990. She chaired the World Commission on Environment and Development which produced the Brundtland Report, published as *Our Common Future* 1987. In 1992 she resigned as leader of the Norwegian Labour Party, a post she had held since 1981.

Brunei country comprising two enclaves on the NW coast of the island of Borneo, bounded to the landward side by Sarawak and to the NW by the South China Sea.

chronology
1888 Brunei became a British protectorate.
1941–45 Occupied by Japan.
1959 Written constitution made Britain responsible for defence and external affairs.
1962 Sultan began rule by decree.
1963 Proposal to join Malaysia abandoned.
1967 Sultan abdicated in favour of his son, Hassanal ◊Bolkiah.
1971 Brunei given internal self-government.
1975 United Nations resolution called for independence for Brunei.
1984 Independence achieved from Britain, with Britain maintaining a small force to protect the oil- and gasfields.
1985 A 'loyal and reliable' political party, the Brunei National Democratic Party (BNDP), legalized.
1986 Death of former sultan, Sir Omar. Formation of multiethnic Brunei National United Party (BNUP).
1988 BNDP banned.

Brüning Heinrich 1885–1970. German politician. Elected to the Reichstag (parliament) 1924, he led the Catholic Centre Party from 1929 and was federal chancellor 1930–32 when political and economic crisis forced his resignation.

Brussels, Treaty of pact of economic, political, cultural, and military alliance established 17 March 1948, for 50 years, by the UK, France, and the Benelux countries, joined by West Germany and Italy 1955. It was the forerunner of the North Atlantic Treaty Organization and the European Community.

Brussilov Aleksei Alekseevich 1853–1926. Russian general, military leader in World War I who achieved major successes against the Austro-Hungarian forces in 1916. Later he was commander of the Red Army 1920, which drove the Poles to within a few miles of Warsaw before being repulsed by them.

Bryan William Jennings 1860–1925. US politician who campaigned unsuccessfully for the presidency three times: as the Populist and Democratic nominee 1896, as an anti-imperialist Democrat 1900, and as a Democratic tariff reformer 1908. He served as President Wilson's secretary of state 1913–15. In the early 1920s he was a leading fundamentalist and opponent of Clarence ◊Darrow in the ◊Scopes monkey trial.

Bryce James, 1st Viscount Bryce 1838–1922. British Liberal politician, professor of civil law at Oxford University 1870–93. He entered Parliament 1880, holding office under Gladstone and Rosebery. He was author of *The American Commonwealth* 1888, ambassador to Washington 1907–13, and improved US-Canadian relations.

Brzezinski Zbigniew 1928–   . US Democrat politician, born in Poland; he taught at Harvard University, USA, and became a US citizen 1949. He was national security adviser to President Carter 1977–81 and chief architect of Carter's human-rights policy.

Buchenwald site of a Nazi ◊concentration camp 1937–45 at a village NE of Weimar, E Germany.

Bukharin Nikolai Ivanovich 1888–1938. Soviet politician and theorist. A moderate, he was the chief Bolshevik thinker after Lenin. Executed on Stalin's orders for treason 1938, he was posthumously rehabilitated 1988.

Bulganin Nikolai 1895–1975. Soviet politician and military leader. His career began in 1918 when he joined the Cheka, the Soviet secret police. He helped to organize Moscow's defence in World War II, became a marshal of the USSR 1947, and was minister of defence 1947–49 and 1953–55. On the fall of Malenkov he became prime minister (chair of Council of Ministers) 1955–58 until ousted by Khrushchev.

Bulgaria country in SE Europe, bounded N by Romania, W by Yugoslavia, S by Greece, SE by Turkey, and E by the Black Sea.

chronology
1908 Bulgaria became a kingdom independent of Turkish rule.
1944 Soviet invasion of German-occupied Bulgaria.
1946 Monarchy abolished and communist-dominated people's republic proclaimed.
1947 Soviet-style constitution adopted.
1949 Death of Georgi ◊Dimitrov, the communist government leader.
1954 Election of Todor ◊Zhivkov as Communist Party general secretary; made nation a loyal satellite of USSR.
1971 Constitution modified; Zhivkov elected president.
1985–89 Large administrative and personnel changes made haphazardly under Soviet stimulus.
1987 New electoral law introduced multicandidate elections.
1989 Programme of 'Bulgarianization' resulted in mass exodus of Turks to Turkey. Nov: Zhivkov ousted by Petar ◊Mladenov. Dec: opposition parties allowed to form.
1990 April: Bulgarian Communist Party (BCP) renamed Bulgarian Socialist Party (BSP). Aug: Dr Zhelyu ◊Zhelev elected president. Nov: government headed by Andrei Lukanov resigned, replaced Dec by coalition led by Dimitur Popov.
1991 July: new constitution adopted. Oct: Union of Democratic Forces (UDF) beat BSP in general election by narrow margin; formation of first noncommunist, UDF-minority government under Filip Dimitrov.
1992 Zhelev became Bulgaria's first directly elected president. Relations with West greatly improved. Dimitrov resigned after vote of no confidence; replaced by Lyuben Berov.

Bulge, Battle of the or *Ardennes offensive* in World War II, Hitler's plan, code-named 'Watch on the Rhine', for a breakthrough by his field marshal ◊Rundstedt aimed at the US line in the Ardennes 16 Dec 1944–28 Jan 1945. There were 77,000 Allied casualties and 130,000 German, including Hitler's last powerful reserve, his Panzer elite. Although US troops were encircled for some weeks at Bastogne, the German counteroffensive failed.

Bülow Bernhard, Prince von 1849–1929. German diplomat and politician. He was chancellor of the German Empire 1900–09 under Kaiser Wilhelm II and, holding that self-interest was the only rule for any state, adopted attitudes to France and Russia that unintentionally reinforced the trend towards opposing European power groups: the ◊Triple Entente (Britain, France, Russia) and Triple Alliance (Germany, Austria–Hungary, Italy).

Bunche Ralph 1904–1971. US diplomat. Grandson of a slave, he was principal director of the UN Department of Trusteeship 1947–54, and UN undersecretary acting as mediator in Palestine 1948–49 and as special representative in the Congo 1960. He taught at Harvard and Howard universities and was involved in the planning of the ◊United Nations. In 1950 he was awarded the Nobel Prize for Peace, the first awarded to a black man.

Burgess Guy (Francis de Moncy) 1910–1963. British spy, a diplomat recruited by the USSR as an agent. He was linked with Kim ◊Philby, Donald Maclean (1913–1983), and Anthony ◊Blunt.

Burkina Faso (formerly *Upper Volta*) landlocked country in W Africa, bounded E by Niger, NW and W by Mali, S by Ivory Coast, Ghana, Togo, and Benin.

chronology
1958 Became a self-governing republic within the French Community.
1960 Independence from France, with Maurice Yaméogo as the first president.
1966 Military coup led by Col Lamizana. Constitution suspended, political activities banned, and a supreme council of the armed forces established.
1969 Ban on political activities lifted.
1970 Referendum approved a new constitution leading to a return to civilian rule.
1974 After experimenting with a mixture of military and civilian rule, Lamizana reassumed full power.
1977 Ban on political activities removed. Referendum approved a new constitution based on civilian rule.
1978 Lamizana elected president.
1980 Lamizana overthrown in bloodless coup led by Col Zerbo.
1982 Zerbo ousted in a coup by junior officers. Major Ouédraogo became president and Thomas Sankara prime minister.
1983 Sankara seized complete power.

1984 Upper Volta renamed Burkina Faso, 'land of upright men'.
1987 Sankara killed in coup led by Blaise Compaoré.
1989 New government party Organization for Popular Democracy–Workers' Party (ODP–MT) formed by merger of other pro-government parties. Coup against Compaoré foiled.
1991 New constitution approved. Compaoré re-elected president.
1992 Multiparty elections won by FP–Popular Front.

Burma former name (to 1989) of ◊Myanmar.

Burma War war 1942–45 during which Burma (now ◊Myanmar) was occupied by Japan. Initially supported by ◊Aung San's Burma National Army, the Japanese captured Rangoon and Mandalay 1942, forcing the withdrawal of General Alexander's British forces to India. During 1943, ◊Chindit guerilla resistance was organized and after a year's heavy fighting at Imphal and Kohima, British, Commonwealth, American, and Chinese nationalist troops reopened the 'Burma Road' between India and China Jan 1945. Rangoon was recaptured May 1945.

Burnham Forbes 1923–1985. Guyanese Marxist-Leninist politician. He was prime minister 1964–80, leading the country to independence 1966 and declaring it the world's first cooperative republic 1970. He was executive president 1980–85. Resistance to the US landing in Grenada 1983 was said to be due to his forewarning the Grenadans of the attack.

Burns John 1858–1943. British labour leader, sentenced to six weeks' imprisonment for his part in the Trafalgar Square demonstration on 'Bloody Sunday' 13 Nov 1887, and leader of the strike in 1889 securing the 'dockers' tanner' (wage of 6d per hour). An Independent Labour member of Parliament 1892–1918, he was the first working-class person to be a member of the cabinet, as president of the Local Government Board 1906–14.

Burundi country in E central Africa, bounded N by Rwanda, W by Zaire, SW by Lake Tanganyika, and SE and E by Tanzania.

chronology
1962 Separated from Ruanda-Urundi, as Burundi, and given independence as a monarchy under King Mwambutsa IV.
1966 King deposed by his son Charles, who became Ntare V; he was in turn deposed by his prime minister, Capt Michel Micombero, who declared Burundi a republic.

1972 Ntare V killed, allegedly by the Hutu ethnic group. Massacres of 150,000 Hutus by the rival Tutsi ethnic group, of which Micombero was a member.

1973 Micombero made president and prime minister.

1974 Union for National Progress (UPRON) declared the only legal political party, with the president as its secretary general.

1976 Army coup deposed Micombero. Col Jean-Baptiste Bagaza appointed president by the Supreme Revolutionary Council.

1981 New constitution adopted, providing for a national assembly.

1984 Bagaza elected president as sole candidate.

1987 Bagaza deposed in coup Sept. Maj Pierre Buyoya headed new Military Council for National Redemption.

1988 Some 24,000 majority Hutus killed by Tutsis.

1992 New constitution approved.

Bush George 1924– . 41st president of the USA 1989–93, a Republican. He was director of the Central Intelligence Agency (CIA) 1976-81 and US vice president 1981–89. As president, his response to the Soviet leader Gorbachev's diplomatic initiatives were initially criticized as inadequate, but his sending of US troops to depose his former ally, General ◊Noriega of Panama, proved a popular move at home. Success in the 1991 Gulf War against Iraq further raised his standing. Domestic economic problems 1991–92 were followed by his defeat in the 1992 presidential elections by Democrat Bill Clinton.

Bustamante (William) Alexander (born Clarke) 1884–1977. Jamaican socialist politician. As leader of the Labour Party, he was the first prime minister of independent Jamaica 1962–67.

Buthelezi Chief Gatsha 1928– . Zulu leader and politician, chief minister of KwaZulu, a black 'homeland' in the Republic of South Africa from 1970. He is the founder (1975) and president of ◊Inkatha, a paramilitary organization for attaining a nonracial democratic political system. He has been accused of complicity in the factional violence between Inkatha and ◊African National Congress supporters that has continued to rack the townships despite his signing of a peace accord with ANC leader, Nelson Mandela, Sept 1991.

Butler Richard Austen ('Rab'), Baron Butler 1902–1982. British Conservative politician. As minister of education 1941–45, he was responsible for the 1944 Education Act; he was chancellor of the Exchequer 1951–55, Lord Privy Seal 1955–59, and foreign minister 1963–64. As a candidate for the prime ministership, he was defeated by Harold Macmillan in 1957 (under whom he was home secretary 1957–62), and by Alec Douglas-Home in 1963.

Butskellism UK term for political policies tending towards the middle ground in an effort to gain popular support; the term was coined 1954 after R A ◊Butler (moderate Conservative) and Hugh ◊Gaitskell (moderate Labour politician).

Byng Julian, 1st Viscount of Vimy 1862–1935. British general in World War I, commanding troops in Turkey and France, where, after a victory at Vimy Ridge, he took command of the Third Army.

C

cacique term for person involved in nepotism or fraud in Spain. Originally a word for Indian chiefs in colonial Spanish America, in late 19th- and early 20th-century Spain it came to mean the local political boss who 'delivered' votes to the main parties in Madrid, Spain.

Caetano Marcello 1906–1980. Portuguese right-wing politician. Professor of administrative law at Lisbon from 1940, he succeeded the dictator Salazar as prime minister from 1968 until his exile after the military coup of 1974. He was granted political asylum in Brazil.

Callaghan (Leonard) James, Baron Callaghan 1912– . British Labour politician. As chancellor of the Exchequer 1964-67, he introduced corporation and capital-gains taxes, and resigned following devaluation. He was home secretary 1967–70 and prime minister 1976-79 in a period of increasing economic stress.

Cambodia (formerly *Khmer Republic* 1970–76, *Democratic Kampuchea* 1976–79, and *People's Republic of Kampuchea* 1979–89) country in SE Asia, bounded N and NW by Thailand, N by Laos, E and SE by Vietnam, and SW by the Gulf of Thailand.

chronology
1863–1941 French protectorate.
1941–45 Occupied by Japan.
1946 Recaptured by France.
1953 Independence achieved from France.
1970 Prince Sihanouk overthrown by US-backed Lon Nol.
1975 Lon Nol overthrown by ◊Khmer Rouge.
1976–78 Khmer Rouge introduced an extreme communist programme, forcing urban groups into rural areas, which brought about over 2.5 million deaths from famine, disease, and maltreatment.
1978–79 Vietnamese invasion and installation of ◊Heng Samrin government.

1982 The three main anti-Vietnamese resistance groups formed an alliance under Prince Sihanouk.

1987 Vietnamese troop withdrawal began.

1989 Sept: completion of Vietnamese withdrawal. Nov: United Nations peace proposal rejected by Phnom Penh government.

1991 Oct: Peace agreement signed in Paris, providing for a UN Transitional Authority in Cambodia (UNTAC) to administer country in transition period in conjunction with all-party Supreme National Council; communism abandoned. Nov: Sihanouk returned as head of state.

1992 Political prisoners released; freedom of speech and party formation restored. Oct: Khmer Rouge refused to disarm in accordance with peace process. Dec: UN Security Council voted to impose limited trade embargo on area of country controlled by Khmer Rouge guerrillas.

1993 General election set for May.

Cambon Paul 1843–1924. French diplomat who was ambassador to London during the years leading to the outbreak of World War I, and a major figure in the creation of the Anglo-French entente during 1903–04.

Cambrai, Battles of two battles in World War I at Cambrai in NE France: *First Battle* Nov–Dec 1917, the town was almost captured by the British when large numbers of tanks were used for the first time.
Second Battle 26 Aug–5 Oct 1918, the town was taken during the final British offensive.

Cameroon country in W Africa, bounded NW by Nigeria, NE by Chad, E by the Central African Republic, S by Congo, Gabon, and Equatorial Guinea, and W by the Atlantic.

chronology

1884 Treaty signed establishing German rule.

1916 Captured by Allied forces in World War I.

1922 Divided between Britain and France.

1946 French Cameroon and British Cameroons made UN trust territories.

1960 French Cameroon became the independent Republic of Cameroon. Ahmadou Ahidjo elected president.

1961 Northern part of British Cameroon merged with Nigeria and southern part joined the Republic of Cameroon to become the Federal Republic of Cameroon.

1966 One-party regime introduced.

1972 New constitution made Cameroon a unitary state, the United Republic of Cameroon.

1973 New national assembly elected.

1982 Ahidjo resigned and was succeeded by Paul Biya.

1983 Biya began to remove his predecessor's supporters; accused by Ahidjo of trying to create a police state. Ahidjo went into exile in France.

1984 Biya re-elected; defeated a plot to overthrow him. Country's name changed to Republic of Cameroon.

1988 Biya re-elected.

1990 Widespread public disorder. Biya granted amnesty to political prisoners.

1991 Constitutional changes made.

1992 Ruling Democratic Assembly of the Cameroon People (RDPC) won in first multiparty elections in 28 years. Biya's presidential victory challenged by opposition.

Campaign for Nuclear Disarmament (CND) nonparty-political British organization advocating the abolition of nuclear weapons worldwide. CND seeks unilateral British initiatives to help start the multilateral process and end the arms race. It was founded 1958.

Campbell-Bannerman Henry 1836–1908. British Liberal politician, prime minister 1905–08. It was during his term of office that the South African colonies achieved self-government, and the Trades Disputes Act 1906 was passed.

Camp David official country home of US presidents, situated in the Appalachian mountains, Maryland; it was originally named Shangri-la by F D Roosevelt, but was renamed Camp David by Eisenhower (after his grandson).

Camp David Agreements two framework agreements signed 1978 by Israeli prime minister Begin and Egyptian president Sadat at Camp David, Maryland, USA, under the guidance of US president Carter, covering an Egypt–Israel peace treaty and phased withdrawal of Israel from Sinai, which was completed 1982, and an overall Middle East settlement including the election by the West Bank and Gaza Strip Palestinians of a 'self-governing authority'. The latter issue has stalled repeatedly over questions of who should represent the Palestinians and what form the self-governing body should take.

Canada country occupying the northern part of the North American continent, bounded S by the USA, N by the Arctic Ocean, NW by Alaska, E by the Atlantic Ocean, and W by the Pacific Ocean.

chronology
1867 Dominion of Canada founded.
1949 Newfoundland joined Canada.
1957 Progressive Conservatives returned to power after 22 years in opposition.
1961 New Democratic Party (NDP) formed.
1963 Liberals elected under Lester Pearson.
1968 Pearson succeeded by Pierre ◊Trudeau.
1979 Joe Clark, leader of the Progressive Conservatives, formed a minority government; defeated on budget proposals.
1980 Liberals under Trudeau returned with a large majority. Québec referendum rejected demand for independence.
1982 Canada Act removed Britain's last legal control over Canadian affairs; 'patriation' of Canada's constitution.
1983 Clark replaced as leader of the Progressive Conservatives by Brian Mulroney.
1984 Trudeau retired and was succeeded as Liberal leader and prime minister by John Turner. Progressive Conservatives won the federal election with a large majority, and Mulroney became prime minister.
1988 Conservatives re-elected with reduced majority on platform of free trade with the USA.
1989 Free-trade agreement signed. Turner resigned as Liberal Party leader, and Ed Broadbent as NDP leader.
1990 Collapse of Meech Lake accord. Canada joined the coalition opposing Iraq's invasion of Kuwait.
1991 Constitutional reform package proposed.
1992 Gradual withdrawal of Canadian forces in Europe announced. Self-governing homeland for Inuit approved. Constitutional reform package, the Charlottetown agreement, rejected in national referendum.
1993 Feb: Mulroney resigned leadership of Conservative Party but remained prime minister until a successor was appointed.

Cape Verde group of islands in the Atlantic, W of Senegal (W Africa).

chronology
1951–74 Ruled as an overseas territory by Portugal.

1974 Moved towards independence through a transitional Portuguese–Cape Verde government.

1975 Independence achieved from Portugal. National people's assembly elected. Aristides Pereira became the first president.

1980 Constitution adopted providing for eventual union with Guinea-Bissau.

1981 Union with Guinea-Bissau abandoned and the constitution amended; became one-party state.

1991 First multiparty elections held. New party, Movement for Democracy (MPD), won majority in assembly. Pereira replaced by Mascarenhas Monteiro.

capitalism economic system in which the principal means of production, distribution, and exchange are in private (individual or corporate) hands and competitively operated for profit. A *mixed economy* combines the private enterprise of capitalism and a degree of state monopoly, as in nationalized industries.

Capone Al(phonse 'Scarface') 1898–1947. US gangster. During the ◊Prohibition period, he built a formidable criminal organization in Chicago. He was brutal in his pursuit of dominance, killing seven members of a rival gang in the ◊St Valentine's Day massacre. He was imprisoned 1931–39 for income-tax evasion, the only charge that could be sustained against him.

Caradon Baron. Title of Hugh ◊Foot, British Labour politician.

Cárdenas Lázaro 1895–1970. Mexican centre-left politician and general, president 1934–40. A civil servant in early life, Cárdenas took part in the revolutionary campaigns 1915–29 that followed the fall of President Díaz (1830–1915). As president of the republic, he attempted to achieve the goals of the revolution by building schools, distributing land to the peasants, and developing transport and industry. He was minister of defence 1943–45.

Carlos I 1863–1908. King of Portugal, of the Braganza-Coburg line, from 1889 until he was assassinated in Lisbon with his elder son Luis. He was succeeded by his younger son Manuel.

Carlsson Ingvar (Gösta) 1934–   . Swedish socialist politician, leader of the Social Democratic Party, deputy prime minister 1982–86 and prime minister 1986–91.

Carlucci Frank (Charles) 1930–   . US politician. A former diplomat and deputy director of the CIA, he was national security adviser 1986–87 and defence secretary 1987–89 under Reagan, supporting Soviet–US arms reduction.

Carol I 1839–1914. First king of Romania 1881–1914. A prince of the house of Hohenzollern-Sigmaringen, he was invited to become prince of Romania, then part of the Ottoman Empire, 1866. In 1877, in alliance with Russia, he declared war on Turkey, and the Congress of Berlin 1878 recognized Romanian independence.

Carol II 1893–1953. King of Romania 1930–40. Son of King Ferdinand, he married Princess Helen of Greece and they had a son, Michael. In 1925 he renounced the succession because of his affair with Elena Lupescu and went into exile in Paris. Michael succeeded to the throne 1927, but in 1930 Carol returned to Romania and was proclaimed king. In 1938 he introduced a new constitution under which he practically became an absolute ruler. He was forced to abdicate by the pro-Nazi ◊Iron Guard Sept 1940, went to Mexico, and married his mistress 1947.

Carrington Peter Alexander Rupert, 6th Baron Carrington 1919–   . British Conservative politician. He was defence secretary 1970–74, and led the opposition in the House of Lords 1964–70 and 1974–79. While foreign secretary 1979–82, he negotiated independence for Zimbabwe, but resigned after failing to anticipate the Falklands crisis. He was secretary general of NATO 1984–88. He chaired EC-sponsored peace talks on Yugoslavia 1991.

Carson Edward Henry, Baron Carson 1854–1935. Irish politician and lawyer who played a decisive part in the trial of the writer Oscar Wilde. In the years before World War I he led the movement in Ulster to resist Irish ◊Home Rule by force of arms if need be.

Carter Jimmy (James Earl) 1924–   . 39th president of the USA 1977–81, a Democrat. In 1976 he narrowly wrested the presidency from Gerald Ford. Features of his presidency were the return of the Panama Canal Zone to Panama, the Camp David Agreements for peace in the Middle East, and the Iranian seizure of US embassy hostages. He was defeated by Ronald Reagan 1980.

Carter Doctrine assertion 1980 by President Carter of a vital US interest in the Persian Gulf region (prompted by the Soviet invasion of Afghanistan and instability in Iran): any outside attempt at control would be met by military force if necessary.

Carver George Washington 1864–1943. US agricultural chemist. Born a slave in Missouri, he was kidnapped and raised by his former owner, Moses Carver. He devoted his life to improving the economy of the US South and the condition of blacks. He advocated the diversification of crops, promoted peanut production, and was a pioneer in the field of plastics.

Casablanca Conference World War II meeting of the US and UK leaders Roosevelt and Churchill, 14–24 Jan 1943, at which the Allied demand for the unconditional surrender of Germany, Italy, and Japan was issued.

Casement Roger David 1864–1916. Irish nationalist. While in the British consular service, he exposed the ruthless exploitation of the people of the Belgian Congo and Peru, for which he was knighted 1911 (degraded 1916). He was hanged for treason by the British for his involvement in the Irish nationalist cause.

Castle Barbara, Baroness Castle (born Betts) 1911–   . British Labour politician, a cabinet minister in the Labour governments of the 1960s and 1970s. She led the Labour group in the European Parliament 1979–89.

Castro Cipriano 1858–1924. Venezuelan dictator 1899-1908, known as 'the Lion of the Andes'. When he refused to pay off foreign debts 1902, British, German, and Italian ships blockaded the country. He presided over a corrupt government. There were frequent rebellions during his rule, and opponents of his regime were exiled or murdered.

Castro (Ruz) Fidel 1927–   . Cuban communist politician, prime minister 1959-76 and president from 1976. He led two unsuccessful coups against the right-wing ◊Batista regime and led the revolution that overthrew the dictator 1959. He raised the standard of living for most Cubans but dealt harshly with dissenters.

Catalonia (Spanish *Cataluña*, Catalan *Catalunya*) autonomous region of NE Spain with a long tradition of independence. It enjoyed autonomy 1932–39 but lost its privileges for supporting the republican cause in the Spanish Civil War (see ◊Civil War, Spanish). Autonomy and official use of the Catalan language were restored 1980.

Cat and Mouse Act popular name for the *Prisoners, Temporary Discharge for Health, Act* 1913; an attempt by the UK Liberal government under Herbert Asquith to reduce embarrassment caused by the incarceration of ◊suffragettes accused of violent offences against property.

Cavaco Silva Anibal 1939–   . Portuguese politician, finance minister 1980–81, and prime minister and Social Democratic Party (PSD) leader from 1985. Under his leadership Portugal joined the European Community 1985 and the Western European Union 1988.

Cavell Edith Louisa 1865–1915. British matron of a Red Cross hospital in Brussels, Belgium, in World War I, who helped Allied soldiers escape to the Dutch frontier. She was court-martialled by the Germans and condemned to death.

CDU abbreviation for *Christian Democratic Union*, a right-of-centre political party in Germany.

Ceauşescu Nicolae 1918–1989. Romanian politician, leader of the Romanian Communist Party (RCP), in power 1965–89. He pursued a policy line independent of and critical of the USSR. He appointed family members, including his wife *Elena Ceauşescu*, to senior state and party posts, and governed in an increasingly repressive manner, zealously implementing schemes that impoverished the nation. The Ceauşescus were overthrown in a bloody revolutionary coup Dec 1989 and executed.

CEDA (acronym for *Confederación Español de Derechas Autónomas*) federation of right-wing parties under the leadership of José Maria Gil Robles, founded during the Second Spanish Republic 1933 to provide a right-wing coalition in the Spanish Cortes. Supporting the Catholic and monarchist causes, the federation was uncommitted as to the form of government.

Central African Federation or (CAF) grouping imposed by the British government 1953, incorporating the territories of Nyasaland and Northern and Southern Rhodesia. Although it established representative government along federal and multiracial lines, an underlying function was to prevent the spread of Afrikaner nationalism into central Africa. It was dismembered 1963 in the face of African demands for independence in Nyasaland and Northern Rhodesia, and the intransigence of the minority white community in Southern Rhodesia.

Central African Republic landlocked country in Central Africa, bordered NE and E by Sudan, S by Zaire and the Congo, W by Cameroon, and NW by Chad.

chronology

1960 Central African Republic achieved independence from France; David Dacko elected president.

1962 The republic made a one-party state.

1965 Dacko ousted in military coup led by Col ◊Bokassa.

1966 Constitution rescinded and national assembly dissolved.

1972 Bokassa declared himself president for life.

1977 Bokassa made himself emperor of the Central African Empire.

1979 Bokassa deposed by Dacko following violent repressive measures by the self-styled emperor, who went into exile.

1981 Dacko deposed in a bloodless coup, led by General André Kolingba, and an all-military government established.

1983 Clandestine opposition movement formed.

1984 Amnesty for all political party leaders announced. President Mitterrand of France paid a state visit.

1985 New constitution promised, with some civilians in the government.

1986 Bokassa returned from France, expecting to return to power; he was imprisoned and his trial started. General Kolingba re-elected. New constitution approved by referendum.

1988 Bokassa found guilty and received death sentence, later commuted to life imprisonment.

1991 Government announced that a national conference would be held in response to demands for a return to democracy.

1992 Abortive debate held on political reform; multiparty elections promised but then postponed.

Central Intelligence Agency (CIA) US intelligence organization established 1947. It has actively intervened overseas, generally to undermine left-wing regimes or to protect US financial interests; for example, in the Congo (now Zaire) and Nicaragua. From 1980 all covert activity by the CIA has by law to be reported to Congress, preferably beforehand, and must be authorized by the president. In 1990 the CIA's estimated budget was $10–12 billion. Robert James Woolsey became CIA director 1993.

central planning system by which the state takes complete control over the running of the national economy. For example, in the Soviet Union from the 1920s, targets and strategies were all decided centrally, leaving little or no room for private initiative or enterprise.

Central Powers originally the signatories of the Triple Alliance 1882: Germany, Austria-Hungary, and Italy. During the World War I, Italy remained neutral before joining the ◊Allies.

Central Treaty Organization (CENTO) military alliance that replaced the ◊Baghdad Pact 1959; it collapsed when the withdrawal of Iran, Pakistan, and Turkey 1979 left the UK as the only member.

Centre Party (German *Zentrumspartei*) German political party established 1871 to protect Catholic interests. Although alienated by Chancellor Bismarck's ◊*Kulturkampf* 1873–78, in the following years the *Zentrum* became an essential component in the government of imperial Germany. The party continued to play a part in the politics of Weimar Germany before being barred by Hitler in the summer of 1933.

Chad landlocked country in central N Africa, bounded N by Libya, E by Sudan, S by the Central African Republic, and W by Cameroon, Nigeria, and Niger.

chronology
1960 Independence achieved from France, with François Tombalbaye as president.
1963 Violent opposition in the Muslim north, led by the Chadian National Liberation Front (Frolinat), backed by Libya.
1968 Revolt quelled with France's help.
1975 Tombalbaye killed in military coup led by Félix Malloum. Frolinat continued its resistance.
1978 Malloum tried to find a political solution by bringing the former Frolinat leader Hissène Habré into his government but they were unable to work together.
1979 Malloum forced to leave the country; an interim government was set up under General Goukouni. Habré continued his opposition with his Army of the North (FAN).
1981 Habré now in control of half the country. Goukouni fled and set up a 'government in exile'.
1983 Habré's regime recognized by the Organization for African Unity (OAU), but in the north Goukouni's supporters, with Libya's help, fought on. Eventually a cease-fire was agreed, with latitude 16°N dividing the country.
1984 Libya and France agreed to a withdrawal of forces.

1985 Fighting between Libyan-backed and French-backed forces intensified.

1987 Chad, France, and Libya agreed on cease-fire proposed by OAU.

1988 Full diplomatic relations with Libya restored.

1989 Libyan troop movements reported on border; Habré re-elected, amended constitution.

1990 President Habré ousted in coup led by Idriss Deby. New constitution adopted.

1991 Several anti-government coups foiled.

1992 Anti-government coup foiled. Two new opposition parties approved.

Chadli Benjedid 1929– . Algerian socialist politician, president 1979–92. An army colonel, he supported ◊Boumédienne in the overthrow of ◊Ben Bella 1965, and succeeded Boumédienne 1979, pursuing more moderate policies. Chadli resigned Jan 1992 following a victory for Islamic fundamentalists in the first round of assembly elections.

Chamberlain (Arthur) Neville 1869–1940. British Conservative politician, son of Joseph Chamberlain. He was prime minister 1937-40; his policy of appeasement towards the fascist dictators Mussolini and Hitler (with whom he concluded the ◊Munich Agreement 1938) failed to prevent the outbreak of World War II. He resigned 1940 following the defeat of the British forces in Norway.

Chamberlain (Joseph) Austen 1863–1937. British Conservative politician, elder son of Joseph Chamberlain; as foreign secretary 1924-29 he negotiated the Pact of ◊Locarno, for which he won the Nobel Peace Prize 1925, and signed the ◊Kellogg–Briand pact to outlaw war 1928.

Chamorro Violeta Barrios de *c.* 1939– . President of Nicaragua from 1990. With strong US support, she was elected to be the candidate for the National Opposition Union (UNO) 1989, winning the presidency from David Ortega Saavedra Feb 1990 and thus ending the period of Sandinista rule.

Charles (Mary) Eugenia 1919– . Dominican politician, prime minister from 1980; cofounder and first leader of the centrist Dominica Freedom Party (DFP). Two years after Dominica's independence the DFP won the 1980 general election and she became the Caribbean's first female prime minister.

Charles (Karl Franz Josef) 1887–1922. Emperor of Austria and king of Hungary from 1916, the last of the Habsburg emperors. He succeeded his great-uncle Franz Josef 1916 but was forced to withdraw to Switzerland 1918, although he refused to abdicate. In 1921 he attempted unsuccessfully to regain the crown of Hungary and was deported to Madeira, where he died.

Chavez Cesar Estrada 1927–   . US labour organizer who founded the National Farm Workers Association 1962 and, with the support of the AFL-CIO and other major unions, embarked on a successful campaign to unionize California grape workers. He led boycotts of citrus fruits, lettuce, and grapes in the early 1970s, but disagreement and exploitation of migrant farm labourers continued despite his successes.

Checkpoint Charlie Western-controlled crossing point for non-Germans between West Berlin and East Berlin, opened 1961 as the only crossing point between the Allied and Soviet sectors. Its dismantling in June 1990 was seen as a symbol of the ending of the ◊Cold War.

Cheka secret police operating in the USSR 1917–23. It originated from the tsarist Okhrana (the security police under the tsar 1881-1917), and became successively the OGPU (GPU) 1923-34, NKVD 1934-46, MVD 1946-53, and the ◊KGB from 1954.

chemical warfare use in war of gaseous, liquid, or solid substances intended to have a toxic effect on humans, animals, or plants. Together with biological warfare, it was banned by the Geneva Protocol 1925 and the United Nations in 1989 also voted for a ban. The total US stockpile 1989 was estimated at 30,000 tonnes and the Soviet stockpile at 50,000 tonnes. In June 1990, the USA and USSR agreed bilaterally to reduce their stockpile to 5,000 tonnes each by 2002. The USA began replacing its stocks with new nerve-gas binary weapons.

Chernenko Konstantin 1911–1985. Soviet politician, leader of the Soviet Communist Party (CPSU) and president 1984–85. He was a protégé of Brezhnev and from 1978 a member of the Politburo.

Chetnik member of a Serbian nationalist group that operated underground during the German occupation of Yugoslavia during World War II. Led by Col Draza ◊Mihailović, the Chetniks initially received aid from the Allies, but this was later transferred to the communist partisans led by Tito. The term has also popularly been applied to Serb militia forces in the 1991-92 Yugoslav civil war.

Chiang Ching alternative transliteration of ◊Jiang Qing, Chinese actress, third wife of Mao Zedong.

Chiang Ching-kuo 1910–1988. Taiwanese politician, son of Chiang Kai-shek, prime minister 1971–78, president 1978–88.

Chiang Kai-shek (Pinyin *Jiang Jie Shi*) 1887–1975. Chinese nationalist ◊Guomindang (Kuomintang) general and politician, president of China 1928–31 and 1943–49, and of Taiwan from 1949, where he set up a US-supported right-wing government on his expulsion from the mainland by the communist forces.He was a commander in the civil war that lasted from the end of imperial rule 1911 to the Second ◊Sino-Japanese War and beyond, having split with the communist leader Mao Zedong 1927.

Chifley Ben (Joseph Benedict) 1885–1951. Australian Labor prime minister 1945–49. He united the party in fulfilling a welfare and nationalization programme 1945–49 (although he failed in an attempt to nationalize the banks 1947) and initiated an immigration programme and the Snowy Mountains hydroelectric project.

Childers (Robert) Erskine 1870–1922. British civil servant and, from 1921, Irish Sinn Féin politician, author of the spy novel *The Riddle of the Sands* 1903. He was executed as a Republican terrorist.

Chile South American country, bounded N by Peru and Bolivia, E by Argentina, and S and W by the Pacific Ocean.

chronology
1818 Achieved independence from Spain.
1964 Christian Democratic Party (PDC) formed government under Eduardo ◊Frei.
1970 Dr Salvador ◊Allende became the first democratically elected Marxist president; he embarked on an extensive programme of nationalization and social reform.
1973 Government overthrown by the CIA-backed military, led by General Augusto ◊Pinochet. Allende killed. Policy of repression began during which all opposition was put down and political activity banned.
1983 Growing opposition to the regime from all sides, with outbreaks of violence.
1988 Referendum on whether Pinochet should serve a further term resulted in a clear 'No' vote.
1989 President Pinochet agreed to constitutional changes to allow pluralist

politics. Patricio Aylwin (PDC) elected president (his term would begin 1990); Pinochet remained as army commander in chief.

1990 Aylwin reached accord on end to military junta government. Pinochet censured by president.

1992 Future US–Chilean free-trade agreement announced.

Chilean Revolution in Chile, the presidency of Salvador ◊Allende 1970–73, the Western hemisphere's first democratically elected Marxist-oriented president of an independent state.

China the largest country in E Asia, bounded N by Mongolia; NW by Tajikistan, Kyrgyzstan, Kazakhstan, and Afghanistan; SW by India, Nepal, and Bhutan; S by Myanmar (Burma), Laos, and Vietnam; SE by the South China Sea; E by the East China Sea, North Korea, and Yellow Sea; NE by Russia.

chronology
1949 People's Republic of China proclaimed by Mao ◊Zedong.
1954 Soviet-style constitution adopted.
1956-57 ◊Hundred Flowers Movement encouraged criticism of the government.
1958-60 ◊Great Leap Forward commune experiment to achieve 'true communism'.
1960 Withdrawal of Soviet technical advisers.
1962 Sino-Indian border war.
1962-65 Economic recovery programme under ◊Liu Shaoqi; Maoist 'socialist education movement' rectification campaign.
1966-69 Great Proletarian Cultural Revolution; Liu Shaoqi overthrown.
1969 Ussuri River border clashes with USSR.
1970-76 Reconstruction under Mao and Zhou Enlai.
1971 Entry into United Nations.
1972 US president Nixon visited Beijing.
1975 New state constitution. Unveiling of ◊Zhou's 'Four Modernizations' programme.
1976 Deaths of Zhou Enlai and Mao Zedong; appointment of ◊Hua Guofeng as prime minister and Communist Party chair. Vice Premier ◊Deng Xiaoping in hiding. ◊Gang of Four arrested.
1977 Rehabilitation of Deng Xiaoping.
1979 Economic reforms introduced. Diplomatic relations opened with USA. Punitive invasion of Vietnam.

1980 ◊Zhao Ziyang appointed prime minister.

1981 Hu Yaobang succeeded Hua Guofeng as party chair. Imprisonment of Gang of Four.

1982 New state constitution adopted.

1984 'Enterprise management' reforms for industrial sector.

1986 Student prodemocracy demonstrations.

1987 Hu was replaced as party leader by Zhao, with ◊Li Peng as prime minister. Deng left Politburo but remained influential.

1988 ◊Yang Shangkun replaced Li Xiannian as state president. Economic reforms encountered increasing problems; inflation rocketed.

1989 Over 2,000 killed in prodemocracy student demonstrations in Tiananmen Square; international sanctions imposed.

1991 March: European Community and Japanese sanctions lifted. May: normal relations with USSR resumed. Sept: UK prime minister John Major visited Beijing. Nov: relations with Vietnam normalized.

1992 China promised to sign 1968 Nuclear Non-Proliferation Treaty. Historic visit by Japan's emperor.

1993 ◊Jiang Zemin, Chinese Communist Party general secretary, set to replace Yang Shangkun as president.

Chindit member of an Indian division of the British army in World War II that carried out guerrilla operations against the Japanese in Burma (now Myanmar) under the command of Brigadier General Orde Wingate (1903–44). The name derived from the mythical Chinthay—half lion, half eagle—placed at the entrance of Burmese pagodas to scare away evil spirits.

Chinese Revolution series of great political upheavals in China 1911–49 that eventually led to Communist Party rule and the establishment of the People's Republic of China. In 1912, a nationalist revolt overthrew the imperial Manchudynasty. Led by Sun Yat-sen 1923–25 and by Chiang Kai-shek 1925–49, the nationalists, or Guomindang, were increasing challenged by the growing communist movement. The 10,000 km/6,000 mi *Long March* to the NW by the communists 1934–35 to escape from attacks by the Guomindang forces resulted in Mao Zedong's emergence as communist leader. During World War II 1939–45, the various Chinese political groups pooled military resources against the Japanese invaders. After World War II, the conflict reignited into open civil war 1946–49, until the Guomindang were defeated at Nanking and forced to flee to Taiwan.

Communist rule was established in the People's Republic of China under the leadership of Mao.

Chirac Jacques 1932– . French conservative politician, prime minister 1974–76 and 1986–88. He established the neo-Gaullist Rassemblement pour la République (RPR) 1976, and became mayor of Paris 1977.

Chissano Joaquim 1939– . Mozambique nationalist politician, president from 1986; foreign minister 1975–86. In Oct 1992 Chissano signed a peace accord with the leader of the rebel Mozambique National Resistance (MNR) party, bringing to an end 16 years of civil war.

Choonhavan Chatichai 1922– . Thai conservative politician, prime minister of Thailand 1988–91. He promoted a peace settlement in neighbouring Cambodia as part of a vision of transforming Indochina into a thriving open-trade zone. Despite economic success, he was ousted in a bloodless military coup 1991.

Chou En-lai alternative transliteration of ◊Zhou Enlai.

Christian X 1870–1947. King of Denmark and Iceland from 1912, when he succeeded his father Frederick VIII. He married Alexandrine, Duchess of Mecklenburg-Schwerin, and was popular for his democratic attitude. During World War II he was held prisoner by the Germans in Copenhagen. He was succeeded by Frederick IX.

Chun Doo-hwan 1931– . South Korean military ruler who seized power 1979, president 1981–88 as head of the newly formed Democratic Justice Party.

Churchill Winston (Leonard Spencer) 1874–1965. British Conservative politician, prime minister 1940-45 and 1951-55. In Parliament from 1900, as a Liberal until 1923, he held a number of ministerial offices, including First Lord of the Admiralty 1911-15 and chancellor of the Exchequer 1924-29. Absent from the cabinet in the 1930s, he returned Sept 1939 to lead a coalition government 1940-45, negotiating with Allied leaders in World War II to achieve the unconditional surrender of Germany 1945; he led a Conservative government 1951-55. He received the Nobel Prize for Literature 1953.

Ciano Galeazzo 1903–1944. Italian Fascist politician. Son-in-law of the dictator Mussolini, he was foreign minister and member of the Fascist

Supreme Council 1936–43. He voted against Mussolini at the meeting of the Grand Council July 1943 that overthrew the dictator, but was later tried for treason and shot by the Fascists.

CIS abbreviation for ◊*Commonwealth of Independent States*, established 1992 by 11 former Soviet republics.

civil-rights movement general term for efforts by American black people to improve their status in society after World War II. Following their significant contribution to the national effort in wartime, they began a sustained campaign for full civil rights which challenged racial discrimination. Despite favourable legislation such as the Civil Rights Act 1964 and the 1965 Voting Rights Act, growing discontent among urban blacks in northern states led to outbreaks of civil disorder such as the Watts riots in Los Angeles, Aug 1965. Another riot in the city 1992, following the acquittal of policemen charged with beating a black motorist, demonstrated continuing problems in American race relations.

Civil War, Spanish war 1936–39 precipitated by a military revolt led by General Franco against the Republican government. Inferior military capability led to the gradual defeat of the Republicans by 1939, and the establishment of Franco's dictatorship.

Franco's insurgents (Nationalists, who were supported by Fascist Italy and Nazi Germany) seized power in the south and northwest, but were suppressed in areas such as Madrid and Barcelona by the workers' militia. The loyalists (Republicans) were aided by the USSR and the volunteers of the International Brigade, which included several writers, among them George Orwell.

Clark Joe (Joseph) Charles 1939–   . Canadian Progressive Conservative politician who became party leader 1976, and May 1979 defeated Pierre ◊*Trudeau* at the polls to become the youngest prime minister in Canada's history. Following the rejection of his government's budget, he was defeated in a second election Feb 1980. He became secretary of state for external affairs (foreign minister) 1984 in the ◊Mulroney government.

Clark Mark (Wayne) 1896–1984. US general in World War II. In 1942 he became Chief of Staff for ground forces, and deputy to General Eisenhower. He led a successful secret mission by submarine to get information in North Africa to prepare for the Allied invasion, and commanded the 5th Army in the invasion of Italy.

Clarke Kenneth (Harry) 1940– . British Conservative politician, member of Parliament from 1970, a cabinet minister from 1985, education secretary 1990–92, home secretary from 1992, and chancellor of the Exchequer 1993.

Clay Lucius DuBignon 1897–1978. US commander in chief of the US occupation forces in Germany 1947–49. He broke the Soviet blockade of Berlin 1948 after 327 days, with an airlift—a term he brought into general use—which involved bringing all supplies into West Berlin by air.

Clemenceau Georges 1841–1929. French politician and journalist (prominent in the defence of Alfred ◊Dreyfus). He was prime minister 1906–09 and 1917–20. After World War I he presided over the peace conference in Paris that drew up the Treaty of ◊Versailles, but failed to secure for France the Rhine as a frontier.

Clinton Bill (William Jefferson) 1946– . 42nd president of the USA from 1993. A Democrat, he served as governor of Arkansas 1979-81, and 1983-93, establishing a liberal and progressive reputation. He won a successful 1992 presidential campaign, against the incumbent George Bush, by centring on domestic issues and economic recovery. He became the first Democrat in the White House for 13 years.

CND abbreviation for ◊*Campaign for Nuclear Disarmament*.

Cold War ideological, political, and economic tensions 1945–90 between the USSR and Eastern Europe on the one hand and the USA and Western Europe on the other. The Cold War was exacerbated by propaganda, covert activity by intelligence agencies, and economic sanctions; it intensified at times of conflict anywhere in the world. Arms-reduction agreements between the USA and USSR in the late 1980s, and a diminution of Soviet influence in Eastern Europe, symbolized by the opening of the Berlin Wall 1989, led to a reassessment of positions, and the 'war' officially ended 1990.

collective farm farm in which a group of farmers pool their land, domestic animals, and agricultural implements, retaining as private property enough only for the members' own requirements. The profits of the farm are divided among its members. In cooperative farming, farmers retain private ownership of the land.

collectivization policy pursued by the Soviet leader Stalin in the USSR after 1928 to reorganize agriculture by taking land into state ownership or creating ◊collective farms. Much of this was achieved during the first two ◊Five-Year Plans but only with much coercion and loss of life among the peasantry.

Collins Michael 1890–1922. Irish nationalist. He was a Sinn Féin leader, a founder and director of intelligence of the Irish Republican Army 1919, minister for finance in the provisional government of the Irish Free State 1922 (see ◊Ireland, Republic of), commander of the Free State forces in the civil war, and for ten days head of state before being killed by Irishmen opposed to the partition treaty with Britain.

Collor de Mello Fernando 1949– . Brazilian politician, president 1990–92. He founded the centre-right National Reconstruction Party (PRN) 1989 and won that year's presidential election by promising to root out government corruption and entrenched privileges. However, rumours of his misconduct led to his constitutional removal from office by a vote of impeachment 1992.

Colombia country in South America, bounded N by the Caribbean Sea, W by the Pacific Ocean, NW corner by Panama, E and NE by Venezuela, SE by Brazil, and SW by Peru and Ecuador.

chronology
1886 Full independence achieved from Spain.
1930 Liberals in power.
1946 Conservatives in power.
1948 Left-wing mayor of Bogotá assassinated; widespread outcry.
1949 Start of civil war, 'La Violencia', during which over 250,000 people died.
1957 Hoping to halt the violence, Conservatives and Liberals agreed to form a National Front, sharing the presidency.
1970 National Popular Alliance (ANAPO) formed as a left-wing opposition to the National Front.
1974 National Front accord temporarily ended.
1975 Civil unrest because of disillusionment with the government.
1978 Liberals, under Julio Turbay, revived the accord and began an intensive fight against drug dealers.
1982 Liberals maintained their control of congress but lost the presidency. The Conservative president, Belisario Betancur, granted guerrillas an amnesty and freed political prisoners.

1984 Minister of justice assassinated by drug dealers; campaign against them stepped up.

1986 Virgilio Barco Vargas, Liberal, elected president by record margin.

1989 Drug cartel assassinated leading presidential candidate; Vargas declared antidrug war; bombing campaign by drug lords killed hundreds; police killed José Rodríguez Gacha, one of the most wanted cartel leaders.

1990 Cesar Gaviria Trujillo elected president. Liberals maintained control of congress.

1991 New constitution prohibited extradition of Colombians wanted for trial in other countries; several leading drug traffickers arrested. Oct: Liberal Party won general election.

1992 One of leading drug barons, Pablo Escobar, escaped from prison.

1993 Escobar continued to defy government.

Colombo Plan plan for cooperative economic and social development in Asia and the Pacific, established 1950. The 26 member countries are Afghanistan, Australia, Bangladesh, Bhutan, Cambodia, Canada, Fiji, India, Indonesia, Iran, Japan, South Korea, Laos, Malaysia, Maldives, Myanmar (Burma), Nepal, New Zealand, Pakistan, Papua New Guinea, Philippines, Singapore, Sri Lanka, Thailand, UK, and USA. They meet annually to discuss economic and development plans such as irrigation, hydroelectric schemes, and technical training.

Comecon (acronym for *Co*uncil for *M*utual *Econ*omic Assistance, or *CMEA*) economic organization 1949–91, linking the USSR with Bulgaria, Czechoslovakia, Hungary, Poland, Romania, East Germany (1950–90), Mongolia (from 1962), Cuba (from 1972), and Vietnam (from 1978), with Yugoslavia as an associated member. Albania also belonged 1949–61. Its establishment was prompted by the ◊Marshall Plan.

Cominform (acronym for *Com*munist *Inform*ation Bureau) organization 1947–56 established by the Soviet politician Andrei Zhdanov (1896–1948) to exchange information between European communist parties. Yugoslavia was expelled 1948.

Comintern acronym from *Com*munist ◊*Intern*ational.

Committee of Imperial Defence informal group established 1902 to coordinate planning of the British Empire's defence forces. Initially meeting on a temporary basis, it was established permanently 1904. Members were usually cabinet ministers concerned with defence, military leaders, and key civil servants.

Commonwealth conference any consultation between the prime ministers (or defence, finance, foreign, or other ministers) of the sovereign independent members of the British Commonwealth. These are informal discussion meetings, and the implementation of policies is decided by individual governments.

Commonwealth Development Corporation organization founded as the Colonial Development Corporation 1948 to aid the development of dependent Commonwealth territories; the change of name and extension of its activities to include those now independent were announced 1962.

Commonwealth Immigration Acts successive acts that attempted to regulate the entry into the UK of British subjects from the Commonwealth. The Commonwealth Immigration Act, passed by the Conservative government 1962, ruled that Commonwealth immigrants entering Britain must have employment or be able to offer required skills.

Commonwealth of Independent States (CIS) successor body to the ◊Union of Soviet Socialist Republics, initially formed as a new commonwealth of Slav republics on 8 Dec 1991 by the presidents of the Russian Federation, Belarus, and Ukraine. On 21 Dec, eight of the nine remaining non-Slav republics—Moldova, Tajikistan, Armenia, Azerbaijan, Turkmenistan, Kazakhstan, Kyrgyzstan, and Uzbekistan – joined the CIS at a meeting held in Kazakhstan's capital, Alma Ata. The CIS formally came into existence in Jan 1992 when President Gorbachev resigned and the Soviet government voted itself out of existence. It has no real, formal political institutions and its role is uncertain. Its headquarters are in Minsk (Mensk), Belarus.

Commonwealth, the (British) voluntary association of 50 countries and their dependencies that once formed part of the ◊British Empire and are now independent sovereign states. They are all regarded as 'full members of the Commonwealth'. Additionally, there are some 20 territories that are not completely sovereign and remain dependencies of the UK or another of the fully sovereign members, and are regarded as 'Commonwealth countries'. Heads of government meet every two years, apart from those of Nauru and Tuvalu; however, Nauru and Tuvalu have the right to participate in all functional activities. The Commonwealth has no charter or constitution, and is founded more on tradition and sentiment than on political or economic factors.

communism revolutionary socialism based on the theories of the political philosophers Karl Marx and Friedrich Engels, emphasizing common ownership of the means of production and a planned economy. The principle held is that each should work according to their capacity and receive according to their needs. Politically, it seeks the overthrow of capitalism through a proletarian revolution. The first communist state was the USSR after the revolution of 1917. Revolutionary socialist parties and groups united to form communist parties in other countries (in the UK 1920). After World War II, communism was enforced in those countries that came under Soviet occupation. China emerged after 1961 as a rival to the USSR in world communist leadership, and other countries attempted to adapt communism to their own needs. The late 1980s saw a movement for more individual freedoms in many communist countries, culminating in the abolition or overthrow of communist rule in Eastern European countries and Mongolia, and further state repression in China. The failed hard-line coup in the USSR against President Gorbachev 1991 resulted in the effective abandonment of communism there.

Comoros group of islands in the Indian Ocean between Madagascar and the east coast of Africa. Three of them—Njazidja, Nzwani, and Mwali—form the republic of Comoros; the fourth island, Mayotte, is a French dependency.

chronology

1975 Independence achieved from France, but the island of Mayotte remained part of France. Ahmed Abdallah elected president. The Comoros joined the United Nations.

1976 Abdallah overthrown by Ali Soilih.

1978 Soilih killed by mercenaries working for Abdallah. Islamic republic proclaimed and Abdallah elected president.

1979 The Comoros became a one-party state; powers of the federal government increased.

1985 Constitution amended to make Abdallah head of government as well as head of state.

1989 Abdallah killed by French mercenaries who took control of government; under French and South African pressure, mercenaries left Comoros, turning authority over to French administration and interim president Said Mohammad Djohar.

1990 Antigovernment coup foiled.

1992 Third transitional government appointed. Antigovernment coup foiled.

1993 Jan: general election failed to provide any one party with overall assembly majority. President Djohar appointed Halidi Abderamane Ibrahim prime minister.

concentration camp prison camp for civilians in wartime or under totalitarian rule. A system of hundreds of concentration camps was developed by the Nazis in Germany and occupied Europe (1933-45) to imprison Jews and political and ideological opponents after Hitler became chancellor Jan 1933. The most infamous camps in World War II were the extermination camps of Auschwitz, Belsen, Dachau, Maidanek, Sobibor, and Treblinka. The total number of people who died at the camps exceeded 6 million, and some inmates were subjected to medical experimentation before being killed.

At Oswiecim (Auschwitz-Birkenau), a vast camp complex was created for imprisonment and slave labour as well as the extermination of over 4 million people in gas chambers or by other means. In addition to Jews, the victims included Gypsies, homosexuals, and other 'misfits' or 'unwanted' people. At Maidanek, about 1.5 million people were exterminated, cremated, and their ashes used as fertilizer. Many camp officials and others responsible were tried after 1945 for war crimes, and executed or imprisoned. Foremost was Adolf ◊Eichmann, the architect of the extermination system, who was tried and executed by the state of Israel 1961.

Conference on Security and Cooperation in Europe (CSCE) international forum attempting to reach agreement in security, economics, science, technology, and human rights. The CSCE first met at the ◊Helsinki Conference in Finland 1975. By the end of March 1992, having admitted the former republics of the USSR, as well as Croatia and Slovenia, its membership had risen to 51 states.

Confindustria in European history, a general confederation of industry established in Italy 1920 with the aim of countering working-class agitation. It contributed large funds to the fascist movement, which, in turn, used its *squadristi* against the workers. After Mussolini's takeover of power in 1922, Confindustria became one of the major groups of the fascist corporative state.

Congo country in W central Africa, bounded N by Cameroon and the Central African Republic, E and S by Zaire, W by the Atlantic Ocean, and NW by Gabon.

chronology
1910 Became part of French Equatorial Africa.
1960 Achieved independence from France, with Abbé Youlou as the first president.
1963 Youlou forced to resign. New constitution approved, with Alphonse Massamba-Débat as president.
1964 The Congo became a one-party state.
1968 Military coup, led by Capt Marien Ngouabi, ousted Massamba-Débat.
1970 A Marxist state, the People's Republic of the Congo, was announced, with the Congolese Labour Party (PCT) as the only legal party.
1977 Ngouabi assassinated. Col Yhombi-Opango became president.
1979 Yhombi-Opango handed over the presidency to the PCT, who chose Col Denis ♢Sassou-Nguessou as his successor.
1984 Sassou-Nguessou elected for another five-year term.
1990 The PCT abandoned Marxist-Leninism and promised multiparty politics.
1991 1979 constitution suspended. Country renamed the Republic of Congo.
1992 New constitution approved and multiparty elections held, giving Pan-African Union for Social Democracy (UPADS) the most assembly seats.

Congress of Racial Equality (CORE) US nonviolent civil-rights organization, founded in Chicago 1942.

Connell James 1850–1929. Irish socialist who wrote the British Labour Party anthem 'The Red Flag' during the 1889 London strike.

Conservative Party UK political party, one of the two historic British parties; the name replaced *Tory* in general use from 1830 onwards. Traditionally the party of landed interests, it broadened its political base under Benjamin Disraeli's leadership in the 19th century. The present Conservative Party's free-market capitalism is supported by the world of finance and the management of industry.

Contadora Group alliance formed between Colombia, Mexico, Panama, and Venezuela Jan 1983 to establish a general peace treaty for Central America. It was named after Contadora, the island of the Pearl Group in the Gulf of Panama where the first meeting was held.

containment US policy (adopted from 1947) that was designed to prevent the spread of communism.

Contra member of a Central American right-wing guerrilla force attempting to overthrow the democratically elected Nicaraguan Sandinista government 1979–90. The Contras, many of them mercenaries or former members of the deposed dictator Somoza's guard (see ◊Nicaraguan Revolution), operated mainly from bases outside Nicaragua, mostly in Honduras, with covert US funding, as revealed by the ◊Irangate hearings 1986–87.

Cook Robin Finlayson 1946–   . English Labour politician. A member of the moderate-left Tribune Group, he entered Parliament 1974 and became a leading member of Labour's shadow cabinet, specializing in health matters. When John Smith assumed the party leadership July 1992, Cook remained in the shadow cabinet as spokesman for trade and industry.

Coolidge (John) Calvin 1872–1933. 30th president of the USA 1923-29, a Republican. As governor of Massachusetts 1919, he was responsible for crushing a Boston police strike. As Warren ◊Harding's vice president 1921-23, he succeeded to the presidency on Harding's death (2 Aug 1923). He won the 1924 presidential election, and his period of office was marked by economic growth.

Cooperative Party political party founded in Britain 1917 by the cooperative movement to maintain its principles in parliamentary and local government. A written constitution was adopted 1938. The party had strong links with the Labour Party; from 1946 Cooperative Party candidates stood in elections as Cooperative and Labour Candidates and, after the 1959 general election, agreement was reached to limit the party's candidates to 30.

Corfu incident international crisis 27 Aug–27 Sept 1923 that marked the first assertion of power in foreign affairs by the Italian Fascist government. In 1923 an international commission was determining the frontier between Greece and Albania. On 27 Aug 1923, its chief, Italian general Tellini, was found (with four of his staff) murdered near the Albanian border, but on Greek territory. The Italian government under Benito Mussolini, backed by Italians, Fascist and anti-Fascist, sent an ultimatum to the Greek government demanding compensation, which was rejected. On 31 Aug Mussolini ordered the Italian bombardment and occupation of the Greek island of Corfu. The Greeks appealed to the League of Nations and, under pressure from Britain and France, Mussolini withdrew from Corfu on 27 Sept 1923. Greece had to accept most of the Italian demands, including the payment of a large indemnity.

corporatism belief that the state in capitalist democracies should intervene to a large extent in the economy to ensure social harmony. In Austria, for example, corporatism results in political decisions often being taken after discussions between chambers of commerce, trade unions, and the government.

Corregidor island fortress off the Bataan Peninsula at the mouth of Manila Bay, Luzon, the Philippines. On 6 May 1942, Japanese forces captured Corregidor and its 10,000 US and Filipino defenders, completing their conquest of the Philippines. US forces recaptured Corregidor in Feb 1945.

Cosgrave Liam 1920–   . Irish Fine Gael politician, prime minister of the Republic of Ireland 1973–77. As party leader 1965–77, he headed a Fine Gael–Labour coalition government from 1973. Relations between the Irish and UK governments improved under his premiership.

Cosgrave William Thomas 1880–1965. Irish politician. He took part in the ◊Easter Rising 1916 and sat in the Sinn Féin cabinet of 1919–21. Head of the Free State government 1922–33, he founded and led the Fine Gael opposition 1933–44. His eldest son is Liam Cosgrave.

Costa Rica country in Central America, bounded N by Nicaragua, SE by Panama, E by the Caribbean Sea, and W by the Pacific Ocean.

chronology
1821 Independence achieved from Spain.
1949 New constitution adopted. National army abolished. José Figueres, cofounder of the National Liberation Party (PLN), elected president; he embarked on ambitious socialist programme.
1958–73 Mainly conservative administrations.
1974 PLN regained the presidency and returned to socialist policies.
1978 Rodrigo Carazo, conservative, elected president. Sharp deterioration in the state of the economy.
1982 Luis Alberto Monge (PLN) elected president. Harsh austerity programme introduced to rebuild the economy. Pressure from the USA to abandon neutral stance and condemn Sandinista regime in Nicaragua.
1983 Policy of neutrality reaffirmed.

1985 Following border clashes with Sandinista forces, a US-trained antiguerrilla guard formed.

1986 Oscar ◊Arias Sánchez won the presidency on a neutralist platform.

1987 Oscar Arias Sánchez won Nobel Prize for Peace for devising a Central American peace plan.

1990 Rafael Calderón, Christian Socialist Union Party (PUSC), elected president.

Council of Europe body constituted 1949 in Strasbourg, France (still its headquarters), to secure 'a greater measure of unity between the European countries'. The widest association of European states, it has a *Committee* of foreign ministers, a *Parliamentary Assembly* (with members from national parliaments), and a *European Commission* investigating violations of human rights.

Country Party (official name *National Country Party* from 1975) Australian political party representing the interests of the farmers and people of the smaller towns; it holds the power balance between Liberals and Labor. It developed from about 1860, gained strength after the introduction of preferential voting 1918, and has been in coalition with the Liberals from 1949.

coup d'état or *coup* forcible takeover of the government of a country by elements from within that country, generally carried out by violent or illegal means. It differs from a revolution in typically being carried out by a small group (for example, of army officers or opposition politicians) to install its leader as head of government, rather than being a mass uprising by the people.

Craig James 1871–1940. Ulster Unionist politician, the first prime minister of Northern Ireland 1921–40. Craig became a member of Parliament 1906, and was a highly effective organizer of Unionist resistance to Home Rule. As prime minister he carried out systematic discrimination against the Catholic minority, abolishing proportional representation 1929 and redrawing constituency boundaries to ensure Protestant majorities.

Craxi Bettino 1934– . Italian socialist politician, leader of the Italian Socialist Party (PSI) from 1976, prime minister 1983–87.

Cresson Edith 1934– . French politician and founder member of the Socialist Party, prime minister 1991–92. Cresson held successive ministerial portfolios in François Mitterrand's government 1981–86 and 1988–90.

Her government was troubled by a struggling economy, a series of strikes, and unrest in many of the country's poor suburban areas, which eventually forced her resignation.

Cripps (Richard) Stafford 1889–1952. British Labour politician, expelled from the Labour Party 1939–45 for supporting a 'Popular Front' against Chamberlain's ◊appeasement policy. He was ambassador to Moscow 1940–42, minister of aircraft production 1942–45, and chancellor of the Exchequer 1947–50.

Croatia (Serbo-Croatian *Hrvatska*) country in central Europe, bounded N by Slovenia and Hungary, W by the Adriatic Sea, and E by Bosnia-Herzegovina and the Yugoslavian republic of Serbia.

chronology
1918 Became part of the kingdom that united the Serbs, Croats, and Slovenes.
1929 The kingdom of Croatia, Serbia, and Slovenia became Yugoslavia. Croatia continued its campaign for autonomy.
1941 Became a Nazi puppet state following German invasion.
1945 Became constituent republic of Yugoslavia.
1970s Separatist demands resurfaced. Crackdown against anti-Serb separatist agitators.
1989 Formation of opposition parties permitted.
1990 April–May: Communists defeated by ◊Tudjman-led Croatian Democratic Union (HDZ) in first free election since 1938. Sept: 'sovereignty' declared. Dec: new constitution adopted.
1991 Feb: assembly called for Croatia's secession. March: Serb-dominated Krajina announced secession from Croatia. June: Croatia declared independence; military conflict with Serbia; internal civil war ensued. July onwards: civil war intensified. Oct: Croatia formally seceded from Yugoslavia.
1992 Jan: United Nations peace accord reached in Sarajevo; Croatia's independence recognized by the European Community. March–April: UN peacekeeping forces drafted into Croatia. April: independence recognized by USA. May: became a member of the United Nations. Aug: Tudjman directly elected president; HDZ won assembly elections. Sept: Tudjman requested withdrawal of UN forces on expiry of mandate 1993.
1993 Jan: Croatian forces launched offensive to retake parts of Serb-held Krajina, violating the 1992 UN peace accord.

Croker Richard 1841–1922. US politician, 'boss' of Tammany Hall, the Democratic Party political machine in New York 1886–1902.

Crossman Richard (Howard Stafford) 1907–1974. British Labour politician. He was minister of housing and local government 1964–66 and of health and social security 1968–70. His posthumous *Crossman Papers* 1975 revealed confidential cabinet discussion.

Cuba island country in the Caribbean Sea, the largest of the West Indies, off the S coast of Florida and to the E of Mexico.

chronology
1901 Cuba achieved independence; Tomás Estrada Palma became first president of the Republic of Cuba.
1933 Fulgencia ◊Batista seized power.
1944 Batista retired.
1952 Batista seized power again to begin an oppressive regime.
1953 Fidel ◊Castro led an unsuccessful coup against Batista.
1956 Second unsuccessful coup by Castro.
1959 Batista overthrown by Castro. Constitution of 1940 replaced by a 'Fundamental Law', making Castro prime minister, his brother Raúl Castro his deputy, and 'Che' ◊Guevara his number three.
1960 All US businesses in Cuba appropriated without compensation; USA broke off diplomatic relations.
1961 USA sponsored an unsuccessful invasion at the Bay of Pigs. Castro announced that Cuba had become a communist state, with a Marxist-Leninist programme of economic development.
1962 Cuba expelled from the Organization of American States. Soviet nuclear missiles installed but subsequently removed from Cuba at US insistence.
1965 Cuba's sole political party renamed Cuban Communist Party (PCC). With Soviet help, Cuba began to make considerable economic and social progress.
1972 Cuba became a full member of the Moscow-based Council for Mutual Economic Assistance.
1976 New socialist constitution approved; Castro elected president.
1976-81 Castro became involved in extensive international commitments, sending troops as Soviet surrogates, particularly to Africa.
1982 Cuba joined other Latin American countries in giving moral support to Argentina in its dispute with Britain over the Falklands.

1984 Castro tried to improve US-Cuban relations by discussing exchange of US prisoners in Cuba for Cuban 'undesirables' in the USA.

1988 Peace accord with South Africa signed, agreeing to withdrawal of Cuban troops from Angola.

1989 Reduction in Cuba's overseas military activities.

1991 Soviet troops withdrawn.

1992 Castro affirmed continuing support of communism.

Cuban missile crisis confrontation in international relations 1962 when Soviet rockets were installed in Cuba and US president Kennedy compelled Soviet leader Khrushchev, by an ultimatum, to remove them. The drive by the USSR to match the USA in nuclear weaponry dates from this event.

Cultural Revolution Chinese mass movement 1966-69 begun by Communist Party chair Mao Zedong, directed against the upper middle class—bureaucrats, artists, and academics—who were killed, imprisoned, humiliated, or 'resettled'. Intended to 'purify' Chinese communism, it was also an attempt by Mao to renew his political and ideological pre-eminence inside China. Half a million people are estimated to have been killed.

Cuno Wilhelm 1876–1933. German industrialist and politician who was briefly chancellor of the Weimar Republic 1923.

Curley James Michael 1874–1958. US Democrat politician. He was a member of the US House of Representatives 1912–14, several times mayor of Boston between 1914 and 1934, when he was elected governor. He lost a bid for the US Senate 1936 and did not hold political office again until elected to the House 1942. His fourth and last mayoral term began 1946, during which time he spent six months in federal prison on a mail-fraud conviction.

Curragh 'Mutiny' demand March 1914 by the British general Hubert Gough and his officers, stationed at Curragh, Ireland, that they should not be asked to take part in forcing Protestant Ulster to participate in Home Rule. They were subsequently allowed to return to duty, and after World War I the solution of partition was adopted.

Curtin John 1885–1945. Australian Labor politician, prime minister and minister of defence 1941–45. He was elected leader of the Labor Party 1935. As prime minister, he organized the mobilization of Australia's resources to meet the danger of Japanese invasion during World War II.

Curzon George Nathaniel, 1st Marquess Curzon of Kedleston 1859–1925. British Conservative politician, viceroy of India 1899–1905. During World War I, he was a member of the cabinet 1916–19. As foreign secretary 1919–24, he set up a British protectorate over Persia.

Curzon Line Polish-Soviet frontier proposed after World War I by the territorial commission of the Versailles conference 1919, based on the eastward limit of areas with a predominantly Polish population. It acquired its name after British foreign secretary Lord Curzon suggested in 1920 that the Poles, who had invaded the USSR, should retire to this line pending a Russo-Polish peace conference. The frontier established 1945 generally follows the Curzon Line.

Cyprus (*Republic of Cyprus* in the south, and *Turkish Republic of Northern Cyprus* in the north) island in the Mediterranean Sea, off the S coast of Turkey and W coast of Syria.

chronology
1878 Came under British administration.
1955 Guerrilla campaign began against the British for enosis (union with Greece), led by Archbishop ◊Makarios and General ◊Grivas.
1956 Makarios and enosis leaders deported.
1959 Compromise agreed and Makarios returned to be elected president of an independent Greek-Turkish Cyprus.
1960 Independence achieved from Britain, with Britain retaining its military bases.
1963 Turks set up their own government in northern Cyprus. Fighting broke out between the two communities.
1964 United Nations peacekeeping force installed.
1971 Grivas returned to start a guerrilla war against the Makarios government.
1974 Grivas died. Military coup deposed Makarios, who fled to Britain. Nicos Sampson appointed president. Turkish army sent to northern Cyprus to confirm Turkish Cypriots' control; military regime in southern Cyprus collapsed; Makarios returned. Northern Cyprus declared itself the Turkish Federated State of Cyprus (TFSC), with Rauf ◊Denktaş as president.
1977 Makarios died; succeeded by Spyros ◊Kyprianou.
1983 An independent Turkish Republic of Northern Cyprus proclaimed but recognized only by Turkey.
1984 UN peace proposals rejected.

1985 Summit meeting between Kyprianou and Denktaş failed to reach agreement.

1988 Georgios Vassiliou elected president. Talks with Denktaş began, under UN auspices.

1989 Vassiliou and Denktaş agreed to draft an agreement for the future reunification of the island, but peace talks were abandoned Sept.

1991 Turkish offer of peace talks rejected by Cyprus and Greece.

1992 UN-sponsored peace talks collapsed.

1993 Glafkos Clerides replaced Vassiliou as Greek president.

Czechoslovakia former country in E central Europe.

Czech Republic landlocked country in E central Europe, bounded NE by Poland, E and SE by the Slovak Republic, S by Austria, and W and NW by Germany.

chronology

1526–1918 Under Habsburg domination.

1918 Independence achieved from Austro-Hungarian Empire; Czechs joined Slovaks in forming Czechoslovakia as independent nation.

1948 Communists assumed power in Czechoslovakia.

1968 Czech Socialist Republic created under new federal constitution.

1989 Nov: pro-democracy demonstrations in Prague; new political parties formed, including Czech-based Civic Forum under Václav ◊Havel; Communist Party stripped of powers; political parties legalized. Dec: new 'grand coalition' government formed, including former dissidents; Havel appointed state president. Amnesty granted to 22,000 prisoners; calls for USSR to withdraw troops.

1990 July: Havel re-elected president in multiparty elections.

1991 Civic Forum split into Civil Democratic Party (CDP) and Civic Movement (CM); evidence of increasing Czech and Slovak separatism.

1992 June: Václav Klaus, leader of the Czech-based CDP, became prime minister; Havel resigned following Slovak gains in assembly elections. Aug: creation of separate Czech and Slovak states agreed.

1993 Jan: Czech Republic became sovereign state, with Klaus as prime minister. Havel elected president of the new republic. Admitted into United Nations, Conference on Security and Cooperation in Europe, and Council of Europe.

D

Dachau site of a Nazi ◊concentration camp during World War II, in Bavaria, Germany.

Daladier Edouard 1884–1970. French Radical politician. As prime minister April 1938–March 1940, he signed the ◊Munich Agreement 1938 (by which the Sudeten districts of Czechoslovakia were ceded to Germany) and declared war on Germany 1939. He resigned 1940 because of his unpopularity for failing to assist Finland against Russia. He was arrested on the fall of France 1940 and was a prisoner in Germany 1943-45. Following the end of World War II he was re-elected to the Chamber of Deputies 1946–58.

Dalai Lama 14th incarnation 1935–   . Spiritual and temporal head of the Tibetan state until 1959, when he went into exile in protest against Chinese annexation and oppression. His people have continued to demand his return.

Daley Richard Joseph 1902–1976. US politician and controversial mayor of Chicago 1955-76. He built a formidable political machine and ensured a Democratic presidential victory 1960 when J F Kennedy was elected. He hosted the turbulent national Democratic convention 1968.

Dalton Hugh, Baron Dalton 1887–1962. British Labour politician and economist. Chancellor of the Exchequer from 1945, he oversaw nationalization of the Bank of England, but resigned 1947 after making a disclosure to a lobby correspondent before a budget speech.

Darlan Jean François 1881–1942. French admiral and politician. He entered the navy 1899, and was appointed admiral and commander in chief 1939. He commanded the French navy 1939–40, took part in the evacuation of Dunkirk, and entered the Pétain cabinet as naval minister. In 1941 he was appointed vice premier, and became strongly anti-British and pro-German, but in 1942 he was dropped from the cabinet by Laval and sent to N Africa, where he was assassinated.

Darrow Clarence (Seward) 1857–1938. US lawyer, born in Ohio, a champion of liberal causes and defender of the underdog. He defended many trade-union leaders, including Eugene ◊Debs 1894. He was counsel for the defence in the Nathan Leopold and Richard Loeb murder trial in Chicago 1924, and in the ◊Scopes monkey trial. Darrow matched wits in the trial with prosecution attorney William Jennings ◊Bryan. He was an opponent of capital punishment.

Davis Angela 1944– . US left-wing activist for black rights, prominent in the student movement of the 1960s. In 1970 she went into hiding after being accused of supplying guns used in the murder of a judge who had been seized as a hostage in an attempt to secure the release of three black convicts. She was captured, tried, and acquitted. At the University of California she studied under Herbert Marcuse, and was assistant professor of philosophy at UCLA 1969–70. In 1980 she was the Communist vice-presidential candidate.

Davison Emily 1872–1913. English militant suffragette who died after throwing herself under the king's horse at the Derby at Epsom (she was trampled by the horse). She joined the Women's Social and Political Union in 1906 and served several prison sentences for militant action such as stone throwing, setting fire to pillar boxes, and bombing Lloyd George's country house.

Dawes Charles Gates 1865–1951. US Republican politician. In 1923 he was appointed by the Allied Reparations Commission president of the committee that produced the *Dawes Plan*, a $200 million loan that enabled Germany to pay enormous war debts after World War I. It reduced tensions temporarily in Europe but was superseded by the ◊Young Plan (which reduced the total reparations bill) 1929. Dawes was made US vice president (under Calvin Coolidge) 1924, received the Nobel Peace Prize 1925, and was ambassador to Britain 1929–32.

Dayan Moshe 1915–1981. Israeli general and politician. As minister of defence 1967 and 1969–74, he was largely responsible for the victory over neighbouring Arab states in the 1967 Six-Day War, but he was criticized for Israel's alleged unpreparedness in the 1973 October War and resigned along with Prime Minister Golda Meir. Foreign minister from 1977, Dayan resigned 1979 in protest over the refusal of the Begin government to negotiate with the Palestinians.

D-day 6 June 1944, the day of the Allied invasion of Normandy under the command of General Eisenhower, with the aim of liberating Western Europe from German occupation. The Anglo-American invasion fleet landed on the Normandy beaches on the stretch of coast between the Orne River and St Marcouf. Artificial harbours known as 'Mulberries' were constructed and towed across the Channel so that equipment and armaments could be unloaded onto the beaches. After overcoming fierce resistance the allies broke through the German defences; Paris was liberated on 25 Aug, and Brussels on 2 Sept.

D-day is also military jargon for any day on which a crucial operation is planned. D+1 indicates the day after the start of the operation.

Deakin Alfred 1856–1919. Australian politician, prime minister 1903–04, 1905–08, and 1909–10. In his second administration, he enacted legislation on defence and pensions.

Debray Régis 1941– . French Marxist theorist. He was associated with Che ◊Guevara in the revolutionary movement in Latin America in the 1960s. In 1967 he was sentenced to 30 years' imprisonment in Bolivia but was released after three years. His writings on Latin American politics include *Strategy for Revolution* 1970. He became a specialist adviser to President Mitterrand of France on Latin American affairs.

Debs Eugene V(ictor) 1855–1926. US labour leader and socialist who organized the Social Democratic Party 1897. He was the founder and first president of the American Railway Union 1893, and was imprisoned for six months in 1894 for defying a federal injunction to end the Pullman strike in Chicago. He was socialist candidate for the presidency in every election from 1900 to 1920, except that of 1916.

decolonization gradual achievement of independence by former colonies of the European imperial powers which began after World War I. The process of decolonization accelerated after World War II and the movement affected every continent: India and Pakistan gained independence from Britain 1947; Algeria gained independence from France 1962.

defiance campaign in South Africa, the joint action of non-violent demonstrations and civil disobedience organized by the ◊African National Congress and the Indian Congress Party 1952. Police and press were given notice before trained volunteers trespassed on 'whites-only' areas, broke curfews, or assembled without their passes. The campaigners' aim was to overcrowd the prisons and embarrass the authorities. Over 8,300 arrests were made.

De Gasperi Alcide de 1881–1954. Italian politician. A founder of the Christian Democrat Party, he was prime minister 1945–53 and worked for European unification.

de Gaulle Charles André Joseph Marie 1890–1970. French general and first president of the Fifth Republic 1958-69. He organized the ◊Free French troops fighting the Nazis 1940-44, was head of the provisional French government 1944-46, and leader of his own Gaullist party. In 1958 the national assembly asked him to form a government during France's economic recovery and to solve the crisis in Algeria. He became president at the end of 1958, having changed the constitution to provide for a presidential system, and served until 1969.

de Klerk F(rederik) W(illem) 1936–   . South African National Party politician, president from 1989. Trained as a lawyer, he entered the South African parliament 1972. He served in the cabinets of B J Vorster and P W Botha 1978-89, and replaced Botha as National Party leader Feb 1989 and as state president Aug 1989. Projecting himself as a pragmatic conservative who sought gradual reform of the apartheid system, he won the Sept 1989 elections for his party, but with a reduced majority. In Feb 1990 he ended the ban on the ◊African National Congress opposition movement and released its effective leader, Nelson Mandela. In Feb 1991 de Klerk promised the end of all apartheid legislation and a new multiracial constitution, and by June of the same year had repealed all racially discriminating laws. In March 1992 a nationwide, whites-only referendum gave de Klerk a clear mandate to proceed with plans for major constitutional reform to end white minority rule.

Delcassé Théophile 1852–1923. French politician. He became foreign minister 1898, but had to resign 1905 because of German hostility; he held that post again 1914–15. To a large extent he was responsible for the ◊Entente Cordiale 1904 with Britain.

Delors Jacques 1925–   . French socialist politician, finance minister 1981–84. As president of the European Commission from 1984 he has overseen significant budgetary reform and the move towards a free European Community market in 1992, with increased powers residing in Brussels.

de Maiziere Lothar 1940– . German politician, leader 1989–90 of the conservative Christian Democratic Union in East Germany. He became premier after East Germany's first democratic election April 1990 and negotiated the country's reunion with West Germany. In Dec 1990 he resigned from Chancellor Kohl's cabinet and as deputy leader of the CDU, following allegations that he had been an informer to the Stasi (East German secret police). In Sept 1991, he resigned as deputy chairman of the CDU and from the legislature, effectively leaving active politics.

Demirel Suleyman 1924– . Turkish politician. Leader from 1964 of the Justice Party, he was prime minister 1965–71, 1975–77, and 1979–80. He favoured links with the West, full membership in the European Community, and foreign investment in Turkish industry.

De Mita Luigi Ciriaco 1928– . Italian conservative politician, leader of the Christian Democratic Party (DC) from 1982, prime minister 1988-90. He entered the Chamber of Deputies 1963 and held a number of ministerial posts in the 1970s before becoming DC secretary general.

Democratic Party one of the two main political parties of the USA. It tends to be the party of the working person, as opposed to the Republicans, the party of big business, but the divisions between the two are not clear cut. Its stronghold since the Civil War has traditionally been industrial urban centres and the Southern states, but conservative Southern Democrats were largely supportive of Republican positions and helped elect President Reagan.

Deng Xiaoping or *Teng Hsiao-ping* 1904– . Chinese political leader. A member of the Chinese Communist Party (CCP) from the 1920s, he took part in the Long March 1934–36. He was in the Politburo from 1955 until ousted in the Cultural Revolution 1966–69. Reinstated in the 1970s, he gradually took power and introduced a radical economic modernization programme. He retired from the Politburo 1987 and from his last official position (as chair of State Military Commission) March 1990, but remained influential behind the scenes.

Denikin Anton Ivanovich 1872–1947. Russian general. He distinguished himself in the ◊Russo-Japanese War 1904–05 and World War I. After the outbreak of the Bolshevik Revolution 1917 he organized a volunteer army of 60,000 Whites (loyalists) but was routed 1919 and escaped to France. He wrote a history of the Revolution and the Civil War.

Denktaş Rauf R 1924–   . Turkish-Cypriot nationalist politician. In 1975 the Turkish Federated State of Cyprus (TFSC) was formed in the northern third of the island, with Denktaş as its head, and in 1983 he became president of the breakaway Turkish Republic of Northern Cyprus (TRNC).

Denmark peninsula and islands in N Europe, bounded N by the Skagerrak, E by the Kattegat, S by Germany, and W by the North Sea.

chronology
1940–45 Occupied by Germany.
1945 Iceland's independence recognized.
1947 Frederik IX succeeded Christian X.
1948 Home rule granted for Faeroe Islands.
1949 Became a founding member of NATO.
1960 Joined European Free Trade Association (EFTA).
1972 Margrethe II became Denmark's first queen in nearly 600 years.
1973 Left EFTA and joined European Economic Community (EEC).
1979 Home rule granted for Greenland.
1985 Strong non-nuclear movement in evidence.
1990 General election; another coalition government formed.
1992 Rejection of ◊Maastricht Treaty in national referendum; government requested modifications (codicils) to treaty prior to second national referendum, planned for 1993.
1993 Poul Schlüter resigned; replaced by Poul Nyrup Rasmussen at head of Social Democrat-led coalition government.

depression in economics, a period of low output and investment, with high unemployment. The term is most often used to refer to the world economic crisis precipitated by the Wall Street crash of 29 Oct 1929 when millions of dollars were wiped off US share values in a matter of hours. This forced the closure of many US banks involved in stock speculation and led to the recall of US overseas investments. This loss of US credit had serious repercussions on the European economy, especially that of Germany, and led to a steep fall in the levels of international trade as countries attempted to protect their domestic economies. Although most European countries experienced a slow recovery during the mid-1930s, the main impetus for renewed economic growth was provided by rearmament programmes later in the decade.

Derby Edward George Villiers Stanley, 17th Earl of Derby 1865–1948. British Conservative politician, member of Parliament from 1892. He was secretary of war 1916–18 and 1922–24, and ambassador to France 1918–20.

De Roburt Hammer 1923–1992. President of Nauru 1968–76, 1978–83, 1987–89. During the country's occupation 1942–45, he was deported to Japan. He became head chief of Nauru 1956 and was elected the country's first president 1968. He secured only a narrow majority in the 1987 elections and in 1989 was ousted on a no-confidence motion.

Desai Morarji 1896–   . Indian politician. An early follower of Mahatma Gandhi, he was prime minister 1977–79, as leader of the ◊Janata party, after toppling Indira Gandhi. Party infighting led to his resignation of both the premiership and the party leadership.

Desert Rats nickname of the British 8th Army in N Africa during World War II. Their uniforms had a shoulder insignia bearing a jerboa (N African rodent, capable of great leaps). The Desert Rats' most famous victories include the expulsion of the Italian army from Egypt in Dec 1940 when they captured 130,000 prisoners, and the Battle of El ◊Almein. Their successors, the 7th Armoured Brigade, fought as part of the British 1st Armoured Division in the 1991 Gulf War.

détente (French) reduction of political tension and the easing of strained relations between nations, for example, the ending of the Cold War 1989–90, although it was first used in the 1970s to describe the easing East–West relations, trade agreements, and cultural exchanges.

deterrence underlying conception of the nuclear arms race: the belief that a potential aggressor will be discouraged from launching a 'first strike' nuclear attack by the knowledge that the adversary is capable of inflicting 'unacceptable damage' in a retaliatory strike. This doctrine is widely known as that of *mutual assured destruction (MAD)*. Three essential characteristics of deterrence are: the 'capability to act', 'credibility', and the 'will to act'.

de Valera Eámon 1882–1975. Irish nationalist politician, prime minister of the Irish Free State/Eire/Republic of Ireland 1932–48, 1951–54, and 1957–59, and president 1959–73. Repeatedly imprisoned, he participated in the ◊Easter Rising 1916 and was leader of the nationalist ◊Sinn Féin party 1917–26, when he formed the republican ◊Fianna Fáil party; he directed negotiations with Britain 1921 but refused to accept the partition of Ireland until 1937.

development in the social sciences, the acquisition by a society of industrial techniques and technology; hence the common classification of the 'developed' nations of the First and Second Worlds and the poorer, 'developing' or 'underdeveloped' nations of the Third World. The assumption that development in the sense of industrialization is inherently good has been increasingly questioned since the 1960s.

de Wet Christiaan Rudolf 1854–1922. Boer general and politician. He served in the South African Wars 1880 and 1899. When World War I began, he headed a pro-German rising of 12,000 Afrikaners but was defeated, convicted of treason, and imprisoned. He was sentenced to six years' imprisonment for his part in the uprising, but was released 1915.

Dewey George 1837–1917. US naval officer. He was appointed chief of the Bureau of Equipment 1889 and of the Board of Inspection and Survey 1895. As commodore, Dewey was dispatched to the Pacific 1896. He destroyed the Spanish fleet in Manila harbour at the outbreak of the Spanish-American War 1898. Dewey was promoted to the rank of admiral of the navy (the highest naval rank ever awarded) 1899. He retired from active service 1900.

Dewey Thomas Edmund 1902–1971. US public official. He was Manhattan district attorney 1937-38 and served as governor of New York 1942-54. Dewey was twice the Republican presidential candidate, losing to F D Roosevelt 1944 and to Truman 1948, the latter race being one of the greatest electoral upsets in US history.

Díaz Porfirio 1830–1915. Dictator of Mexico 1877–80 and 1884–1911. After losing the 1876 election, he overthrew the government and seized power. He was supported by conservative landowners and foreign capitalists, who invested in railways and mines. He centralized the state at the expense of the peasants and Indians, and dismantled all local and regional leadership. He faced mounting and revolutionary opposition in his final years and was forced into exile 1911.

Diefenbaker John George 1895–1979. Canadian Progressive Conservative politician, prime minister 1957–63; he was defeated after criticism of the proposed manufacture of nuclear weapons in Canada.

Dien Bien Phu, Battle of decisive battle in the ◊Indochina War at a French fortress in North Vietnam, near the Laotian border. French troops were besieged 13 March–7 May 1954 by the communist Vietminh. The fall of Dien Bien Phu resulted in the end of French control of Indochina.

Dilke Charles Wentworth 1843–1911. British Liberal politician, member of Parliament 1868–86 and 1892–1911. A Radical, he supported a minimum wage and legalization of trade unions.

Dillinger John 1903–1934. US bank robber and murderer. In 1923 he was convicted of armed robbery and spent the next ten years in state prison. Released in 1933, he led a gang on a robbery spree throughout the Midwest, staging daring raids on police stations to obtain guns. Named 'Public Enemy Number One' by the Federal Bureau of Investigation (FBI), Dillinger led the authorities on a long chase. He was finally betrayed by his mistress, the mysterious 'Lady in Red,' and was killed by FBI agents in Chicago as he left a cinema.

Dimitrov Georgi 1882–1949. Bulgarian communist, prime minister from 1946. He was elected a deputy in 1913 and from 1919 was a member of the executive of the Comintern, an international communist organization (see the ◊International). In 1933 he was arrested in Berlin and tried with others in Leipzig for allegedly setting fire to the parliament building (see ◊Reichstag fire). Acquitted, he went to the USSR, where he became general secretary of the Comintern until its dissolution in 1943.

Dinkins David 1927– . Mayor of New York City from Jan 1990, a Democrat. He won a reputation as a moderate and consensual community politician and was Manhattan borough president before succeeding Edward I Koch to become New York's first black mayor.

Diouf Abdou 1935– . Senegalese left-wing politician, president from 1980. He became prime minister 1970 under President Leopold Senghor and, on his retirement, succeeded him, being re-elected in 1983 and 1988. His presidency has been characterized by authoritarianism.

Diplock court in Northern Ireland, a type of court established 1972 by the British government under Lord Diplock (1907–1985) to try offences linked with guerrilla violence. The right to jury trial was suspended and the court consisted of a single judge, because potential jurors were allegedly being intimidated and were unwilling to serve. Despite widespread criticism, the Diplock courts have remained in operation.

dissident in one-party states, a person intellectually dissenting from the official line. Dissidents have been sent into exile, prison, labour camps, and mental institutions, or deprived of their jobs. In the USSR the number of imprisoned dissidents declined from more than 600 in 1986 to fewer than

100 in 1990, of whom the majority were ethnic nationalists. In China the number of prisoners of conscience increased after the 1989 Tiananmen Square massacre, and in South Africa, despite the release of Nelson Mandela in 1990, numerous political dissidents remained in jail.

Distributism campaign for land reform publicized by English writer G K Chesterton in his group the Distributist League, the journal of which he published from 1925. The movement called for a revival of smallholdings and a turn away from industrialization. Supporters included many Conservatives and traditional clergy.

Djibouti country on the E coast of Africa, at the S end of the Red Sea, bounded E by the Gulf of Aden, SE by Somalia, and S, W, and N by Ethiopia.

chronology
1884 Annexed by France as part of French Somaliland.
1967 French Somaliland became the French Territory of the Afars and the Issas.
1977 Independence achieved from France; Hassan Gouled elected president.
1979 All political parties combined to form the People's Progress Assembly (RPP).
1981 New constitution made RPP the only legal party. Gouled re-elected. Treaties of friendship signed with Ethiopia, Somalia, Kenya, and Sudan.
1984 Policy of neutrality reaffirmed.
1987 Gouled re-elected for a final term.
1991 Amnesty International accused secret police of brutality.
1992 Djibouti elected member of UN Security Council 1993–95.

Djilas Milovan 1911–   . Yugoslav political writer and dissident. A former close wartime colleague of Marshal Tito, in 1953 he was dismissed from high office and subsequently imprisoned because of his advocacy of greater political pluralism. He was released 1966 and formally rehabilitated 1989.

Dobrynin Anataloy Fedorovich 1919–   . Soviet diplomat, ambassador to the USA 1962–86, emerging during the 1970s as a warm supporter of ◊détente.

Doe Samuel Kenyon 1950–1990. Liberian politician and soldier, head of state 1980–90. He seized power in a coup. Having successfully put down an uprising April 1990, Doe was deposed and killed by rebel forces Sept 1990.

Doi Takako 1929– . Japanese socialist politician, leader of the Social Democratic Party of Japan (SDJP), formerly the Japan Socialist Party (JSP), 1986–1991. The country's first female major party leader, she was largely responsible for the SDJP's revival in the late 1980s. Her resignation followed the party's crushing defeat in local elections in April 1991.

dollar diplomacy disparaging description of US foreign policy in the early 20th century. The US sought political influence over foreign governments (China 1909 and 1912; Haiti 1910; Nicaragua and Honduras 1911; Dominican Republic 1916) by encouraging American financiers to make loans to countries whose indebtedness could then be used to promote US interests. Dollar diplomacy sometimes resulted in US military intervention (such as marines in Nicaragua 1912-25) to prop up client regimes.

Dollfuss Engelbert 1892–1934. Austrian Christian Socialist politician. He was appointed chancellor in 1932, and in 1933 suppressed parliament and ruled by decree. In Feb 1934 he crushed a protest by the socialist workers by force, and in May Austria was declared a 'corporative' state. The Nazis attempted a coup d'état on 25 July; the Chancellery was seized and Dollfuss murdered.

Dominica island in the E Caribbean, between Guadeloupe and Martinique, the largest of the Windward Islands, with the Atlantic Ocean to the E and the Caribbean Sea to the W.

chronology
1763 Became British possession.
1978 Independence achieved from Britain. Patrick John, leader of Dominica Labour Party (DLP), elected prime minister.
1980 Dominica Freedom Party (DFP), led by Eugenia Charles, won convincing victory in general election.
1981 Patrick John implicated in plot to overthrow government.
1982 John tried and acquitted.
1985 John retried and found guilty. Regrouping of left-of-centre parties resulted in new Labour Party of Dominica (LPD). DFP, led by Eugenia Charles, re-elected.
1990 Charles elected to a third term.
1991 Integration into Windward Islands confederation proposed.

Dominican Republic country in the West Indies (E Caribbean), occupying the eastern two-thirds of the island of Hispaniola, with Haiti covering the western third; the Atlantic Ocean is to the E and the Caribbean Sea to the W.

chronology
1844 Dominican Republic established.
1930 Military coup established dictatorship of Rafael ◊Trujillo.
1961 Trujillo assassinated.
1962 First democratic elections resulted in Juan ◊Bosch, founder of the Dominican Revolutionary Party (PRD), becoming president.
1963 Bosch overthrown in military coup.
1965 US Marines intervene to restore order and protect foreign nationals.
1966 New constitution adopted. Joaquín Balaguer, leader of Christian Social Reform Party (PRSC), became president.
1978 PRD returned to power, with Silvestre Antonio Guzmán as president.
1982 PRD re-elected, with Jorge Blanco as president.
1985 Blanco forced by International Monetary Fund to adopt austerity measures to save the economy.
1986 PRSC returned to power, with Balaguer re-elected president.
1990 Balaguer re-elected by a small majority.

Dominions the name formerly applied to the self-governing divisions of the ◊British Empire—for example Australia, New Zealand, Canada, and South Africa.

domino theory idea popularized by US president Eisenhower in 1954 that if one country came under communist rule, adjacent countries were likely to fall to communism as well.

Dönitz Karl 1891–1980. German admiral, originator of the wolf-pack submarine technique, which sank 15 million tonnes of Allied shipping in World War II. He succeeded Hitler in 1945, capitulated, and was imprisoned 1946–56.

Donovan William Joseph 1883–1959. US military leader and public official. Donovan served as US district attorney 1922–24 and as assistant to the US attorney general 1925–29. He was national security adviser to Presidents Hoover and F D Roosevelt and founded the Office of Strategic Services (OSS) 1942. As OSS director 1942–45, Donovan coordinated US intelligence during World War II.

Dos Santos José Eduardo 1942– . Angolan left-wing politician, president from 1979, a member of the People's Movement for the Liberation of

Angola (MPLA). By 1989, he had negotiated the withdrawal of South African and Cuban forces, and in 1991 a peace agreement to end the civil war. In Sept 1992 his victory in multiparty elections was disputed by ◊UNITA rebel leader Jonas Savimbi, and fighting resumed.

Douglas-Home Alec Douglas-Home, Baron Home of the Hirsel 1903– . British Conservative politician. He was foreign secretary 1960–63, and succeeded Harold Macmillan as prime minister 1963. He renounced his peerage (as 14th Earl of Home) to fight (and lose) the general election 1964, and resigned as party leader 1965. He was again foreign secretary 1970–74, when he received a life peerage. The playwright William Douglas-Home was his brother.

Doumer Paul 1857–1932. French politician. He was elected president of the Chamber in 1905, president of the Senate in 1927, and president of the republic in 1931. He was assassinated by Gorgulov, a White Russian emigré.

Doumergue Gaston 1863–1937. French prime minister Dec 1913–June 1914 (during the time leading up to World War I); president 1924–31; and premier again Feb–Nov 1934 at head of 'national union' government.

Dreadnought class of battleships built for the British navy after 1905 and far superior in speed and armaments to anything then afloat. The first modern battleship to be built, it was the basis of battleship design for more than 50 years. The first Dreadnought was launched 1906, with armaments consisting entirely of big guns.

Drees Willem 1886–1988. Dutch socialist politician, prime minister 1948–58. Chair of the Socialist Democratic Workers' Party from 1911 until the German invasion of 1940, he returned to politics in 1947, after being active in the resistance movement. In 1947, as the responsible minister, he introduced a state pension scheme.

Dresden capital of the state of Saxony, Germany. It was one of the most beautiful German cities until its devastation by Allied fire-bombing on the night 13–14 Feb 1945, 15.5 sq km/6 sq mi of the inner town being destroyed, and deaths being estimated at 35,000–135,000.

Dreyfus Alfred 1859–1935. French army officer, victim of miscarriage of justice, anti-Semitism, and cover-up. Employed in the War Ministry, in 1894 he was accused of betraying military secrets to Germany, court-martialled, and sent to the penal colony on ◊Devil's Island, French Guiana. When his innocence was discovered 1896 the military establishment tried to conceal it, and the implications of the Dreyfus affair were passionately discussed in the press until he was exonerated in 1906.

Druse or *Druze* religious sect in the Middle East of some 500,000 people. They are monotheists, preaching that the Fatimid caliph al-Hakim (996–1021) is God; their scriptures are drawn from the Bible, the Koran, and Sufi allegories. Druse militia groups form one of the three main factions involved in the Lebanese civil war (the others are Amal Shi'ite Muslims and Christian Maronites). The Druse military leader (from the time of his father's assassination 1977) is Walid Jumblatt.

Dual Entente alliance between France and Russia that lasted from 1893 until the Bolshevik Revolution of 1917.

Duarte José Napoleon 1925–1990. El Salvadorean politician, president 1980–82 and 1984–88. He was mayor of San Salvador 1964–70, and was elected president 1972, but exiled by the army 1982. On becoming president again 1984, he sought a negotiated settlement with the left-wing guerrillas 1986, but resigned on health grounds.

Dubček Alexander 1921–1992. Czechoslovak politician, chair of the federal assembly 1989–92. He was a member of the Slovak ◊resistance movement during World War II, and became first secretary of the Communist Party 1967–69. He launched a liberalization campaign (called the ◊Prague Spring) that was opposed by the USSR and led to the Soviet invasion of Czechoslovakia 1968. He was arrested by Soviet troops and expelled from the party 1970. In 1989 he gave speeches at prodemocracy rallies, and after the fall of the hardline regime, he was elected speaker of the National Assembly in Prague, a position to which he was re-elected 1990. He was fatally injured in a car crash Sept 1992.

Du Bois W(illiam) E(dward) B(urghardt) 1868–1963. US educator and social critic. Du Bois was one of the early leaders of the National Association for the Advancement of Colored People (NAACP) and the editor of its journal *Crisis* 1909-32. As a staunch advocate of black American rights, he came into conflict with Booker T ◊Washington opposing the latter's policy of compromise on the issue of slavery.

Duce (Italian 'leader') title bestowed on the fascist dictator Benito ◊Mussolini by his followers and later adopted as his official title.

Dukakis Michael 1933– . US Democrat politician, governor of Massachusetts 1974–78 and 1982–90, presiding over a high-tech economic boom, the 'Massachusetts miracle'. He was a presidential candidate 1988.

Dulles Alan 1893–1969. US lawyer, director of the Central Intelligence Agency (CIA) 1953–61. He helped found the CIA 1950. He was embroiled in the ◊Bay of Pigs, Cuba, controversial invasion attempt, among others, which forced his resignation. He was the brother of John Foster Dulles.

Dulles John Foster 1888–1959. US politician. Senior US adviser at the founding of the United Nations, he was largely responsible for drafting the Japanese peace treaty of 1951. As secretary of state 1952–59, he was the architect of US Cold War foreign policy, secured US intervention in South Vietnam after the expulsion of the French 1954, and was critical of Britain during the Suez Crisis 1956.

Duma in Russia, before 1917, an elected assembly that met four times following the short-lived 1905 revolution. With progressive demands the government could not accept, the Duma was largely powerless. After the abdication of Nicholas II, the Duma directed the formation of a provisional government.

Dumbarton Oaks 18th-century mansion in Washington DC, USA, used for conferences and seminars. It was the scene of a conference held 1944 that led to the foundation of the United Nations.

Duncan-Sandys Duncan (Edwin) British politician; see ◊Sandys, Duncan Edwin.

Durban riots inter-racial conflict between Zulus and Indians in Durban, South Africa in Jan 1949. The riots, in which 142 people were killed and 1,087 injured, began when a black youth was killed by an Indian shopkeeper. The violence was symptomatic of longstanding social and economic divisions between the two communities. Paradoxically, the riots accelerated cooperation between the ◊African National Congress and Indian leaders.

Duvalier François 1907–1971. Right-wing president of Haiti 1957–71. Known as *Papa Doc*, he ruled as a dictator, organizing the Tontons Macoutes ('bogeymen') as a private security force to intimidate and assassinate opponents of his regime. He rigged the 1961 elections in order to have his term of office extended until 1967, and in 1964 declared himself president for life. He was excommunicated by the Vatican for harassing the church, and was succeeded on his death by his son Jean-Claude Duvalier.

Duvalier Jean-Claude 1951–   . Right-wing president of Haiti 1971–86. Known as *Baby Doc*, he succeeded his father François Duvalier, becoming, at the age of 19, the youngest president in the world. He continued to receive support from the USA but was pressured into moderating some elements of his father's regime, yet still tolerated no opposition. In 1986, with Haiti's economy stagnating and with increasing civil disorder, Duvalier fled to France, taking much of the Haitian treasury with him.

E

Eanes António dos Santos Ramalho 1935– . Portuguese politician. He helped plan the 1974 coup that ended the Caetano regime, and as army chief of staff put down a left-wing revolt Nov 1975. He was president 1976–86.

Eastern Front battlefront between Russia and Germany during World War I and World War II.

Easter Rising or *Easter Rebellion* in Irish history, a republican insurrection that began on Easter Monday, April 1916, in Dublin. It was inspired by the Irish Republican Brotherhood (IRB) in an unsuccessful attempt to overthrow British rule in Ireland. It was led by Patrick Pearce of the IRB and James Connolly of Sinn Féin.

East Pakistan former province of ◊Pakistan, now Bangladesh.

East Timor disputed territory on the island of Timor in the Malay Archipelago; prior to 1975, it was a Portuguese colony for almost 460 years. Following Portugal's withdrawal, civil war broke out and the left-wing Revolutionary Front of Independent East Timor (Fretilin) occupied the capital, calling for independence. In opposition, troops from neighbouring Indonesia invaded the territory, declaring East Timor (*Loro Sae*) the 17th province of Indonesia July 1976. This claim is not recognized by the United Nations.

Eban Abba 1915– . Israeli diplomat and politician, ambassador in Washington 1950–59 and foreign minister 1966–74.

Ecuador country in South America, bounded N by Colombia, E and S by Peru, and W by the Pacific Ocean.

chronology
1830 Independence achieved from Spain.
1925-48 Great political instability; no president completed his term of office.
1948-55 Liberals in power.
1956 First conservative president in 60 years.

1960 Liberals returned, with José Velasco as president.

1961 Velasco deposed and replaced by the vice president.

1962 Military junta installed.

1968 Velasco returned as president.

1972 A coup put the military back in power.

1978 New democratic constitution adopted.

1979 Liberals in power but opposed by right- and left-wing parties.

1982 Deteriorating economy provoked strikes, demonstrations, and a state of emergency.

1983 Austerity measures introduced.

1984-85 No party with a clear majority in the national congress; Febres Cordero narrowly won the presidency for the Conservatives.

1988 Rodrigo Borja Cevallos elected president for moderate left-wing coalition.

1989 Guerrilla left-wing group, *Alfaro Vive, Carajo* ('Alfaro lives, Dammit'), numbering about 1,000, laid down arms after nine years.

1992 United Republican Party (PUR) leader, Sixto Duran Ballen, elected president; Social Christian Party (PSC) became largest party in congress.

Eden Anthony, 1st Earl of Avon 1897–1977. British Conservative politician, foreign secretary 1935–38, 1940–45, and 1951–55; prime minister 1955–57, when he resigned after the failure of the Anglo-French military intervention in the ◊Suez Crisis.

Edward VII 1841–1910. King of Great Britain and Ireland from 1901. As Prince of Wales he was a prominent social figure, but his mother Queen Victoria considered him too frivolous to take part in political life. In 1860 he made the first tour of Canada and the USA ever undertaken by a British prince.

Edward VIII 1894–1972. King of Great Britain and Northern Ireland Jan–Dec 1936, when he renounced the throne to marry Wallis Warfield Simpson (see ◊abdication crisis). He was created Duke of Windsor and was governor of the Bahamas 1940–45, subsequently settling in France.

EEC abbreviation for *European Economic Community*; see ◊European Community.

EFTA acronym for ◊*European Free Trade Association*.

Egypt country in NE Africa, bounded N by the Mediterranean Sea, E by the Suez Canal and Red Sea, S by Sudan, and W by Libya.

chronology

1914 Egypt became a British protectorate.

1936 Independence achieved from Britain. King Fuad succeeded by his son Farouk.

1946 Withdrawal of British troops except from Suez Canal Zone.

1952 Farouk overthrown by army in bloodless coup.

1953 Egypt declared a republic, with General Neguib as president.

1956 Neguib replaced by Col Gamal ◊Nasser. Nasser announced national-ization of Suez Canal; Egypt attacked by Britain, France, and Israel. Cease-fire agreed because of US intervention.

1958 Short-lived merger of Egypt and Syria as United Arab Republic (UAR). Subsequent attempts to federate Egypt, Syria, and Iraq failed.

1967 Six-Day War with Israel ended in Egypt's defeat and Israeli occupa-tion of Sinai and Gaza Strip.

1970 Nasser died suddenly, succeeded by Anwar ◊Sadat.

1973 Attempt to regain territory lost to Israel led to fighting; cease-fire arranged by US secretary of state Henry Kissinger.

1977 Sadat's visit to Israel to address the Israeli parliament was criticized by Egypt's Arab neighbours.

1978–79 ◊Camp David talks in the USA resulted in a treaty between Egypt and Israel. Egypt expelled from the Arab League.

1981 Sadat assassinated, succeeded by Hosni ◊Mubarak.

1983 Improved relations between Egypt and the Arab world; only Libya and Syria maintained a trade boycott.

1984 Mubarak's party victorious in the people's assembly elections.

1987 Mubarak re-elected. Egypt readmitted to Arab League.

1988 Full diplomatic relations with Algeria restored.

1989 Improved relations with Libya; diplomatic relations with Syria restored. Mubarak proposed a peace plan.

1991 Participation in Gulf War on US-led side. Major force in convening Middle East peace conference in Spain.

1992 Outbreaks of violence between Muslims and Christians. Earthquake devastated Cairo.

Eichmann (Karl) Adolf 1906–1962. Austrian Nazi. As an ◊SS official during Hitler's regime (1933–1945), he was responsible for atrocities against Jews and others, including the implementation of genocide. He managed to escape at the fall of Germany 1945, but was discovered in

Argentina 1960, abducted by Israeli agents, tried in Israel 1961 for ◊war crimes, and executed.

Eighth Route Army the Chinese *Red Army*, formed 1927 when the communists broke away from the ◊Guomindang (nationalists) and established a separate government in Jiangxi in SE China. When Japan invaded China 1937 the Red Army was recognized as a section of the national forces under the name Eighth Route Army and led by ◊Zhu De.

Einstein Albert 1879–1955. German-born US physicist who formulated the theories of ◊relativity, and worked on radiation physics and thermodynamics. In 1905 he published the special theory of relativity, and in 1915 issued his general theory of relativity. He received the Nobel Prize for Physics 1921. His latest conception of the basic laws governing the universe was outlined in his ◊unified field theory, made public 1953.

Eisenhower Dwight David ('Ike') 1890–1969. 34th president of the USA 1953–60, a Republican. A general in World War II, he commanded the Allied forces in Italy 1943, then the Allied invasion of Europe, and from Oct 1944 all the Allied armies in the West. As president he promoted business interests at home and conducted the ◊Cold War abroad. His vice president was Richard Nixon.

Elizabeth II 1926–   . Queen of Great Britain and Northern Ireland from 1952, the elder daughter of George VI. She married her third cousin, Philip, the Duke of Edinburgh, 1947. They have four children: Charles, Anne, Andrew, and Edward.

Princess Elizabeth Alexandra Mary was born in London 21 April 1926; she was educated privately, and assumed official duties at 16. During World War II she served in the Auxiliary Territorial Service, and by an amendment to the Regency Act she became a state counsellor on her 18th birthday. On the death of George VI in 1952 she succeeded to the throne while in Kenya with her husband and was crowned on 2 June 1953.

El Salvador country in Central America, bounded N and E by Honduras, S and SW by the Pacific Ocean, and NW by Guatemala.

chronology
1821 Independence achieved from Spain.
1931 Peasant unrest followed by a military coup.
1961 Following a coup, the conservative National Conciliation Party (PCN) was established and came to power.

1969 ◊Football war with Honduras.

1972 Allegations of human-rights violations and growth of left-wing guerrilla activities. General Carlos Romero elected president.

1979 A coup replaced Romero with a military-civilian junta.

1980 Archbishop Oscar Romero assassinated; country on verge of civil war. José ◊Duarte became first civilian president since 1931.

1981 Mexico and France recognized the guerrillas as a legitimate political force but the USA actively assisted the government in its battle against them.

1982 Assembly elections boycotted by left-wing parties and held amid considerable violence.

1986 Duarte sought a negotiated settlement with the guerrillas.

1988 Duarte resigned.

1989 Alfredo Cristiani, National Republican Alliance (ARENA), became president in rigged elections; rebel attacks intensified.

1991 United Nations-sponsored peace accord signed by representatives of the government and the socialist guerrilla group, the Farabundo Marti Liberation Front (FMLN).

1992 Peace accord validated; FMLN became political party.

Eminent Persons Group group of seven Commonwealth nations' politicians deputed by Commonwealth leaders in Dec 1985 to visit South Africa to report on the political situation there. It was chaired jointly by Malcolm Fraser of Australia and Olusegun Obasanjo, former head of the Nigerian government. Its report, *Mission to South Africa* 1986, proposed among other things the abolition of ◊apartheid.

Empire Marketing Board organization formed 1926 to encourage self-sufficiency within the British Empire. Its mandate was to promote the sale of empire foodstuffs which, in turn, would benefit British exports of manufactured goods and protect domestic industry from European and American competition. It was abolished 1933.

Empire Settlement Act British act of Parliament 1922 which provided for the first large-scale state-assisted migration programme undertaken by the British government. Over 400,000 people received state subsidies totalling £6 million which helped them travel to a variety of imperial destinations, mainly in the dominions, during the inter-war period. The legislation was renewed 1937 and 1952 but operations and costs were on a much smaller scale.

enabling act legislative enactment enabling or empowering a person or corporation to take certain actions. Perhaps the best known example of an Enabling Law was that passed in Germany in March 1933 by the Reichstag and Reichsrat. It granted Hitler's cabinet dictatorial powers until April 1937, and effectively terminated parliamentary government in Germany until 1950. The law firmly established the Nazi dictatorship by giving dictatorial powers to the government.

enosis movement, developed from 1930, for the union of ◊Cyprus with Greece. The campaign (led by ◊EOKA and supported by Archbishop Makarios) intensified from the 1950s. In 1960 independence from Britain, without union, was granted, and increased demands for union led to its proclamation 1974. As a result, Turkey invaded Cyprus, ostensibly to protect the Turkish community, and the island was effectively partitioned.

Entente Cordiale agreement reached by Britain and France 1904 recognizing British interests in Egypt and French interests in Morocco. It formed the basis for Anglo-French cooperation before the outbreak of World War I 1914.

Enver Pasha 1881–1922. Turkish politician and soldier. He led the military revolt 1908 that resulted in the ◊Young Turks' revolution (see ◊Turkey). He was killed fighting the Bolsheviks in Turkestan.

EOKA acronym for *Ethnikí Organósis Kipriakóu Agónos* (National Organization of Cypriot Struggle) an underground organization formed by General George ◊Grivas 1955 to fight for the independence of Cyprus from Britain and ultimately its union (*enosis*) with Greece. In 1971, 11 years after the independence of Cyprus, Grivas returned to the island to form EOKA B and to resume the fight for *enosis*, which had not been achieved by the Cypriot government.

Equatorial Guinea country in W central Africa, bounded N by Cameroon, E and S by Gabon, and W by the Atlantic Ocean; also five offshore islands including Bioko, off the coast of Cameroon.

chronology
1885 Mainland territory came under Spanish rule; colony known as Spanish Guinea.
1968 Independence achieved from Spain. Francisco Macias Nguema became first president, soon assuming dictatorial powers.

1979 Macias overthrown and replaced by his nephew, Teodoro Obiang Nguema Mbasogo, who established a military regime. Macias tried and executed

1982 Obiang elected president unopposed for another seven years. New constitution adopted.

1989 Obiang re-elected president.

1992 New constitution adopted; elections held, but president continued to nominate candidates for top government posts.

Erhard Ludwig 1897–1977. West German Christian Democrat politician, chancellor of the Federal Republic 1963–66. The 'economic miracle' of West Germany's recovery after World War II is largely attributed to Erhard's policy of social free enterprise which he initiated during his period as federal economics minister (1949–63).

Ershad Hussain Mohammad 1930– . Military ruler of Bangladesh 1982–90. He became chief of staff of the Bangladeshi army 1979 and assumed power in a military coup 1982. As president from 1983, Ershad introduced a successful rural-oriented economic programme. He was re-elected 1986 and lifted martial law, but faced continuing political opposition, which forced him to resign Dec 1990. In 1991 he was formally charged with the illegal possession of arms, convicted, and sentenced to ten years' imprisonment. He received a further sentence of three years' imprisonment Feb 1992 after being convicted of corruption.

Estonia country in N Europe, bounded E by Russia, S by Latvia, and N and W by the Baltic Sea.

chronology

1918 Estonia declared its independence. March: Soviet forces, who had tried to regain control from occupying German forces during World War I, were overthrown by German troops. Nov: Soviet troops took control after German withdrawal.

1919 Soviet rule overthrown with help of British navy; Estonia declared a democratic republic.

1934 Fascist coup replaced government.

1940 Estonia incorporated into USSR.

1941–44 German occupation during World War II.

1944 USSR regained control.

1980 Beginnings of nationalist dissent.

1988 Adopted own constitution, with power of veto on all centralized Soviet legislation. Popular Front (Rahvarinne) established to campaign for democracy. Estonia's supreme soviet (state assembly) voted to declare the republic 'sovereign' and autonomous in all matters except military and foreign affairs; rejected by USSR as unconstitutional.

1989 Estonian replaced Russian as main language.

1990 Feb: Communist Party monopoly of power abolished; multiparty system established. March: pro-independence candidates secured majority after republic elections; coalition government formed with Popular Front leader Edgar Savisaar as prime minister; Arnold Rüütel became president. May: prewar constitution partially restored.

1991 March: independence plebiscite overwhelmingly approved. Aug: full independence declared after abortive anti-Gorbachev coup; Communist Party outlawed. Sept: independence recognized by Soviet government and Western nations; admitted into United Nations and CSCE (Conference on Security and Cooperation in Europe).

1992 Jan: Savisaar resigned owing to his government's inability to alleviate food and energy shortages; new government formed by Tiit Vahl. June: New constitution approved. Sept: presidential election inconclusive; right-wing Fatherland Group did well in general election. Oct: Meri chosen by parliament to replace Rüütel.

Ethiopia (formerly also known as *Abyssinia*) country in E Africa, bounded NE by Djibouti and the Red Sea, E and SE by Somalia, S by Kenya, and W and NW by Sudan.

chronology

1889 Abyssinia reunited by Menelik II.

1930 ◊Haile Selassie became emperor.

1962 Eritrea annexed by Haile Selassie; resistance movement began.

1974 Haile Selassie deposed and replaced by a military government led by General Teferi Benti. Ethiopia declared a socialist state.

1977 Teferi Benti killed and replaced by Col ◊Mengistu Haile Mariam.

1977–79 'Red Terror' period in which Mengistu's regime killed thousands of people.

1981-85 Ethiopia spent at least $2 billion on arms.

1984 WPE declared the only legal political party.

1985 Worst famine in more than a decade; Western aid sent and forcible internal resettlement programmes undertaken.

1987 New constitution adopted, Mengistu Mariam elected president. New famine; food aid hindered by guerrillas.

1988 Mengistu agreed to adjust his economic policies in order to secure assistance from the International Monetary Fund (IMF). Influx of refugees from Sudan.

1989 Coup attempt against Mengistu foiled. Peace talks with Eritrean rebels mediated by former US president Carter reported some progress.

1990 Rebels captured port of Massawa. Mengistu announced new reforms.

1991 Mengistu overthrown; transitional government set up by Ethiopian People's Revolutionary Democratic Front (EPRDF). Eritrean People's Liberation Front (EPLF) secured Eritrea; Eritrea's right to secede recognized; Meles Zenawi elected Ethiopia's new head of state and government. Isaias Afwerki became secretary general of provisional government in Eritrea.

1993 April: overwhelming majority voted in favour of Eritrean independence in referendum.

Eurocommunism policy followed by communist parties in Western Europe to seek power within the framework of national political initiative rather than by revolutionary means. In addition, Eurocommunism enabled these parties to free themselves from total reliance on the USSR.

European Atomic Energy Commission (Euratom) organization established by the second Treaty of Rome 1957, which seeks the cooperation of member states of the European Community in nuclear research and the rapid and large-scale development of nonmilitary nuclear energy.

European Community (EC) political and economic alliance consisting of the European Coal and Steel Community (1952), European Economic Community (EEC, popularly called the Common Market, 1957), and the European Atomic Energy Commission (Euratom, 1957). The original six members—Belgium, France, West Germany, Italy, Luxembourg, and the Netherlands—were joined by the UK, Denmark, and the Republic of Ireland 1973, Greece 1981, and Spain and Portugal 1986. Association agreements—providing for free trade within ten years and the possibility of full EC membership—were signed with Czechoslovakia, Hungary, and Poland 1991, subject to ratification, and with Romania 1992. The aims of the EC include the expansion of trade, reduction of competition, the abolition of restrictive trading practices, the encouragement of free movement of capital and labour within the community, and the establishment of a closer union among European people. The ◊Maastricht Treaty 1991 provides the framework for closer economic and political union but there have been delays over its ratification.

European Defence Community supranational western European army planned after World War II and designed to counterbalance the military superiority of the USSR in eastern Europe. Although a treaty was signed 1952, a thaw in East-West relations lessened the need for this force and negotiations were instead directed to the formation of the Western European Union in 1955.

European Free Trade Association (EFTA) organization established 1960 consisting of Austria, Finland, Iceland, Norway, Sweden, Switzerland, and (from 1991) Liechtenstein, previously a nonvoting associate member. There are no import duties between members.

F

Fabius Laurent 1946– . French politician, leader of the Socialist Party from 1992. As prime minister 1984–86, he introduced a liberal, free-market economic programme, but his career was damaged by the 1985 Greenpeace sabotage scandal.

Fadden Artie (Arthur) 1895–1973. Australian politician, leader of the ◊Country Party 1941–58 and prime minister Aug–Oct 1941.

Fahd 1921– . King of Saudi Arabia from 1982, when he succeeded his half-brother Khalid. As head of government, he has been active in trying to bring about a solution to the Middle East conflicts.

Fair Deal the policy of social improvement advocated by Harry S Truman, President of the USA 1945–53. The Fair Deal proposals, first mooted in 1945 after the end of World War II, aimed to extend the ◊New Deal on health insurance, housing development, and the laws to maintain farming prices. Although some bills became law—for example a Housing Act, a higher minimum wage, and wider social security benefits—the main proposals were blocked by a hostile Congress.

Faisal Ibn Abdul Aziz 1905–1975. King of Saudi Arabia from 1964. He was the younger brother of King Saud, on whose accession 1953 he was declared crown prince. He was prime minister from 1953–60 and from 1962–75. In 1964 he emerged victorious from a lengthy conflict with his brother and adopted a policy of steady modernization of his country. He was assassinated by his nephew.

Faisal I 1885–1933. King of Iraq 1921–33. An Arab nationalist leader during World War I, he was instrumental in liberating the Near East from Ottoman control and was declared king of Syria in 1918 but deposed by the French in 1920. The British then installed him as king in Iraq, where he continued to foster pan-Arabism.

Falange Española former Spanish Fascist Party, founded 1933 by José Antonio de Rivera (1903–1936), son of military ruler Miguel ◊Primo de

Rivera. It was closely modelled in programme and organization on the Italian fascists and on the Nazis. In 1937, when ◊Franco assumed leadership, it was declared the only legal party, and altered its name to Traditionalist Spanish Phalanx.

Falkender Marcia, Baroness Falkender (Marcia Williams) 1932– . British political secretary to Labour prime minister Harold Wilson from 1956. She was influential in the 'kitchen cabinet' of the 1964–70 government, as described in her book *Inside No 10* 1972.

Falklands War war between Argentina and Britain over disputed sovereignty of the Falkland Islands initiated when Argentina invaded and occupied the islands 2 April 1982. On the following day, the United Nations Security Council passed a resolution calling for Argentina to withdraw. A British task force was immediately dispatched and, after a fierce conflict in which over 1,000 Argentine and British lives were lost, 12,000 Argentine troops surrendered and the islands were returned to British rule 14-15 June 1982.

Fang Lizhi 1936–   . Chinese political dissident and astrophysicist. He advocated human rights and Western-style pluralism and encouraged his students to campaign for democracy. In 1989, after the Tiananmen Square massacre, he sought refuge in the US embassy in Beijing and, over a year later, received official permission to leave China.

Farouk 1920–1965. King of Egypt 1936–52. He succeeded his father ◊Fuad I. In 1952 a coup headed by General Muhammed Neguib and Colonel Gamal Nasser compelled him to abdicate, and his son Fuad II was temporarily proclaimed in his place.

fascism political ideology that denies all rights to individuals in their relations with the state; specifically, the totalitarian nationalist movement founded in Italy 1919 by ◊Mussolini and followed by Hitler's Germany 1933.

Fascism was essentially a product of the economic and political crisis of the years after World War I. Units called *fasci di combattimento* (combat groups), from the Latin *fasces*, were originally established to oppose communism. The fascist party, the *Partitio Nazionale Fascista*, controlled Italy 1922–43. Fascism protected the existing social order by forcible suppression of the working-class movement and by providing scapegoats for popular anger such as outsiders who lived within the state: Jews, foreigners, or blacks; it also prepared the citizenry for the economic and psychological mobilization of war.

Fatah, al- Palestinian nationalist organization founded 1956 to bring about an independent state of Palestine. Also called the Palestine National Liberation Movement, it is the main component of the ◊Palestine Liberation Organization. Its leader is Yassir ◊Arafat.

Faulkner Brian 1921–1977. Northern Ireland Unionist politician. He was the last prime minister of Northern Ireland 1971–72 before the Stormont Parliament was suspended.

Fawcett Millicent Garrett 1847–1929. English suffragette, younger sister of Elizabeth Garrett ◊Anderson. A non-militant, she rejected the violent acts of some of her contemporaries in the suffrage movement. She joined the first Women's Suffrage Committee 1867 and became president of the Women's Unionist Association 1889.

February Revolution the first of the two political uprisings of the ◊Russian revolution in 1917 that led to the overthrow of the tsar and the end of the ◊Romanov dynasty.

Federal Bureau of Investigation (FBI) agency of the US Department of Justice that investigates violations of federal law not specifically assigned to other agencies, being particularly concerned with internal security. The FBI was established 1908 and built up a position of powerful autonomy during the autocratic directorship of J Edgar Hoover 1924–72. William Sessions, a former judge, has been director since 1987.

Ferdinand 1861–1948. King of Bulgaria 1908–18. Son of Prince Augustus of Saxe-Coburg-Gotha, he was elected prince of Bulgaria 1887 and, in 1908, proclaimed Bulgaria's independence of Turkey and assumed the title of tsar. In 1915 he entered World War I as Germany's ally, and in 1918 abdicated.

Ferdinand 1865–1927. King of Romania from 1914, when he succeeded his uncle Charles I. In 1916 he declared war on Austria. After the Allied victory in World War I, Ferdinand acquired Transylvania and Bukovina from Austria-Hungary, and Bessarabia from Russia. In 1922 he became king of this Greater Romania. His reign saw agrarian reform and the introduction of universal suffrage.

Ferraro Geraldine 1935– . US Democrat politician, vice-presidential candidate in the 1984 election.

Fianna Fáil Republic of Ireland political party, founded by the Irish nationalist de Valera 1926. It has been the governing party in the Republic of Ireland 1932–48, 1951–54, 1957–73, 1977–81, 1982, and 1987– . It aims at the establishment of a united and completely independent all-Ireland republic.

fifth column group within a country secretly aiding an enemy attacking from without. The term originated 1936 during the Spanish Civil War, when General Mola boasted that Franco supporters were attacking Madrid with four columns and that they had a 'fifth column' inside the city.

Fiji country comprising 844 islands and islets in the SW Pacific Ocean, about 100 of which are inhabited.

chronology
1874 Fiji became a British crown colony.
1970 Independence achieved from Britain; Ratu Sir Kamisese Mara elected as first prime minister.
1987 April: general election brought to power an Indian-dominated coalition led by Dr Timoci Bavadra. May: military coup by Col Sitiveni ◊Rabuka removed new government at gunpoint; Governor General Ratu Sir Penaia Ganilau regained control within weeks. Sept: second military coup by Rabuka proclaimed Fiji a republic and suspended the constitution. Oct: Fiji ceased to be a member of the Commonwealth. Dec: civilian government restored with Rabuka retaining control of security as minister for home affairs.
1990 New constitution, favouring indigenous Fijians, introduced.
1992 General election produced coalition government; Col Rabuka named as president.

Filene Edward Albert 1860–1937. US businessman renowned for his innovative retailing methods. One of his most imaginative merchandising ideas was the 'bargain basement,' where prices were dramatically lowered on certain goods. Incorporating his father's dry goods store in Boston as William Filene's Sons 1891, Filene was committed to employee profit-sharing and for that reason was removed by his partners 1928.

final solution (to the Jewish question; German *Endlosung der Judenfrage*) euphemism used by the Nazis to describe the extermination of Jews (and other racial groups and opponents of the regime) before and during World War II. See ◊Holocaust.

Fine Gael Republic of Ireland political party founded 1933 by W J ◊Cosgrave and led by Alan Dukes from 1987. It is socially liberal but fiscally conservative.

Finland country in Scandinavia, bounded N by Norway, E by Russia, S and W by the Baltic Sea, and NW by Sweden.

chronology
1809 Finland annexed by Russia.
1917 Independence declared from Russia.
1920 Soviet regime acknowledged independence.
1939 Defeated by USSR in Winter War.
1941 Allowed Germany to station troops in Finland to attack USSR; USSR bombed Finland.
1944 Concluded separate armistice with USSR.
1948 Finno-Soviet Pact of Friendship, Cooperation, and Mutual Assistance signed.
1955 Finland joined the United Nations and the Nordic Council.
1956 Urho Kekkonen elected president; re-elected 1962, 1968, 1978.
1973 Trade treaty with European Economic Community signed.
1977 Trade agreement with USSR signed.
1982 Mauno Koivisto elected president; re-elected 1988.
1989 Finland joined Council of Europe.
1991 Big swing to the centre in general election. New coalition government formed.
1992 Formal application for European Community membership.

Finlandization political term for the tendency of a small state to shape its foreign policy so as to accommodate a much more powerful neighbour, taken from the example of Finland's foreign policy with respect to the USSR.

First World War another name for ◊World War I, 1914–18.

Fisher Andrew 1862–1928. Australian Labor politician. Born in Scotland, he went to Australia 1885, and entered the Australian parliament in 1901. He was prime minister 1908–09, 1910–13, and 1914–15, and Australian high commissioner to the UK 1916–21.

Fisher John Arbuthnot, First Baron Fisher 1841–1920. British admiral, First Sea Lord 1904–10, when he carried out many radical reforms and innovations, including the introduction of the dreadnought battleship.

FitzGerald Garret 1926–   . Irish politician. As *Taoiseach* (prime minister) 1981-82 and again 1982–86, he was noted for his attempts to solve the Northern Ireland dispute, ultimately by participating in the ◊Anglo-Irish agreement 1985. He tried to remove some of the overtly Catholic features of the constitution to make the Republic more attractive to Northern Protestants. He retired as leader of the Fine Gael Party 1987.

five-year plan long-term strategic plan for the development of a country's economy. Five-year plans were from 1928 the basis of economic planning in the USSR, aimed particularly at developing heavy and light industry in a primarily agricultural country. They have since been adopted by many other countries.

Flynn John 1880–1951. Australian missionary. Inspired by the use of aircraft to transport the wounded of World War I, he instituted in 1928 the *flying doctor* service in Australia, which can be summoned to the outback by radios in individual homesteads.

FNLA abbreviation for *Front National de Libération de l'Angola* (French 'National Front for the Liberation of Angola').

Foch Ferdinand 1851–1929. Marshal of France during World War I. He was largely responsible for the Allied victory at the first battle of the ◊Marne Sept 1914, and commanded on the NW front Oct 1914–Sept 1916. He was appointed commander in chief of the Allied armies in the spring of 1918, and launched the Allied counter-offensive in July that brought about the negotiation of an armistice to end the war.

Foot Michael 1913–   . British Labour politician and writer. A leader of the left-wing Tribune Group, he was secretary of state for employment 1974–76, Lord President of the Council and leader of the House 1976–79, and succeeded James Callaghan as Labour Party leader 1980–83.

Football War popular name for a five-day war between El Salvador and Honduras which began on 14 July 1969, when Salvadorean planes bombed Tegucigelpa. Its army entered Honduras, but the ◊Organization of American States arranged a cease-fire, by which time about 2,000 lives had been lost.

Ford Gerald R(udolph) 1913–   . 38th president of the USA 1974–77, a Republican. He was elected to the House of Representatives 1949, was nominated to the vice-presidency by Richard Nixon 1973 following the resignation of Spiro ◊Agnew, and became president 1974, when Nixon was forced to resign following the ◊Watergate scandal. He pardoned Nixon and gave amnesty to those who had resisted the draft for the Vietnam War.

Ford Henry 1863–1947. US automobile manufacturer, who built his first car 1896 and founded the Ford Motor Company 1903. His Model T (1908–27) was the first car to be constructed solely by assembly-line methods and to be mass marketed; 15 million of these cars were made and sold.

Formosa alternative name for ◊Taiwan.

Forrestal James Vincent 1892–1949. US Democratic politician. As under secretary from 1940 and secretary of the navy from 1944, he organized its war effort, accompanying the US landings on the Japanese island Iwo Jima. He was the first secretary of the Department of Defense 1947–49, a post created to unify the three armed forces at the end of World War II.

Four Freedoms, the four kinds of liberty essential to human dignity as defined in an address to the US Congress by President F D ◊Roosevelt 6 Jan 1941: freedom of speech and expression, freedom of worship, freedom from want, freedom from fear.

Fourteen Points the terms proposed by President Wilson of the USA in his address to Congress 8 Jan 1918, as a basis for the settlement of World War I. The creation of the ◊League of Nations was one of the points.

Fourth Republic the French constitutional regime that was established between 1944 and 1946 and lasted until 4 Oct 1958: from liberation after Nazi occupation during World War II to the introduction of a new constitution by General de Gaulle.

Fowler (Peter) Norman 1938–   . British Conservative politician. He was a junior minister in the Heath government, transport secretary in the first Thatcher administration 1979, social services secretary 1981, and employment secretary 1987–89. In May 1992 he succeeded Chris Patten as Conservative Party chairman.

France country in W Europe, bounded NE by Belgium and Germany, E by Germany, Switzerland, and Italy, S by the Mediterranean Sea, SW by Spain and Andorra, and W by the Atlantic Ocean.

chronology

1944-46 Provisional government headed by General Charles ◊de Gaulle; start of Fourth Republic.

1954 Indochina achieved independence.

1956 Morocco and Tunisia achieved independence.

1957 Entry into the European Economic Community.

1958 Recall of de Gaulle after Algerian crisis; start of Fifth Republic.

1959 De Gaulle became president.

1962 Algeria achieved independence.

1966 France withdrew from military wing of NATO.

1968 'May events' crisis.

1969 De Gaulle resigned after referendum defeat; Georges Pompidou became president.

1974 ◊Giscard d'Estaing elected president.

1981 François Mitterrand elected Fifth Republic's first socialist president.

1986 'Cohabitation' experiment, with the conservative Jacques ◊Chirac as prime minister.

1988 Mitterrand re-elected. Moderate socialist Michel ◊Rocard became prime minister. Matignon Accord on future of New Caledonia approved by referendum.

1989 Greens gained 11% of vote in elections to European Parliament.

1991 French forces were part of the US-led coalition in the Gulf War. Edith ◊Cresson became France's first woman prime minister. Mitterrand's popularity rating fell rapidly.

1992 March: Socialist Party humiliated in regional and local elections; Greens and National Front polled strongly. April: Cresson replaced by Pierre ◊Bérégovoy. Sept: referendum narrowly endorsed ◊Maastricht Treaty.

1993 March: Socialist Party suffered heavy defeat in National Assembly elections. Edouard Balladur appointed prime minister.

Franco Francisco (Paulino Hermenegildo Teódulo Bahamonde) 1892–1975. Spanish dictator from 1939. As a general, he led the insurgent Nationalists to victory in the Spanish ◊Civil War 1936–39, supported by Fascist Italy and Nazi Germany, and established a dictatorship. In 1942 Franco reinstated a Cortes (Spanish parliament), which in 1947 passed an act by which he became head of state for life.

Franco-German entente resumption of friendly relations between France and Germany, designed to erase the enmities of successive wars. It was initiated by the French president de Gaulle's visit to West Germany 1962, followed by the Franco-German Treaty of Friendship and Co-operation 1963.

Frankfurter Felix 1882–1965. Austrian-born US jurist and Supreme Court justice. As a supporter of liberal causes, Frankfurter was one of the founders of the American Civil Liberties Union 1920. Appointed to the US Supreme Court 1939 by F D Roosevelt, he opposed the use of the judicial veto to advance political ends. He received the Presidential Medal of Freedom 1963.

Franz Ferdinand or Francis Ferdinand 1863–1914. Archduke of Austria. He became heir to his uncle, Emperor Franz Joseph, in 1884 but while visiting Sarajevo 28 June 1914, he and his wife were assassinated by a Serbian nationalist. Austria used the episode to make unreasonable demands on Serbia that ultimately precipitated World War I.

Franz Joseph or Francis Joseph 1830–1916. Emperor of Austria-Hungary from 1848, when his uncle, Ferdinand I, abdicated. After the suppression of the 1848 revolution, Franz Joseph tried to establish an absolute monarchy but had to grant Austria a parliamentary constitution 1861 and Hungary equality with Austria 1867. He was defeated in the Italian War 1859 and the Prussian War 1866. In 1914 he made the assassination of his heir and nephew Franz Ferdinand the excuse for attacking Serbia, thus precipitating World War I.

Fraser (John) Malcolm 1930– . Australian Liberal politician, prime minister 1975–83; nicknamed 'the Prefect' because of a supposed disregard of subordinates.

Fraser Peter 1884–1950. New Zealand Labour politician, born in Scotland. He held various cabinet posts 1935–40, and was prime minister 1940–49.

Frederick IX 1899–1972. King of Denmark from 1947. He was succeeded by his daughter who became Queen ◊Margrethe II.

Frederick William 1882–1951. Last crown prince of Germany, eldest son of Wilhelm II. During World War I he commanded a group of armies on the western front. In 1918, he retired into private life.

Free French in World War II, movement formed by General Charles ◊de Gaulle in the UK June 1940, consisting of French soldiers who continued to fight against the Axis after the Franco-German armistice. They took the name *Fighting France* 1942 and served in many campaigns, among them General Leclerc's advance from Chad to Tripolitania 1942, the Syrian campaigns 1941, the campaigns in the Western Desert, the Italian campaign, the liberation of France, and the invasion of Germany. Their emblem was the Cross of Lorraine, a cross with two bars.

free trade economic system where governments do not interfere in the movement of goods between countries; there are thus no taxes on imports. In the modern economy, free trade tends to hold within economic groups such as the European Community (EC), but not generally, despite such treaties as ◊GATT 1948 and subsequent agreements to reduce tariffs. The opposite of free trade is protectionism.

Frei Edwardo 1911–1982. Chilean president 1964–70. Elected as the only effective anti-Marxist candidate, he pursued a moderate programme of 'Chileanization' of US-owned copper interests. His regime was plagued by inflation and labour unrest, but saw considerable economic development.

Frelimo (acronym for *Fr*ont for th*e Li*beration of *Mo*zambique) nationalist group aimed at gaining independence for Mozambique from the occupying Portuguese. It began operating from S Tanzania 1963 and continued until victory 1975.

French John Denton Pinkstone, 1st Earl of Ypres 1852–1925. British field marshal. In the second ◊South African War 1899–1902, he relieved Kimberley and took Bloemfontein; in World War I he was Commander in Chief of the British Expeditionary Force in France 1914–15; he resigned after being criticized as indecisive.

French Community former association consisting of France and those overseas territories joined with it by the constitution of the Fifth Republic, following the 1958 referendum. Many of the constituent states withdrew during the 1960s, and it no longer formally exists, but in practice all former French colonies have close economic and cultural as well as linguistic links with France.

French Equatorial Africa federation of French territories in West Africa. Founded 1910, it consisted of Gabon, Middle Congo, Chad, and Ubangi-Shari (now the Central African Republic), and was ruled from Brazzaville. The federation supported the ◊Free French in World War II and was given representation in the French Fourth Republic 1944-58. In 1958, the states voted for autonomy and the federation was dissolved.

Freyberg Bernard Cyril, Baron Freyberg 1889–1963. New Zealand soldier and administrator born in England. He fought in World War I, and during World War II he commanded the New Zealand expeditionary force. He was governor general of New Zealand 1946–52.

Friedan Betty 1921–   . US liberal feminist. Her book *The Feminine Mystique* 1963 started the contemporary women's movement, both in the US and the UK. She was a founder of the National Organization for Women (NOW) 1966 (and its president 1966–70), the National Women's Political Caucus 1971, and the First Women's Bank 1973. Friedan also helped to organize the Women's Strike for Equality 1970 and called the First International Feminist Congress 1973.

front-line states the black nations of southern Africa in the 'front line' of the struggle against the segregationist policies of South Africa: Mozambique, Tanzania, and Zambia, as well as Botswana and Zimbabwe.

Fuad I 1868–1936. King of Egypt from 1922. Son of the Khedive Ismail, he succeeded his elder brother Hussein Kiamil as sultan of Egypt 1917; when Egypt was declared independent 1922 he assumed the title of king.

Fuad II 1952–   . King of Egypt 1952–53, between the abdication of his father ◊Farouk and the establishment of the republic. He was a grandson of Fuad I.

Führer or *Fuehrer* title adopted by Adolf ◊Hitler as leader of the Nazi Party.

Fujimori Alberto 1939–   . President of Peru from July 1990. As leader of the newly formed Cambio 90 (Change 90) he campaigned on a reformist ticket and defeated his more experienced Democratic Front opponent. With no assembly majority, and faced with increasing opposition to his policies, he imposed military rule early 1992.

Fulbright (James) William 1905–   . US Democratic politician. A US senator 1945-75, he was responsible for the *Fulbright Act* 1946, which provided grants for thousands of Americans to study abroad and for overseas students to study in the USA. Fulbright chaired the Senate Foreign Relations Committee 1959–74, and was a strong internationalist and supporter of the ◊United Nations.

Fuller Melville Weston 1833–1910. US jurist and chief justice of the US Supreme Court 1888-1910. Fuller endorsed court options that limited state and federal strengths to regulate private business. He sided with the majority of the Court in *Pollack* v *Farmers Loan and Trust Co* 1895, which held invalid a flat-rate US income tax leading to passage of the 16th Amendment to the Constitution in 1913, authorizing an income tax.

fundamentalism in religion, an emphasis on basic principles or articles of faith. *Christian fundamentalism* emerged in the USA just after World War I (as a reaction to theological modernism and the historical criticism of the Bible) and insisted on belief in the literal truth of everything in the Bible. *Islamic fundamentalism* insists on strict observance of Muslim Shari'a law.

Fusion government South African coalition government formed 1933 which saw the merger of J B M ◊Hertzog's Nationalist Party and J C ◊Smuts' South African Party the following year. The United South African National Party, as it became, attempted to cultivate a broader white unity in South Africa in the face of growing political and economic uncertainty.

G

Gabon country in central Africa, bounded N by Cameroon, E and S by the Congo, W by the Atlantic Ocean, and NW by Equatorial Guinea.

chronology
1889 Gabon became part of the French Congo.
1960 Independence from France achieved; Léon M'ba became the first president.
1967 Attempted coup by rival party foiled with French help. M'ba died; he was succeeded by his protégé Albert-Bernard Bongo.
1968 One-party state established.
1973 Bongo re-elected; converted to Islam, he changed his first name to Omar.
1986 Bongo re-elected.
1989 Coup attempt against Bongo defeated.
1990 Gabonese Democratic Party (PDG) won first multiparty elections since 1964 amidst allegations of ballot-rigging.

Gaddafi alternative form of ◊Khaddhafi, Libyan leader.

Gaitskell Hugh (Todd Naylor) 1906–1963. British Labour politician. In 1950 he became minister of economic affairs, and then chancellor of the Exchequer until Oct 1951. In 1955 he defeated Aneurin Bevan for the succession to Attlee as party leader, and tried to reconcile internal differences on nationalization and disarmament. He was re-elected leader in 1960.

Gallegos Rómulo 1884–1969. Venezuelan politician and writer. He was Venezuela's first democratically elected president 1948 before being overthrown by a military coup the same year. He was also a professor of philosophy and literature. His novels include *La trepadora/The Climber* 1925 and *Doña Bárbara* 1929.

Galtieri Leopoldo 1926– . Argentine general, president 1981–82. A leading member from 1979 of the ruling right-wing military junta and commander of the army, Galtieri became president in 1981. Under his leadership the junta ordered the seizure 1982 of the Falkland Islands (Malvinas), a British colony in the SW Atlantic claimed by Argentina. After the surrender of his forces he resigned as army commander and was replaced as president. He and his fellow junta members were tried for abuse of human rights and court-martialled for their conduct of the war; he was sentenced to 12 years in prison in 1986.

Gambia, The country in W Africa, bounded N, E, and S by Senegal and W by the Atlantic Ocean.

chronology
1843 The Gambia became a crown colony.
1965 Independence achieved from Britain as a constitutional monarchy within the Commonwealth, with Dawda K Jawara as prime minister.
1970 Declared itself a republic, with Jawara as president.
1972 Jawara re-elected.
1981 Attempted coup foiled with the help of Senegal.
1982 Formed with Senegal the Confederation of Senegambia; Jawara re-elected.
1987 Jawara re-elected.
1989 Confederation of Senegambia dissolved.
1990 Gambian troops contributed to the stabilizing force in Liberia.

Gamelin Maurice Gustave 1872–1958. French commander in chief of the Allied armies in France at the outset of World War II 1939. Replaced by Maxime Weygand after the German breakthrough at Sedan 1940, he was tried by the ◊Vichy government as a scapegoat before the Riom 'war guilt' court 1942. He refused to defend himself and was detained in Germany until released by the Allies 1945.

Gamsakhurdia Zviad 1939–   . Georgian politician, president 1990-92. He was an active anti-communist and became head of state after nationalist success in parliamentary elections. Directly elected to the post by a huge margin in May 1991, Gamsakhurdia's increasingly dictatorial style led to his forced removal and he fled to Armenia.

Gandhi Indira (born Nehru) 1917–1984. Indian politician, prime minister of India 1966–77 and 1980–84, and leader of the Congress Party 1966–77 and subsequently of the Congress (I) party. She was assassinated 1984 by members of her Sikh bodyguard, resentful of her use of troops to clear malcontents from the Sikh temple at Amritsar.

Gandhi Mohandas Karamchand, called *Mahatma* ('Great Soul') 1869–1948. Indian nationalist leader. A pacifist, he led the struggle for Indian independence from the UK by advocating nonviolent noncooperation (*satyagraha*, defence of and by truth) from 1915. He was imprisoned several times by the British authorities and was influential in the nationalist Congress Party and in the independence negotiations 1947. He was assassinated by a Hindu nationalist in the violence that followed the partition of British India into India and Pakistan.

Gandhi Rajiv 1944–1991. Indian politician, prime minister from 1984 (following his mother Indira Gandhi's assassination) to Nov 1989. As prime minister, he faced growing discontent with his party's elitism and lack of concern for social issues. He was assassinated by a bomb at an election rally.

Gang of Four in Chinese history, the chief members of the radical faction that played a key role in directing the ◊Cultural Revolution and tried to seize power after the death of the communist leader Mao Zedong 1976. It included his widow, ◊Jiang Qing; the other members were three young Shanghai politicians: Zhang Chunqiao, Wang Hongwen, and Yao Wenyuan. The coup failed and the Gang of Four were arrested. Publicly tried in 1980, they were found guilty of treason.

García Perez Alan 1949– . Peruvian politician, leader of the moderate, left-wing APRA party; president 1985–90. He inherited an ailing economy and was forced to trim his socialist programme.

Garner John Nance 1868–1967. US political leader and vice president of the USA 1933-41. He served in the US House of Representatives 1903–33. A Democratic leader in the House, he was chosen as Speaker 1931. He later served as vice president during Franklin Roosevelt's first two terms. Opposing Roosevelt's reelection in 1940, Garner retired from public life.

Garvey Marcus (Moziah) 1887–1940. Jamaican political thinker and activist, an early advocate of black nationalism. He founded the UNIA (Universal Negro Improvement Association) in 1914, and moved to the USA in 1916, where he established branches in New York and other northern cities. Aiming to achieve human rights and dignity for black people through black pride and economic self-sufficiency, he was considered one of the first militant black nationalists. He led a Back to Africa movement for black Americans to establish a black-governed country in Africa. The Jamaican cult of Rastafarianism is based largely on his ideas.

GATT acronym for ◊*General Agreement on Tariffs and Trade*.

Gaulle Charles de. French politician, see Charles ◊de Gaulle.

gaullism political philosophy deriving from the views of Charles ◊de Gaulle but not necessarily confined to Gaullist parties, or even to France. Its basic tenets are the creation and preservation of a strongly centralized state and an unwillingness to enter into international obligations at the expense of national interests.

Gaviria (Trujillo) Cesar 1947– . Colombian Liberal Party politician, president from 1990; he was finance minister 1986–87 and minister of government 1987–89. He has supported the extradition of drug traffickers wanted in the USA and has sought more US aid in return for stepping up the drug war.

Geingob Hage Gottfried 1941– . Namibian politician and prime minister. Geingob was appointed founding director of the United Nations Institute for Namibia in Lusaka, 1975. He became first prime minister of an independent Namibia March 1990.

Gemayel Amin 1942– . Lebanese politician, a Maronite Christian; president 1982–88. He succeeded his brother, president-elect *Bechir Gemayel* (1947–1982), on his assassination on 14 Sept 1982. The Lebanese parliament was unable to agree on a successor when his term expired, so separate governments were formed under rival Christian and Muslim leaders.

General Agreement on Tariffs and Trade (GATT) organization within the United Nations founded 1948 with the aim of encouraging ◊free trade between nations through low tariffs, abolitions of quotas, and curbs on subsidies.

General Belgrano Argentine battle cruiser torpedoed and sunk on 2 May 1982 by the British nuclear-powered submarine *Conqueror* during the ◊Falklands War.

general strike refusal to work by employees in several key industries, with the intention of paralysing the economic life of a country. In British history, the General Strike was a nationwide strike called by the Trade Union Congress on 3 May 1926 in support of the miners' union. Elsewhere, the general strike was used as a political weapon by anarchists and others, especially in Spain and Italy.

Geneva Protocol international agreement 1925 designed to prohibit the use of poisonous gases, chemical weapons, and bacteriological methods of warfare. It came into force 1928 but was not ratified by the USA until 1974.

Genscher Hans-Dietrich 1927–   . German politician, chair of the West German Free Democratic Party (FDP) 1974–85, foreign minister 1974–92. A skilled and pragmatic tactician, Genscher became the reunified Germany's most popular politician.

George I 1845–1913. King of Greece 1863–1913. The son of Christian IX of Denmark, he was nominated to the Greek throne and, in spite of early unpopularity, became a highly successful constitutional monarch. He was assassinated by a Greek, Schinas, at Salonika.

George II 1890–1947. King of Greece 1922–23 and 1935–47. He became king on the expulsion of his father Constantine I 1922 but was himself overthrown 1923. Restored by the military 1935, he set up a dictatorship under Ioannis ◊Metaxas, and went into exile during the German occupation 1941–45.

George V 1865–1936. King of Great Britain from 1910, when he succeeded his father Edward VII. He was the second son, and became heir 1892 on the death of his elder brother Albert, Duke of Clarence. In 1893, he married Princess Victoria Mary of Teck (Queen Mary), formerly engaged to his brother. During World War I he made several visits to the front. In 1917, he abandoned all German titles for himself and his family. The name of the royal house was changed from Saxe-Coburg-Gotha (popularly known as Brunswick or Hanover) to Windsor.

George VI 1895–1952. King of Great Britain from 1936, when he succeeded after the abdication of his brother Edward VIII, who had succeeded their father George V. Created Duke of York 1920, he married in 1923 Lady Elizabeth Bowes-Lyon (1900–   ), and their children are Elizabeth II and Princess Margaret. During World War II, he visited the Normandy and Italian battlefields.

Georgetown, Declaration of call, at a conference in Guyana of non-aligned countries 1972, for a multipolar system to replace the two world power blocs, and for the Mediterranean Sea and Indian Ocean to be neutral.

Georgia, Republic of country in the Caucasus of SE Europe, bounded N by Russia, E by Azerbaijan, S by Armenia, and W by the Black Sea.

chronology
1918–21 Independent republic.
1921 Uprising quelled by Red Army and Soviet republic established.
1922-36 Linked with Armenia and Azerbaijan as the Transcaucasian Republic.
1936 Became separate republic within USSR.
1981-88 Increasing demands for autonomy, spearheaded from 1988 by the Georgian Popular Front.
1989 March–April: Abkhazians demanded secession from Georgia, provoking inter-ethnic clashes. April: Georgian Communist Party (GCP) leadership purged. July: state of emergency imposed in Abkhazia; inter-ethnic clashes in South Ossetia. Nov: economic and political sovereignty declared.
1990 March: GCP monopoly ended. Oct: nationalist coalition triumphed in supreme soviet elections. Nov: Zviad ⚭Gamsakhurdia became president. Dec: GCP seceded from Communist Party of USSR; calls for Georgian independence.
1991 April: declared independence. May: Gamsakhurdia popularly elected president. Aug: GCP outlawed and all relations with USSR severed. Sept: anti-Gamsakhurdia demonstrations; state of emergency declared. Dec: Georgia failed to join new Commonwealth of Independent States (CIS).
1992 Jan: Gamsakhurdia fled to Armenia; Sigua appointed prime minister; Georgia admitted into Conference on Security and Cooperation in Europe (CSCE). Eduard Shevardnadze appointed interim president. July: admitted into United Nations (UN). Aug: fighting started between Georgian troops and Abkhazian separatists in Abkhazia in NW. Oct: ⚭Shevardnadze elected chair of new parliament. Clashes in South Ossetia and Abkhazia continued.
1993 Inflation at 1,500%.

German expansion aggressive territorial expansion of ⚭Germany during the 1930s before the outbreak of World War II.

German Spring offensive Germany's final offensive on the Western Front during World War I. By early 1918, German forces outnumbered the Allies on the Western Front. Germany staged three separate offensives, which culminated in the Second Battle of the Marne, fought between 15 July and 6 Aug. It marked the turning point of World War I. After winning the battle the Allies advanced steadily, and by Sept, Germany had lost all the territory it had gained during the spring.

Germany Federal Republic of; country in central Europe, bounded N by the North and Baltic Seas and Denmark, E by Poland and the Czech Republic, S by Austria and Switzerland, and W by France, Luxembourg, Belgium, and the Netherlands.

chronology
1945 Germany surrendered; country divided into four occupation zones (US, French, British, Soviet).
1948 Blockade of West Berlin.
1949 Establishment of Federal Republic under the 'Basic Law' Constitution with Konrad ◊Adenauer as chancellor; establishment of the German Democratic Republic as an independent state.
1953 Uprising in East Berlin suppressed by Soviet troops.
1954 Grant of full sovereignty to both West Germany and East Germany.
1957 West Germany was a founder-member of the European Economic Community; recovery of Saarland from France.
1961 Construction of Berlin Wall.
1963 Retirement of Chancellor Adenauer.
1964 Treaty of Friendship and Mutual Assistance signed between East Germany and USSR.
1969 Willy ◊Brandt became chancellor of West Germany.
1971 Erich ◊Honecker elected Socialist Unity Party (SED) leader in East Germany.
1972 Basic Treaty between West Germany and East Germany; treaty ratified 1973, normalizing relations between the two.
1974 Resignation of Brandt; Helmut ◊Schmidt became chancellor.
1975 East German friendship treaty with USSR renewed for 25 years.
1982 Helmut ◊Kohl became West German chancellor.
1987 Official visit of Honecker to the Federal Republic.
1988 Death of Franz-Josef ◊Strauss, leader of the West German Bavarian Christian Social Union (CSU).
1989 West Germany: rising support for far right in local and European elections, declining support for Kohl. East Germany: mass exodus to West Germany began. Honecker replaced by Egon ◊Krenz. National borders opened in Nov, including Berlin Wall. Reformist Hans Modrow appointed prime minister. Krenz replaced.

1990 March: East German multiparty elections won by a coalition led by the right-wing Christian Democratic Union (CDU). 3 Oct: official reunification of East and West Germany. 2 Dec: first all-German elections since 1932, resulting in a victory for Kohl.

1991 Kohl's popularity declined after tax increase. The CDU lost its Bundesrat majority to the Social Democratic Party (SPD). Racism continued with violent attacks on foreigners.

1992 Neo-Nazi riots against immigrants continued.

1993 Jan: unemployment exceeded 7%; 1% decline in national output predicted for 1993. Honecker allowed to leave for exile in Chile. March: support for CDU slumped in state election in Hesse; Republicans captured 8% of vote.

Germany, East (German Democratic Republic, GDR) country 1949–90, formed from the Soviet zone of occupation in the partition of Germany following World War II. East Germany became a sovereign state 1954, and was reunified with West Germany Oct 1990. See ◊Germany, Federal Republic of.

Germany, West (Federal Republic of Germany) country 1949-90, formed from the British, US, and French occupation zones in the partition of Germany following World War II; reunified with East Germany Oct 1990. For history before 1949, see ◊Germany, history; for history after 1949, see ◊Germany, Federal Republic of.

Gestapo (contraction of *Ge*heime *Sta*ats*po*lizei) Nazi Germany's secret police, formed 1933, and under the direction of Heinrich Himmler from 1936. The Gestapo used torture and terrorism to stamp out anti-Nazi resistance. It was declared a criminal organization at the Nuremberg Trials 1946.

Ghana country in W Africa, bounded N by Burkina Faso, E by Togo, S by the Gulf of Guinea, and W by the Ivory Coast.

chronology
1957 Independence achieved from Britain, within the Commonwealth, with Kwame ◊Nkrumah as president.

1960 Ghana became a republic.

1964 Ghana became a one-party state.

1966 Nkrumah deposed and replaced by General Joseph Ankrah.

1969 Ankrah replaced by General Akwasi Afrifa, who initiated a return to civilian government.

1970 Edward Akufo-Addo elected president.

1972 Another coup placed Col Acheampong at the head of a military government.

1978 Acheampong deposed in a bloodless coup led by Frederick Akuffo; another coup put Flight-Lt Jerry Rawlings in power.

1979 Return to civilian rule under Hilla Limann.

1981 Rawlings seized power again, citing the incompetence of previous governments. All political parties banned.

1989 Coup attempt against Rawlings foiled.

1992 New multiparty constitution approved. Partial lifting of ban on political parties. Nov: Rawlings won presidency in national elections.

1993 Fourth republic of Ghana formally inaugurated in Rawlings's presence.

Gheorgiu-Dej Gheorge 1901–1965. Romanian communist politician. A member of the Romanian Communist Party from 1930, he played a leading part in establishing a communist regime 1945. He was prime minister 1952–55 and state president 1961–65. Although retaining the support of Moscow, he adopted an increasingly independent line during his final years.

Gierek Edward 1913– . Polish Communist politician. He entered the Politburo of the ruling Polish United Workers' Party (PUWP) in 1956 and was party leader 1970–80. His industrialization programme plunged the country heavily into debt and sparked a series of ◊Solidarity-led strikes.

Giolitti Giovanni 1842–1928. Italian liberal politician, born in Mondovi. He was prime minister 1892–93, 1903–05, 1906–09, 1911–14, and 1920–21. He opposed Italian intervention in World War I and pursued a policy of broad coalitions, which proved ineffective in controlling Fascism after 1921.

Giscard d'Estaing Valéry 1926– . French conservative politician, president 1974–81. He was finance minister to de Gaulle 1962–66 and Pompidou 1969–74. As leader of the Union pour la Démocratie Française, which he formed in 1978, Giscard sought to project himself as leader of a 'new centre'.

glasnost former Soviet leader Mikhail ◊Gorbachev's policy of liberalizing various aspects of Soviet life, such as introducing greater freedom of expression and information and opening up relations with Western countries. *Glasnost* was introduced and adopted by the Soviet government 1986.

Goebbels (Paul) Josef 1897–1945. German Nazi leader. As minister of propaganda from 1933, he brought all cultural and educational activities under Nazi control and built up sympathetic movements abroad to carry on the 'war of nerves' against Hitler's intended victims. On the capture of Berlin by the Allies, he poisoned himself.

Goering (German *Göring*) Hermann Wilhelm 1893–1946. Nazi leader, German field marshal from 1938. He was part of Hitler's inner circle, and with Hitler's rise to power was appointed commissioner for aviation from 1933 and built up the Luftwaffe (airforce). He built a vast economic empire in occupied Europe, but later lost favour and was expelled from the party in 1945. Tried at Nuremberg for war crimes, he poisoned himself before he could be executed.

Goh Chok Tong 1941– . Singapore politician, prime minister from 1990. A trained economist, Goh became a member of Parliament for the ruling People's Action Party 1976. Rising steadily through the party ranks, he was appointed deputy prime minister 1985, and subsequently chosen by the cabinet as Lee Kuan Yew's successor.

Gokhale Gopal Krishna 1866–1915. Indian political adviser and friend of Mohandas Gandhi, leader of the Moderate group in the Indian National Congress before World War I.

Goldman Emma 1869–1940. US political organizer, feminist and co-editor of the anarchist monthly *Mother Earth* 1906-17. In 1908 her citizenship was revoked and in 1919 she was deported to Russia. Breaking with the Bolsheviks 1921, she spent the rest of her life in exile. Her writings include *My Disillusionment in Russia* 1923 and *Living My Life* 1931.

gold standard system under which a country's currency is exchangeable for a fixed weight of gold on demand at the central bank. It was almost universally applied 1870–1914, but by 1937 no single country was on the full gold standard. Britain abandoned the gold standard 1931; the USA abandoned it 1971. Holdings of gold are still retained because it is an internationally recognized commodity, which cannot be legislated upon or manipulated by interested countries.

Goldwater Barry 1909– . US Republican politician, presidential candidate in the 1964 election, when he was heavily defeated by Lyndon Johnson. Many of Goldwater's ideas were later adopted by the Republican right and the Reagan administration.

Gómez Juan Vicente 1864–1935. Venezuelan dictator 1908–35. The discovery of oil during his rule attracted US, British, and Dutch oil interests and made Venezuela one of the wealthiest countries in Latin America. Gómez amassed a considerable personal fortune and used his well-equipped army to dominate the civilian population.

Gompers Samuel 1850–1924. US labour leader. His early career in the Cigarmakers' Union led him to found and lead the ◊American Federation of Labor 1886. Gompers advocated nonpolitical activity within the existing capitalist system to secure improved wages and working conditions for members.

Gomułka Władysław 1905–1982. Polish Communist politician, party leader 1943–48 and 1956–70. He introduced moderate reforms, including private farming and tolerance for Roman Catholicism.

González Márquez Felipe 1942– . Spanish socialist politician, leader of the Socialist Workers' Party (PSOE), prime minister from 1982. Although re-elected in the 1989 election, his popularity suffered from economic upheaval and allegations of corruption.

Good Neighbor policy the efforts of US administrations between the two World Wars to improve relations with Latin American and Caribbean states. The phrase was first used by President F D Roosevelt in his inaugural speech March 1933 to describe the foreign policy of his ◊New Deal.

Gorbachev Mikhail Sergeyevich 1931– . Soviet president, in power 1985–91. He was a member of the Politburo from 1980. As general secretary of the Communist Party (CPSU) 1985–91, and president of the Supreme Soviet 1988–91, he introduced liberal reforms at home (*perestroika* and ◊*glasnost*), proposed the introduction of multiparty democracy, and attempted to halt the arms race abroad. He became head of state 1989.

He was awarded the Nobel Peace Prize 1990 but his international reputation suffered in the light of harsh state repression of nationalist demonstrations in the Baltic states. Following an abortive coup attempt by hardliners Aug 1991, international acceptance of independence for the Baltic states, and accelerated moves towards independence in other republics, Gorbachev's power base as Soviet president was greatly weakened and in Dec 1991 he resigned.

Gore Al(bert) 1948– . US politician, vice president from 1993. A Democrat, he became a member of the House of Representatives 1977–79, and was elected senator for Tennessee 1985–92. Like his running mate, Bill ◊Clinton, he is on the conservative wing of the party, but holds liberal views on such matters as women's rights and abortion.

Goria Giovanni 1943–   . Italian Christian Democrat (DC) politician, prime minister 1987–88. He entered the Chamber of Deputies 1976 and held a number of posts, including treasury minister, until he was asked to form a coalition government in 1987.

Göring Hermann. German spelling of ◊Goering, Nazi leader.

Gorton John Grey 1911–   . Australian Liberal politician. He was minister for education and science 1966–68, and prime minister 1968–71.

Gould Bryan (Charles) 1939–   . British Labour politician, member of the shadow cabinet from 1986 to 1992.

Gow Ian 1937–1990. British Conservative politician. After qualifying as a solicitor, he became member of Parliament for Eastbourne 1974. He became parliamentary private secretary to the then prime minister, Margaret Thatcher, 1979, and her close ally. He secured steady promotion but resigned his post as minister of state 1985 in protest at the signing of the ◊Anglo-Irish Agreement. A strong critic of terrorist acts, he was killed by an IRA car bomb.

Gowon Yakubu 1934–   . Nigerian politician, head of state 1966–75. Educated at Sandhurst military college in the UK, he became chief of staff, and in the military coup of 1966 seized power. After the Biafran civil war 1967–70, he reunited the country with his policy of 'no victor, no vanquished'. In 1975 he was overthrown by a military coup.

GPU name (1922–23) for the security service of the Soviet Union; later the ◊KGB.

Gramsci Antonio 1891–1937. Italian Marxist who attempted to unify social theory and political practice. He helped to found the Italian Communist Party 1921 and was elected to parliament 1924, but was imprisoned by the Fascist leader Mussolini from 1926; his *Quaderni di carcere/Prison Notebooks* were published posthumously 1947.

Grandi Dino 1895–1988. Italian politician who challenged Mussolini for leadership of the Italian Fascist Party in 1921 and was subsequently largely responsible for Mussolini's downfall in July 1943.

Graziani Rodolfo 1882–1955. Italian general. He was commander in chief of Italian forces in North Africa during World War II but was defeated by British forces 1940, and subsequently replaced. Later, as defence minister in the new Mussolini government, he failed to reorganize a republican Fascist army, was captured by the Allies 1945, tried by an Italian military court, and finally released 1950.

Great Leap Forward change in the economic policy of the People's Republic of China introduced by ◊Mao Zedong under the second five-year plan of 1958–62. The aim was to achieve rapid and simultaneous agricultural and industrial growth through the creation of large new agro-industrial communes. The inefficient and poorly planned allocation of state resources led to the collapse of the strategy by 1960 and the launch of a 'reactionary programme', involving the use of rural markets and private subsidiary plots. More than 20 million people died in the Great Leap famines of 1959–61.

Great Patriotic War (1941–45) war between the USSR and Germany during ◊World War II. When Germany invaded the USSR in June 1941, the Soviet troops retreated. Stalin remained in Moscow and the Soviet forces, inspired to fight on by his patriotic speeches, launched a counter-offensive. In 1942 the Germans failed to take Leningrad and Moscow, and launched an attack towards the river Volga and to capture oil wells at Baku. In Aug 1942 the Germans attacked Stalingrad but it was held by the Russians. A substantial German force was forced to surrender at Stalingrad in Jan 1943. The Red Army, under the command of Marshal Zhukov, gradually forced the Germans back and by Feb 1945 the Russians had reached the German border. In April 1945 the Russians, who had made tremendous sacrifices (20 million dead and millions more wounded) entered Berlin. In May 1945 the war ended.

Great Society political slogan coined 1965 by US President Lyndon B Johnson to describe the ideal society to be created by his administration (1963-68), and to which all other nations would aspire. The programme included extensive social welfare legislation, most of which was subsequently passed by Congress.

Great War another name for ◊World War I.

Greece country in SE Europe, comprising the S Balkan peninsula, bounded N by Yugoslavia and Bulgaria, NW by Albania, NE by Turkey, E by the Aegean Sea, S by the Mediterranean Sea, and W by the Ionian Sea.

chronology

1829 Independence achieved from Turkish rule.

1912–13 Balkan Wars; Greece gained much land.

1941–44 German occupation of Greece.

1946 Civil war between royalists and communists; communists defeated.

1949 Monarchy re-established with Paul as king.

1964 King Paul succeeded by his son Constantine.

1967 Army coup removed the king; Col George Papadopoulos became prime minister. Martial law imposed, all political activity banned.

1973 Republic proclaimed, with Papadopoulos as president.

1974 Former premier Constantine ◊Karamanlis recalled from exile to lead government. Martial law and ban on political parties lifted; restoration of the monarchy rejected by a referendum.

1975 New constitution adopted, making Greece a democratic republic.

1980 Karamanlis resigned as prime minister and was elected president.

1981 Greece became full member of European Economic Community. Andreas ◊Papandreou elected Greece's first socialist prime minister.

1983 Five-year military and economic cooperation agreement signed with USA; ten-year economic cooperation agreement signed with USSR.

1985 Papandreou re-elected.

1988 Relations with Turkey improved. Major cabinet reshuffle after mounting criticism of Papandreou.

1989 Papandreou defeated. Tzannis Tzannetakis became prime minister; his all-party government collapsed. Xenophon Zolotas formed new unity government. Papandreou charged with corruption.

1990 New Democracy Party (ND) won half of parliamentary seats in general election but no outright majority; Constantine Mitsotakis became premier; formed new all-party government. Karamanlis re-elected president.

1992 Papandreou acquitted. Greece opposed recognition of independence of the Yugoslav breakaway republic of Macedonia. Decisive parliamentary vote to ratify ◊Maastricht Treaty.

Greenham Common site of a continuous peace demonstration 1981–90 on common land near Newbury, Berkshire, UK, outside a US airbase. The women-only camp was established Sept 1981 in protest against the siting of US cruise missiles in the UK. The demonstrations ended with the closure of the base. Greenham Common reverted to standby status, and the last US cruise missiles were withdrawn March 1991.

Green Party political party aiming to 'preserve the planet and its people', based on the premise that incessant economic growth is unsustainable. The leaderless party structure reflects a general commitment to decentralization. Green parties sprang up in W Europe in the 1970s and in E Europe from 1988. Parties in different countries are linked to one another but unaffiliated with any pressure group.

green revolution in agriculture, a popular term for the change in methods of arable farming in Third World countries. The intent is to provide more and better food for their populations, albeit with a heavy reliance on chemicals and machinery. It was instigated in the 1940s and 1950s, but abandoned by some countries in the 1980s. Much of the food produced is exported as cash crops, so that local diet does not always improve.

Grenada island country in the Caribbean, the southernmost of the Windward Islands.

chronology
1974 Independence achieved from Britain; Eric Gairy elected prime minister.
1979 Gairy removed in bloodless coup led by Maurice Bishop; constitution suspended and a People's Revolutionary Government established.
1982 Relations with the USA and Britain deteriorated as ties with Cuba and the USSR strengthened.
1983 After Bishop's attempt to improve relations with the USA, he was overthrown by left-wing opponents. A coup established the Revolutionary Military Council (RMC), and Bishop and three colleagues were executed. The USA invaded Grenada, accompanied by troops from other E Caribbean countries; RMC overthrown, 1974 constitution reinstated.
1984 The newly formed New National Party (NNP) won 14 of the 15 seats in the house of representatives and its leader, Herbert Blaize, became prime minister.
1989 Herbert Blaize lost leadership of NNP, remaining as head of government; he died and was succeeded by Ben Jones.
1990 Nicholas Braithwaite of the National Democratic Congress (NDC) became prime minister.
1991 Integration into Windward Islands confederation proposed.

Grey Edward, 1st Viscount Grey of Fallodon 1862–1933. British Liberal politician, nephew of Charles Grey. As foreign secretary 1905–16 he negotiated an entente with Russia 1907, and backed France against Germany in the ◊Agadir Incident of 1911. In 1914 he said: 'The lamps are going out all over Europe; we shall not see them lit again in our lifetime.'

Grimond Jo(seph), Baron Grimond 1913–   . British Liberal politician. As leader of the party 1956–67, he aimed at making it 'a new radical party to take the place of the Socialist Party as an alternative to Conservatism'.

Grivas George 1898–1974. Greek Cypriot general who from 1955 led the underground group EOKA's attempts to secure the union (Greek *enosis*) of Cyprus with Greece.

Gromyko Andrei 1909–1989. President of the USSR 1985–88. As ambassador to the USA from 1943, he took part in the ◊Tehran, ◊Yalta, and ◊Potsdam conferences; as United Nations representative 1946–49, he exercised the Soviet veto 26 times. He was foreign minister 1957–85. It was Gromyko who formally nominated Mikhail Gorbachev as Communist Party leader 1985.

Grosz Károly 1930–   . Hungarian Communist politician, prime minister 1987–88. As leader of the ruling Hungarian Socialist Workers' Party (HSWP) 1988–89, he sought to establish a flexible system of 'socialist pluralism'.

Guatemala country in Central America, bounded N and NW by Mexico, E by Belize and the Caribbean Sea, SE by Honduras and El Salvador, and SW by the Pacific Ocean.

chronology
1839 Independence achieved from Spain.
1954 Col Carlos Castillo became president in US-backed coup, halting land reform.
1963 Military coup made Col Enrique Peralta president.
1966 Cesar Méndez elected president.
1970 Carlos Araña elected president.
1974 General Kjell Laugerud became president. Widespread political violence precipitated by the discovery of falsified election returns in March.
1978 General Fernando Romeo became president.
1981 Growth of antigovernment guerrilla movement.
1982 General Angel Anibal became president. Army coup installed General Ríos Montt as head of junta and then as president; political violence continued.

1983 Montt removed in coup led by General Mejía Victores, who declared amnesty for the guerrillas.

1985 New constitution adopted; Guatemalan Christian Democratic Party (PDCG) won congressional elections; Vinicio Cerezo elected president.

1989 Coup attempt against Cerezo foiled. Over 100,000 people killed, and 40,000 reported missing since 1980.

1991 Jorge Serrano Elías of the Solidarity Action Movement elected president. Diplomatic relations with Belize established.

Guderian Heinz 1888–1954. German general in World War II. He created the Panzer (German 'armour') divisions that formed the ground spearhead of Hitler's ◊*Blitzkrieg* attack strategy, achieving a significant breakthrough at Sedan in Ardennes, France 1940, and leading the advance to Moscow 1941.

Guernica town in the Basque province of Vizcaya, N Spain. It was almost completely destroyed 1937 by German bombers aiding General Franco in the Spanish Civil War and rebuilt 1946. The bombing inspired a painting by Pablo Picasso and a play by dramatist Fernando Arrabal (1932–   ).

Guevara 'Che' Ernesto 1928–1967. Latin American revolutionary. He was born in Argentina and trained there as a doctor, but left his homeland 1953 because of his opposition to the right-wing president Perón. In effecting the Cuban revolution of 1959, he was second only to Castro and Castro's brother Raúl. In 1965 he went to the Congo to fight against white mercenaries, and then to Bolivia, where he was killed in an unsuccessful attempt to lead a peasant rising. He was an orthodox Marxist and renowned for his guerrilla techniques.

Guinea country in W Africa, bounded N by Senegal, NE by Mali, SE by the Ivory Coast, S by Liberia and Sierra Leone, W by the Atlantic Ocean, and NW by Guinea-Bissau.

chronology

1958 Full independence achieved from France; Sékou Touré elected president.

1977 Strong opposition to Touré's rigid Marxist policies forced him to accept return to mixed economy.

1980 Touré returned unopposed for fourth seven-year term.

1984 Touré died. Bloodless coup established a military committee for national recovery, led by Col Lansana Conté.

1985 Attempted coup against Conté while he was out of the country was foiled by loyal troops.
1990 Sent troops to join the multinational force that attempted to stabilize Liberia.
1991 Antigovernment general strike by National Confederation of Guinea Workers (CNTG).

Guinea-Bissau country in W Africa, bounded N by Senegal, E and SE by Guinea, and SW by the Atlantic Ocean.

chronology
1956 African Party for the Independence of Portuguese Guinea and Cape Verde (PAIGC) formed to secure independence from Portugal.
1973 Two-thirds of the country declared independent, with Luiz Cabral as president of a state council.
1974 Independence achieved from Portugal.
1980 Cape Verde decided not to join a unified state. Cabral deposed, and João Vieira became chair of a council of revolution.
1981 PAIGC confirmed as the only legal party, with Vieira as its secretary general.
1982 Normal relations with Cape Verde restored.
1984 New constitution adopted, making Vieira head of government as well as head of state.
1989 Vieira re-elected.
1991 Other parties legalized.
1992 Multiparty electoral commission established.

gulag Russian term for the system of prisons and labour camps used to silence dissidents and opponents of the Soviet regime. In the Stalin era (1920s–1930s), thousands of prisoners died from the harsh conditions of these remote camps.

Gulf War war 16 Jan–28 Feb 1991 between Iraq and a coalition of 28 nations led by the USA. (It is also another name for the ◊Iran–Iraq War). The invasion and annexation of Kuwait by Iraq on 2 Aug 1990 provoked a build-up of US troops in Saudi Arabia, eventually totalling over 500,000. The UK subsequently deployed 42,000 troops, France 15,000, Egypt 20,000, and other nations smaller contingents. An air offensive lasting six weeks, in which 'smart' weapons came of age, destroyed about one-third of Iraqi equipment and inflicted massive casualties. A 100-hour ground war followed, which effectively destroyed the remnants of the 500,000-strong Iraqi army in or near Kuwait.

Gummer John Selwyn 1939– . British Conservative politician, secretary of state for agriculture from 1989. He was minister of state for employment 1983–84, paymaster general 1984–85, minister for agriculture 1985–89, and chair of the party 1983–85.

Guomindang Chinese National People's Party, founded 1894 by ◊Sun Yat-sen, which overthrew the Manchu Empire 1912. From 1927 the right wing, led by ◊Chiang Kai-shek, was in conflict with the left, led by Mao Zedong until the Communist victory 1949 (except for the period of the Japanese invasion 1937-45). It survives as the dominant political party of Taiwan, where it is still spelled *Kuomintang*.

Gustaf V 1858–1950. King of Sweden from 1907, when he succeeded his father Oscar II. He married Princess Victoria, daughter of the Grand Duke of Baden 1881, thus uniting the reigning Bernadotte dynasty with the former royal house of Vasa.

Gustaf VI 1882–1973. King of Sweden from 1950, when he succeeded his father Gustaf V. He was an archaeologist and expert on Chinese art. He was succeeded by his grandson Carl XVI Gustaf.

Guyana country in South America, bounded N by the Atlantic Ocean, E by Surinam, S and SW by Brazil, and NW by Venezuela.

chronology
1831 Became British colony under name of British Guiana.
1953 Assembly elections won by left-wing People's Progressive Party (PPP); Britain suspended constitution and installed interim administration, fearing communist takeover.
1961 Internal self-government granted; Cheddi ◊Jagan became prime minister.
1964 People's National Congress (PNC) leader Forbes ◊Burnham led PPP–PNC coalition.
1966 Independence achieved from Britain.
1970 Guyana became a republic within the Commonwealth.
1981 Forbes Burnham became first executive president under new constitution.
1985 Burnham died; succeeded by Desmond Hoyte.

1992 PPP had decisive victory in assembly elections; Jagan returned as prime minister.

Gysi Gregor 1948–   . German politician, elected leader of the Communist Party Dec 1989 following the resignation of Egon ◊Krenz. A lawyer, Gysi had acted as defence counsel for dissidents during the 1960s.

H

Haakon VII 1872–1957. King of Norway from 1905. Born Prince Charles, the second son of Frederick VIII of Denmark, he was elected king of Norway on separation from Sweden, and in 1906 he took the name Haakon. In World War II he carried on the resistance from Britain during the Nazi occupation of his country. He returned 1945.

Haganah Zionist military organization in Palestine. It originated under the Turkish rule of the Ottoman Empire before World War I to protect Jewish settlements, and many of its members served in the British forces in both world wars. After World War II it condemned guerrilla activity, opposing the British authorities only passively. It formed the basis of the Israeli army after Israel was established 1948.

Haig Alexander (Meigs) 1924–   . US general and Republican politician. He became President Nixon's White House Chief of Staff at the height of the ♢Watergate scandal, was NATO commander 1974–79, and secretary of state to President Reagan 1981–82.

Haig Douglas, 1st Earl Haig 1861–1928. British army officer, commander in chief in World War I. His Somme offensive in France in the summer of 1916 made considerable advances only at enormous cost to human life, and his Passchendaele offensive in Belgium from July to Nov 1917 achieved little at a similar loss. He was created field marshal 1917 and, after retiring, became first president of the British Legion 1921.

Haile Selassie Ras (Prince) Tafari ('the Lion of Judah') 1892–1975. Emperor of Ethiopia 1930–74. He pleaded unsuccessfully to the League of Nations against Italian conquest of his country 1935–36, and lived in the UK until his restoration 1941. He was deposed by a military coup 1974 and died in captivity the following year.

Followers of the Rastafarian religion believe that Haile Selassie was the Messiah, the incarnation of God (Jah).

Hailsham Quintin Hogg, Baron Hailsham of St Marylebone 1907–   . British lawyer and Conservative politician. The 2nd Viscount Hailsham, he renounced the title in 1963 to re-enter the House of Commons, and was then able to contest the Conservative Party leadership elections, but took a life peerage 1970 on his appointment as Lord Chancellor 1970–74. He was Lord Chancellor again 1979–87.

Haiti country in the Caribbean, occupying the W part of the island of Hispaniola; to the E is the Dominican Republic.

chronology
1804 Independence achieved from France.
1915 Haiti invaded by USA; remained under US control until 1934.
1957 Dr François Duvalier (Papa Doc) elected president.
1964 Duvalier pronounced himself president for life.
1971 Duvalier died, succeeded by his son, Jean-Claude (Baby Doc); thousands murdered during ◊Duvalier era.
1986 Duvalier deposed; replaced by Lt-Gen Henri Namphy as head of a governing council.
1988 Feb: Leslie Manigat became president. Namphy staged a military coup in June, but another coup in Sept led by Brig-Gen Prosper Avril replaced him with a civilian government under military control.
1989 Coup attempt against Avril foiled; US aid resumed.
1990 Opposition elements expelled; Ertha Pascal-Trouillot acting president.
1991 Jean-Bertrand ◊Aristide elected president but later overthrown in military coup led by Brig-Gen Raoul Cedras. Efforts to reinstate Aristide failed. Joseph Nerette became interim head of state.
1992 Economic sanctions imposed since 1991 were eased by the USA but increased by the Organization of American States (OAS). Marc Bazin appointed premier.

Haldane Richard Burdon, Viscount Haldane 1856–1928. British Liberal politician. As secretary for war 1905–12, he sponsored the army reforms that established an expeditionary force, backed by a territorial army and under the unified control of an imperial general staff. He was Lord Chancellor 1912–15 and in the Labour government of 1924. His writings on German philosophy led to accusations of his having pro-German sympathies.

Halifax Edward Frederick Lindley Wood, Earl of Halifax 1881–1959. British Conservative politician, viceroy of India 1926–31. As foreign secretary 1938–40 he was associated with Chamberlain's ◊'appeasement' policy. He received an earldom 1944 for services to the Allied cause while ambassador to the USA 1941–46.

Halsey William Frederick 1882–1959. US admiral, known as 'Bull'. He was the commander of the Third Fleet in the S Pacific from 1942 during World War II. The Japanese signed the surrender document ending World War II on his flagship, the battleship *Missouri*.

Hamaguchi Osachi, also known as *Hamaguchi Yūkō* 1870–1931. Japanese politician, prime minister 1929–30. His policies created social unrest and alienated military interests. His acceptance of the terms of the London Naval Agreement 1930 was also unpopular. Shot by an assassin Nov 1930, he died of his wounds nine months later.

Hammarskjöld Dag 1905–1961. Swedish secretary general of the United Nations 1953–61. He opposed Britain over the ◊Suez Crisis 1956. His attempts to solve the problem of the Congo (now Zaire), where he was killed in a plane crash, were criticized by the USSR. He was awarded the Nobel Peace Prize 1961.

Haq Fazlul 1873–1962. Leader of the Bengali Muslim peasantry. He was a member of the Viceroy's Defence Council, established 1941, and was Bengal's first Indian prime minister 1937–43.

Hardie (James) Keir 1856–1915. Scottish socialist, member of Parliament 1892–95 and 1900–15. He worked in the mines as a boy and in 1886 became secretary of the Scottish Miners' Federation. In 1888 he was the first Labour candidate to stand for Parliament; he entered Parliament independently as a Labour member 1892 and was a chief founder of the ◊Independent Labour Party 1893.

Harding (Allan Francis) John, 1st Baron Harding of Petherton 1896–1989. British field marshal. He was Chief of Staff in Italy during World War II. As governor of Cyprus 1955–57, during the period of political agitation prior to independence 1960, he was responsible for the deportation of Makarios III from Cyprus 1955.

Harding Warren G(amaliel) 1865–1923. 29th president of the USA 1921–23, a Republican. He opposed US membership of the League of Nations. There was corruption among members of his cabinet (the ◊Teapot Dome Scandal), with the secretary of the interior later convicted for taking bribes.

Harriman (William) Averell 1891–1986. US diplomat, administrator of ◊lend-lease in World War II, Democratic secretary of commerce in Truman's administration 1946–48, negotiator of the Nuclear Test Ban Treaty with the USSR 1963, and governor of New York 1955–58.

Harris Arthur Travers 1892–1984. British marshal of the Royal Air Force in World War II. Known as 'Bomber Harris', he was commander in chief of Bomber Command 1942–45. He was an autocratic and single-minded leader, and was criticized for his policy of civilian-bombing of selected cities in Germany; he authorized the fire-bombing raids on Dresden, in which more than 100,000 died.

Hart Gary 1936– . US Democrat politician, senator for Colorado from 1974. In 1980 he contested the Democratic nomination for the presidency, and stepped down from his Senate seat 1986 to run, again unsuccessfully, in the 1988 presidential campaign.

Hassan II 1929– . King of Morocco from 1961. From 1976 he undertook the occupation of Western Sahara when it was ceded by Spain.

Hattersley Roy 1932– . British Labour politician. On the right wing of the Labour Party, he was prices secretary 1976–79, and deputy leader of the party 1983–1992.

Hatton Derek 1948– . British left-wing politician, former deputy leader of Liverpool Council. A leading member of the Militant Tendency, Hatton was removed from office and expelled from the Labour Party 1987.

Haughey Charles 1925– . Irish Fianna Fáil politician of Ulster descent. Dismissed 1970 from Jack Lynch's cabinet for alleged complicity in IRA gun-running, he was afterwards acquitted. He was prime minister 1979–81, March–Nov 1982, and 1986–92, when he was replaced by Albert Reynolds.

Havel Václav 1936– . Czech playwright and politician, president of Czechoslovakia 1989–92 and president of the Czech Republic from 1993. His plays include *The Garden Party* 1963 and *Largo Desolato* 1985, about a dissident intellectual. Havel became widely known as a human-rights activist. He was imprisoned 1979–83 and again 1989 for support of Charter 77, a human-rights manifesto. As president of Czechoslovakia he sought to preserve a united republic, but resigned in recognition of the breakup of the federation 1992. In 1993 he became president of the newly independent Czech Republic.

Havers Robert Michael Oldfield, Baron Havers 1923–1992. British lawyer, Lord Chancellor 1987–88. After a successful legal career he became Conservative member of Parliament for Wimbledon 1970 and was solicitor general under Edward Heath and attorney general under Margaret Thatcher. He was made a life peer 1987 and served briefly, and unhappily, as Lord Chancellor before retiring 1988.

Hawke Bob (Robert) 1929– . Australian Labor politician, prime minister 1983–91, on the right wing of the party. He was president of the Australian Council of Trade Unions 1970–80. He announced his retirement from politics 1992.

Hayden William (Bill) 1933– . Australian Labor politician. He was leader of the Australian Labor Party and of the opposition 1977–83, and minister of foreign affairs 1983. He became governor general 1989.

Hayek Friedrich August von 1899–1992. Austrian economist. Born in Vienna, he taught at the London School of Economics 1931–50. His *The Road to Serfdom* 1944 was a critical study of socialist trends in Britain. He won the 1974 Nobel Prize for Economics with Gunnar Myrdal.

Haywood William Dudley 1869–1928. US labour leader. One of the founders of the Industrial Workers of the World (IWW, 'Wobblies') 1905, Haywood was arrested for conspiracy to murder an antiunion politician. His acquittal in 1907 made him a labour hero. Arrested again for sedition during World War I, he spent his later years in exile in the Soviet Union.

H-bomb abbreviation for *hydrogen bomb*. See ◊nuclear warfare

Healey Denis (Winston) 1917– . British Labour politician. While minister of defence 1964–70 he was in charge of the reduction of British forces east of Suez. He was chancellor of the Exchequer 1974–79. In 1976 he contested the party leadership, losing to James Callaghan, and again in 1980, losing to Michael Foot, to whom he was deputy leader 1980–83. In 1987 he resigned from the shadow cabinet.

Heath Edward (Richard George) 1916– . British Conservative politician, party leader 1965–75. As prime minister 1970–74 he took the UK into the European Community but was brought down by economic and industrial relations crises at home. He was replaced as party leader by Margaret Thatcher 1975, and became increasingly critical of her policies and her opposition to the UK's full participation in the EC. In 1990 he undertook a mission to Iraq in an attempt to secure the release of British hostages.

Hearst Patty (Patricia) 1955–   . US socialite. A granddaughter of the newspaper tycoon William Randolph Hearst, she was kidnapped 1974 by an urban guerrilla group, the Symbionese Liberation Army. She joined her captors in a bank robbery, was sought, tried, convicted, and imprisoned 1976–79.

Hearst William Randolph 1863–1951. US newspaper publisher, celebrated for his introduction of banner headlines, lavish illustration, and the sensationalist approach known as 'yellow journalism'. A campaigner in numerous controversies, and a strong isolationist, he was said to be the model for Citizen Kane in the 1941 film of that name by Orson Welles.

Heffer Eric 1922–1991. English Labour politician, member of Parliament for Walton, Liverpool 1964–91. He held a ◊ministerial post 1974–75, joined Michael Foot's shadow cabinet 1981, and was regularly elected to Labour's National Executive Committee, but found it difficult to follow the majority view.

Hekmatyar Gulbuddin 1949–   . Afghani Islamic fundamentalist guerrilla leader. He became a ◊mujaheddin guerrilla in the 1980s, leading the fundamentalist faction of the Hizb-i Islami (Islamic Party), dedicated to the overthrow of the Soviet-backed communist regime in Kabul. He refused to countenance participation in any interim 'national unity' government that was to include Afghan communists. Hekmatyar resisted the takeover of Kabul by moderate mujaheddin forces April 1992 and refused to join the interim administration, continuing to bombard the city until being driven out. A renewed bombardment in Aug lead to his faction being barred from government posts.

Helms Richard 1913–   . US director of the Central Intelligence Agency 1966–73, when he was dismissed by President Nixon. In 1977 he was convicted of lying before a congressional committee because his oath as chief of intelligence compelled him to keep secrets from the public. He was originally with the Office of Strategic Services, before it developed into the CIA 1947.

Helsinki Conference international meeting 1975 at which 35 countries, including the USSR and the USA, attempted to reach agreement on cooperation in security, economics, science, technology, and human rights. This established the ◊Conference on Security and Cooperation in Europe (CSCE).

Heng Samrin 1934– . Cambodian politician. A former Khmer Rouge commander 1976-78, who had become disillusioned with its brutal tactics, he led an unsuccessful coup against ◊Pol Pot 1978 and established the Kampuchean People's Revolutionary Party (KPRP) in Vietnam, before returning 1979 to head the new Vietnamese-backed government. He was replaced as prime minister by the reformist Hun Sen 1985.

Henlein Konrad 1898–1945. Sudeten-German leader of the Sudeten Nazi Party in Czechoslovakia, and closely allied with Hitler's Nazis. He was partly responsible for the destabilization of the Czechoslovak state 1938, which led to the ◊Munich Agreement and secession of the Sudetenland to Germany.

Herriot Edouard 1872–1957. French Radical socialist politician. An opponent of Poincaré, who as prime minister carried out the French occupation of the Ruhr, Germany, he was briefly prime minister 1924–25, 1926, and 1932. As president of the chamber of deputies 1940, he opposed the policies of the right-wing Vichy government and was arrested and later taken to Germany; he was released 1945 by the Soviets.

Hertling Count Georg von 1843–1919. German politician who was appointed imperial chancellor Nov 1917. He maintained a degree of support in the Reichstag (parliament) but was powerless to control the military leadership under ◊Ludendorff.

Hertzog James Barry Munnik 1866–1942. South African politician, prime minister 1924–39, founder of the Nationalist Party 1913 (the United South African National Party from 1933). He opposed South Africa's entry into both world wars.

His motion against South Africa's participation in World War II was rejected 1939, bringing about his resignation.

Heseltine Michael (Ray Dibdin) 1933– . English Conservative politician, member of Parliament from 1966 (for Henley from 1974), secretary of state for the environment 1990-92, and for trade and industry from 1992. Heseltine was minister of the environment 1979-83, when he succeeded John Nott as minister of defence Jan 1983 but resigned Jan 1986 over the Westland affair and was then seen as a major rival to Margaret Thatcher. In Nov 1990, Heseltine's challenge to Thatcher's leadership of the

Conservative Party brought about her resignation, though he lost the leadership election to John Major. In Oct 1992, adverse public reaction to his pit-closure programme forced the government to backtrack and review their policy.

Hess (Walter Richard) Rudolf 1894–1987. German Nazi leader. Imprisoned with Hitler 1924–25, he became his private secretary, taking down ◊*Mein Kampf* from his dictation. In 1932 he was appointed deputy *Führer* to Hitler. On 10 May 1941 he landed by air in the UK with his own compromise peace proposals and was held a prisoner of war until 1945, when he was tried at Nuremberg as a war criminal and sentenced to life imprisonment. He died in Spandau prison, Berlin.

Heydrich Reinhard 1904–1942. German Nazi, head of the party's security service and Heinrich ◊Himmler's deputy. He was instrumental in organizing the ◊final solution, the policy of genocide used against Jews and others. 'Protector' of Bohemia and Moravia from 1941, he was ambushed and killed the following year by three members of the Czechoslovak forces in Britain, who had landed by parachute. Reprisals followed, including several hundred executions and the massacre in ◊Lidice.

hijacking illegal seizure or taking control of a vehicle and/or its passengers or goods. The term dates from 1923 and originally referred to the robbing of freight lorries. In recent times it (and its derivative, 'skyjacking') has been applied to the seizure of aircraft, usually in flight, by an individual or group, often with some political aim. International treaties (Tokyo 1963, The Hague 1970, and Montreal 1971) encourage cooperation against hijackers and make severe penalties compulsory.

Hill Joe *c*. 1872–1915. Swedish-born US labour organizer. A member of the Industrial Workers of the World (IWW, 'Wobblies'), he was convicted of murder on circumstantial evidence in Salt Lake City, Utah, 1914. Despite calls by President Wilson and the Swedish government for a re-trial, Hill was executed 1915, becoming a martyr for the labour movement.

Hill Octavia 1838–1912. English campaigner for housing reform and public open spaces. She cofounded the National Trust 1894.

Hillsborough Agreement another name for the ◊Anglo- Irish Agreement 1985.

Himmler Heinrich 1900–1945. German Nazi leader, head of the ◊SS elite corps from 1929, the police and the ◊Gestapo secret police from 1936, and supervisor of the extermination of the Jews in E Europe. During World War II he replaced Goering as Hitler's second-in-command. He was captured May 1945 and committed suicide.

Hindenburg Paul Ludwig Hans von Beneckendorf und Hindenburg 1847–1934. German field marshal and right-wing politician. During World War I he was supreme commander and, with Ludendorff, practically directed Germany's policy until the end of the war. He was president of Germany 1925–33.

Hindenburg Line German western line of World War I fortifications built 1916–17.

Hirohito (regnal era name *Shōwa*) 1901–1989. Emperor of Japan from 1926, when he succeeded his father Taishō (Yoshihito). After the defeat of Japan in World War II 1945, he was made a figurehead monarch by the US-backed 1946 constitution. He is believed to have played a reluctant role in General ◊Tōjō's prewar expansion plans. He was succeeded by his son Akihito.

Hiroshima industrial city and port on the south coast of Honshu Island, Japan, destroyed by the first wartime use of an atomic bomb 6 Aug 1945. More than 10 sq km/4 sq mi were obliterated, with very heavy damage outside that area. Casualties totalled at least 137,000 out of a population of 343,000; 78,150 were found dead, others died later. The city has largely been rebuilt since the war.

Hiss Alger 1904–   . US diplomat and liberal Democrat, a former State Department official, imprisoned 1950 for perjury when he denied having been a Soviet spy. There are doubts about the justice of Hiss's conviction.

Hitler Adolf 1889–1945. German Nazi dictator, born in Austria. He was *Führer* (leader) of the Nazi Party from 1921 and author of *Mein Kampf/My Struggle* 1925–27. As chancellor of Germany from 1933 and head of state from 1934, he created a dictatorship by playing party and state institutions against each other and continually creating new offices and appointments. His position was not seriously challenged until the 'Bomb Plot' 20 July 1944 (see ◊July plot) to assassinate him. In foreign affairs, he reoccupied the Rhineland and formed an alliance with the Italian Fascist Mussolini

1936, annexed Austria 1938, and occupied the Sudetenland under the ◊Munich Agreement. The rest of Czechoslovakia was annexed March 1939. The Hitler–Stalin pact was followed in Sept by the invasion of Poland and the declaration of war by Britain and France (see ◊World War II). He committed suicide as Berlin fell.

Hitler–Stalin pact nonaggression treaty signed by Germany and the USSR 23 Aug 1939. Under the terms of the treaty both countries agreed to remain neutral and to refrain from acts of aggression against each other if either went to war. Secret clauses allowed for the partition of Poland— Hitler was to acquire western Poland, Stalin the eastern part. On 1 Sept 1939 Hitler invaded Poland. The pact ended when Hitler invaded Russia on 22 June 1941. See also ◊World War II.

Hoare–Laval Pact plan for a peaceful settlement to the Italian invasion of Ethiopia in Oct 1935. It was devised by Samuel Hoare (1880–1959), British foreign secretary, and Pierre ◊Laval, French premier, at the request of the ◊League of Nations. Realizing no European country was willing to go to war over Ethiopia, Hoare and Laval proposed official recognition of Italian claims. Public outcry in Britain against the pact's seeming approval of Italian aggression was so great that the pact had to be disowned and Hoare was forced to resign.

Hobson John Atkinson 1858–1940. British economist and publicist who was a staunch opponent of the Boer War 1899-1902. He condemned it as a conflict orchestrated by and fought for the preservation of finance capitalism at the expense of the British working class.

Ho Chi Minh adopted name of Nguyen Tat Thanh 1890–1969. North Vietnamese communist politician, premier and president 1954–69. Having trained in Moscow shortly after the Russian Revolution, he headed the communist ◊Vietminh from 1941 and fought against the French during the ◊Indochina War 1946–54, becoming president and prime minister of the republic at the armistice. Aided by the communist bloc, he did much to develop industrial potential. He relinquished the premiership 1955, but continued as president. In the years before his death, Ho successfully led his country's fight against US-aided South Vietnam in the ◊Vietnam War 1954–75.

Ho Chi Minh Trails North Vietnamese troop and supply routes to South Vietnam via Laos during the ◊Vietnam War 1954-75. In an unsuccessful attempt to disrupt the Trail between 1964 and 1973, the USA dropped 2 million tonnes of bombs in Laos, a country with which it was not at war.

Hodza Milan 1878–1944. Czechoslovak politician, prime minister 1936–38. He and President Beneš were forced to agree to the secession of the Sudeten areas of Czechoslovakia to Germany before resigning 22 Sept 1938 (see ◊Munich Agreement).

Hoess Rudolf 1900–1947. German commandant of Auschwitz concentration camp 1940–43. Under his control, more than 2.5 million people were exterminated. Arrested by Allied military police in 1946, he was handed over to the Polish authorities, who tried and executed him in 1947.

Hoffa Jimmy (James Riddle) 1913–*c*. 1975. US labour leader, president of the International Brotherhood of Teamsters (transport workers) from 1957. He was jailed 1967–71 for attempted bribery of a federal court jury after he was charged with corruption. He was released by President Nixon with the stipulation that he did not engage in union activities, but was evidently attempting to reassert influence when he disappeared. He is generally believed to have been murdered.

Hoffman Abbie (Abbot) 1936–1989. US left-wing political activist, founder of the Yippies (Youth International Party), a political offshoot of the hippies. He was a member of the Chicago Seven, a radical group tried for attempting to disrupt the 1968 Democratic Convention.

Holkeri Harri 1937–   . Finnish politician, prime minister 1987–91. Joining the centrist National Coalition Party (KOK) at an early age, he eventually became its national secretary.

Holland John Philip 1840–1914. Irish engineer who developed some of the first submarines. He began work in Ireland in the late 1860s and emigrated to the USA 1873. His first successful boat was launched 1881 and, after several failures, he built the *Holland* 1893, which was bought by the US Navy two years later.

Holland Sidney George 1893–1961. New Zealand politician, leader of the National Party 1940-57 and prime minister 1949-57.

Hollis Roger 1905–1973. British civil servant, head of the secret intelligence service MI5 1956–65. He was alleged to have been a double agent together with Kim Philby, but this was denied by the KGB 1991.

Holocaust, the the annihilation of more than 16 million people by the Hitler regime 1933–45 in the numerous extermination and ◊concentration camps, most notably Auschwitz, Sobibor, Treblinka, and Maidanek in Poland, and Belsen, Buchenwald, and Dachau in Germany. Of the victims who died during imprisonment or were exterminated, more than 6 million were Jews (over 67% of European Jewry); 10 million were Ukrainian, Polish, and Russian civilians and prisoners of war, Romanies, socialists, homosexuals, and others (labelled 'defectives'). Victims were variously starved, tortured, experimented on, and worked to death. Many thousands were executed in gas chambers, shot, or hanged. It was euphemistically termed the ◊final solution.

Holt Harold Edward 1908–1967. Australian Liberal politician, prime minister 1966–67. His brief prime ministership was dominated by the Vietnam War, to which he committed increased Australian troops.

Holyoake Keith Jacka 1904–1983. New Zealand National Party politician, prime minister 1957 (for two months) and 1960–72 during which time he was also foreign minister.

home front the organized sectors of domestic activity in wartime, mainly associated with World Wars I and II. Features of the UK home front in World War II included the organization of the black-out, evacuation, air-raid shelters, the Home Guard, rationing, and distribution of gas masks. With many men on active military service, women were called upon to carry out jobs previously undertaken only by men.

Home Guard unpaid force formed in Britain May 1940 to repel the expected German invasion, and known until July 1940 as the Local Defence Volunteers.

It consisted of men aged 17–65 who had not been called up, formed part of the armed forces of the crown, and was subject to military law. Over 2 million strong in 1944, it was disbanded 31 Dec 1945, but revived 1951, then placed on a reserve basis 1955, and ceased activities 1957.

homeland or *Bantustan* before 1980, name for the ◊Black National States in the Republic of South Africa.

Homelands Policy South Africa's apartheid policy which set aside ◊Black National States for black Africans.

Home Rule, Irish movement to repeal the Act of Union 1801 that joined Ireland to Britain and to establish an Irish parliament responsible for internal affairs. In 1870 Isaac Butt (1813–1879) formed the Home Rule Association and the movement was led in Parliament from 1880 by Charles Parnell. After 1918 the demand for an independent Irish republic replaced that for home rule.

Home Rule League demand for Indian home rule, established Sept 1916. The Indian demand for home rule was inspired by the unsuccessful ◊Easter rising in Ireland the previous April. It was launched by theosophist and educationalist Annie ◊Besant, who received support from the leading Indian nationalist Bal Gangadhar Tilak (1856-1920), and was briefly interned in Madras 1917. The organization faded after the introduction of the India Act 1919 and the initiation of Mahatma ◊Gandhi's non-cooperation campaign.

Honduras country in Central America, bounded N by the Caribbean Sea, SE by Nicaragua, S by the Pacific Ocean, SW by El Salvador, and W and NW by Guatemala.

chronology
1838 Independence achieved from Spain.
1980 After more than a century of mostly military rule, a civilian government was elected, with Dr Roberto Suazo as president; the commander in chief of the army, General Gustavo Alvarez, retained considerable power.
1983 Close involvement with the USA in providing naval and air bases and allowing Nicaraguan counter-revolutionaries (◊'Contras') to operate from Honduras.
1984 Alvarez ousted in coup led by junior officers, resulting in policy review towards USA and Nicaragua.
1985 José Azcona elected president after electoral law changed, making Suazo ineligible for presidency.
1989 Government and opposition declared support for Central American peace plan to demobilize Nicaraguan Contras based in Honduras; Contras and their dependents in Honduras in 1989 thought to number about 55,000.
1990 Rafael Callejas, National Party (PN), inaugurated as president.
1992 Border dispute with El Salvador dating from 1861 finally resolved.

Honecker Erich 1912– . German communist politician, in power 1973–89, elected chair of the council of state (head of state) 1976. He governed in an outwardly austere and efficient manner and, while favouring East–West détente, was a loyal ally of the USSR. In Oct 1989, following a wave of prodemocracy demonstrations, he was replaced as leader of the

Socialist Unity Party (SED) and head of state by Egon ◊Krenz, and in Dec expelled from the Communist Party.

Hoover Herbert Clark 1874–1964. 31st president of the USA 1929–33, a Republican. He was secretary of commerce 1921–28. Hoover lost public confidence after the stock-market crash of 1929, when he opposed direct government aid for the unemployed in the Depression that followed.

Hoover J(ohn) Edgar 1895–1972. US director of the Federal Bureau of Investigation (FBI) from 1924. He built up a powerful network for the detection of organized crime. His drive against alleged communist activities after World War II, and his opposition to the Kennedy administration and others brought much criticism over abuse of power.

Hooverville colloquial term for any shantytown built by the unemployed and destitute in the USA during the Depression 1929–40, named after US president Herbert ◊Hoover whose policies were blamed for the plight of millions. He also lent his name to 'Hoover blankets' (newspapers) and 'Hoover flags' (turned-out, empty pockets).

Hopkins Harry Lloyd 1890–1946. US government official. Originally a social worker, in 1935 he became head of the WPA (Works Progress Administration), which was concerned with Depression relief work. After a period as secretary of commerce 1938–40, he was appointed supervisor of the ◊lend-lease programme 1941, and undertook missions to Britain and the USSR during World War II.

Hore-Belisha Leslie, Baron Hore-Belisha 1895–1957. British politician. A National Liberal, he was minister of transport 1934–37, introducing *Belisha beacons* to mark pedestrian crossings. As war minister from 1937, until removed by Chamberlain 1940 on grounds of temperament, he introduced peacetime conscription 1939.

Horthy Nicholas Horthy de Nagybánya 1868–1957. Hungarian politician and admiral. Leader of the counterrevolutionary White government, he became regent 1920 on the overthrow of the communist Bela Kun regime by Romanian and Czechoslovak intervention. He represented the conservative and military class, and retained power until World War II, trying (although allied to Hitler) to retain independence of action. In 1944 he tried to negotiate a surrender to the USSR but Hungary was taken over by the Nazis and he was deported to Germany. He was released from German captivity the same year by the Western Allies and allowed to go to Portugal, where he died.

Houphouët-Boigny Félix 1905– . Ivory Coast right-wing politician. He held posts in French ministries, and became president of the Republic of the Ivory Coast on independence 1960, maintaining close links with France, which helped to boost an already thriving economy and encourage political stability. Pro-Western and opposed to communist intervention in Africa, Houphouët-Boigny has been strongly criticized for maintaining diplomatic relations with South Africa. He was re-elected for a seventh term 1990 in multiparty elections, amid allegations of ballot rigging and political pressure.

House Edward Mandell 1858–1938. US politician and diplomat. He was instrumental in obtaining the presidential nomination for Woodrow Wilson 1912 and later served as Wilson's closest adviser. During World War I 1914-1918, House served as US liaison with Great Britain and was an important behind-the-scenes participant in the 1919 Versailles Peace Conference.

House Un-American Activities Committee (HUAC) Congressional committee, established 1938, noted for its public investigating into alleged subversion, particularly of communists. First headed by Martin Dies, it achieved its greatest notoriety during the 1950s through its hearings on communism in the movie industry. It was later renamed the House Internal Security Committee.

Howe Geoffrey 1926– . British Conservative politician, member of Parliament for Surrey East. Under Edward Heath he was solicitor general 1970–72 and minister for trade 1972–74; as chancellor of the Exchequer 1979–83 under Margaret Thatcher, he put into practice the monetarist policy which reduced inflation at the cost of a rise in unemployment. In 1983 he became foreign secretary, and in 1989 deputy prime minister and leader of the House of Commons. On 1 Nov 1990 he resigned in protest at Thatcher's continued opposition to Britain's greater integration in Europe

Hoxha Enver 1908–1985. Albanian Communist politician, the country's leader from 1954. He founded the Albanian Communist Party 1941, and headed the liberation movement 1939–44. He was prime minister 1944–54, combining with foreign affairs 1946–53, and from 1954 was first secretary of the Albanian Party of Labour. In policy he was a Stalinist and independent of both Chinese and Soviet communism.

Hsuan Tung name adopted by Henry ◊P'u-i on becoming emperor of China 1908

Hua Guofeng or *Hua Kuofeng* 1920– . Chinese politician, leader of the Chinese Communist Party (CCP) 1976–81, premier 1976–80. He dominated Chinese politics 1976–77, seeking economic modernization without major structural reform. From 1978 he was gradually eclipsed by Deng Xiaoping. Hua was ousted from the Politburo Sept 1982 but remained a member of the CCP Central Committee.

Huai-Hai, Battle of decisive campaign 1948–49 in the Chinese Civil War (1946–49). The name is derived from the two main defensive positions held by the nationalist ◊Guomindang force: the Huang (Huai) River in Shandong and Jiangsu provinces, and the Lung Hai railway. Communist forces from the E and W captured Xuzchou (Soochow), a key railway junction, on 1 Dec 1948. On 6 Jan 1949 they secured a crushing victory at Yungchung to the SW, facilitating an advance on Shanghai, which fell in the spring of 1949.

Hughes William Morris 1864–1952. Australian politician, prime minister 1915–23; originally Labor, he headed a national cabinet. After resigning as prime minister 1923, he held many other cabinet posts 1934–41.

Hukbalahap movement left-wing Filipino peasant resistance campaign 1942–54. Formed to challenge the Japanese wartime occupation of the Philippines 1942–45, it carried out guerrilla attacks against the Japanese from its base in central Luzon. After World War II, it opposed the Filipino landed elite and its American allies and established an alternative government in Luzon. During the Korean War, a government military campaign 1950–54 defeated the 'Huks'.

Hull Cordell 1871–1955. US Democratic politician. As F D Roosevelt's secretary of state 1933–44, he opposed German and Japanese aggression. He was identified with the Good Neighbour Policy of nonintervention in Latin America. In his last months of office he paved the way for a system of collective security, for which he was called 'father' of the United Nations. He was awarded the Nobel Peace Prize 1945.

Hume John 1937– . Northern Ireland Catholic politician, leader of the Social Democrat Party (SDLP) from 1979. Hume was a founder member of the Credit Union Party, which later became the SDLP.

Humphrey Hubert Horatio 1911–1978. US political leader, vice presi-dent 1965-69. He was elected to the US Senate 1948, serving for three terms, dis-tinguishing himself an eloquent and effective promoter of key legislation. He was an unsuccessful presidential candidate 1960. Serving as vice pres-ident under L B Johnson, he made another unsuccessful run for the presi-dency 1968. He was re-elected to the Senate in 1970 and 1976.

Hundred Flowers campaign in Chinese history, a movement 1956–57 of open political and intellectual debate, encouraged by ◊Mao Zedong. The campaign was intended to rouse the bureaucracy and to weaken the posi-tion of the Chinese Communist Party's then dominant pro-Soviet 'right wing'. It rapidly got out of hand, resulting in excessive censure of party personnel.

Hungarian uprising national uprising against Soviet dominance of ◊Hungary in 1956.

Hungary country in central Europe, bounded N by the Slovak Republic, NE by Ukraine, E by Romania, S by Yugoslavia and Croatia, and W by Austria and Slovenia.

chronology
1918 Independence achieved from Austro-Hungarian empire.
1919 A communist state formed for 133 days.
1920–44 Regency formed under Admiral ◊Horthy, who joined Hitler's attack on the USSR.
1945 Liberated by USSR.
1946 Republic proclaimed; Stalinist regime imposed.
1949 Soviet-style constitution adopted.
1956 Hungarian national uprising; workers' demonstrations in Budapest; democratization reforms by Imre ◊Nagy overturned by Soviet tanks, János ◊Kádár installed as party leader.
1968 Economic decentralization reforms.
1983 Competition introduced into elections.
1987 VAT and income tax introduced.
1988 Kádár replaced by Károly ◊Grosz. First free trade union recognized; rival political parties legalized.
1989 May: border with Austria opened. July: new four-person collective leadership of the Hungarian Socialist Workers' Party (HSWP). Oct: new 'transitional constitution' adopted, founded on multiparty democracy and

new presidentialist executive. HSWP changed name to Hungarian Socialist Party (HSP), with ◊Nyers as new leader. Kádár 'retired'.

1990 HSP reputation damaged by 'Danubegate' bugging scandal. March–April: elections won by right-of-centre coalition, headed by Hungarian Democratic Forum (MDF). May: József Antall, leader of the MDF, appointed premier. Aug: Arpád Göncz elected president.

1991 Jan: devaluation of currency. June: legislation approved to compensate owners of land and property expropriated under communist government. Last Soviet troops departed. Dec: EC association pact signed.

1992 March: EC pact came into effect.

hunger march procession of the unemployed, a feature of social protest in interwar Britain.

The first took place from Glasgow to London in 1922 and another in 1929. In 1932 the National Unemployed Workers' Movement organized the largest demonstration, with groups converging on London from all parts of the country, but the most emotive was probably the ◊Jarrow Crusade of 1936, when 200 unemployed shipyard workers marched to the capital.

Hun Sen 1950– . Cambodian political leader, prime minister from 1985. Originally a member of the Khmer Rouge army, he defected in 1977 to join Vietnam-based anti-Khmer Cambodian forces. His leadership has been characterized by the promotion of economic liberalization and a thawing in relations with exiled non-Khmer opposition forces as a prelude to a compromise political settlement. In Oct 1991, following a peace accord ending 13 years of civil war in Cambodia, Hun Sen agreed to rule the country in conjunction with the United Nations Transitional Authority in Cambodia (UNTAC) and representatives of the warring factions until UN-administered elections 1993.

Hurd Douglas (Richard) 1930– . English Conservative politician, home secretary 1986–89, appointed foreign secretary 1989 in the reshuffle that followed Nigel Lawson's resignation as chancellor of the Exchequer. In Nov 1990 he was an unsuccessful candidate in the Tory leadership contest following Margaret Thatcher's unexpected resignation. He retained his post as foreign secretary in Prime Minister John Major's new cabinet formed after the 1992 general election.

Husák Gustáv 1913–1991. Leader of the Communist Party of Czechoslovakia (CCP) 1969–87 and president 1975–89. After the 1968 ◊Prague

Spring of liberalization, his task was to restore control, purge the CCP, and oversee the implementation of a new, federalist constitution. He was deposed in the popular uprising of Nov–Dec 1989 and expelled from the Communist Party Feb 1990.

Hussein ibn Ali *c.* 1854–1931. Leader of the Arab revolt 1916–18 against the Turks. He proclaimed himself king of the Hejaz 1916, accepted the caliphate 1924, but was unable to retain it due to internal fighting. He was deposed 1924 by Ibn Saud.

Hussein ibn Talal 1935– . King of Jordan from 1952. Great-grandson of Hussein ibn Ali, he became king following the mental incapacitation of his father, Talal. By 1967 he had lost all his kingdom west of the river Jordan in the ◊Arab-Israeli Wars, and in 1970 suppressed the ◊Palestine Liberation Organization acting as a guerrilla force against his rule on the remaining East Bank territories. In recent years, he has become a moderating force in Middle Eastern politics. After Iraq's annexation of Kuwait 1990 he attempted to mediate between the opposing sides, at the risk of damaging his relations with both sides.

Hussein Saddam 1937– . Iraqi politician, in power from 1968, president from 1979, progressively eliminating real or imagined opposition factions as he gained increasing dictatorial control. Ruthless in the pursuit of his objectives, he fought a bitter war against Iran 1980–88, with US economic aid, and dealt harshly with Kurdish rebels seeking independence, using chemical weapons against civilian populations. In 1990 he annexed Kuwait, to universal condemnation, before being driven out by a US-dominated coalition army Feb 1991. Iraq's defeat in the ◊Gulf War undermined Saddam's position as the country's leader; when the Kurds rebelled again after the end of the war, he sent the remainder of his army to crush them, bringing international charges of genocide against him and causing hundreds of thousands of Kurds to flee their homes in northern Iraq. His continued indiscriminate bombardment of Shi'ites in southern Iraq caused the UN to impose a 'no-fly zone' in the area Aug 1992. Alleging infringements of the zone, US-led warplanes bombed strategic targets in Iraq Jan 1993, forcing Hussein to back down and comply with repeated UN requests for access to inspect his arms facilities.

Hu Yaobang 1915–1989. Chinese politician, Communist Party (CCP) chair 1981–87. A protégé of the communist leader Deng Xiaoping, Hu presided over a radical overhaul of the party structure and personnel 1982–86. His death ignited the prodemocracy movement, which was eventually crushed in ◊Tiananmen Square in June 1989.

Hyde Douglas 1860–1949. Irish scholar and politician. Founder president of the Gaelic League 1893–1915, he was president of Eire 1938–45. He was the first person to write a book in modern Irish and to collect Irish folklore, as well as being the author of the first literary history of Ireland. His works include *Love Songs of Connacht* 1894.

Ibarruri Dolores, known as *La Pasionaria* (`the passion flower') 1895–1989. Spanish Basque politician, journalist, and orator; she was first elected to the Cortes in 1936. She helped to establish the Popular Front government and was a Loyalist leader in the Civil War. When Franco came to power in 1939 she left Spain for the USSR, where she was active in the Communist Party. She returned to Spain in 1977 after Franco's death and was re-elected to the Cortes (at the age of 81) in the first parliamentary elections for 40 years.

Ibn Saud 1880–1953. First king of Saudi Arabia from 1932. His father was the son of the sultan of Nejd, at whose capital, Riyadh, Ibn Saud was born. In 1891 a rival group seized Riyadh, and Ibn Saud went into exile with his father, who resigned his claim to the throne in his son's favour. In 1902 Ibn Saud recaptured Riyadh and recovered the kingdom, and by 1921 he had brought all central Arabia under his rule. In 1924 he invaded the Hejaz, of which he was proclaimed king in 1926.

Iceland island country in the N Atlantic Ocean, situated S of the Arctic Circle, between Greenland and Norway.

chronology
1944 Independence achieved from Denmark.
1949 Joined NATO and Council of Europe.
1953 Joined Nordic Council.
1976 'Cod War' with UK.
1979 Iceland announced 320-km/200-mi exclusive fishing zone.
1983 Steingrímur Hermannsson appointed to lead a coalition government.
1985 Iceland declared itself a nuclear-free zone.
1987 New coalition government formed by Thorsteinn Pálsson after general election.
1988 Vigdís Finnbogadóttir re-elected president for a third term; Hermannsson led new coalition.
1991 Davíd Oddsson led new IP–SDP (Independence Party and Social

Democratic Party) centre-right coalition, becoming prime minister in the general election.

1992 Iceland defied world ban to resume whaling industry.

Ickes Harold LeClair 1874–1952. US public official. A liberal Republican, he was appointed secretary of the interior by F D Roosevelt 1933. As director of the Public Works Administration (PWA, established 1935), he administered Roosevelt's New Deal development projects. He served briefly under President Truman, but resigned from the cabinet 1946.

Iglesias Pablo 1850–1925. Spanish politician, founder of the Spanish Socialist Party (Partido Socialista Obrero Español, PSOE) in 1879. In 1911 he became the first socialist deputy to be elected to the *Cortes* (Spanish parliament).

Iliescu Ion 1930– . Romanian president from 1990. A former member of the Romanian Communist Party (PCR) and of Nicolae Ceauşescu's government, Iliescu swept into power on Ceauşescu's fall as head of the National Salvation Front.

imperialism policy of extending the power and rule of a government beyond its own boundaries. A country may attempt to dominate others by direct rule or by less obvious means such as control of markets for goods or raw materials. The latter is often called neocolonialism.

Independent Labour Party (ILP) British socialist party, founded in Bradford 1893 by the Scottish member of Parliament Keir Hardie. In 1900 it joined with trades unions and Fabians in founding the Labour Representation Committee, the nucleus of the ◊Labour Party. Many members left the ILP to join the Communist Party 1921, and in 1932 all connections with the Labour Party were severed. After World War II the ILP dwindled, eventually becoming extinct. James Maxton (1885–1946) was its chair 1926–46.

India country in S Asia, bounded N by China, Nepal, and Bhutan; E by Myanmar; NW by Pakistan; and SE, S, and SW by the Indian Ocean. Situated in the NE of India, N of the Bay of Bengal, is Bangladesh.

chronology
1947 Independence achieved from Britain.
1950 Federal republic proclaimed.
1962 Border skirmishes with China.
1964 Death of Prime Minister Jawaharlal ◊Nehru. Border war with Pakistan over Kashmir.

1966 Indira ◊Gandhi became prime minister.

1971 War with Pakistan leading to creation of Bangladesh.

1975–77 State of emergency proclaimed.

1977–79 ◊Janata Party government in power.

1980 Indira Gandhi returned in landslide victory.

1984 Indira Gandhi assassinated; her son Rajiv Gandhi elected with record majority.

1987 Signing of 'Tamil' Colombo peace accord with Sri Lanka; Indian Peacekeeping Force (IPKF) sent there. Public revelation of Bofors corruption scandal.

1988 New opposition party, Janata Dal, established by former finance minister V P ◊Singh. Voting age lowered from 21 to 18.

1989 Congress (I) lost majority in general election, after Gandhi associates implicated in financial misconduct; Janata Dal minority government formed, with V P Singh prime minister.

1990 Central rule imposed in Jammu and Kashmir. V P Singh resigned; new minority Janata Dal government formed by Chandra Shekhar. Interethnic and religious violence in Punjab and elsewhere.

1991 Central rule imposed in Tamil Nadu. Shekhar resigned; elections called for May. May: Rajiv Gandhi assassinated. June: elections resumed, resulting in a Congress (I) minority government led by P V Narasimha Rao. Separatist violence continued.

1992 Congress (I) won control of state assembly and a majority in parliament in Punjab state elections. Split in Janata Dal opposition resulted in creation of National Front coalition party (including rump of Janata Dal party). Widespread communal violence killed over 1,200 people, mainly Muslims, following destruction of a mosque in Ayodhya, N India, by Hindu extremists.

1993 Sectarian violence in Bombay left 500 dead.

India Acts legislation passed 1858, 1919, and 1939 which formed the basis of British rule in India until independence 1947. The 1858 Act abolished the administrative functions of the ◊East India Company, replacing them with direct rule from London. The 1919 Act increased Indian participation at local and provincial levels but did not meet nationalist demands for complete internal self-government (◊Montagu-Chelmsford reforms). The 1939 Act outlined a federal structure but was never implemented.

Indian National Congress (INC) official name for the Congress Party of India.

Indochina War successful war of independence 1946-54 between the nationalist forces of what was to become Vietnam and France, the occupying colonial power.

Indonesia country in SE Asia, made up of over 13,000 islands situated on or near the equator, between the Indian and Pacific oceans.

chronology
1942 Occupied by Japan; nationalist government established.
1945 Japanese surrender; nationalists declared independence under Ahmed Sukarno.
1949 Formal transfer of Dutch sovereignty.
1950 Unitary constitution established.
1963 Western New Guinea (Irian Jaya) ceded by the Netherlands.
1965-66 Attempted communist coup; General T N J ◊Suharto imposed emergency administration, carried out massacre of hundreds of thousands.
1967 Sukarno replaced as president by Suharto.
1975 Guerrillas seeking independence for S Moluccas seized train and Indonesian consulate in the Netherlands, held Western hostages.
1976 Forced annexation of former Portuguese colony of East Timor.
1986 Institution of 'transmigration programme' to settle large numbers of Javanese on sparsely populated outer islands, particularly Irian Jaya.
1988 Partial easing of travel restrictions to East Timor. Suharto re-elected for fifth term.
1989 Foreign debt reaches $50 billion; Western creditors offer aid on condition that concessions are made to foreign companies and that austerity measures are introduced.
1991 Democracy forums launched to promote political dialogue. Massacre in East Timor.
1992 The ruling Golkar party won the assembly elections.
1993 President Suharto re-elected for sixth consecutive five-year term.

Industrial Workers of the World (IWW) labour movement founded in Chicago, USA 1905, and in Australia 1907, the members of which were popularly known as the *Wobblies*. The IWW was dedicated to the overthrow of capitalism and the creation of a single union for workers, but divided on tactics.

Inkatha South African political organization formed 1975 by Chief Gatsha ◊Buthelezi, leader of 6 million Zulus, the country's biggest ethnic group.

Inkatha's avowed aim is to create a nonracial democratic political situation. Inkatha has tried to work with the white regime and, as a result, Buthelezi has been widely regarded as a collaborator. Fighting between Inkatha and ◊African National Congress members cost more than 1,000 lives in the first five months of 1990. In 1991, revelations that Inkatha had received covert financial aid from the South African government during 1989–90 increased the ANC's distrust of its motives.

INLA abbreviation for ◊Irish National Liberation Army.

Intermediate Nuclear Forces Treaty agreement signed 8 Dec 1987 between the USA and the USSR to eliminate all ground-based nuclear missiles in Europe that were capable of hitting only European targets (including European Russia). It reduced the countries' nuclear arsenals by some 2,000 (4% of the total). The treaty included provisions for each country to inspect the other's bases.

International, the coordinating body established by labour and socialist organizations, including:

First International or *International Working Men's Association* 1864–72, formed in London under Karl ◊Marx.

Second International 1889–1940, founded in Paris.

Third (Socialist) International or *Comintern* 1919–43, formed in Moscow by the Soviet leader Lenin, advocating from 1933 a popular front (communist, socialist, liberal) against the German dictator Hitler.

Fourth International or *Trotskyist International* 1936, somewhat indeterminate, anti-Stalinist.

Revived Socialist International 1951, formed in Frankfurt, Germany, a largely anti-communist association of social democrats.

International Brigade international volunteer force on the Republican side in the Spanish ◊Civil War 1936–39.

International Monetary Fund (IMF) specialized agency of the ◊United Nations, headquarters Washington DC, established under the 1944 ◊Bretton Woods agreement and operational since 1947. It seeks to promote international monetary cooperation and the growth of world trade, and to smooth multilateral payment arrangements among member states. IMF standby loans are available to members in balance-of-payments difficulties (the amount being governed by the member's quota), usually on the basis that the country must agree to take certain corrective measures.

Intifada Palestinian uprising; also the title of the involved *Liberation Army of Palestine*, a loosely organized group of adult and teenage Palestinians active since 1987 in attacks on armed Israeli troops in the occupied territories of Palestine. Their campaign for self-determination includes stone-throwing and petrol bombing.

Invergordon Mutiny incident in the British Atlantic Fleet, Cromarty Firth, Scotland, 15 Sept 1931. Ratings refused to prepare the ships for sea following the government's cuts in their pay; the cuts were consequently modified.

IRA abbreviation for ◊Irish Republican Army.

Iran (*Persia* until 1935) country in SW Asia, bounded N by Armenia, Azerbaijan, the Caspian Sea, and Turkmenistan; E by Afghanistan and Pakistan; S and SW by the Gulf of Oman and the Persian Gulf; W by Iraq; and NW by Turkey.

chronology
1946 British, US, and Soviet forces left Iran.
1951 Oilfields nationalized by Prime Minister Muhammad Mossadeq.
1953 Mossadeq deposed and the US-backed shah, Muhammad Reza Shah Pahlavi, took full control of the government.
1975 The shah introduced single-party system.
1978 Opposition to the shah organized from France by Ayatollah ◊Khomeini.
1979 Shah left the country; Khomeini returned to create Islamic state. Revolutionaries seized US hostages at embassy in Tehran; US economic boycott.
1980 Start of Iran–Iraq War.
1981 US hostages released.
1984 Egyptian peace proposals rejected.
1985 Fighting intensified in Iran–Iraq War.
1988 Cease-fire; talks with Iraq began.
1989 Khomeini called for the death of British writer Salman Rushdie. June: Khomeini died; Ali Khamenei elected interim Leader of the Revolution; speaker of Iranian parliament Hoshemi ◊Rafsanjani elected president. Secret oil deal with Israel revealed.
1990 Generous peace terms with Iraq accepted. Normal relations with UK restored.

1991 Imprisoned British business executive released. Nearly one million Kurds arrived in Iran from Iraq, fleeing persecution by Saddam Hussein after the Gulf War.

1992 Pro-Rafsanjani moderates won assembly elections.

Irangate US political scandal 1987 involving senior members of the Reagan administration (called this to echo the Nixon administration's ◊Watergate). Congressional hearings 1986–87 revealed that the US government had secretly sold weapons to Iran in 1985 and traded them for hostages held in Lebanon by pro-Iranian militias, and used the profits to supply right-wing Contra guerrillas in Nicaragua with arms. The attempt to get around the law (Boland amendment) specifically prohibiting military assistance to the Contras also broke other laws in the process.

Iran–Iraq War or *Gulf War* war between Iran and Iraq 1980–88, claimed by the former to have begun with the Iraqi offensive 21 Sept 1980, and by the latter with the Iranian shelling of border posts 4 Sept 1980. Occasioned by a boundary dispute over the Shatt-al-Arab waterway, it fundamentally arose because of Saddam Hussein's fear of a weakening of his absolute power base in Iraq by Iran's encouragement of the Shi'ite majority in Iraq to rise against the Sunni government. An estimated 1 million people died in the war.

Iraq country in SW Asia, bounded N by Turkey, E by Iran, SE by the Persian Gulf and Kuwait, S by Saudi Arabia, and W by Jordan and Syria.

chronology
1920 Iraq became a British League of Nations protectorate.
1921 Hashemite dynasty established, with Faisal I installed by Britain as king.
1932 Independence achieved from British protectorate status.
1958 Monarchy overthrown; Iraq became a republic.
1963 Joint Ba'athist-military coup headed by Col Salem Aref.
1968 Military coup put Maj-Gen al-Bakr in power.
1979 Al-Bakr replaced by Saddam ◊Hussein.
1980 War between Iraq and Iran broke out.
1985 Fighting intensified.
1988 Cease-fire; talks began with Iran. Iraq used chemical weapons against Kurdish rebels seeking greater autonomy.
1989 Unsuccessful coup against President Hussein; Iraq launched ballistic missile in successful test.

1990 Peace treaty favouring Iran agreed. Aug: Iraq invaded and annexed Kuwait, precipitating another Gulf crisis. US forces massed in Saudi Arabia at request of King Fahd. United Nations resolutions ordered Iraqi withdrawal from Kuwait and imposed total trade ban on Iraq; UN resolution sanctioning force approved. All foreign hostages released.

1991 16 Jan: US-led forces began aerial assault on Iraq; Iraq's infrastructure destroyed by bombing. 23–28 Feb: land–sea–air offensive to free Kuwait successful. Uprisings of Kurds and Shi'ites brutally suppressed by surviving Iraqi troops. Talks between Kurdish leaders and Saddam Hussein about Kurdish autonomy. Allied troops withdrew after establishing 'safe havens' for Kurds in the north, leaving a rapid-reaction force near the Turkish border. Allies threatened to bomb strategic targets in Iraq if full information about nuclear facilities denied to UN.

1992 UN imposed a 'no-fly zone' over S Iraq to protect Shi'ites.

1993 Jan: Iraqi incursions into the 'no-fly zone' prompted US-led alliance aircraft to bomb 'strategic' targets in Iraq. Relations subsequently improved.

Ireland, Republic of country occupying the main part of the island of Ireland, NW Europe. It is bounded E by the Irish Sea, S and W by the Atlantic Ocean, and NE by Northern Ireland.

chronology

1937 Independence achieved from Britain.

1949 Eire left the Commonwealth and became the Republic of Ireland.

1973 ◊Fianna Fáil defeated after 40 years in office; Liam ◊Cosgrave formed a coalition government.

1977 Fianna Fáil returned to power, with Jack ◊Lynch as prime minister.

1979 Lynch resigned, succeeded by Charles ◊Haughey.

1981 Garret ◊FitzGerald formed a coalition.

1983 New Ireland Forum formed, but rejected by the British government.

1985 ◊Anglo-Irish Agreement signed.

1986 Protests by Ulster Unionists against the agreement.

1987 General election won by Charles Haughey.

1988 Relations with UK at low ebb because of disagreement over extradition decisions.

1989 Haughey failed to win majority in general election. Progressive Democrats given cabinet positions in coalition government.

1990 Mary ◊Robinson elected president; John Bruton became ◊Fine Gael leader.

1992 Jan: Haughey resigned after losing parliamentary majority. Feb: Albert Reynolds became Fianna Fáil leader and prime minister. June: National referendum approved ratification of Maastricht Treaty. Nov: Reynolds lost confidence vote; election result inconclusive.
1993 Fianna Fáil–Labour coalition formed.

Irgun short for *Irgun Zvai Leumi* (National Military Society), a Jewish guerrilla group active against the British administration in Palestine 1946–48. Their bombing of the King David Hotel in Jerusalem 22 July 1946 resulted in 91 fatalities.

Irish National Liberation Army (INLA) guerrilla organization committed to the end of British rule in Northern Ireland and the incorporation of Ulster into the Irish Republic. The INLA was a 1974 offshoot of the Irish Republican Army (IRA). Among the INLA's activities was the killing of British politician Airey Neave in 1979.

Irish Republican Army (IRA) militant Irish nationalist organization whose aim is to create a united Irish socialist republic including Ulster. The paramilitary wing of ◊Sinn Féin, it was founded 1919 by Michael ◊Collins and fought a successful war against Britain 1919-21. It came to the fore again 1939 with a bombing campaign in Britain, having been declared illegal in 1936 . Its activities intensified from 1968 onwards, as the civil- rights disorders ('the Troubles') in Northern Ireland developed. In 1970 a group in the north broke away to become the *Provisional IRA*; its objective is the expulsion of the British from Northern Ireland.

Iron Curtain in Europe after World War II, the symbolic boundary of the ◊Cold War between capitalist West and communist East. The term was popularized by the UK prime minister Winston Churchill from 1945.

Iron Guard pro-fascist group controlling Romania in the 1930s. To counter its influence, King Carol II established a dictatorship 1938 but the Iron Guard forced him to abdicate 1940.

Isaacs Rufus Daniel, 1st Marquess of Reading 1860–1935. British Liberal lawyer and politician. As Lord Chief Justice he tried the Irish nationalist Roger ◊Casement in 1916. Viceroy of India 1921–26; foreign secretary 1931.

Israel country in SW Asia, bounded N by Lebanon, E by Syria and Jordan, S by the Gulf of Aqaba, and W by Egypt and the Mediterranean Sea.

chronology

1948 Independent State of Israel proclaimed with David ◊Ben-Gurion as prime minister; attacked by Arab nations, Israel won the War of Independence. Many displaced Arabs settled in refugee camps in the Gaza Strip and West Bank.

1952 Col Gamal ◊Nasser of Egypt stepped up blockade of Israeli ports and support of Arab guerrillas in Gaza.

1956 Israel invaded Gaza and Sinai.

1959 Egypt renewed blockade of Israeli trade through Suez Canal.

1963 Ben-Gurion resigned, succeeded by Levi Eshkol.

1964 ◊Palestine Liberation Organization (PLO) founded with the aim of overthrowing the state of Israel.

1967 Israel victorious in the Six-Day War. Gaza, West Bank, E Jerusalem, Sinai, and Golan Heights captured.

1968 Israel Labour Party formed, led by Golda Meir.

1969 Golda ◊Meir became prime minister.

1973–74 ◊Yom Kippur War: Israel attacked by Egypt and Syria. Golda Meir succeeded by Yitzhak ◊Rabin.

1975 Suez Canal reopened.

1977 Menachem ◊Begin elected prime minister. Egyptian president addressed the Knesset.

1978 ◊Camp David talks.

1979 Egyptian-Israeli agreement signed. Israel agreed to withdraw from Sinai.

1980 Jerusalem declared capital of Israel.

1981 Golan Heights formally annexed.

1982 Israel pursued PLO fighters into Lebanon.

1983 Agreement reached for withdrawal from Lebanon.

1985 Israeli prime minister Shimon ◊Peres had secret talks with King Hussein of Jordan.

1986 Yitzhak ◊Shamir took over from Peres under power-sharing agreement.

1988 Criticism of Israel's handling of Palestinian uprising in occupied territories; PLO acknowledged Israel's right to exist.

1989 New Likud–Labour coalition government formed under Shamir. Limited progress achieved on proposals for negotiations leading to elections in occupied territories.

1990 Coalition collapsed due to differences over peace process; international condemnation of Temple Mount killings. New Shamir right-wing coalition formed.

1991 Shamir gave cautious response to Middle East peace proposals. Some Palestinian prisoners released. Peace talks began in Barcelona.

1992 Jan: Shamir lost majority in Knesset when fundamentalists withdrew from coalition. June: Labour Party, led by Yitzhak Rabin, won elections; coalition formed under Rabin. Aug: US–Israeli loan agreement signed. Dec: Palestinians expelled in face of international criticism.

1993 Jan: UN condemned expulsion of Palestinians. Ban on contacts with PLO formally lifted. Feb: government allowed 100 of 400 expelled Palestinians to return. March: Ezer Weizman elected president; Binyamin 'Bibi' Netanyahu elected leader of Likud party.

Italy country in S Europe, bounded N by Switzerland and Austria, E by Slovenia, Croatia, and the Adriatic Sea, S by the Ionian and Mediterranean seas, and W by the Tyrrhenian and Ligurian seas and France. It includes the Mediterranean islands of Sardinia and Sicily.

chronology

1946 Monarchy replaced by a republic.

1948 New constitution adopted.

1954 Trieste returned to Italy.

1976 Communists proposed establishment of broad-based, left–right government, the 'historic compromise'; rejected by Christian Democrats.

1978 Christian Democrat Aldo ◊Moro, architect of the historic compromise, kidnapped and murdered by Red Brigade guerrillas.

1983 Bettino ◊Craxi, a Socialist, became leader of broad coalition government.

1987 Craxi resigned; succeeding coalition fell within months.

1988 Christian Democrats' leader Ciriaco de Mita established a five-party coalition including the Socialists.

1989 De Mita resigned after disagreements within his coalition government; succeeded by Giulio ◊Andreotti. De Mita lost leadership of Christian Democrats; Communists formed 'shadow government'.

1991 Referendum approved electoral reform.

1992 April: ruling coalition lost its majority in general election; President Cossiga resigned, replaced by Oscar Luigi Scalfaro in May. Giuliano Amato, deputy leader of Democratic Party of the Left (PDS), accepted premiership. Sept: lira devalued and Italy withdrew from the Exchange Rate Mechanism.

1993 Feb–March: investigation of corruption network exposed Mafia links with several notable politicians, including Craxi and Andreotti. Craxi resigned Socialist Party leadership; replaced by Giorgio Benvenutu. April: referendum results showed Italian people strongly in favour of majority electoral system. Amato resigned premiership; Carlo Ciampi named as his successor.

Ivory Coast (French *Côte d'Ivoire*) country in W Africa, bounded N by Mali and Burkina Faso, E by Ghana, S by the Gulf of Guinea, and W by Liberia and Guinea.

chronology
1904 Became part of French West Africa.
1958 Achieved internal self-government.
1960 Independence achieved from France, with Félix ◊Houphouët-Boigny as president of a one-party state.
1985 Houphouët-Boigny re-elected, unopposed.
1986 Name changed officially from Ivory Coast to Côte d'Ivoire.
1990 Houphouët-Boigny and Democratic Party of the Ivory Coast (PDCI) re-elected.

Iwo Jima, Battle of intense fighting between Japanese and US forces 19 Feb–17 March 1945 during World War II. In Feb 1945, US marines landed on the island of Iwo Jima, a Japanese air base, intending to use it to prepare for a planned final assault on mainland Japan. The Japanese defences were so strong that 5,000 US marines were killed before the island was captured from the Japanese.

IWW abbreviation for ◊*Industrial Workers of the World*.

J

Jackson Jesse 1941– . US Democrat politician, a cleric and campaigner for minority rights. He contested his party's 1984 and 1988 presidential nominations in an effort to increase voter registration and to put black issues on the national agenda. He is an eloquent public speaker.

Jagan Cheddi (Berrat) 1918– . Guyanese left-wing politician. Educated in British Guyana and the USA, he led the People's Progressive Party (PPA) from 1950, and was the first prime minister of British Guyana 1961–64. As candidate for president 1992, he opposed privatization as leading to 'recolonization'. In Aug elections the PPA won a decisive victory, and Jagan as veteran leader replaced Desmond Hoyte.

Jakeš Miloš 1922– . Czech communist politician, a member of the Politburo from 1981 and party leader 1987–89. A conservative, he supported the Soviet invasion of Czechoslovakia in 1968. He was forced to resign in Nov 1989 following a series of pro-democracy mass rallies.

Jamaica island in the Caribbean Sea, S of Cuba and W of Haiti.

chronology

1655 Captured by British.

1944 Internal self-government introduced.

1962 Independence achieved from Britain, with Alexander Bustamante of the Jamaica Labour Party (JLP) as prime minister.

1967 JLP re-elected under Hugh Shearer.

1972 Michael ◊Manley of the People's National Party (PNP) became prime minister.

1980 JLP elected, with Edward Seaga as prime minister.

1983 JLP re-elected, winning all 60 seats.

1988 Island badly damaged by Hurricane Gilbert.

1989 PNP won a decisive victory with Michael Manley returning as prime minister.

1992 Manley resigned, succeeded by P J Patterson.

1993 March: landslide victory for PNP in general election.

Jameson Leander Starr 1853–1917. British colonial administrator. In South Africa, early in 1896, he led the *Jameson Raid* from Mafeking into Transvaal to support the non-Boer colonists there, in an attempt to overthrow the government (for which he served some months in prison). Returning to South Africa, he succeeded Cecil Rhodes as leader of the Progressive Party of Cape Colony, where he was prime minister 1904–08.

Janata alliance of political parties in India formed 1971 to oppose Indira Gandhi's Congress Party. Victory in the election brought Morarji ◊Desai to power as prime minister but he was unable to control the various groups within the alliance and resigned 1979. His successors fared little better, and the elections of 1980 overwhelmingly returned Indira Gandhi to office.

Japan country in NE Asia, occupying a group of islands of which the four main ones are Hokkaido, Honshu, Kyushu, and Shikoku. Japan is situated between the Sea of Japan (to the W) and the N Pacific (to the E), E of North and South Korea.

chronology
1902 Formed alliance with Britain.
1904–05 War with Russia; Russia ceded southern half of Sakhalin.
1910 Japan annexed Korea.
1914 Joined Allies in World War I.
1918 Received German Pacific islands as mandates.
1931–32 War with China; renewed 1937.
1941 Japan attacked US fleet at Pearl Harbor 7 Dec.
1945 World War II ended with Japanese surrender. Allied control commission took power. Formosa and Manchuria returned to China.
1946 Framing of 'peace constitution'. Emperor Hirohito became figurehead ruler.
1952 Full sovereignty regained.
1958 Joined United Nations.
1968 Bonin and Volcano Islands regained.
1972 Ryukyu Islands regained.
1974 Prime Minister ◊Tanaka resigned over Lockheed bribes scandal.
1982 Yasuhiro ◊Nakasone elected prime minister.
1985 Yen revalued.
1987 Noboru ◊Takeshita chosen to succeed Nakasone.
1988 Recruit scandal cast shadow over government and opposition parties.
1989 Emperor Hirohito died; succeeded by his son Akihito. Many cabinet

ministers implicated in Recruit scandal and Takeshita resigned; succeeded by Sosuke ◊Uno. Aug: Uno resigned after sex scandal; succeeded by Toshiki Kaifu.

1990 Feb: new house of councillors' elections won by the Liberal Democratic Party (LDP). Public-works budget increased by 50% to encourage imports.

1991 Japan contributed billions of dollars to the Gulf War and its aftermath. Kaifu succeeded by Kiichi ◊Miyazawa.

1992 Over 100 politicians implicated in new financial scandal. Emperor Akihito made first Japanese imperial visit to China. Trade surpluses reached record levels.

1993 Worst recession of postwar era; trade surpluses, however, again reached record levels.

Jarrow Crusade march in 1936 from Jarrow to London, protesting at the high level of unemployment following the closure of Palmer's shipyard in the town.

Jaruzelski Wojciech 1923– . Polish general, communist leader from 1981, president 1985–90. He imposed martial law for the first year of his rule, suppressed the opposition, and banned trade-union activity, but later released many political prisoners. In 1989, elections in favour of the free trade union Solidarity forced Jaruzelski to speed up democratic reforms, overseeing a transition to a new form of 'socialist pluralist' democracy and stepping down as president 1990.

Jayawardene Junius Richard 1906– . Sri Lankan politician. Leader of the United Nationalist Party from 1973, he became prime minister 1977 and the country's first president 1978–88.

Jellicoe John Rushworth, 1st Earl 1859–1935. British admiral who commanded the Grand Fleet 1914–16 during World War I; the only action he fought was the inconclusive battle of ◊Jutland. He was First Sea Lord 1916–17, when he failed to push the introduction of the convoy system to combat U-boat attack. Created 1st Earl 1925.

Jenkins Roy (Harris), Lord Jenkins 1920– . British politician. He became a Labour minister 1964, was home secretary 1965–67 and 1974–76, and chancellor of the Exchequer 1967–70. He was president of the European Commission 1977–81. In 1981 he became one of the founders of the Social Democratic Party and was elected 1982, but lost his seat 1987.

In the same year, he was elected chancellor of Oxford University and made a life peer.

Jewish Agency administrative body created by the British mandate power in Palestine 1929 to oversee the Jewish population and immigration. In 1948 it took over as the government of an independent Israel.

Jiang Zemin 1926–   . Chinese political leader. The son-in-law of ◊Li Xiannian, he joined the Chinese Communist Party's politburo in 1967 after serving in the Moscow embassy and as mayor of Shanghai. He succeeded ◊Zhao Ziyang as party leader after the Tiananmen Square massacre of 1989. A cautious proponent of economic reform coupled with unswerving adherence to the party's 'political line', he subsequently replaced ◊Deng Xiaoping as head of the influential central military commission.

Jiang Jie Shi alternate transcription of ◊Chiang Kai-shek.

Jiang Qing or *Chiang Ching* 1914–1991. Chinese communist politician, third wife of the party leader Mao Zedong. In 1960 she became minister for culture, and played a key role in the 1966–69 Cultural Revolution as the leading member of the Shanghai-based Gang of Four, who attempted to seize power 1976. Jiang was imprisoned 1981.

Jinnah Muhammad Ali 1876–1948. Indian politician, Pakistan's first governor general from 1947. He was president of the ◊Muslim League 1916, 1934–48, and by 1940 was advocating the need for a separate state of Pakistan; at the 1946 conferences in London he insisted on the partition of British India into Hindu and Muslim states.

Jodl Alfred 1892–1946. German general. In World War II he drew up the Nazi government's plan for the attack on Yugoslavia, Greece, and the USSR. In Jan 1945 he became Chief of Staff and headed the delegation that signed Germany's surrender in Reims 7 May 1945. He was tried for war crimes in Nuremberg 1945–46 and hanged.

Joffre Joseph Jacques Césaire 1852–1931. Marshal of France during World War I. He was chief of general staff 1911. The German invasion of Belgium 1914 took him by surprise, but his stand at the Battle of the ◊Marne resulted in his appointment as supreme commander of all the French armies 1915. His failure to make adequate preparations at Verdun 1916 and the military disasters on the ◊Somme led to his replacement by Nivelle in Dec 1916.

Johnson Hiram Warren 1866–1945. US politician. He was the 'Bull Moose' party candidate for vice president in Theodore Roosevelt's unsuccessful bid to regain the presidency 1912. Elected to the US Senate 1917, Johnson served there until his death. He was an unyielding isolationist, opposing US involvement in World War I as well as membership in the League of Nations and World Court.

Johnson Lyndon Baines 1908–1973. 36th president of the USA 1963–69, a Democrat. He was elected to Congress 1937–49 and the Senate 1949–60. Born in Texas, he brought critical Southern support as J F Kennedy's vice-presidential running mate 1960, and became president on Kennedy's assassination. After the ◊Tonkin Gulf Incident, which escalated US involvement in the ◊Vietnam War, support won by Johnson's Great Society legislation (civil rights, education, alleviation of poverty) dissipated, and he declined to run for re-election 1968.

Jonathan Chief (Joseph) Leabua 1914–1987. Lesotho politician. A leader in the drive for independence, Jonathan became prime minister of Lesotho in 1965. His rule was ended by a coup in 1986.

Jordan country in SW Asia, bounded N by Syria, NE by Iraq, E, SE and S by Saudi Arabia, S by the Gulf of Aqaba, and W by Israel.

chronology
1946 Independence achieved from Britain as Transjordan.
1949 New state of Jordan declared.
1950 Jordan annexed West Bank.
1953 Hussein ibn Talai officially became king of Jordan.
1958 Jordan and Iraq formed Arab Federation that ended when the Iraqi monarchy was deposed.
1967 Israel captured and occupied West Bank. Martial law imposed.
1976 Lower house dissolved, political parties banned, elections postponed until further notice.
1982 Hussein tried to mediate in Arab-Israeli conflict.
1984 Women voted for the first time.
1985 Hussein and Yassir ◊Arafat put forward framework for Middle East peace settlement. Secret meeting between Hussein and Israeli prime minister.
1988 Hussein announced decision to cease administering the West Bank as part of Jordan, passing responsibility to ◊Palestine Liberation Organization, and the suspension of parliament.

1989 Prime Minister Zaid al-Rifai resigned; Hussein promised new parliamentary elections following criticism of economic policies. Riots over price increases up to 50% following fall in oil revenues. First parliamentary elections for 22 years; Muslim Brotherhood won 25 of 80 seats but exiled from government; martial law lifted.
1990 Hussein unsuccessfully tried to mediate after Iraq's invasion of Kuwait. Massive refugee problems as thousands fled to Jordan from Kuwait and Iraq.
1991 24 years of martial law ended; ban on political parties lifted.
1992 Political parties allowed to register.

Joseph Keith (Sinjohn), Baron 1918–   . British Conservative politician. A barrister, he entered Parliament 1956. He held ministerial posts 1962–64, 1970–74, 1979–81, and was secretary of state for education and science 1981–86. He was made a life peer 1987.

Joyce William 1906–1946. Born in New York, son of a naturalized Irish-born American, he carried on fascist activity in the UK as a 'British subject'. During World War II he made propaganda broadcasts from Germany to the UK, his upper-class accent earning him the nickname *Lord Haw Haw*. He was hanged for treason.

July Plot or *July Conspiracy* in German history, an unsuccessful attempt to assassinate the dictator Adolf Hitler and to overthrow the Nazi regime 20 July 1944. Colonel von Stauffenberg planted a bomb under the conference table at Hitler's headquarters at Rastenburg, East Prussia. Believing that Hitler had been killed, Stauffenberg flew to Berlin to join Field Marshal von Witzleben and General von Beck to proclaim a government headed by resistance leader and former lord mayor of Leipzig Carl Goerdeler. Hitler was only injured, telephone communications remained intact, and counter measures were taken in Berlin by Major Ernst Remer. Reprisals were savage: 150 alleged conspirators were executed, while 15 prominent persons, including Field Marshal Rommel, committed suicide and many others were imprisoned.

Jutland, Battle of naval battle of World War I, fought between England and Germany on 31 May 1916, off the W coast of Jutland. Its outcome was indecisive, but the German fleet remained in port for the rest of the war.

K

Kádár János 1912–1989. Hungarian Communist leader, in power 1956–88, after suppressing the national uprising. As Hungarian Socialist Workers' Party (HSWP) leader and prime minister 1956–58 and 1961–65, Kádár introduced a series of market-socialist economic reforms, while retaining cordial political relations with the USSR.

Kaifu Toshiki 1932– . Japanese conservative politician, prime minister 1989–91. A protégé of former premier Takeo Miki, he was selected as a compromise choice as Liberal Democratic Party (LDP) president and prime minister Aug 1989, following the resignation of Sosuke Uno. Kaifu resigned Nov 1991, having lost the support of important factional leaders in the LDP, and was replaced by Kiichi Miyazawa.

Kalinin Mikhail Ivanovich 1875–1946. Soviet politician, founder of the newspaper *Pravda*. He was prominent in the 1917 October Revolution, and in 1919 became head of state (president of the Central Executive Committee of the Soviet government until 1937, then president of the Presidium of the Supreme Soviet until 1946).

Kaltenbrunner Ernst 1901–1946. Austrian Nazi leader. After the annexation of Austria 1938 he joined police chief Himmler's staff, and as head of the Security Police (SD) from 1943 was responsible for the murder of millions of Jews (see the ◊Holocaust) and Allied soldiers in World War II. After the war, he was tried at Nuremberg for war crimes and hanged.

Kamenev Lev Borisovich 1883–1936. Russian leader of the Bolshevik movement after 1917 who, with Stalin and Zinoviev, formed a ruling triumvirate in the USSR after Lenin's death 1924. His alignment with the Trotskyists led to his dismissal from office and from the Communist Party by Stalin 1926. Arrested 1934 after Kirov's assassination, Kamenev was secretly tried and sentenced, then retried, condemned, and shot 1936 for allegedly plotting to murder Stalin.

kamikaze pilots of the Japanese air force in World War II who deliberately crash-dived their planes, loaded with bombs, usually onto ships of the US Navy.

KANU (acronym for *K*enya *A*frican *N*ational *U*nion) political party founded 1944 and led by Jomo ◊Kenyatta from 1947, when it was the Kenya African Union; it became KANU on independence. The party formed Kenyatta's political power base in 1963 when he became prime minister; in 1964 he became the first president of Kenya.

Karamanlis Constantinos 1907–   . Greek politician of the New Democracy Party. A lawyer and an anticommunist, he was prime minister Oct 1955–March 1958, May 1958–Sept 1961, and Nov 1961–June 1963 (when he went into self-imposed exile because of a military coup). He was recalled as prime minister on the fall of the regime of the 'colonels' in July 1974, and was president 1980–85.

Karmal Babrak 1929–   . Afghani communist politician, president 1979–86. In 1965 he formed what became the banned People's Democratic Party of Afghanistan (PDPA) 1977. As president, with Soviet backing, he sought to broaden the appeal of the PDPA but encountered wide resistance from the ◊Mujaheddin Muslim guerrillas.

Kassem Abdul Karim 1914–1963. Iraqi politician, prime minister from 1958; he adopted a pro-Soviet policy. Kassem pardoned the leaders of the pro-Egyptian party who tried to assassinate him 1959. He was executed after the 1963 coup.

Katō Taka-akira 1860–1926. Japanese politician, prime minister 1924–26. After a long political career with several terms as foreign minister, Katōl led probably the most democratic and liberal regime of the Japanese Empire.

Katsura Tarō 1847–1913. Prince of Japan, army officer, politician, and prime minister (1901–06, 1908–11, 1912–13). He was responsible for the Anglo-Japanese treaty of 1902 (an alliance against Russia), the successful prosecution of the Russo-Japanese war 1904–05, and the annexation of Korea 1910.

Katyn Forest forest near Smolensk, SW of Moscow, Russia, where 4,500 Polish officer prisoners of war (captured in the German-Soviet partition of Poland 1940) were shot; 10,000 others were killed elsewhere. In 1989 the USSR accepted responsibility for the massacre.

Kaunda Kenneth (David) 1924– . Zambian politician, president 1964–91. Imprisoned in 1958–60 as founder of the Zambia African National Congress, he became in 1964 the first prime minister of Northern Rhodesia, then the first president of independent Zambia. In 1973 he introduced one-party rule. He supported the nationalist movement in Southern Rhodesia, now Zimbabwe, and survived a coup attempt 1980 thought to have been promoted by South Africa. He was elected chair of the Organization of African Unity 1987. In 1990 he was faced with wide anti-government demonstrations, leading to the acceptance of a multiparty political system. He lost the first multiparty election, in Nov 1991, to Frederick Chiluba.

Kautsky Karl 1854–1938. German socialist theoretician who opposed the reformist ideas of Edouard ◊Bernstein from within the Social Democratic Party. In spite of his Marxist ideas he remained in the party when its left wing broke away to form the German Communist Party (KPD).

Kazakhstan country in central Asia, bounded N by Russia, W by the Caspian Sea, E by China, and S by Turkmenistan, Uzbekistan, and Kyrgyzstan.

chronology
1920 Autonomous republic in USSR.
1936 Joined the USSR and became a full union republic.
1950s Site of Nikita Khrushchev's ambitious 'Virgin Lands' agricultural extension programme.
1960s A large influx of Russian settlers turned the Kazakhs into a minority in their own republic.
1986 Riots in Alma-Alta after Gorbachev ousted local communist leader.
1989 June: Nursuttan ◊Nazarbayev became leader of the Kazakh Communist Party (KCP) and instituted economic and cultural reform programmes.
1990 Feb: Nazarbayev became head of state.
1991 March: support pledged for continued union with USSR; Aug: Nazarbayev condemned attempted anti-Gorbachev coup; KCP abolished and replaced by Independent Socialist Party of Kazakhstan (SPK). Dec: joined new Commonwealth of Independent States (CIS); independence recognized by USA.
1992 Jan: admitted into Conference on Security and Cooperation in Europe (CSCE). March: became a member of the United Nations (UN). May: trade agreement with USA.

1993 Jan: new constitution adopted, increasing the authority of the president and making Kazakh the state language.

Keating Paul 1954–   . Australian politician, Labor Party (ALP) leader and prime minister from 1991. He was treasurer and deputy leader of the ALP 1983–91.

Kefauver (Carey) Estes 1903–1963. US Democratic politician. He was elected to the US House of Representatives 1939 and served in the US Senate 1948 until his death. He was an unsuccessful candidate for the Democratic presidential nomination 1952 and 1956.

Keitel Wilhelm 1882–1946. German field marshal in World War II, chief of the supreme command from 1938 and Hitler's chief military adviser. He signed Germany's unconditional surrender in Berlin 8 May 1945. Tried at Nuremberg for war crimes, he was hanged.

Kellogg Frank Billings 1856–1937. US political leader and diplomat. Elected to the US Senate 1916, he was appointed US ambassador to Great Britain by President Harding 1922 and secretary of state 1925. He formulated the ◊Kellogg–Briand Pact 1927, the international antiwar resolution, for which he was awarded the Nobel Peace Prize 1929

Kellogg–Briand pact agreement negotiated 1927 between the USA and France to renounce war and seek settlement of disputes by peaceful means. It took its name from the US secretary of state Frank B Kellogg (1856–1937) and the French foreign minister Aristide Briand. Most other nations subsequently signed. Some successes were achieved in settling South American disputes, but the pact made no provision for measures against aggressors and became ineffective in the 1930s, with Japan in Manchuria, Italy in Ethiopia, and Hitler in central Europe.

Kelly Petra 1947–1992. German politician and activist. She was a vigorous campaigner against nuclear power and other environmental issues and founded the German Green Party 1972. She was a member of parliament 1983–1990, but then fell out with her party over her assertive and domineering style of leadership. She died at the hands of her lover, the former general Gert Bastian.

Kemal Atatürk Mustafa. Turkish politician; see ◊Atatürk.

Kennedy Edward (Moore) 'Ted' 1932–   . US Democratic politician. He aided his brothers John and Robert Kennedy in the presidential campaign of

1960, and entered politics as a senator for Massachusetts 1962. He failed to gain the presidential nomination 1980, largely because of questions about his delay in reporting a car crash at Chappaquiddick Island, near Cape Cod, Massachusetts, in 1969, in which his passenger, Mary Jo Kopechne, was drowned.

Kennedy John F(itzgerald) 'Jack' 1917–1963. 35th president of the USA 1961–63, a Democrat; the first Roman Catholic and the youngest person to be elected president. In foreign policy he carried through the unsuccessful ♢Bay of Pigs invasion of Cuba, and in 1963 secured the withdrawal of Soviet missiles from the island. His programme for reforms at home, called the *New Frontier*, was posthumously executed by Lyndon Johnson. Kennedy was assassinated while on a visit to Dallas, Texas, on 22 Nov 1963 by Lee Harvey Oswald (1939–1963), who was within a few days shot dead by Jack Ruby (1911–1967).

Kennedy Joseph Patrick 1888–1969. US industrialist and diplomat; ambassador to the UK 1937–40. A self-made millionaire, he ventured into the film industry, then set up the Securities and Exchange Commission (SEC) for F D Roosevelt. He groomed each of his four sons—Joseph Patrick Kennedy Jr (1915–1944), John F ♢Kennedy, Robert ♢Kennedy, and Edward ♢Kennedy – for a career in politics. His eldest son, Joseph, was killed in action with the naval air force in World War II.

Kennedy Robert (Francis) 1925–1968. US Democratic politician and lawyer. He was presidential campaign manager for his brother John F ♢Kennedy 1960, and as attorney general 1961–64 pursued a racket-busting policy and promoted the Civil Rights Act of 1964. He was also a key aide to his brother. When John Kennedy's successor, Lyndon Johnson, preferred Hubert H Humphrey for the 1964 vice-presidential nomination, Kennedy resigned and was elected senator for New York. In 1968 he campaigned for the Democratic Party's presidential nomination, but during a campaign stop in California was assassinated by Sirhan Bissara Sirhan (1944–   ), a Jordanian.

Kent Bruce 1929–   . British peace campaigner who was general secretary for the Campaign for Nuclear Disarmament 1980–85. He has published numerous articles on disarmament, Christianity, and peace. He was a Catholic priest until 1987.

Kenya country in E Africa, bounded N by Sudan and Ethiopia, E by Somalia, SE by the Indian Ocean, SW by Tanzania, and W by Uganda.

chronology
1920 Kenya became a British colony.
1944 African participation in politics began.
1950 Mau Mau campaign began.
1953 Nationalist leader Jomo ◊Kenyatta imprisoned by British authorities.
1956 Mau Mau campaign defeated, Kenyatta released.
1963 Achieved internal self-government, with Kenyatta as prime minister.
1964 Independence achieved from Britain as a republic within the Commonwealth, with Kenyatta as president.
1967 East African Community (EAC) formed with Tanzania and Uganda.
1977 Collapse of EAC.
1978 Death of Kenyatta. Succeeded by Daniel arap ◊Moi.
1982 Attempted coup against Moi foiled.
1983 Moi re-elected unopposed.
1984 Over 2,000 people massacred by government forces at Wajir.
1985-86 Thousands of forest villagers evicted and their homes destroyed to make way for cash crops.
1988 Moi re-elected. 150,000 evicted from state- owned forests.
1989 Moi announced release of all known political prisoners. Confiscated ivory burned in attempt to stop elephant poaching.
1990 Despite antigovernment riots, Moi refused multiparty politics.
1991 Increasing demands for political reform; Moi promised multiparty politics.
1992 Constitutional amendment passed. Dec: Moi re-elected in first direct elections despite allegations of fraud.

Kenyatta Jomo. Assumed name of Kamau Ngengi *c.* 1894–1978. Kenyan nationalist politician, prime minister from 1963, as well as the first president of Kenya from 1964 until his death. He led the Kenya African Union from 1947 (◊*KANU* from 1963) and was active in liberating Kenya from British rule.

Kerekou Mathieu (Ahmed) 1933–   . Benin socialist politician and soldier, president 1980–91. In 1972, when deputy head of the Dahomey army, he led a coup to oust the ruling president and establish his own military government. He embarked on a programme of 'scientific socialism', changing his country's name to Benin to mark this change of direction. In 1987 he resigned from the army and confirmed a civilian administration. He was re-elected president 1989, but lost to Nicéphore Soglo in the 1991 presidential elections.

Kerensky Alexandr Feodorovich 1881–1970. Russian revolutionary politician, prime minister of the second provisional government before its collapse Nov 1917, during the ◊Russian Revolution. He was overthrown by the Bolshevik revolution and fled to France 1918 and to the USA 1940.

Kerr John Robert 1914–1990. Australian lawyer who as governor general 1974–77 controversially dismissed the prime minister, Gough Whitlam, and his government 1975.

Kesselring Albert 1885–1960. German field marshal in World War II, commander of the Luftwaffe (air force) 1939–40, during the invasions of Poland and the Low Countries and the early stages of the Battle of Britain. He later served under Field Marshal Rommel in N Africa, took command in Italy 1943, and was commander in chief on the western front March 1945. His death sentence for war crimes at the Nuremberg trials 1947 was commuted to life imprisonment, but he was released 1952.

Keynes John Maynard, 1st Baron Keynes 1883–1946. English economist, whose *The General Theory of Employment, Interest, and Money* 1936 proposed the prevention of financial crises and unemployment by adjusting demand through government control of credit and currency. He is responsible for that part of economics now known as *macroeconomics*.

KGB secret police of the USSR, the *Komitet Gosudarstvennoy Bezopasnosti*/Committee of State Security, which was in control of frontier and general security and the forced-labour system. KGB officers held key appointments in all fields of daily life, reporting to administration offices in every major town. The KGB was superseded by the Russian Federal Security Agency on the demise of the Soviet Union 1991.

Khaddhafi or *Gaddafi* or *Qaddafi*, Moamer al 1942– . Libyan revolutionary leader. Overthrowing King Idris 1969, he became virtual president of a republic, although he nominally gave up all except an ideological role 1974. He favours territorial expansion in N Africa reaching as far as Zaire, has supported rebels in Chad, and has proposed mergers with a number of countries. His theories, based on those of the Chinese communist leader Mao Zedong, are contained in a *Green Book*.

Khalaf Salah, also known as *Abu Iyad* 1933–1991. Palestinian nationalist leader. He became a refugee in 1948 when Israel became independent, and was one of the four founder members—with Yassir Arafat—of the PLO in the 1960s. One of its most senior members, he was involved with the ◊Black September group, and is believed to have orchestrated their campaign of terrorist attacks such as the 1972 killing of 11 Israeli atheletes at the Munich Olympics. He later argued for a diplomatic as well as a terrorist campaign. He was assassinated by an Arab dissident follower of Abu Nidal.

Khama Seretse 1921–1980. Botswanan politician, prime minister of Bechuanaland 1965, and first president of Botswana from 1966 until his death.

Khe Sanh in the Vietnam War, US Marine outpost near the Laotian border and just south of the demilitarized zone between North and South Vietnam. Garrisoned by 4,000 Marines, it was attacked unsuccessfully by 20,000 North Vietnamese troops 21 Jan–7 April 1968.

Khmer Rouge communist movement in Cambodia (Kampuchea) formed in the 1960s. Controlling the country 1974–78, it was responsible for mass deportations and executions under the leadership of ◊Pol Pot. Since then it has conducted guerrilla warfare, and in 1991 gained representation in the governing body. The leader of the Khmer Rouge from 1985 is Khieu Samphan.

Khomeini Ayatollah Ruhollah 1900–1989. Iranian Shi'ite Muslim leader, born in Khomein, central Iran. Exiled for opposition to the Shah from 1964, he returned when the Shah left the country 1979, and established a fundamentalist Islamic republic. His rule was marked by a protracted war with Iraq, and suppression of opposition within Iran, executing thousands of opponents.

Khrushchev Nikita Sergeyevich 1894–1971. Soviet politician, secretary general of the Communist Party 1953–64, premier 1958–64. He emerged as leader from the power struggle following Stalin's death and was the first official to denounce Stalin, in 1956. His de-Stalinization programme gave rise to revolts in Poland and Hungary 1956. Because of problems with the economy and foreign affairs (a breach with China 1960; conflict with the USA in the ◊Cuban missile crisis 1962), he was ousted by Leonid Brezhnev and Alexei Kosygin.

Kilmuir David Patrick Maxwell Fyfe, 1st Earl of Kilmuir 1900–1967. British lawyer and Conservative politician. He was solicitor-general 1942–45 and attorney-general in 1945 during the Churchill governments. He was home secretary 1951–54 and lord chancellor 1954–62.

Kim Dae Jung 1924– . South Korean social-democratic politician. As a committed opponent of the regime of General Park Chung Hee, he suffered imprisonment and exile. He was a presidential candidate in 1971 and 1987.

Kim Il Sung 1912– . North Korean communist politician and marshal. He became prime minister 1948 and president 1972, retaining the presidency of the Communist Workers' party. He likes to be known as the 'Great Leader' and has campaigned constantly for the reunification of Korea. His son *Kim Jong Il* (1942–), known as the 'Dear Leader', has been named as his successor.

Kim Young Sam 1927– . South Korean democratic politician. A member of the National Assembly from 1954 and president of the New Democratic Party (NDP) from 1974, he lost his seat and was later placed under house arrest because of his opposition to President Park Chung Hee. In 1983 he led a pro-democracy hunger strike but in 1987 failed to defeat Roh Tae-Woo in the presidential election. In 1990 he merged the NDP with the ruling party to form the new Democratic Liberal Party (DLP).

King Martin Luther Jr 1929–1968. US civil-rights campaigner, black leader, and Baptist minister. He first came to national attention as leader of the Montgomery, Alabama, bus boycott 1955, and was one of the organizers of the massive (200,000 people) march on Washington DC 1963 to demand racial equality. An advocate of nonviolence, he was awarded the Nobel Peace Prize 1964. He was assassinated in Memphis, Tennessee, by James Earl Ray (1928–).

King William Lyon Mackenzie 1874–1950. Canadian Liberal prime minister 1921–26, 1926–30, and 1935–48. He maintained the unity of the English- and French-speaking populations, and was instrumental in establishing equal status for Canada with Britain.

Kinnock Neil 1942– . British Labour politician, party leader 1983–92. Born and educated in Wales, he was elected to represent a Welsh constituency in Parliament 1970 (Islwyn from 1983). He was further left than prime ministers Wilson and Callaghan, but as party leader (in succession to Michael Foot) adopted a moderate position, initiating a major policy review 1988–89. He resigned as party leader after Labour's defeat in the 1992 general election.

Kiribati republic in the W central Pacific Ocean, comprising three groups of coral atolls: the 16 Gilbert Islands, 8 uninhabited Phoenix Islands, 8 of the 11 Line Islands, and the volcanic island of Banaba.

chronology
1892 Gilbert and Ellice Islands proclaimed a British protectorate.
1937 Phoenix Islands added to colony.
1950s UK tested nuclear weapons on Kiritimati (formerly Christmas Island).
1962 USA tested nuclear weapons on Kiritimati.
1975 Ellice Islands separated to become Tuvalu.
1977 Gilbert Islands achieved internal self-government.
1979 Independence achieved from Britain, within the Commonwealth, as the Republic of Kiribati, with Ieremia Tabai as president.
1982 and 1983 Tabai re-elected.
1985 Fishing agreement with Soviet state-owned company negotiated, prompting formation of Kiribati's first political party, the opposition Christian Democrats.
1987 Tabai re-elected.
1991 Tabai re-elected but not allowed under constitution to serve further term; Teatao Teannaki elected president.

Kirk Norman 1923–1974. New Zealand Labour politician, prime minister 1972–74. He entered parliament 1957 and led the Labour Party from 1964. During his office as prime minister he withdrew New Zealand troops from the Vietnam War and attempted to block French nuclear tests in the Pacific.

Kirkpatrick Jeane 1926–   . US politician and professor of political science. She served as US ambassador to the United Nations 1981–85. Originally a Democrat, she often spoke out against Communism and left-wing causes. She joined the Republican Party 1985.

Kirov Sergei Mironovich 1886–1934. Russian Bolshevik leader who joined the party 1904 and played a prominent part in the 1918–20 civil war. As one of ◊Stalin's closest associates, he became first secretary of the Leningrad Communist Party. His assassination, possibly engineered by Stalin, led to the political trials held during the next four years as part of the purge.

Kishi Nobusuke 1896–1987. Japanese politician and prime minister 1957–60. A government minister during World War II and imprisoned

1945, he was never put on trial and returned to politics 1953. During his premiership, Japan began a substantial rearmament programme and signed a new treaty with the USA that gave greater equality in the relationship between the two states.

Kissinger Henry 1923– . German-born US diplomat. After a brilliant academic career at Harvard University, he was appointed national security adviser 1969 by President Nixon, and was secretary of state 1973–77. His missions to the USSR and China improved US relations with both countries, and he took part in negotiating US withdrawal from Vietnam 1973 and in Arab-Israeli peace negotiations 1973–75. Nobel Peace Prize 1973.

Kitchener Horatio Herbert, Earl Kitchener of Khartoum 1850–1916. British soldier and administrator. He defeated the Sudanese dervishes at Omdurman 1898 and reoccupied Khartoum. In South Africa, he was Chief of Staff 1900–02 during the Boer War, and commanded the forces in India 1902–09. He was appointed war minister on the outbreak of World War I, and drowned when his ship was sunk on the way to Russia.

Knesset the Israeli parliament, consisting of a single chamber of 120 deputies elected for a period of four years.

Kohl Helmut 1930– . German conservative politician, leader of the Christian Democratic Union (CDU) from 1976, West German chancellor (prime minister) 1982–90. He oversaw the reunification of East and West Germany 1989–90 and in 1990 won a resounding victory to become the first chancellor of reunited Germany. His miscalculation of the true costs of reunification and their subsequent effects on the German economy led to a dramatic fall in his popularity.

Kolchak Alexander Vasilievich 1875–1920. Russian admiral, commander of the White forces in Siberia after the Russian Revolution. He proclaimed himself Supreme Ruler of Russia 1918, but was later handed over to the Bolsheviks by his own men and shot.

kolkhoz Russian term for a ◊collective farm, as opposed to a ◊sovkhoz or state-owned farm.

Kollontai Alexandra 1872–1952. Russian revolutionary, politician, and writer. In 1905 she published *On the Question of the Class Struggle*, and, as commissar for public welfare, was the only female member of the first Bolshevik government. She campaigned for domestic reforms such as acceptance of free love, simplification of divorce laws, and collective child care.

Komsomol Russian name for the All-Union Leninist Communist Youth League of the former Soviet Union. Founded 1918, it acted as the youth section of the Communist Party.

Koniev Ivan Stepanovich 1898–1973. Soviet marshal who in World War II liberated Ukraine from the invading German forces 1943 and advanced from the south on Berlin to link up with the British-US forces. He commanded all Warsaw Pact forces 1955–60.

Konoe Fumimaro, Prince 1891–1946. Japanese politician and prime minister 1937–39 and 1940–41. Entering politics in the 1920s, Konoe was active in trying to curb the power of the army in government and preventing an escalation of the war with China. He helped to engineer the fall of the ◊Tōjō government 1944 but committed suicide after being suspected of war crimes.

Korea, North country in E Asia, bounded NE by Russia, N and NW by China, E by the Sea of Japan, S by South Korea, and W by the Yellow Sea.

chronology
1910 Korea formally annexed by Japan.
1945 Russian and US troops entered Korea, forced surrender of Japanese, and divided the country in two. Soviet troops occupied ◊North Korea.
1948 Democratic People's Republic of Korea declared.
1950 North Korea invaded South Korea to unite the nation, beginning the Korean War.
1953 Armistice agreed to end Korean War.
1961 Friendship and mutual assistance treaty signed with China.
1972 New constitution, with executive president, adopted. Talks took place with South Korea about possible reunification.
1980 Reunification talks broke down.
1983 Four South Korean cabinet ministers assassinated in Rangoon, Burma (Myanmar), by North Korean army officers.
1985 Increased relations with the USSR.
1989 Increasing evidence shown of nuclear-weapons development.
1990 Diplomatic contacts with South Korea and Japan suggested the beginning of a thaw in North Korea's relations with the rest of the world.
1991 Became a member of the United Nations. Signed nonaggression agreement with South Korea; agreed to ban nuclear weapons.

1992 Signed Nuclear Safeguards Agreement, allowing international inspection of its nuclear facilities. Also signed a pact with South Korea for mutual inspection of nuclear facilities. Passed legislation making foreign investment in the country attractive. Yon Hyong Muk replaced by Kang Song San.

1993 March: government announced it was pulling out of Nuclear Non-Proliferation Treaty.

Korean War war 1950–53 between North Korea (supported by China) and South Korea, aided by the United Nations (the troops were mainly US). North Korean forces invaded the South 25 June 1950, and the Security Council of the United Nations, owing to a walk-out by the USSR, voted to oppose them. The North Koreans held most of the South when US reinforcements arrived Sept 1950 and forced their way through to the North Korean border with China. The Chinese retaliated, pushing them back to the original boundary Oct 1950; truce negotiations began 1951, although the war did not end until 1953.

Korea, South country in E Asia, bounded N by North Korea, E by the Sea of Japan, S by the Korea Strait, and W by the Yellow Sea.

chronology
1910 Korea formally annexed by Japan.
1945 Russian and US troops entered Korea, forced surrender of Japanese, and divided the country in two. US military government took control of South Korea.
1948 Republic proclaimed.
1950–53 War with North Korea.
1960 President Syngman ◊Rhee resigned amid unrest.
1961 Military coup by General ◊Park Chung-Hee. Industrial growth programme.
1979 Assassination of President Park.
1980 Military takeover by General Chun Doo Hwan.
1987 Adoption of more democratic constitution after student unrest. ◊Roh Tae Woo elected president.
1988 Former president Chun, accused of corruption, publicly apologized and agreed to hand over his financial assets to the state. Seoul hosted Summer Olympic Games.
1989 Roh reshuffled cabinet, threatened crackdown on protesters.
1990 Two minor opposition parties united with Democratic Justice Party to

form ruling Democratic Liberal Party (DLP). Diplomatic relations established with the USSR.

1991 Violent mass demonstrations against the government. New opposition grouping, the Democratic Party, formed. Prime Minister Ro Jai Bong replaced by Chung Won Shik. Entered United Nations (UN). Nonaggression and nuclear pacts signed with North Korea.

1992 DLP lost absolute majority in March general election; substantial gains made by Democratic Party and newly formed Unification National Party (UNP), led by Chung Ju Wong. Diplomatic relations with China established. Dec: ◊Kim Young Sam, DLP candidate, won the presidential election.

1993 Feb: Kim Young Sam assumed office. ◊Kim Dae Jung and Chung Ju Yung announced their retirement from active politics. Hwang In Sung appointed prime minister.

Kornilov Lavr 1870–1918. Russian general, commander in chief of the army, who in Aug 1917 launched an attempted coup, backed by officers, against the revolutionary prime minister, ◊Kerensky. The coup failed, but brought down the provisional government, thus clearing the way for the Bolsheviks to seize power.

Kosygin Alexei Nikolaievich 1904–1980. Soviet politician, prime minister 1964–80. He was elected to the Supreme Soviet 1938, became a member of the Politburo 1946, deputy prime minister 1960, and succeeded Khrushchev as premier (while Brezhnev succeeded him as party secretary). In the late 1960s Kosygin's influence declined.

Kravchuk Leonid 1934–   . Ukrainian politician, president from July 1990. Formerly a member of the Ukrainian Communist Party (UCP), he became its ideology chief in the 1980s. After the suspension of the UCP Aug 1991, Kravchuk became an advocate of independence and market-centred economic reform.

Krenz Egon 1937–   . German communist politician. A member of the East German Socialist Unity Party (SED) from 1955, he joined its politburo 1983 and was a hardline protégé of Erich ◊Honecker, succeeding him as party leader and head of state 1989 after widespread prodemocracy demonstrations. Pledging a 'new course', Krenz opened the country's western border and promised more open elections, but his conversion to pluralism proved weak in the face of popular protest and he resigned Dec 1989 after only a few weeks as party general secretary and head of state.

Krishna Menon Vengalil Krishnan 1897–1974. Indian politician who was a leading light in the Indian nationalist movement. He represented India at the United Nations 1952–62, and was defence minister 1957–62, when he was dismissed by Nehru following China's invasion of N India.

Kristallnacht 'night of (broken) glass' 9–10 Nov 1938 when the Nazi Sturmabteilung (SA) militia in Germany and Austria mounted a concerted attack on Jews, their synagogues, homes, and shops. It followed the assassination of a German embassy official in Paris by a Polish-Jewish youth. Subsequent measures included German legislation against Jews owning businesses or property, and restrictions on their going to school or leaving Germany. It was part of the ◊Holocaust.

Kronstadt uprising revolt in March 1921 by sailors of the Russian Baltic Fleet at their headquarters in Kronstadt, outside Petrograd (now St Petersburg). On the orders of the leading Bolshevik, Leon Trotsky, Red Army troops, dressed in white camouflage, crossed the ice to the naval base and captured it on 18 March. The leaders were subsequently shot.

Kropotkin Peter Alexeivich, Prince Kropotkin 1842–1921. Russian anarchist. Imprisoned for revolutionary activities 1874, he escaped to the UK 1876 and later moved to Switzerland. Expelled from Switzerland 1881, he went to France, where he was imprisoned 1883-86. He lived in Britain until 1917, when he returned to Moscow. Among his works are *Memoirs of a Revolutionist* 1899, *Mutual Aid* 1902, and *Modern Science and Anarchism* 1903.

Kubitschek Juscelino 1902–1976. Brazilian president 1956–61. His term as president saw political peace, civil liberty, and rapid economic growth at the cost of high inflation and corruption. He had a strong commitment to public works and the construction of Brasília as the nation's capital.

Ku Klux Klan US secret society dedicated to white supremacy, founded 1866 in the southern states of the USA to oppose Reconstruction after the American Civil War and to deny political rights to the black population. Members wore hooded white robes to hide their identity, and burned crosses at their night-time meetings. Today the Klan has evolved into a paramilitary extremist group that has forged loose ties with other white supremacist groups.

kulak Russian term for a peasant who could afford to hire labour and often acted as village usurer. The kulaks resisted the Soviet government's policy of collectivization, and in 1930 they were 'liquidated as a class', with up to 5 million being either killed or deported to Siberia.

Kulturkampf German word for a policy introduced by Chancellor Bismarck in Germany 1873 that isolated the Catholic interest and attempted to reduce its power in order to create a political coalition of liberals and agrarian conservatives. The alienation of such a large section of the German population as the Catholics could not be sustained, and the policy was abandoned after 1876 to be replaced by an anti-socialist policy.

Kun Béla 1885–1938. Hungarian politician who created a Soviet republic in Hungary March 1919, which was overthrown Aug 1919 by a Western blockade and Romanian military actions. The succeeding regime under Admiral Horthy effectively liquidated both socialism and liberalism in Hungary.

Küng Hans 1928–   . Swiss Roman Catholic theologian who was barred from teaching by the Vatican 1979 'in the name of the Church' because he had cast doubt on papal infallibility, and on whether Christ was the son of God.

Kuomintang original spelling of the Chinese nationalist party, now known (outside Taiwan) as ◊Guomindang.

Kurd member of the Kurdish culture, living mostly in the Taurus and Sagros mountains of W Iran and N Iraq in the region called Kurdistan. Although divided among more powerful states, the Kurds have nationalist aspirations; there are some 8 million in Turkey (where they suffer from discriminatory legislation), 5 million in Iran, 4 million in Iraq, 500,000 in Syria, and 500,000 in Azerbaijan, Armenia, and Georgia. Several million live elsewhere in Europe. Some 1 million Kurds were made homeless and 25,000 killed as a result of chemical-weapon attacks by Iraq 1984–89, and in 1991 more than 1 million were forced to flee their homes in N Iraq. The Kurdish languages (Kurmanji, Sorani Kurdish, Guraní, and Zaza) are members of the Indo-Iranian branch of the Indo-European family, and the Kurds are a non-Arab, non-Turkic ethnic group. The Kurds are predominantly Sunni Muslims, although there are some Shi'ites in Iran.

Kuwait country in SW Asia, bounded N and NW by Iraq, E by the Persian Gulf, and S and SW by Saudi Arabia.

chronology
1914 Britain recognized Kuwait as an independent sovereign state.
1961 Full independence achieved from Britain, with Sheik Abdullah al-Salem al-Sabah as emir.

1965 Sheik Abdullah died; succeeded by his brother, Sheik Sabah.

1977 Sheik Sabah died; succeeded by Crown Prince Jabir.

1983 Shi'ite guerrillas bombed targets in Kuwait; 17 arrested.

1986 National assembly suspended.

1987 Kuwaiti oil tankers reflagged, received US Navy protection; missile attacks by Iran.

1988 Aircraft hijacked by pro-Iranian Shi'ites demanding release of convicted guerrillas; Kuwait refused.

1989 Two of the convicted guerrillas released.

1990 Prodemocracy demonstrations suppressed. Kuwait annexed by Iraq. Emir set up government in exile in Saudi Arabia.

1991 Feb: Kuwait liberated by US-led coalition forces; extensive damage to property and environment. New government omitted any opposition representatives. Trials of alleged Iraqi collaborators criticized.

1992 Oct: reconstituted national assembly elected on restricted franchise, with opposition party winning majority of seats.

1993 Jan: incursions by Iraq into Kuwait again created tension; US-led air strikes restored calm.

Kyprianou Spyros 1932– . Cypriot politician, president 1977–88. Foreign minister 1961–72, he founded the federalist, centre-left Democratic Front (DIKO) 1976.

Kyrgyzstan or *Kirghizia* country in central Asia, bounded N by Kazakhstan, E by China, W by Uzbekistan, and S by Tajikistan.

chronology

1917–1924 Part of an independent Turkestan republic.

1924 Became autonomous republic within USSR.

1936 Became full union republic within USSR.

1990 June: ethnic clashes resulted in state of emergency being imposed in Bishkek. Nov: Askar Akayev chosen as state president.

1991 March: Kyrgyz voters endorsed maintenance of Union in USSR referendum. Aug: President Akayev condemned anti-Gorbachev attempted coup in Moscow; Kyrgyz Communist Party, which supported the coup, suspended. Oct: Akayev directly elected president. Dec: joined new Commonwealth of Independent States (CIS) and independence recognized by USA.

1992 Jan: admitted into Conference on Security and Cooperation in Europe (CSCE); March: became a member of the United Nations (UN). Dec: Supreme Soviet (parliament) renamed the Uluk Kenesh.

L

Labor Party in Australia, a political party based on socialist principles. It was founded in 1891 and first held office in 1904. It formed governments 1929–31 and 1939–49, but in the intervening periods internal discord provoked splits, and reduced its effectiveness. It returned to power under Gough Whitlam 1972–75, and again under Bob Hawke from 1983.

Labour Party UK political party based on socialist principles, originally formed to represent workers. It was founded in 1900 and first held office in 1924. The first majority Labour government 1945–51 introduced ⟡nationalization and the National Health Service, and expanded social security. Labour was again in power 1964–70 and 1974–79. The party leader is elected by Labour members of Parliament.

Labour Representation Committee in British politics, a forerunner 1900–1906 of the Labour Party. The committee was founded in Feb 1900 after a resolution drafted by Ramsay ⟡Macdonald and moved by the Amalgamated Society of Railway Workers (now the National Union of Railwaymen) was carried at the 1899 Trades Union Congress (TUC). The resolution called for a special congress of the TUC parliamentary committee to campaign for more Labour members of Parliament. Ramsay MacDonald became its secretary. Following his efforts, 29 Labour members of Parliament were elected in the 1906 general election, and the Labour Representation Committee was renamed the Labour Party.

La Follette Robert Marion 1855–1925. US political leader. A US senator 1906-25, he was a leader of the national progressive reform movement and unsuccessfully ran for president on the Progressive ticket 1924. His memoirs *Autobiography, A Personal Narrative of Political Experiences* appeared in 1913.

Lafontaine Oskar 1943– . German socialist politician, federal deputy chair of the Social Democrat Party (SPD) from 1987. Leader of the Saar regional branch of the SPD from 1977 and former mayor of Saarbrucken, he was nicknamed 'Red Oskar' because of his radical views on military and environmental issues. His attitude became more conservative once he had become minister-president of Saarland in 1985.

La Guardia Fiorello (Henrico) 1882–1947. US Republican politician; congressman 1917, 1919, 1923–33; mayor of New York 1933–45. Elected against the opposition of the powerful Tammany Hall Democratic Party organization, he improved the administration, suppressed racketeering, and organized unemployment relief, slum-clearance schemes, and social services. Although nominally a Republican, he supported the Democratic president F D Roosevelt's ♦New Deal. La Guardia Airport, in New York City, is named after him.

Lahore Resolution meeting in Lahore in March 1940 at which the Indian politician Muhammad Ali ♦Jinnah led the Muslim League in demanding the eventual partition of India and the creation of a Muslim state of Pakistan.

Lamont Norman 1942–   . UK Conservative politician, chief secretary of the Treasury 1989-90, chancellor of the Exchequer from 1990–93. In Sept 1992, despite earlier assurances to the contrary, he was forced to suspend Britain's membership of the European Monetary System (EMS).

Lancaster House Agreement accord reached at a conference held in Sept 1979 at Lancaster House, London, between Britain and representative groups of Rhodesia, including the Rhodesian government under Ian Smith and black nationalist groups. The Agreement enabled a smooth transition to the independent state of Zimbabwe in 1980.

Landon Alf(red Mossman) 1887–1987. US public official. As a popular liberal Republican, Landon ran for president against the incumbent F D Roosevelt 1936 but was overwhelmingly defeated. He later accepted a presidential appointment as US delegate to the 1938 Pan-American Conference.

Landsbergis Vytautas 1932–   . President of Lithuania 1990–1993. He became active in nationalist politics in the 1980s, founding and eventually chairing the anticommunist Sajudis independence movement 1988.

When Sajudis swept to victory in the republic's elections March 1990, Landsbergis chaired the Supreme Council of Lithuania becoming, in effect, president. He immediately drafted the republic's declaration of independence from the USSR which, after initial Soviet resistance, was recognized Sept 1991.

Lange David (Russell) 1942– . New Zealand Labour prime minister 1983–89. Lange, a barrister, was elected to the House of Representatives 1977. Labour had a decisive win in the 1984 general election on a non-nuclear military policy, which Lange immediately put into effect, despite criticism from the USA. He introduced a free-market economic policy and was re-elected 1987. He resigned Aug 1989 over a disagreement with his finance minister.

Lansbury George 1859–1940. British Labour politician, leader in the Commons 1931–35. He was a member of Parliament for Bow 1910–12— when he resigned to force a by-election on the issue of votes for women, which he lost—and again 1922–40. In 1921, while mayor of the London borough of Poplar, he went to prison with most of the council rather than modify their policy of more generous unemployment relief.

Lansdowne Henry Charles, 5th Marquis of Lansdowne 1845–1927. British Liberal Unionist politician, governor-general of Canada 1883–88, viceroy of India 1888–93, war minister 1895–1900, and foreign secretary 1900–06. While at the Foreign Office he abandoned Britain's isolationist policy by forming an alliance with Japan and an entente cordiale with France. His letter of 1917 suggesting an offer of peace to Germany created a controversy.

Laos landlocked country in SE Asia, bounded N by China, E by Vietnam, S by Cambodia, W by Thailand, and NW by Myanmar.

chronology
1893–1945 Laos was a French protectorate.
1945 Temporarily occupied by Japan.
1946 Retaken by France.
1950 Granted semi-autonomy in French Union.
1954 Independence achieved from France.
1960 Right-wing government seized power.
1962 Coalition government established; civil war continued.
1973 Vientiane cease-fire agreement. Withdrawal of US, Thai, and North Vietnamese forces.
1975 Communist-dominated republic proclaimed with Prince Souphanou-vong as head of state.
1986 Phoumi Vongvichit became acting president.
1988 Plans announced to withdraw 40% of Vietnamese forces stationed in the country.

1989 First assembly elections since communist takeover.

1991 Constitution approved. Kaysone Phomvihane elected president. General Khamtay Siphandon named as new premier.

1992 Question of US prisoners of war retained in Laos since the end of Vietnam War unresolved. Nov: Phomvihane died; replaced by Nouhak Phoumsavan. Dec: new national assembly created, replacing supreme people's assembly, and general election held (effectively one-party).

Largo Caballero Francisco 1869–1946. Spanish socialist and leader of the Spanish Socialist Party (PSOE). He became prime minister of the Popular Front government elected in Feb 1936 and remained in office for the first ten months of the Civil War before being replaced in May 1937 by Juan Negrin (1887–1956).

Laski Harold 1893–1950. British political theorist. Professor of political science at the London School of Economics from 1926, he taught a modified Marxism and published *A Grammar of Politics* 1925 and *The American Presidency* 1940. He was chairman of the Labour Party 1945–46.

Lassalle Ferdinand 1825–1864. German socialist. He was imprisoned for his part in the ◊revolution of 1848, during which he met the philosopher Karl ◊Marx, and in 1863 founded the General Association of German Workers (later the Social-Democratic Party). His publications include *The Working Man's Programme* 1862 and *The Open Letter* 1863. He was killed in a duel arising from a love affair.

Lateran Treaties series of agreements that marked the reconciliation of the Italian state with the papacy in 1929. They were hailed as a propaganda victory for the Fascist regime. The treaties involved recognition of the sovereignty of the ◊Vatican City State, the payment of an indemnity for papal possessions lost during unification in 1870, and agreement on the role of the Catholic church within the Italian state in the form of a concordat between Pope Pius XI and the dictator Mussolini.

Latvia country in N Europe, bounded E by Russia, N by Estonia, N and NW by the Baltic Sea, S by Lithuania, and SE by Belarus.

chronology

1917 Soviets and Germans contested for control of Latvia.

1918 Feb: Soviet forces overthrown by Germany. Nov: Latvia declared independence. Dec: Soviet rule restored after German withdrawal.

1919 Soviet rule overthrown by British naval and German forces May–Dec; democracy established.

1934 Coup replaced established government.

1939 German-Soviet secret agreement placed Latvia under Russian influence.

1940 Incorporated into USSR as constituent republic.

1941–44 Occupied by Germany.

1944 USSR regained control.

1980 Nationalist dissent began to grow.

1988 Latvian Popular Front established to campaign for independence. Prewar flag readopted; official status given to Latvian language.

1989 Popular Front swept local elections.

1990 Jan: Communist Party's monopoly of power abolished. March–April: Popular Front secured majority in elections. April: Latvian Communist Party split into pro-independence and pro-Moscow wings. May: unilateral declaration of independence from USSR, subject to transitional period for negotiation.

1991 Jan: Soviet troops briefly seized key installations in Riga. March: overwhelming vote for independence in referendum. Aug: full independence declared at time of anti-Gorbachev coup; Communist Party outlawed. Sept: independence recognized by Soviet government and Western nations; United Nations (UN) membership granted; admitted into Conference on Security and Cooperation in Europe (CSCE).

1992 US reopened its embassy in Latvia. Russia began pullout of ex-Soviet troops, to be completed 1994. July: curbing of rights of non-citizens in Latvia prompted Russia to request minority protection by UN.

Laurier Wilfrid 1841–1919. Canadian politician, leader of the Liberal Party 1887–1919 and prime minister 1896–1911. The first French-Canadian to hold the office, he encouraged immigration into Canada from Europe and the USA, established a separate Canadian navy, and sent troops to help Britain in the Boer War.

Lausanne, Treaty of peace settlement in 1923 between Greece and Turkey after Turkey refused to accept the terms of the Treaty of Sèvres 1920, which would have made peace with the western Allies. It involved the surrender by Greece of Smyrna (now Izmir) to Turkey and the enforced exchange of the Greek population of Smyrna for the Turkish population of Greece.

Laval Pierre 1883–1945. French right-wing politician. He was prime minister and foreign secretary 1931–32, and again 1935–36. In World War II he joined Pétain's ◊Vichy government as vice-premier in June 1940; dismissed in Dec 1940, he was reinstated by Hitler's orders as head of the government and foreign minister in 1942. After the war he was executed.

Law Andrew Bonar 1858–1923. British Conservative politician. Elected leader of the opposition 1911, he became colonial secretary in Asquith's coalition government 1915–16, chancellor of the Exchequer 1916–19, and Lord Privy Seal 1919–21 in Lloyd George's coalition. He formed a Conservative Cabinet 1922, but resigned on health grounds.

Lawrence T(homas) E(dward), known as *Lawrence of Arabia* 1888–1935. British soldier and writer. Appointed to the military intelligence department in Cairo, Egypt, during World War I, he took part in negotiations for an Arab revolt against the Ottoman Turks, and in 1916 attached himself to the emir Faisal. He became a guerrilla leader of genius, combining raids on Turkish communications with the organization of a joint Arab revolt, described in *The Seven Pillars of Wisdom* 1926.

Lawson Nigel 1932– . British Conservative politician. A former financial journalist, he was financial secretary to the Treasury 1979–81, secretary of state for energy 1981–83, and chancellor of the Exchequer from 1983. He resigned 1989 after criticism by government adviser Alan Walters over his policy of British membership of the European Monetary System.

League of Nations international organization formed after World War I to solve international disputes by arbitration. Established in Geneva, Switzerland, 1920, the league included representatives from states throughout the world, but was severely weakened by the US decision not to become a member, and had no power to enforce its decisions. It was dissolved 1946. Its subsidiaries included the *International Labour Organization* and the *Permanent Court of International Justice* in The Hague, Netherlands, both now under the auspices of the ◊United Nations.

Lebanon country in W Asia, bounded N and E by Syria, S by Israel, and W by the Mediterranean Sea.

chronology
1920–41 Administered under French mandate.
1944 Independence achieved.

1948–49 Lebanon joined first Arab war against Israel. Palestinian refugees settled in the south.

1964 ◊Palestine Liberation Organization (PLO) founded in Beirut.

1967 More Palestinian refugees settled in Lebanon.

1971 PLO expelled from Jordan; established headquarters in Lebanon.

1975 Outbreak of civil war between Christians and Muslims.

1976 Cease-fire agreed; Syrian-dominated Arab deterrent force formed to keep the peace but considered by Christians as a occupying force.

1978 Israel invaded S Lebanon in search of PLO fighters. International peacekeeping force established. Fighting broke out again.

1979 Part of S Lebanon declared an 'independent free Lebanon'.

1982 Bachir ◊Gemayel became president but was assassinated before he could assume office; succeeded by his brother Amin Gemayel. Israel again invaded Lebanon. Palestinians withdrew from Beirut under supervision of international peacekeeping force. PLO moved its headquarters to Tunis.

1983 Agreement reached for the withdrawal of Syrian and Israeli troops but abrogated under Syrian pressure.

1984 Most of international peacekeeping force withdrawn. Muslim militia took control of W Beirut.

1985 Lebanon in chaos; many foreigners taken hostage.

1987 Syrian troops sent into Beirut.

1988 Agreement on a Christian successor to Gemayel failed; he established a military government; Selim al-Hoss set up rival government; threat of partition hung over the country.

1989 Christian leader General Michel ◊Aoun declared 'war of liberation' against Syrian occupation; Saudi Arabia and Arab League sponsored talks that resulted in new constitution recognizing Muslim majority; René Muhawad named president, assassinated after 17 days in office; Elias Hrawi named successor; Aoun occupied presidential palace, rejected constitution.

1990 Release of Western hostages began. General Aoun surrendered and legitimate government restored, with Umar Karami as prime minister.

1991 Government extended control to the whole country. Treaty of cooperation with Syria signed. More Western hostages released. General Aoun pardoned.

1992 Karami resigned as prime minister; succeeded by Rashid al-Solh. Remaining Western hostages released. General election boycotted by many Christians; pro-Syrian administration reelected; Rafik al-Hariri became prime minister.

Lebensraum theory developed by Hitler for the expansion of Germany into E Europe, and in the 1930s used by the Nazis to justify their annexation of neighbouring states on the grounds that Germany was overpopulated.

Lebrun Albert 1871–1950. French politician. He became president of the senate in 1931 and in 1932 was chosen as president of the republic. In 1940 he handed his powers over to Marshal Pétain.

Le Duc Tho 1911–1990. North Vietnamese diplomat who was joint winner (with US secretary of state Kissinger) of the 1973 Nobel Peace Prize for his part in the negotiations to end the Vietnam War. He indefinitely postponed receiving the award.

Lee Jennie, Baroness Lee 1904–1988. British socialist politician. She became a member of Parliament for the ◊Independent Labour Party at the age of 24, and in 1934 married Aneurin ◊Bevan. On the left wing of the Labour Party, she was on its National Executive Committee 1958–70 and was minister of education 1967–70, during which time she was responsible for founding the Open University in 1969. She was made a baroness in 1970.

Lee Kuan Yew 1923–   . Singapore politician, prime minister 1959–90. Lee founded the anticommunist Socialist People's Action Party 1954 and entered the Singapore legislative assembly 1955. He was elected the country's first prime minister 1959, and took Singapore out of the Malaysian federation 1965. He remained in power until his resignation 1990, and was succeeded by Goh Chok Tong.

Lee Teng-hui 1923–   . Taiwanese right-wing politician, vice president 1984–88, president and Kuomintang (see ◊Guomindang) party leader from 1988. Lee, the country's first island-born leader, is viewed as a reforming technocrat.

Lehman Herbert Henry 1878–1963. US political leader. In 1932 he became governor of New York, and his subsequent support of F D Roosevelt's reform policies earned his own administration the name 'Little New Deal'. In 1942 Lehman was appointed director of the federal Office of Foreign Relief and Rehabilitation. He served in the US Senate 1949–57.

lend-lease in US history, an act of Congress passed in March 1941 that gave the president power to order 'any defense article for the government of any country whose defense the president deemed vital to the defense of the

USA'. During World War II, the USA negotiated many Lend-Lease agreements, notably with Britain and the Soviet Union.

Lenin Vladimir Ilyich. Adopted name of Vladimir Ilyich Ulyanov 1870–1924. Russian revolutionary, first leader of the USSR, and communist theoretician. Active in the 1905 Revolution, Lenin had to leave Russia when it failed, settling in Switzerland in 1914. He returned to Russia after the February revolution of 1917 (see ◊Russian Revolution). He led the Bolshevik revolution in Nov 1917 and became leader of a Soviet government, concluded peace with Germany, and organized a successful resistance to White Russian (pro-tsarist) uprisings and foreign intervention 1918–20. His modification of traditional Marxist doctrine to fit conditions prevailing in Russia became known as *Marxism-Leninism*, the basis of communist ideology.

Leopold III 1901–1983. King of the Belgians 1934–51. He surrendered to the German army in World War II 1940. Postwar charges against his conduct led to a regency by his brother Charles and his eventual abdication 1951 in favour of his son Baudouin.

Le Pen Jean-Marie 1928– . French extreme right-wing politician. In 1972 he formed the French National Front, supporting immigrant repatriation and capital punishment; the party gained 14% of the national vote in the 1986 election. Le Pen was elected to the European Parliament in 1984.

Lesotho landlocked country in southern Africa, an enclave within South Africa.

chronology
1868 Basutoland became a British protectorate.
1966 Independence achieved from Britain, within the Commonwealth, as the Kingdom of Lesotho, with Moshoeshoe II as king and Chief Leabua ◊Jonathan as prime minister.
1970 State of emergency declared and constitution suspended.
1973 Progovernment interim assembly established; Basotha National Party (BNP) won majority of seats.
1975 Members of the ruling party attacked by guerrillas backed by South Africa.
1985 Elections cancelled because no candidates opposed BNP.
1986 South Africa imposed border blockade, forcing deportation of 60 African National Congress members. General Lekhanya ousted Chief

Jonathan in coup. National assembly abolished. Highlands Water Project agreement signed with South Africa.

1990 Moshoeshoe II dethroned by military council; replaced by his son Mohato as King Letsie III.

1991 Lekhanya ousted in military coup led by Col Elias Tutsoane Ramaema. Political parties permitted to operate.

1992 Ex-king Moshoeshoe returned from exile.

1993 Free elections ended military rule; Ntsu Mokhehle of the Basutoland Congress Party (BCP) became prime minister.

Lévesque René 1922–1987. French-Canadian politician. In 1968 he founded the Parti Québecois, with the aim of an independent Québec, but a referendum rejected the proposal in 1980. He was premier of Québec 1976–85.

Lewis John L(lewellyn) 1880–1969. US labour leader. President of the United Mine Workers (UMW) 1920-60, he was largely responsible for the adoption of national mining safety standards in the USA. His militancy and the miners' strikes during and after World War II, led to President Truman's nationalization of the mines in 1946.

Liaquat Ali Khan Nawabzada 1895–1951. Indian politician, deputy leader of the ◊Muslim League 1940–47, first prime minister of Pakistan from 1947. He was assassinated by objectors to his peace policy with India.

Liberal Party British political party, the successor to the Whig Party, with an ideology of liberalism. In the 19th century, it represented the interests of commerce and industry. Its outstanding leaders were Palmerston, Gladstone, and Lloyd George. From 1914 it declined, and the rise of the Labour Party pushed the Liberals into the middle ground. The Liberals joined forces with the Social Democratic Party (SDP) as the Alliance for the 1983 and 1987 elections. In 1988, a majority of the SDP voted to merge with the Liberals to form the Social and Liberal Democrats.

Liberal Party, Australian political party established 1944 by Robert Menzies, after a Labor landslide, and derived from the former United Australia Party. After the voters rejected Labor's extensive nationalization plans, the Liberals were in power 1949–72 and 1975–83 and were led in succession by Harold Holt, John Gorton, William McMahon (1908–), Billy Snedden (1926–), and Malcolm Fraser.

Liberia country in W Africa, bounded N by Guinea, E by the Ivory Coast, S and SW by the Atlantic Ocean, and NW by Sierra Leone.

chronology
1847 Founded as an independent republic.
1944 William ◊Tubman elected president.
1971 Tubman died; succeeded by William Tolbert.
1980 Tolbert assassinated in coup led by Samuel ◊Doe, who suspended the constitution and ruled through a People's Redemption Council.
1984 New constitution approved. National Democratic Party of Liberia (NDPL) founded by Doe.
1985 NDPL won decisive victory in general election. Unsuccessful coup against Doe.
1990 Rebels under former government minister Charles Taylor controlled nearly entire country by July. Doe killed during a bloody civil war between rival rebel factions. Amos Sawyer became interim head of government.
1991 Amos Sawyer re-elected president. Rebel leader Charles Taylor agreed to work with Sawyer. Peace agreement failed but later revived; UN peacekeeping force drafted into republic.
1992 Monrovia under siege by Taylor's rebel forces.

Libya country in N Africa, bounded N by the Mediterranean Sea, E by Egypt, SE by Sudan, S by Chad and Niger, and W by Algeria and Tunisia.

chronology
1911 Conquered by Italy.
1934 Colony named Libya.
1942 Divided into three provinces: Fezzan (under French control); Cyrenaica, Tripolitania (under British control).
1951 Achieved independence as the United Kingdom of Libya, under King Idris.
1969 King deposed in a coup led by Col Moamer al- ◊Khaddhafi. Revolution Command Council set up and the Arab Socialist Union (ASU) proclaimed the only legal party.
1972 Proposed federation of Libya, Syria, and Egypt abandoned.
1980 Proposed merger with Syria abandoned. Libyan troops began fighting in Chad.
1981 Proposed merger with Chad abandoned.
1986 US bombing of Khaddhafi's headquarters, following allegations of his complicity in terrorist activities.
1988 Diplomatic relations with Chad restored.

1989 USA accused Libya of building a chemical-weapons factory and shot down two Libyan planes; reconciliation with Egypt.

1992 Khaddhafi under international pressure to extradite suspected Lockerbie and UTA (Union de Transports Aerians) bombers for trial outside Libya; sanctions imposed.

Lidice Czechoslovak mining village, replacing one destroyed by the Nazis on 10 June 1942 as a reprisal for the assassination of Reinhard ◊Heydrich. The men were shot, the women sent to concentration camps, and the children taken to Germany. The officer responsible was hanged in 1946.

Lie Trygve (Halvdan) 1896–1968. Norwegian Labour politician and diplomat. He became secretary of the Labour Party in 1926. During the German occupation of Norway in World War II he was foreign minister in the exiled government 1941–46, when he helped retain the Norwegian fleet for the Allies. He became the first secretary general of the United Nations 1946–53, but resigned over Soviet opposition to his handling of the Korean War.

Liebknecht Karl 1871–1919. German socialist, son of Wilhelm Liebknecht. A founder of the German Communist Party, originally known as the Spartacus League (see ◊Spartacist) 1918, he was one of the few socialists who refused to support World War I. He led an unsuccessful revolt with Rosa Luxemburg in Berlin in 1919 and both were murdered by army officers.

Liechtenstein landlocked country in W central Europe, bounded E by Austria and W by Switzerland.

chronology
1921 Adopted Swiss currency.
1923 United with Switzerland in a customs union.
1938 Prince Franz Josef II came to power.
1984 Prince Franz Joseph II handed over power to Crown Prince Hans Adam. Vote extended to women in national elections.
1989 Prince Franz Joseph II died; Hans Adam II succeeded him.
1990 Became a member of the United Nations (UN).
1991 Became seventh member of European Free Trade Association.

Ligachev Egor (Kuzmich) 1920–   . Soviet politician. He joined the Communist Party 1944, and became a member of the Politburo 1985. He was replaced as the party ideologist in 1988 by Vadim Medvedev.

Likud alliance of right-wing Israeli political parties that defeated the Labour Party coalition in the May 1977 election and brought Menachem Begin to power. In 1987 Likud became part of an uneasy national coalition with Labour, formed to solve Israel's economic crisis. In 1989 another coalition was formed under Shamir.

Lima Declaration agreement sponsored by US President F D Roosevelt at the Pan-American Conference Dec 1938 which held that a threat to the peace, security, or territory of any of the American republics would be a source of concern to all the republics. It was designed primarily to safeguard the American continent from the spread of fascism from Europe and provide the USA and other states with a general mandate for intervention if necessary.

Liman von Sanders Otto 1855–1929. German general assigned to the Turkish army to become inspector-general and a Turkish field marshal in Dec 1913. This link between the Turks and the Germans caused great suspicion on the part of the French and Russians.

Lin Biao or *Lin Piao* 1907–1971. Chinese politician and general. He joined the communists in 1927, became a commander of ◊Mao Zedong's Red Army, and led the Northeast People's Liberation Army in the civil war after 1945. He became defence minister in 1959, and as vice chair of the party in 1969 he was expected to be Mao's successor. But in 1972 the government announced that Lin had been killed in an aeroplane crash in Mongolia on 17 Sept 1971 while fleeing to the USSR following an abortive coup attempt.

Li Peng 1928–   . Chinese communist politician, a member of the Politburo from 1985, and head of government from 1987. During the pro-democracy demonstrations of 1989 he supported the massacre of students by Chinese troops and the subsequent execution of others. He sought improved relations with the USSR prior to its demise, and has favoured maintaining firm central and party control over the economy.

Lithuania country in N Europe, bounded N by Latvia, E by Belarus, S by Poland and the Kaliningrad area of Russia, and W by the Baltic Sea.

chronology
1918 Independence declared following withdrawal of German occupying troops at end of World War I; USSR attempted to regain power.
1919 Soviet forces overthrown by Germans, Poles, and nationalist Lithuanians; democratic republic established.

1920–39 Province and city of Vilnius occupied by Poles.

1926 Coup overthrew established government; Antanas Smetona became president.

1939 Secret German-Soviet agreement brought most of Lithuania under Soviet influence.

1940 Incorporated into USSR as constituent republic.

1941 Lithuania revolted against USSR and established own government. During World War II Germany again occupied the country.

1944 USSR resumed rule.

1944–52 Lithuanian guerrillas fought USSR.

1972 Demonstrations against Soviet government.

1980 Growth in nationalist dissent, influenced by Polish example.

1988 Popular front formed, the Sajudis, to campaign for increased autonomy.

1989 Lithuanian declared the state language; flag of independent interwar republic readopted. Communist Party (CP) split into pro-Moscow and nationalist wings. Communist local monopoly of power abolished.

1990 Feb: nationalist Sajudis won elections. March: Vytautas Landsbergis became president; unilateral declaration of independence resulted in temporary Soviet blockade.

1991 Jan: Albertas Shiminas became prime minister. Soviet paratroopers briefly occupied key buildings in Vilnius. Sept: independence recognized by Soviet government and Western nations; Gediminas Vagnorius elected prime minister; CP outlawed; admitted into United Nations (UN) and Conference on Security and Cooperation in Europe (CSCE).

1992 July: Aleksandras Abisala became prime minister. Nov: Democratic Labour Party, led by Algirdas Brazauskas, won majority vote. Dec: Bronislovas Lubys appointed prime minister.

1993 Brazauskas elected president.

Little Entente series of alliances between Czechoslovakia, Romania, and Yugoslavia 1920–21 for mutual security and the maintenance of existing frontiers. Reinforced by the Treaty of Belgrade 1929, the entente collapsed upon Yugoslav cooperation with Germany 1935–38 and the Anglo- French abandonment of Czechoslovakia in 1938.

Little Red Book book of aphorisms and quotations from the speeches and writings by ◊Mao Zedong, in which he adapted Marxist theory to Chinese conditions. Published 1966, the book was printed in huge numbers and read widely at the start of the ◊Cultural Revolution.

Litvinov Maxim 1876–1951. Soviet politician, commissioner for foreign affairs under Stalin from Jan 1931 until his removal from office in May 1939.

Liu Shaoqi or *Liu Shao-chi* 1898–1969. Chinese communist politician, in effective control of government 1960–65. A Moscow-trained labour organizer, he was a firm proponent of the Soviet style of government based around disciplined one-party control, the use of incentive gradings, and priority for industry over agriculture. This was opposed by ◊Mao Zedong, but began to be implemented by Liu while he was state president 1960–65. Liu was brought down during the ◊Cultural Revolution.

Livingstone Ken(neth) 1945– . British left-wing Labour politician. He was leader of the Greater London Council (GLC) 1981–86 and a member of Parliament from 1987. He stood as a candidate for the Labour Party leadership elections 1992.

Li Xiannian 1905–1992. Chinese politician, member of the Chinese Communist Party (CCP) Politburo from 1956. He fell from favour during the 1966–69 Cultural Revolution, but was rehabilitated as finance minister in 1973, supporting cautious economic reform. He was state president 1983–88.

Lloyd Selwyn. See ◊Selwyn Lloyd, British Conservative politician.

Lloyd George David 1863–1945. Welsh Liberal politician, prime minister of Britain 1916–22. A pioneer of social reform, as chancellor of the Exchequer 1908–15 he introduced old-age pensions 1908 and health and unemployment insurance 1911. High unemployment, intervention in the Russian Civil War, and use of the military police force, the ◊Black and Tans, in Ireland eroded his support as prime minister, and the creation of the Irish Free State in 1921 and his pro-Greek policy against the Turks caused the collapse of his coalition government.

Locarno, Pact of series of diplomatic documents initialled in Locarno, Switzerland, 16 Oct 1925 and formally signed in London 1 Dec 1925. The pact settled the question of French security, and the signatories—Britain, France, Belgium, Italy, and Germany—guaranteed Germany's existing frontiers with France and Belgium. Following the signing of the pact, Germany was admitted to the League of Nations.

Lodge Henry Cabot 1850–1924. US politician, Republican senator from 1893, and chair of the Senate Foreign Relations Committee after World

War I. He supported conservative economic legislation at home but expansionist policies abroad. Nevertheless, he influenced the USA to stay out of the ◊League of Nations 1920 as a threat to US sovereignty.

Lodge Henry Cabot, II 1902–1985. US diplomat. He was Eisenhower's presidential campaign manager and the US representative at the United Nations 1953–60. Ambassador to South Vietnam 1963–64 and 1965–67, he replaced W A Harriman as President Nixon's negotiator in the Vietnam peace talks 1969. He was a grandson of Henry Cabot Lodge.

Lomé Convention convention in 1975 that established economic cooperation between the European Community and African, Caribbean, and Pacific countries. It was renewed 1979 and 1985.

London, Treaty of secret treaty signed 26 April 1915 between Britain, France, Russia, and Italy. It promised Italy territorial gains (at the expense of Austria-Hungary) on condition that it entered World War I on the side of the Triple Entente (Britain, France, and Russia). Italy's intervention did not achieve the rapid victories expected, and the terms of the treaty (revealed by Russia 1918), angered the USA. Britain and France refused to honour the treaty and, in the post-war peace treaties, Italy received far less territory than promised.

Long Huey 1893–1935. US Democratic politician, nicknamed 'the Kingfish', governor of Louisiana 1928–31, US senator for Louisiana 1930–35, legendary for his political rhetoric. He was popular with poor white voters for his programme of social and economic reform, which he called the 'Share Our Wealth' programme. It represented a significant challenge to F D Roosevelt's ◊New Deal economic programme.

Longford Frank (Francis Aungier) Pakenham, 7th Earl of Longford 1905– . Anglo-Irish Labour politician. He was brought up a Protestant but is now a leading Catholic. He is an advocate of penal reform.

Long March in Chinese history, the 10,000 km/6,000 mi trek undertaken 1934–35 by ◊Mao Zedong and his communist forces from SE to NW China, under harassment from the Guomindang (nationalist) army.

Louis, Prince of Battenberg 1854–1921. German-born British admiral who took British nationality in 1917 and translated his name to Mountbatten.

Lubbers Rudolph Franz Marie (Ruud) 1939– . Dutch politician, prime minister of the Netherlands from 1982. Leader of the Christian Democratic

Appeal (CDA), he is politically right of centre. He became minister for economic affairs 1973.

Ludendorff Erich von 1865–1937. German general, chief of staff to ◊Hindenburg in World War I, and responsible for the eastern-front victory at the Battle of ◊Tannenberg in 1914. After Hindenburg's appointment as chief of general staff and Ludendorff's as quartermaster-general in 1916, he was also politically influential. He took part in the Nazi rising in Munich in 1923 and sat in the Reichstag (parliament) as a right-wing Nationalist.

Ludwig III 1845–1921. King of Bavaria 1913–18, when he abdicated upon the formation of a republic.

Luftwaffe German air force. In World War I and, as reorganized by the Nazi leader Hermann Goering in 1933, in World War II. The Luftwaffe also covered anti-aircraft defence and the launching of the flying bombs ◊V1 and V2.

Lugard Frederick John Dealtry, 1st Baron Lugard 1858–1945. British colonial administrator. He served in the army 1878–89 and then worked for the British East Africa Company, for whom he took possession of Uganda in 1890. He was high commissioner for N Nigeria 1900–07, governor of Hong Kong 1907–12, and governor general of Nigeria 1914–19.

Lumumba Patrice 1926–1961. Congolese politician, prime minister of Zaire 1960. Imprisoned by the Belgians, but released in time to attend the conference giving the Congo independence in 1960, he led the National Congolese Movement to victory in the subsequent general election. He was deposed in a coup d'état, and murdered some months later.

Lusitania ocean liner sunk by a German submarine on 7 May 1915 with the loss of 1,200 lives, including some Americans; its destruction helped to bring the USA into World War I.

Luthuli or *Lutuli* Albert 1899–1967. South African politician, president of the African National Congress 1952–67. Luthuli, a Zulu tribal chief, preached nonviolence and multiracialism.

Luxembourg landlocked country in W Europe, bounded N and W by Belgium, E by Germany, and S by France.

chronology
1948 With Belgium and the Netherlands, formed the Benelux customs union.

1960 Benelux became fully effective economic union.

1961 Prince Jean became acting head of state on behalf of his mother, Grand Duchess Charlotte.

1964 Grand Duchess Charlotte abdicated; Prince Jean became grand duke.

1974 Dominance of Christian Social Party challenged by Socialists.

1979 Christian Social Party regained pre-eminence.

1991 Pact agreeing European free-trade area signed in Luxembourg.

1992 Voted in favour of ratification of Maastricht Treaty on European union.

Luxembourg Accord French-initiated agreement in 1966 that a decision of the Council of Ministers of the European Community may be vetoed by a member whose national interests are at stake.

Luxemburg Rosa 1870–1919. Polish-born German communist. She helped found the Polish Social Democratic Party in the 1890s (which later became the Polish Communist Party). She was a leader of the left wing of the German Social Democratic Party from 1898 and collaborator with Karl Liebknecht in founding the communist Spartacus League 1918 (see ◊Spartacist). She was murdered with him by army officers during the Jan 1919 Berlin workers' revolt.

Lynch 'Jack' (John) 1917–   . Irish politician, prime minister 1966–73 and 1977–79. A Gaelic footballer and a barrister, in 1948 he entered the parliament of the republic as a Fianna Fáil member.

Lyons Joseph Aloysius 1879–1939. Australian politician, founder of the United Australia Party 1931, prime minister 1932–39.

M

Maastricht Treaty treaty on European union, signed 10 Dec 1991 by leaders of European Community (EC) nations at Maastricht in the Netherlands, at a meeting convened to agree on terms for political union. The treaty was formally endorsed by the European Parliament April 1992 but its subsequent rejection by the Danish in a June referendum placed its future in jeopardy. Survival of the treaty appeared more certain after an Edinburgh summit Dec 1992, at which EC leaders agreed to a set of compromises, including limited Danish participation.

MacArthur Douglas 1880–1964. US general in World War II, commander of US forces in the Far East and, from March 1942, of the Allied forces in the SW Pacific. After the surrender of Japan he commanded the Allied occupation forces there. During 1950 he commanded the UN forces in Korea, but in April 1951, after expressing views contrary to US and UN policy, he was relieved of all his commands by President Truman.

McCarran Patrick 1876–1954. US Democrat politician. He became senator for Nevada 1932, and as an isolationist strongly opposed lend-lease during World War II. He sponsored the McCarran–Walter Immigration and Nationality Act of 1952, which severely restricted entry and immigration to the USA; the act was amended 1965.

McCarthy Eugene (Joseph) 1916– . US politician. He was elected to the US House of Representatives 1948 and to the US Senate 1958. An early opponent of the Vietnam War, he ran for president 1968. Although his upset victory in the New Hampshire primary forced incumbent L B Johnson out of the race, McCarthy lost the Democratic nomination to Hubert Humphrey.

McCarthy Joe (Joseph Raymond) 1908–1957. US right-wing Republican politician. His unsubstantiated claim 1950 that the State Department and US army had been infiltrated by communists started a wave of anticommunist hysteria, wild accusations, and blacklists, which continued until he was discredited 1954. He was censured by the US senate for misconduct.

McCone John Alex 1902–1991. US industrialist, head of the Central Intelligence Agency (CIA) in the 1960s. A devout Catholic and a fervent opponent of communism, he declined to use extreme measures to secure some of the political ends his political masters sought.

MacDonald (James) Ramsay 1866–1937. British politician, first Labour prime minister Jan–Oct 1924 and 1929–31. Failing to deal with worsening economic conditions, he left the party to form a coalition government 1931, which was increasingly dominated by Conservatives, until he was replaced by Stanley Baldwin 1935.

McGovern George (Stanley) 1922– . US politician. A Democrat, he was elected to the US House of Representatives 1956, served as an adviser to the Kennedy administration, and was a US senator 1962-80. He won the presidential nomination 1968, but was soundly defeated by the incumbent Richard Nixon.

Machel Samora 1933–1986. Mozambique nationalist leader, president 1975–86. Machel was active in the liberation front ◊Frelimo from its conception 1962, fighting for independence from Portugal. He became Frelimo leader 1966, and Mozambique's first president from independence 1975 until his death in a plane crash near the South African border.

Mackensen August von 1849–1945. German field marshal. During ◊World War I he achieved the breakthrough at Gorlice and the conquest of Serbia 1915, and in 1916 played a major role in the overthrow of Romania.

MacLennan Robert (Adam Ross) 1936– . Scottish centrist politician; member of Parliament for Caithness and Sutherland from 1966. He left the Labour Party for the Social Democrats (SDP) 1981, and was SDP leader 1988 during merger negotiations with the Liberals. He then became a member of the new Social and Liberal Democrats.

Macleod Iain Norman 1913–1970. British Conservative politician. As colonial secretary 1959–61, he forwarded the independence of former British territories in Africa; he died in office as chancellor of the Exchequer.

Macmillan (Maurice) Harold, 1st Earl of Stockton 1894–1986. British Conservative politician, prime minister 1957–63; foreign secretary 1955 and chancellor of the Exchequer 1955–57. In 1963 he attempted to negotiate British entry into the European Economic Community, but was blocked by French president de Gaulle. Much of his career as prime minister was spent defending the retention of a UK nuclear weapon, and he was responsible for the purchase of US Polaris missiles 1962.

MAD abbreviation for *mutual assured destruction*; the basis of the theory of deterrence by possession of nuclear weapons.

Madagascar island country in the Indian Ocean, off the coast of E Africa, about 400 km/280 mi from Mozambique.

chronology
1896 Became a French colony.
1960 Independence achieved from France, with Philibert Tsiranana as president.
1972 Army took control of the government.
1975 Martial law imposed under a national military directorate. New Marxist constitution proclaimed the Democratic Republic of Madagascar, with Didier Ratsiraka as president.
1976 Front-Line Revolutionary Organization (AREMA) formed.
1977 National Front for the Defence of the Malagasy Socialist Revolution (FNDR) became the sole legal political organization.
1980 Ratsiraka abandoned Marxist experiment.
1983 Ratsiraka re-elected, despite strong opposition from radical socialist National Movement for the Independence of Madagascar (MONIMA) under Monja Jaona.
1989 Ratsiraka re-elected for third term after restricting opposition parties.
1990 Political opposition legalized; 36 new parties created.
1991 Antigovernment demonstrations; opposition to Ratsiraka led to general strike. Nov: Ratsiraka formed new unity government.
1992 Constitutional reform approved. Oct: first multiparty elections won by Democrat coalition.
1993 Albert Zafy, leader of coalition, elected president.

Maginot Line French fortification system along the German frontier from Switzerland to Luxembourg built 1929–36 under the direction of the war minister, André Maginot. It consisted of semi-underground forts joined by underground passages, and protected by antitank defences; lighter fortifications continued the line to the sea. In 1940 German forces pierced the Belgian frontier line and outflanked the Maginot Line.

Maiziere Lothar de 1940–   . German conservative politician, leader of the former East German Christian Democratic Union. He became premier after East Germany's first democratic elections in April 1990, until German reunification Oct 1990.

Major John 1943–   . British Conservative politician, prime minister from Nov 1990.

He was foreign secretary 1989 and chancellor of the Exchequer 1989–90. His earlier positive approach to European Community (EC) matters was hindered during 1991 by divisions within the Conservative Party. Despite continuing public dissatisfaction with the poll tax, the National Health Service, and the recession, Major was returned to power in the April 1992 general election. His subsequent handling of a series of political crises called into question his ability to govern the country effectively.

Makarios III 1913–1977. Cypriot politician, Greek Orthodox archbishop 1950–77. A leader of the Resistance organization ◊EOKA, he was exiled by the British to the Seychelles 1956–57 for supporting armed action to achieve union with Greece (*enosis*). He was president of the republic of Cyprus 1960–77 (briefly deposed by a Greek military coup July–Dec 1974).

Malawi country in SE Africa, bounded N and NE by Tanzania; E, S, and W by Mozambique; and W by Zambia.

chronology
1891 Became the British protectorate Nyasaland.
1964 Independence achieved from Britain, within the Commonwealth, as Malawi.
1966 Became a one-party republic, with Hastings ◊Banda as president.
1971 Banda was made president for life.
1977 Banda released some political detainees and allowed greater freedom of the press.
1986-89 Influx of nearly 1 million refugees from Mozambique.
1992 Calls for multiparty politics. Countrywide industrial riots caused many fatalities. Western aid suspended over human-rights violations. Referendum on constitutional reform promised.
1993 Commission appointed to supervise preparations for the referendum.

Malayan Emergency civil conflict in British-ruled Malaya, officially lasting from 1948 to 1960. The Communist Party of Malaya (CPM) launched an insurrection, calling for immediate Malayan independence. Britain responded by mounting a large-scale military and political counterinsurgency operation, while agreeing to eventual independence. In 1957 Malaya became independent and the state of emergency was ended 1960, although some CPM guerrillas continue to operate.

Malaysia country in SE Asia, comprising the Malay Peninsula, bounded N by Thailand, and surrounded E and S by the South China Sea and W by the Strait of Malacca; and the states of Sabah and Sarawak in the northern part of the island of Borneo (S Borneo is part of Indonesia).

chronology
1826 Became a British colony.
1963 Federation of Malaysia formed, including Malaya, Singapore, Sabah (N Borneo), and Sarawak (NW Borneo).
1965 Secession of Singapore from federation.
1969 Anti-Chinese riots in Kuala Lumpur.
1971 Launch of *bumiputra*, ethnic-Malay-oriented economic policy.
1981 Election of Dr Mahathir bin Mohamad as prime minister.
1982 Mahathir bin Mohamad re-elected.
1986 Mahathir bin Mohamad re-elected.
1987 Arrest of over 100 opposition activists, including Democratic Action Party (DAP) leader, as Malay-Chinese relations deteriorated.
1988 Split in ruling New United Malays' National Organization (UMNO) party over Mahathir's leadership style; new UMNO formed.
1989 Semangat '46 set up by former members of UMNO including ex-premier Tunku Abdul Rahman.
1990 Mahathir bin Mohamad re-elected.
1991 New economic growth programme launched.

Malcolm X adopted name of Malcolm Little 1926–1965. US black nationalist leader. While serving a prison sentence for burglary 1946–53, he joined the ◊Black Muslims sect.

On his release he campaigned for black separatism, condoning violence in self-defence, but 1964 modified his views to found the Islamic, socialist Organization of Afro-American Unity, preaching racial solidarity. He was assassinated.

Maldives group of 1,196 islands in the N Indian Ocean, about 640 km/400 mi SW of Sri Lanka, only 203 of which are inhabited.

chronology
1887 Became a British protectorate.

1953 Long a sultanate, the Maldive Islands became a republic within the Commonwealth.

1954 Sultan restored.

1965 Achieved full independence outside the Commonwealth.

1968 Sultan deposed; republic reinstated with Ibrahim Nasir as president.

1978 Nasir retired; replaced by Maumoon Abdul Gayoom.

1982 Rejoined the Commonwealth.

1983 Gayoom re-elected.

1985 Became a founder member of South Asian Association for Regional Cooperation (SAARC).

1988 Gayoom re-elected. Coup attempt by mercenaries, thought to have the backing of former president Nasir, was foiled by Indian paratroops.

Malenkov Georgi Maximilianovich 1902–1988. Soviet prime minister 1953–55, Stalin's designated successor but abruptly ousted as Communist Party secretary within two weeks of Stalin's death by ◊Khrushchev, and forced out as prime minister 1955 by ◊Bulganin.

Mali landlocked country in NW Africa, bounded to the NE by Algeria, E by Niger, SE by Burkina Faso, S by the Ivory Coast, SW by Senegal and Guinea, and W and N by Mauritania.

chronology

1895 Came under French rule.

1959 With Senegal, formed the Federation of Mali.

1960 Became the independent Republic of Mali, with Modibo Keita as president.

1968 Keita replaced in an army coup by Moussa Traoré.

1974 New constitution made Mali a one-party state.

1976 New national party, the Malian People's Democratic Union, announced.

1983 Agreement between Mali and Guinea for eventual political and economic integration signed.

1985 Conflict with Burkina Faso lasted five days; mediated by International Court of Justice.

1991 Demonstrations against one-party rule. Moussa Traoré ousted in a coup led by Lt-Col Amadou Toumani Toure. New multiparty constitution agreed, subject to referendum.

1992 Referendum endorsed new democratic constitution. Alliance for Democracy in Mali (ADEMA) won multiparty elections; Alpha Oumar Konare elected president.

Malik Yakob Alexandrovich 1906–1980. Soviet diplomat. He was permanent representative at the United Nations 1948–53 and 1968–76, and it was his walkout from the Security Council in Jan 1950 that allowed the authorization of UN intervention in Korea (see ◊Korean War).

Malinovsky Rodion Yakolevich 1898–1967. Russian soldier and politician. In World War II he fought at Stalingrad, commanded in the Ukraine, and led the Soviet advance through the Balkans to capture Budapest 1945. He was minister of defence 1957–67.

Malta island in the Mediterranean Sea, S of Sicily, E of Tunisia, and N of Libya.

chronology
1814 Annexed to Britain by the Treaty of Paris.
1947 Achieved self-government.
1955 Dom ◊Mintoff of the Malta Labour Party (MLP) became prime minister.
1956 Referendum approved MLP's proposal for integration with the UK. Proposal opposed by the Nationalist Party.
1958 MLP rejected the British integration proposal.
1962 Nationalists elected, with Borg Olivier as prime minister.
1964 Independence achieved from Britain, within the Commonwealth. Ten-year defence and economic-aid treaty with UK signed.
1971 Mintoff re-elected. 1964 treaty declared invalid and negotiations began for leasing the NATO base in Malta.
1972 Seven-year NATO agreement signed.
1974 Became a republic.
1979 British military base closed.
1984 Mintoff retired and was replaced by Mifsud Bonnici as prime minister and MLP leader.
1987 Edward Fenech Adami (Nationalist) elected prime minister.
1989 Vincent Tabone elected president. USA–USSR summit held offshore.
1990 Formal application made for EC membership.
1992 Nationalist Party returned to power in general election.

Manchukuo former Japanese puppet state in Manchuria and Jehol 1932–45, ruled by the former Chinese emperor Henry ◊P'u-i.

mandate in history, a territory whose administration was entrusted to Allied states by the League of Nations under the Treaty of Versailles after

World War I. Mandated territories were former German and Turkish possessions (including Iraq, Syria, Lebanon, and Palestine). When the United Nations replaced the League of Nations 1945, mandates that had not achieved independence became known as ◊trust territories.

Mandela Nelson (Rolihlahla) 1918– . South African politician and lawyer, president of the ◊African National Congress (ANC) from 1991. As organizer of the then banned ANC, he was imprisoned 1964. In prison he became a symbol of unity for the worldwide anti-apartheid movement. In Feb 1990 he was released, the ban on the ANC having been lifted, and he entered into negotiations with the government about a multiracial future for South Africa. In Sept 1992, Mandela and President de Klerk agreed to hasten the creation of an interim government under which reforms could take place.

He was married to the South African civil-rights activist Winnie Mandela 1955–92.

Mandela Winnie (Nomzamo) 1934– . Civil-rights activist in South Africa and wife of Nelson Mandela 1955–92. A leading spokesperson for the ◊African National Congress during her husband's imprisonment 1964–90, she has been jailed for a year and put under house arrest several times. In 1989 she was involved in the abduction of four youths, one of whom, Stompie Seipei, was later murdered. Winnie Mandela was convicted of kidnapping and assault, and given a six-year jail sentence May 1991, with the right to appeal. In April 1992 she and Nelson Mandela separated after 33 years of marriage. In the same year she resigned from her ANC leaderships posts, including her seat on the ANC National Executive Committee Sept 1992.

Manhattan Project code name for the development of the atom bomb in the USA in World War II, to which the physicists Enrico Fermi and J Robert Oppenheimer contributed.

Manley Michael (Norman) 1924– . Jamaican politician, leader of the socialist People's National Party from 1969, and prime minister 1972–80 and 1989–92. He resigned the premiership because of ill health March 1992 and was succeeded by P J Patterson. Manley left parliament April 1992. His father, *Norman Manley* (1893–1969), was the founder of the People's National Party and prime minister 1959–62.

Mannerheim Carl Gustav Emil von 1867–1951. Finnish general and politician, leader of the conservative forces in the civil war 1917–18 and regent 1918–19. He commanded the Finnish army 1939–40 and 1941–44, and was president of Finland 1944–46.

Maoism form of communism based on the ideas and teachings of the Chinese communist leader ◊Mao Zedong. It involves an adaptation of ◊Marxism to suit conditions in China and apportions a much greater role to agriculture and the peasantry in the building of socialism, thus effectively bypassing the capitalist (industrial) stage envisaged by Marx.

Mao Zedong or *Mao Tse-tung* 1893–1976. Chinese political leader and Marxist theoretician. A founder of the Chinese Communist Party (CCP) 1921, Mao soon emerged as its leader. He organized the ◊Long March 1934–35 and the war of liberation 1937–49, following which he established a People's Republic and communist rule in China; he headed the CCP and government until his death. His influence diminished with the failure of his 1958–60 ◊Great Leap Forward, but he emerged dominant again during the 1966–69 ◊Cultural Revolution. Mao adapted communism to Chinese conditions, as set out in the ◊*Little Red Book*.

Mapai (Miphlegeth Poale Israel) Israeli Workers' Party or Labour Party, founded 1930. Its leading figure until 1965 was David Ben-Gurion. In 1968, the party allied with two other democratic socialist parties to form the Israeli Labour Party, led initially by Levi Eshkol and later by Golda Meir.

Maquis French ◊resistance movement that fought against the German occupation during World War II.

Marchais Georges 1920–   . Leader of the French Communist Party (PCF) from 1972. Under his leadership, the party committed itself to a 'transition to socialism' by democratic means and entered into a union of the left with the Socialist Party (PS). This was severed 1977, and the PCF returned to a more orthodox pro-Moscow line, since when its share of the vote has decreased.

March on Rome, the means by which Fascist leader Benito Mussolini came to power in Italy 1922. A protracted crisis in government and the threat of civil war enabled him to demand the formation of a Fascist government to restore order. On 29 Oct 1922, King Victor Emmanuel III invited Mussolini to come to Rome to take power. The 'march' was a propaganda myth: Mussolini travelled overnight by train from Milan to Rome, where he formed a government the following day, 30 Oct. Some 25,000 fascist Blackshirts were also transported to the city, where they marched in a ceremonial parade 31 Oct.

Marconi Scandal scandal 1912 in which UK chancellor Lloyd George and two other government ministers were found by a French newspaper to have dealt in shares of the US Marconi company shortly before it was announced that the Post Office had accepted the British Marconi company's bid to construct an imperial wireless chain. A parliamentary select committee, biased towards the Liberal government's interests, found that the other four wireless systems were technically inadequate and therefore the decision to adopt Marconi's tender was not the result of ministerial corruption. The scandal did irreparable harm to Lloyd George's reputation.

Marco Polo bridge incident conflict 1937 between Chinese and Japanese army troops on the border of Japanese-controlled ◊Manchukuo and China that led to full-scale war between the two states. It lasted until the Japanese surrender 1945.

Marcos Ferdinand 1917–1989. Filipino right-wing politician, president from 1965 to 1986, when he was forced into exile in Hawaii by a popular front led by Corazon ◊Aquino. He was backed by the USA when in power, but in 1988 US authorities indicted him and his wife Imelda Marcos for racketeering, embezzlement.

Marcos Imelda 1930– . Filipino politician and socialite, wife of Ferdinand Marcos, in exile 1986–91. She was acquitted 1990 of defrauding US banks. Under indictment for misuse of Philippine state funds, she returned to Manila in Nov 1991 and was an unsuccessful candidate in the 1992 presidential elections.

Margrethe II 1940– . Queen of Denmark from 1972, when she succeeded her father Frederick IX. In 1967, she married the French diplomat Count Henri de Laborde de Monpezat, who took the title Prince Hendrik. Her heir is Crown Prince Frederick (1968–).

Marie 1875–1938. Queen of Romania. She was the daughter of the duke of Edinburgh, second son of Queen Victoria of England, and married Prince Ferdinand of Romania in 1893 (he was king 1922-27). She wrote a number of literary works, notably *Story of My Life* 1934-35. Her son Carol became king of Romania, and her daughters, Elisabeth and Marie, queens of Greece and Yugoslavia respectively.

Markievicz Constance Georgina, Countess Markievicz (born Gore Booth) 1868–1927. Irish nationalist who married the Polish count Markievicz 1900. Her death sentence for taking part in the ◊Easter Rising of 1916 was commuted, and after her release from prison 1917 she was elected to the Westminster Parliament as a Sinn Féin candidate 1918 (technically the first British woman member of Parliament), but did not take her seat.

Markov Georgi 1929–1978. Bulgarian playwright and novelist who fled to the UK 1971; he was assassinated by being jabbed with a poisoned umbrella.

Marne, Battles of the in World War I, two unsuccessful German offensives. In the *First Battle* 6–9 Sept 1914, von Moltke's advance was halted by the British Expeditionary Force and the French under Foch; in the *Second Battle* 15 July–4 Aug 1918, Ludendorff's advance was defeated by British, French, and US troops under the French general Pétain, and German morale crumbled.

Marshall George Catlett 1880–1959. US general and diplomat. He was army Chief of Staff in World War II, secretary of state 1947–49, and secretary of defence Sept 1950–Sept 1951. He initiated the ◊*Marshall Plan* 1947 and received the Nobel Peace Prize 1953.

Marshall John Ross 1912–1988. New Zealand National Party politician, notable for his negotiations of a free-trade agreement with Australia. He was deputy to K J Holyoake as prime minister and succeeded him Feb–Nov 1972.

Marshall Plan programme of US economic aid to Europe, set up at the end of World War II, totalling $13,000 billion 1948–52. Officially known as the European Recovery Programme, it was announced by Secretary of State George C ◊Marshall in a speech at Harvard June 1947, but it was in fact the work of a State Department group led by Dean ◊Acheson. The perceived danger of communist takeover in postwar Europe was the main reason for the aid effort.

Martens Wilfried 1936–   . Prime minister of Belgium 1979–92, member of the Social Christian Party. He was president of the Dutch-speaking CVP 1972–79 and, as prime minister, headed several coalition governments in the period 1979–92 when he was replaced by Jean-Luc Dehaene heading a new coalition.

Marxism philosophical system, developed by the 19th-century German social theorists Karl Marx and Friedrich Engels, also known as *dialectical materialism*. As applied to history, it supposes that the succession of feudalism, capitalism, socialism, and finally the classless society is inevitable. The stubborn resistance of any existing system to change necessitates its complete overthrow in the *class struggle*—in the case of capitalism, by the proletariat—rather than gradual modification.

Marxism has proved one of the most powerful and debated theories in modern history, inspiring both dedicated exponents (Lenin, Trotsky, Stalin, Mao) and bitter opponents. It is the basis of ◊communism.

Mary Queen 1867–1953. Consort of George V of the UK. The daughter of the Duke and Duchess of Teck, the latter a grand-daughter of George II, in 1891 she became engaged to the Duke of Clarence, eldest son of the Prince of Wales (later Edward VII). After his death 1892, she married 1893 his brother George, Duke of York, who succeeded to the throne 1910.

Masaryk Jan (Garrigue) 1886–1948. Czechoslovak politician, son of Tomáš Masaryk. He was foreign minister from 1940, when the Czechoslovak government was exiled in London in World War II. He returned 1945, retaining the post, but as a result of political pressure by the communists committed suicide.

Masaryk Tomáš (Garrigue) 1850–1937. Czechoslovak nationalist politician. He directed the revolutionary movement against the Austrian Empire, founding with Eduard Beneš and Stefanik the Czechoslovak National Council, and in 1918 was elected first president of the newly formed Czechoslovak Republic. Three times re-elected, he resigned 1935 in favour of Beneš.

Masire Quett Ketumile Joni 1925–   . President of Botswana from 1980. In 1962, with Seretse ◊Khama, he founded the Botswana Democratic Party (BDP) and in 1965 was made deputy prime minister. After independence 1966, he became vice president and, on Khama's death 1980, president, continuing a policy of nonalignment.

Massey Vincent 1887–1967. Canadian Liberal Party politician. He was the first Canadian to become governor general of Canada (1952–59).

Massey William Ferguson 1856–1925. New Zealand politician, born in Ireland; prime minister 1912–25. He led the Reform Party, an offshoot of the Conservative Party, and as prime minister before World War I concentrated on controlling militant unions and the newly formed Federation of Labour.

Matsudaira Tsuneo 1877–1949. Japanese diplomat and politician who became the first chair of the Japanese Diet (parliament) after World War II. He negotiated for Japan at the London Naval Conference of 1930 and acted as imperial household minister 1936–45, advising the emperor, but was unsuccessful in keeping Japan out of a war with the Western powers.

Matsukata Masayoshi, Prince 1835–1924. Japanese politician, premier 1891–92 and 1896–98. As minister of finance 1881–91 and 1898–1900, he paved the way for the modernization of the Japanese economy.

Matsuoka Yosuke 1880–1946. Japanese politician, foreign minister 1940–41. A fervent nationalist, Matsuoka led Japan out of the League of Nations when it condemned Japan for the seizure of Manchuria. As foreign minister, he allied Japan with Germany and Italy. At the end of World War II, he was arrested as a war criminal but died before his trial.

Maudling Reginald 1917–1979. British Conservative politician, chancellor of the Exchequer 1962–64, contender for the party leadership 1965, and home secretary 1970–72. He resigned when referred to during the bankruptcy proceedings of the architect John Poulson, since (as home secretary) he would have been in charge of the Metropolitan Police investigating the case.

Mau Mau Kenyan secret guerrilla movement 1952–60, an offshoot of the Kikuyu Central Association banned in World War II. Its aim was to end British colonial rule. This was achieved 1960 with the granting of Kenyan independence and the election of Jomo Kenyatta as Kenya's first prime minister.

Mauritania country in NW Africa, bounded NE by Algeria, E and S by Mali, SW by Senegal, W by the Atlantic Ocean, and NW by Western Sahara.

chronology
1903 Became a French protectorate.
1960 Independence achieved from France, with Moktar Ould Daddah as president.
1975 Western Sahara ceded by Spain. Mauritania occupied the southern area and Morocco the north. Polisario Front formed in Sahara to resist the occupation by Mauritania and Morocco.

1978 Daddah deposed in bloodless coup; replaced by Mohamed Khouna Ould Haidalla. Peace agreed with Polisario Front.

1981 Diplomatic relations with Morocco broken.

1984 Haidalla overthrown by Maaouia Ould Sid Ahmed Taya. Polisario regime formally recognized.

1985 Relations with Morocco restored.

1989 Violent clashes between Mauritanians and Senegalese. Arab-dominated government expelled thousands of Africans into N Senegal; governments had earlier agreed to repatriate each other's citizens (about 250,000).

1991 Amnesty for political prisoners. Multiparty elections promised. Calls for resignation of President Taya.

1992 First multiparty elections won by ruling Democratic and Social Republican Party (PRDS). Diplomatic relations with Senegal resumed.

Mauritius island country in the Indian Ocean, E of Madagascar.

chronology

1968 Independence achieved from Britain within the Commonwealth, with Seewoosagur Ramgoolam as prime minister.

1982 Aneerood Jugnauth became prime minister.

1983 Jugnauth formed a new party, the Mauritius Socialist Movement. Ramgoolam appointed governor general. Jugnauth formed a new coalition government.

1985 Ramgoolam died; was succeeded by Veersamy Ringadoo.

1987 Jugnauth's coalition re-elected.

1990 Attempt to create a republic failed.

1991 Jugnauth's ruling Mauritius Socialist Movement–Mauritius Militant Movement–Rodriguais People's Organization coalition won general election; pledge to secure republican status by 1992.

1992 Mauritius became a republic while remaining a member of the Commonwealth. Ringadoo became interim president.

Mauroy Pierre 1928– . French socialist politician, prime minister 1981–84. He oversaw the introduction of a radical reflationary programme.

May 4th movement Chinese student-led nationalist movement ignited by demonstrations in Beijing 1919. It demanded that China's unpopular warlord government reject the decision by the Versailles peace conference to confirm Japan's rights over the Shandong peninsula that had been asserted in the ◊twenty-one demands 1915.

Mazowiecki Tadeusz 1927–   . Polish politician, founder member of ◊Solidarity, and Poland's first postwar noncommunist prime minister 1989–90. Forced to introduce unpopular economic reforms, he was knocked out in the first round of the Nov 1990 presidential elections, resigning in favour of his former colleague Lech ◊Wałesa.

Mboya Tom 1930–1969. Kenyan politician, a founder of the Kenya African National Union (◊KANU), and minister of economic affairs from 1964 until his assassination.

Medvedev Vadim 1929–   . Soviet communist politician. He was deputy chief of propaganda 1970–78, was in charge of party relations with communist countries 1986–88, and in 1988 was appointed by the Soviet leader Gorbachev to succeed the conservative Ligachev as head of ideology. He adhered to a firm Leninist line.

Meinhof Ulrike 1934–1976. West German urban guerrilla, member of the ◊*Baader–Meinhof gang* in the 1970s.

Mein Kampf book dictated by Adolf ◊Hitler to Rudolf Hess 1923–24 during Hitler's jail sentence for his part in the abortive 1923 Munich beer-hall putsch. Part autobiography, part political philosophy, the book presents Hitler's ideas of German expansion, anticommunism, and anti-Semitism. It was published in two volumes, 1925 and 1927.

Meir Golda 1898–1978. Israeli Labour (*Mapai*) politician. Born in Russia, she emigrated to the USA 1906, and in 1921 went to Palestine. She was foreign minister 1956–66 and prime minister 1969–74. Criticism of the Israelis' lack of preparation for the 1973 Arab-Israeli War led to election losses for Labour and, unable to form a government, she resigned.

Mendes Chico (Filho Francisco) 1944–1988. Brazilian environmentalist and labour leader. Opposed to the destruction of Brazil's rainforests, he organized itinerant rubber tappers into the Workers' Party (PT) and was assassinated by Darci Alves, a cattle rancher's son. Of 488 similar murders in land conflicts in Brazil 1985–89, his was the first to come to trial.

Mendès-France Pierre 1907–1982. French prime minister and foreign minister 1954–55. He extricated France from the war in Indochina, and prepared the way for Tunisian independence.

Menem Carlos (Saul) 1935–   . Argentine politician, president from 1989; leader of the Peronist (Justicialist Party) movement. As president, he introduced sweeping privatization and public spending cuts, released hundreds of political prisoners jailed under the Alfonsín regime, and sent two warships to the Gulf to assist the USA against Iraq in the 1992 Gulf War (the only Latin American country to offer support to the USA). He also improved relations with the UK.

Mengistu Haile Mariam 1937– . Ethiopian soldier and socialist politician, head of state 1977–91 (president 1987–91). He seized power in a coup and was confronted with severe problems of drought and secessionist uprisings, but survived with help from the USSR and the West until his violent overthrow.

Menshevik member of the minority of the Russian Social Democratic Party, who split from the ◊Bolsheviks 1903. The Mensheviks believed in a large, loosely organized party and that, before socialist revolution could occur in Russia, capitalist society had to develop further. During the Russian Revolution they had limited power and set up a government in Georgia, but were suppressed 1922.

Menzies Robert Gordon 1894–1978. Australian politician, leader of the United Australia (now Liberal) Party and prime minister 1939–41 and 1949–66.

Metaxas Ioannis 1870–1941. Greek general and politician, born in Ithaca. He restored ◊George II (1890–1947) as king of Greece, under whom he established a dictatorship as prime minister from 1936, and introduced several necessary economic and military reforms. He led resistance to the Italian invasion of Greece in 1941, refusing to abandon Greece's neutral position.

Mexico country in Central America, bounded N by the USA, E by the Gulf of Mexico, SE by Belize and Guatemala, and SW and W by the Pacific Ocean.

chronology
1917 New constitution introduced, designed to establish permanent democracy.
1983–84 Financial crisis.
1985 Institutional Revolutionary Party (PRI) returned to power. Earthquake in Mexico City.
1986 International Monetary Fund (IMF) loan agreement signed to keep the country solvent until at least 1988.

1988 PRI candidate Carlos ◊Salinas de Gortari elected president. Debt reduction accords negotiated with USA.

1991 PRI won general election. President Salinas promised constitutional reforms.

1992 Public outrage following Guadalajara gas-explosion disaster in which 194 people died and 1,400 were injured.

Michael 1921– . King of Romania 1927–30 and 1940–47. The son of Carol II, he succeeded his grandfather as king 1927 but was displaced when his father returned from exile 1930. In 1940 he was proclaimed king again on his father's abdication, overthrew 1944 the fascist dictatorship of Ion Antonescu (1882–1946), and enabled Romania to share in the victory of the Allies at the end of World War II. He abdicated and left Romania 1947.

Midway Islands two islands in the Pacific, 1,800 km/1,120 mi NW of Honolulu; area 5 sq km/2 sq mi; population (1980) 500. They were annexed by the USA 1867, and are now administered by the US Navy. The naval *Battle of Midway* 3–6 June 1942, between the USA and Japan, was a turning point in the Pacific in World War II; the US victory marked the end of Japanese expansion in the Pacific.

Mihailović Draza 1893–1946. Yugoslav soldier, leader of the guerrilla ◊Chetniks of World War II against the German occupation. His feud with Tito's communists led to the withdrawal of Allied support and that of his own exiled government from 1943. He turned for help to the Italians and Germans, and was eventually shot for treason.

military-industrial complex conjunction of the military establishment and the arms industry, both inflated by Cold War demands. The phrase was first used by US president and former general Dwight D Eisenhower in 1961 to warn Americans of the potential misplacement of power.

Millett Kate 1934– . US radical feminist lecturer, writer, and sculptor whose book *Sexual Politics* 1970 was a landmark in feminist thinking. She was a founding member of the *National Organization of Women* (NOW). Later books include *Flying* 1974, *The Prostitution Papers* 1976, *Sita* 1977, and *The Loony Bin Trip* 1991, describing a period of manic depression and drug therapy.

Milner Alfred, Viscount Milner 1854–1925. British colonial administrator. As governor of Cape Colony 1897–1901, he negotiated with Kruger but did little to prevent the second South African War; and as governor of the

Transvaal and Orange River colonies 1902–05 after their annexation, he reorganized their administration. In 1916 he became a member of Lloyd George's war cabinet.

Milosevic Slobodan 1941– . Serbian communist politician, party chief and president of Serbia from 1986; re-elected Dec 1990 in multiparty elections. Milosevic wielded considerable influence over the Serb-dominated Yugoslav federal army during the 1991–92 civil war and has continued to back Serbian militia in ◊Bosnia-Herzegovina 1992, although publicly disclaiming any intention to 'carve up' the newly independent republic.

Minto Gilbert, 4th Earl of 1845–1914. British colonial administrator who succeeded Curzon as viceroy of India, 1905–10. With John Morley, secretary of state for India, he co-sponsored the ◊Morley-Minto reforms of 1909. The reforms increased Indian representation in government at provincial level, but also created separate Muslim and Hindu electorates which, it was believed, helped the British Raj in the policy of divide and rule.

Mintoff Dom(inic) 1916– . Labour prime minister of Malta 1971–84. He negotiated the removal of British and other foreign military bases 1971–79 and made treaties with Libya.

Mitsotakis Constantine 1918– . Greek politician, leader of the conservative New Democracy Party from 1984, prime minister from April 1990. Minister for economic coordination 1965 (a post he held again 1978–80), he was arrested by the military junta 1967, but escaped from house arrest and lived in exile until 1974. In 1980–81 he was foreign minister.

Mitterrand François 1916– . French socialist politician, president from 1981. He held ministerial posts in 11 governments 1947–58, and founded the French Socialist Party (PS) 1971. In 1985 he introduced proportional representation, allegedly to weaken the growing opposition from left and right. Since 1982 his administrations have combined economic orthodoxy with social reform.

Miyazawa Kiichi 1920– . Japanese politician. After holding a number of key government posts, he became leader of the ruling Liberal Democratic party, and prime minister Nov 1991.

Mladenov Petar 1936– . Bulgarian Communist politician, secretary general of the Bulgarian Communist Party from Nov 1989, after the resignation of ◊Zhivkov, until Feb 1990. He was elected state president in April 1990 but replaced four months later.

Mobutu Sese Seko Kuku Ngbeandu Wa Za Banga 1930–   . Zairean president from 1965. He assumed the presidency in a coup, and created a unitary state under a centralized government. The harshness of some of his policies and charges of corruption have attracted widespread international criticism. In 1991 opposition leaders forced Mobutu to agree formally to give up some of his powers, but the president continued to oppose constitutional reform. His decision Jan 1993 to pay his regular army with near worthless banknotes resulted in mutiny and the accidental shooting of the French ambassador by troops loyal to the president, causing French and Belgium governments to intervene and prepare to evacuate civilians.

Mohamad Mahathir bin 1925–   . Prime minister of Malaysia from 1981 and leader of the United Malays' National Organization (UMNO). His 'look east' economic policy emulates Japanese industrialization.

Moi Daniel arap 1924–   . Kenyan politician, president from 1978. Leader of Kenya African National Union (◊KANU), he became minister of home affairs 1964, vice president 1967, and succeeded Jomo Kenyatta as president. He enjoys the support of Western governments but has been widely criticized for Kenya's poor human-rights record. From 1988 his rule became increasingly authoritarian and in 1991, in the face of widespread criticism, he promised an eventual introduction of multiparty politics. In 1992 he was elected president in the first free elections amid widespread accusations of fraud.

Moldova or *Moldavia* country in E central Europe, bounded N, S, and E by Ukraine, and W by Romania.

chronology
1940 Bessarabia in the E became part of the Soviet Union whereas the W part remained in Romania.
1941 Bessarabia taken over by Romania–Germany.
1944 Red army reconquered Bessarabia.
1946–47 Widespread famine.
1988 A popular front, the Democratic Movement for Perestroika, campaigned for accelerated political reform.
1989 Jan–Feb: nationalist demonstrations in Chisinau. May: Moldavian Popular Front established. July: Mircea Snegur became head of state. Aug:

Moldavian language granted official status triggering clashes between ethnic Russians and Moldavians. Nov: Gagauz-Khalky People's Movement formed to campaign for Gagauz autonomy.

1990 Feb: Popular Front polled strongly in supreme soviet elections. June: economic and political sovereignty declared; renamed Republic of Moldova. Oct: Gagauzi held unauthorized elections to independent parliament; state of emergency declared after inter-ethnic clashes. Trans-Dniester region declared its sovereignty. Nov: state of emergency declared in Trans-Dniester region after inter-ethnic killings.

1991 March: Moldova boycotted the USSR's constitutional referendum. Aug: independence declared after abortive anti-Gorbachev coup; Communist Party outlawed. Dec: Moldova joined new Commonwealth of Independent States (CIS).

1992 Jan: admitted into the Conference on Security and Cooperation in Europe (CSCE). Possible union with Romania discussed. March: state of emergency imposed; admitted into United Nations (UN); diplomatic recognition granted by USA. May: further meeting on unification with Romania; Trans-Dniester region fighting intensified. July: Andrei Sangheli became premier; Moldova agreed to outside peacekeeping force. Aug: talks between Moldova and Russia began; Russian peacekeeping force reportedly deployed in Trans-Dniester region.

Molotov Vyacheslav Mikhailovich. Assumed name of V M Skriabin 1890–1986. Soviet communist politician. He was chair of the Council of People's Commissars (prime minister) 1930–41 and foreign minister 1939–49 and 1953–56. He negotiated the 1939 nonaggression treaty with Germany (the ◊Hitler–Stalin pact), and, after the German invasion 1941, the Soviet partnership with the Allies. His postwar stance prolonged the Cold War and in 1957 he was expelled from the government for Stalinist activities.

Momoh Joseph Saidu 1937– . Sierra Leone soldier and politician, president 1985–92. An army officer who became commander 1983, with the rank of major-general, he succeeded Siaka Stevens as president when he retired; Momoh was endorsed by Sierra Leone's one political party, the All-People's Congress. He dissociated himself from the policies of his predecessor, pledging to fight corruption and improve the economy. In April 1992 he fled to neighbouring Guinea after a military takeover.

Monaco small sovereign state forming an enclave in S France, with the Mediterranean Sea to the south.

chronology
1861 Became an independent state under French protection.
1918 France given a veto over succession to the throne.
1949 Prince Rainier III ascended the throne.
1956 Prince Rainier married US actress Grace Kelly.
1958 Birth of male heir, Prince Albert.
1959 Constitution of 1911 suspended.
1962 New constitution adopted.

Mondale Walter 'Fritz' 1928– . US Democrat politician, unsuccessful presidential candidate 1984. He was a senator 1964–76 from his home state of Minnesota, and vice president to Jimmy Carter 1977–81. After losing the 1984 presidential election to Ronald Reagan, Mondale retired from national politics to resume his law practice.

monetarism economic policy, advocated by the economist Milton Friedman and the Chicago school of economists, that proposes control of a country's money supply to keep it in step with the country's ability to produce goods, with the aim of curbing inflation. Cutting government spending is advocated, and the long-term aim is to return as much of the economy as possible to the private sector, allegedly in the interests of efficiency.

Mongolia (*Outer Mongolia* until 1924; *People's Republic of Mongolia* until 1991) country in E Central Asia, bounded N by Russia and S by China.

chronology
1911 Outer Mongolia gained autonomy from China.
1915 Chinese sovereignty reasserted.
1921 Chinese rule overthrown with Soviet help.
1924 People's Republic proclaimed.
1946 China recognized Mongolia's independence.
1966 20-year friendship, cooperation, and mutual-assistance pact signed with USSR. Relations with China deteriorated.
1984 Yumjaagiyn Tsedenbal, effective leader, deposed and replaced by Jambyn Batmonh.
1987 Soviet troops reduced; Mongolia's external contacts broadened.
1989 Further Soviet troop reductions.
1990 Democratization campaign launched by Mongolian Democratic Union. Punsalmaagiyn Ochirbat's Mongolian People's Revolutionary Party (MPRP) elected in free multiparty elections. Mongolian script readopted.

1991 Massive privatization programme launched as part of move towards a market economy. The word 'Republic' dropped from country's name. GDP declined by 10%.

1992 Jan: New constitution introduced. Economic situation worsened; GDP again declined by 10%. Prime minister Dashiyn Byambasuren's resignation refused. July: Puntsagiyn Jasray appointed new prime minister.

Montagu-Chelmsford reforms changes to the constitution of India 1919, whereby Indians obtained greater control in local and some provincial matters such as health, education, and agriculture, while British administrators still controlled finance and law and order. Arguing that the reforms did not go far enough, Indian nationalists organized a concerted ◊non-cooperation campaign 1920–22 in protest.

Montgomery Bernard Law, 1st Viscount Montgomery of Alamein 1887–1976. British field marshal. In World War II he commanded the 8th Army in N Africa in the Second Battle of El ◊Alamein 1942. As commander of British troops in N Europe from 1944, he received the German surrender 1945.

At the start of World War II he commanded part of the British Expeditionary Force in France 1939–40 and took part in the evacuation from Dunkirk. In Aug 1942 he took command of the 8th Army, then barring the German advance on Cairo; the victory of El Alamein in Oct turned the tide in N Africa and was followed by the expulsion of Field Marshal Rommel from Egypt and rapid Allied advance into Tunisia. In Feb 1943 Montgomery's forces came under US general Eisenhower's command, and they took part in the conquest of Tunisia and Sicily and the invasion of Italy. Montgomery was promoted to field marshal in 1944. In 1948 he became permanent military chair of the Commanders-in-Chief Committee for W European defence, and 1951–58 was deputy Supreme Commander Europe. Created 1st Viscount Montgomery of Alamein 1946.

Montreux, Convention of international agreement 1936 allowing Turkey to remilitarize the Dardenelles.

Morgenthau Plan proposals for Germany after World War II, originated by Henry Morgenthau Jr (1891–1967), US secretary of the treasury, calling for the elimination of war industries in the Ruhr and Saar basins and the conversion of Germany 'into a country primarily agricultural and pastoral in character'. The plan had already been dropped by the time the Allied leaders Churchill, Roosevelt, and Stalin met at Yalta Feb 1945.

Morley John, 1st Viscount Morley of Blackburn 1838–1923. British Liberal politician and writer. He entered Parliament in 1883, and was secretary for Ireland in 1886 and 1892–95. As secretary for India 1905–10, he prepared the way (with Viceroy Gilbert ◊Minto) for more representative government.

Morley-Minto reforms measures announced 1909 to increase the participation of Indians in their country's government. Introduced by John Morley (1838-1923), secretary of state for India, and Lord Minto (1845-1914), viceroy of India, they did not affect the responsibility of government, which remained in British hands, but did give Indians wider opportunities to be heard.

Moro Aldo 1916–1978. Italian Christian Democrat politician. Prime minister 1963–68 and 1974–76, he was expected to become Italy's president, but he was kidnapped and shot by Red Brigade urban guerrillas.

Moroccan Crises two periods of international tension 1905 and 1911 following German objections to French expansion in Morocco. Their wider purpose was to break up the Anglo-French entente 1904, but both crises served to reinforce the entente and isolate Germany.

Morocco country in NW Africa, bounded N and NW by the Mediterranean Sea, E and SE by Algeria, and S by Western Sahara.

chronology
1912 Morocco divided into French and Spanish protectorates.
1956 Independence achieved as the Sultanate of Morocco.
1957 Sultan restyled king of Morocco.
1961 Hassan II came to the throne.
1969 Former Spanish province of Ifni returned to Morocco.
1972 Major revision of the constitution.
1975 Western Sahara ceded by Spain to Morocco and Mauritania.
1976 Guerrilla war in Western Sahara with the Polisario Front. Sahrawi Arab Democratic Republic (SADR) established in Algiers. Diplomatic relations between Morocco and Algeria broken.
1979 Mauritania signed a peace treaty with Polisario.
1983 Peace formula for Western Sahara proposed by the Organization of African Unity (OAU); Morocco agreed but refused to deal directly with Polisario.
1984 Hassan signed an agreement for cooperation and mutual defence with Libya.

1987 Cease-fire agreed with Polisario, but fighting continued.
1988 Diplomatic relations with Algeria restored.
1989 Diplomatic relations with Syria restored.
1992 Mohamed Lamrani appointed prime minister; new constitution approved in national referendum.

Morrison Herbert Stanley, Baron Morrison of Lambeth 1888–1965. British Labour politician. He was a founder member and later secretary of the London Labour Party 1915–45, and a member of the London County Council 1922–45. He entered Parliament in 1923, and organized the Labour Party's general election victory in 1945. He was twice defeated in the contest for leadership of the party, once to Clement Attlee in 1932, and then to Hugh Gaitskell 1955. A skilful organizer, he lacked the ability to unite the party.

Mosley Oswald (Ernald) 1896–1980. British politician, founder of the British Union of Fascists (BUF) 1932. He was a member of Parliament 1918–31, then led the BUF until his internment 1940–43 during World War II. In 1946 Mosley was denounced when it became known that Italy had funded his prewar efforts to establish ◊fascism in Britain, but in 1948 he resumed fascist propaganda with his Union Movement, the revived BUF.

Mossadeq Muhammad 1880–1967. Iranian prime minister 1951–53. A dispute arose with the Anglo-Iranian Oil Company when he called for the nationalization of Iran's oil production, and when he failed in his attempt to overthrow the shah, he was arrested by loyalist forces with support from the USA. From 1956 he was under house arrest.

Mountbatten Louis, 1st Earl Mountbatten of Burma 1900–1979. British admiral and administrator. In World War II he became chief of combined operations 1942 and commander in chief in SE Asia 1943. As last viceroy of India 1947 and first governor general of India until 1948, he oversaw that country's transition to independence. He was killed by an Irish Republican Army bomb aboard his yacht in the Republic of Ireland.

Mozambique country in SE Africa, bounded N by Zambia, Malawi, and Tanzania; E and S by the Indian Ocean; SW by South Africa and Swaziland; and W by Zimbabwe.

chronology
1962 ◊Frelimo (liberation front) established.
1975 Independence achieved from Portugal as a socialist republic, with

Samora ◊Machel as president and Frelimo as the sole legal party.
1977 Renamo resistance group formed.
1983 Re-establishment of good relations with Western powers.
1984 ◊Nkomati accord of nonaggression signed with South Africa.
1986 Machel killed in air crash; succeeded by Joaquim ◊Chissano.
1988 Tanzania announced withdrawal of its troops. South Africa provided training for Mozambican forces.
1989 Frelimo offered to abandon Marxist-Leninism; Chissano re-elected. Renamo continued attacks on government facilities and civilians.
1990 One-party rule officially ended. Partial cease-fire agreed.
1991 Peace talks resumed in Rome, delaying democratic process. Attempted antigovernment coup thwarted.
1992 Aug: peace accord agreed upon, but fighting continued. Oct: peace accord signed, but awaited ratification by government.

MPLA (abbreviation for *M*ovimento *P*opular de *Libertaçaõ de A*ngola/Popular Movement for the Liberation of Angola) socialist organization founded in the early 1950s that sought to free Angola from Portuguese rule 1961–75 before being involved in the civil war against its former allies ◊UNITA and ◊FNLA 1975–76. The MPLA took control of the country, but UNITA guerrilla activity continues, supported by South Africa.

Mubarak Hosni 1928–   . Egyptian politician, president from 1981. Vice president to Anwar Sadat from 1975, Mubarak succeeded him on his assassination. He has continued to pursue Sadat's moderate policies, and has significantly increased the freedom of the press and of political association, while trying to repress the growing Islamic fundamentalist movement.

Mugabe Robert (Gabriel) 1925–   . Zimbabwean politician, prime minister from 1980 and president from 1987. He was in detention in Rhodesia for nationalist activities 1964–74, then carried on guerrilla warfare from Mozambique. As leader of ◊ZANU he was in an uneasy alliance with Joshua ◊Nkomo of ZAPU (Zimbabwe African People's Union) from 1976. The two parties merged 1987.

Mujaheddin (Arabic *mujahid* 'fighters', from *jihad* 'holy war') Islamic fundamentalist guerrillas of contemporary Afghanistan and Iran.

Mukden, Battle of taking of Mukden (now Shenyang), NE China, from

Russian occupation by the Japanese 1905, during the ◊Russo-Japanese War. Mukden was later the scene of a surprise attack (the 'Mukden incident') 18 Sept 1931 by the Japanese on the Chinese garrison, which marked the beginning of their invasion of China.

Mulberry Harbour prefabricated floating harbour, used on D-day in World War II, to assist in the assault on the German-held French coast of Normandy.

Muldoon Robert David 1921–1992. New Zealand National Party politician, prime minister 1975–84, during which time he pursued austere economic policies such as a wage-and-price policy to control inflation.

Mulroney Brian 1939– . Canadian politician, Progressive Conservative Party leader from 1983, prime minister from 1984. He achieved a landslide in the 1984 election, and won the 1988 election on a platform of free trade with the USA, but with a reduced majority. Opposition within Canada to the Meech Lake agreement, a prerequisite to signing the 1982 Constitution, continued to plague Mulroney in his second term. By 1991 his public-opinion standing had fallen to an unprecedented low level. A revised reform package Oct 1992 failed to gain voters' approval.

Munich Agreement pact signed on 29 Sept 1938 by the leaders of the UK (Neville ◊Chamberlain), France (Edouard ◊Daladier), Germany (Hitler), and Italy (Mussolini), under which Czechoslovakia was compelled to surrender its Sudeten-German districts (the ◊*Sudetenland*) to Germany. Chamberlain claimed it would guarantee 'peace in our time', but it did not prevent Hitler from seizing the rest of Czechoslovakia in March 1939.

Museveni Yoweri Kaguta 1945– . Ugandan general and politician, president from 1986. He led the opposition to Idi Amin's regime 1971–78 and was minister of defence 1979–80 but, unhappy with Milton Obote's autocratic leadership, formed the National Resistance Army (NRA). When Obote was ousted in a coup in 1985, Museveni entered into a brief power-sharing agreement with his successor, Tito Okello, before taking over as president. Museveni leads a broad-based coalition government.

Muslim Brotherhood movement founded by members of the Sunni branch of Islam in Egypt in 1928. It aims at the establishment of a theocratic Islamic state and is headed by a 'supreme guide'. It is also active in Jordan, Sudan, and Syria.

Muslim League Indian political organization. The All India Muslim League was founded 1906 under the leadership of the Aga Khan. In 1940 the league, led by Muhammad Ali ♢Jinnah, demanded an independent Muslim state. The ♢Congress Party and the Muslim League won most seats in the 1945 elections for an Indian central legislative assembly. In 1946 the Indian constituent assembly was boycotted by the Muslim League. It was partly the activities of the league that led to the establishment of Pakistan.

Mussolini Benito 1883–1945. Italian dictator 1925-43. As founder of the Fascist Movement (see ♢fascism) 1919 and prime minister from 1922, he became known as *Il Duce* ('the leader'). He invaded Ethiopia 1935–36, intervened in the Spanish Civil War 1936–39 in support of Franco, and conquered Albania 1939. In June 1940 Italy entered World War II supporting Hitler. Forced by military and domestic setbacks to resign 1943, Mussolini established a breakaway government in N Italy 1944–45, but was killed trying to flee the country.

Mustafa Kemal Turkish leader who assumed the name of ♢Atatürk.

Muzorewa Abel (Tendekayi) 1925– . Zimbabwean politician and Methodist bishop. He was president of the African National Council 1971–85 and prime minister of Rhodesia/Zimbabwe 1979–80. He was detained for a year in 1983–84. He is leader of the minority United Africa National Council.

MVD acronym for the Soviet Ministry of Internal Affairs, name (1946–53) of the Soviet secret police; later the ♢KGB.

Mwinyi Ali Hassan 1925– . Tanzanian socialist politician, president from 1985, when he succeeded Julius Nyerere. He began a revival of private enterprise and control of state involvement and spending.

Myanmar formerly (until 1989) *Burma* country in SE Asia, bounded NW by India and Bangladesh, NE by China, SE by Laos and Thailand, and SW by the Bay of Bengal.

chronology
1886 United as province of British India.
1937 Became crown colony in the British Commonwealth.
1942–45 Occupied by Japan.
1948 Independence achieved from Britain. Left the Commonwealth.
1962 General ♢Ne Win assumed power in army coup.

1973–74 Adopted presidential-style 'civilian' constitution.

1975 Opposition National Democratic Front formed.

1986 Several thousand supporters of opposition leader ◊Suu Kyi arrested.

1988 Government resigned after violent demonstrations. General ◊Saw Maung seized power in military coup Sept; over 1,000 killed.

1989 Martial law declared; thousands arrested including advocates of democracy and human rights. Country renamed Myanmar and capital Yangon.

1990 Breakaway opposition group formed 'parallel government' on rebel-held territory.

1991 Martial law and human-rights abuses continued. Military offensives continued. Opposition leader, Aung San Suu Kyi, received Nobel Prize for Peace.

1992 Jan–April: Pogrom against Muslim community in Arakan province, W Myanmar, carried out with army backing. April: Saw Maung replaced by Than Shwe. Several political prisoners liberated. Sept: martial law lifted, but restrictions on political freedom remained.

1993 Constitutional convention held in Yangon to discuss adoption of proposed new constitution.

My Lai massacre killing of 109 civilians in My Lai, a village in South Vietnam, by US troops in March 1968. An investigation in 1969 was followed by the conviction of Lt William Calley, commander of the platoon.

N

NAACP abbreviation for ◊*National Association for the Advancement of Colored People*, a US civil rights organization.

Nadir Shah (Khan) *c*. 1880–1933. King of Afghanistan from 1929. Nadir played a key role in the 1919 Afghan War, but was subsequently forced into exile in France. He returned to Kabul in 1929 to seize the throne and embarked on an ambitious modernization programme. This alienated the Muslim clergy and in 1933 he was assassinated by fundamentalists. His successor as king was his son ◊Zahir Shah.

Nagasaki industrial port (coal, iron, shipbuilding) on Kyushu Island, Japan; population (1990) 444,600. On 9 Aug 1945, three days after ◊Hiroshima, the second atom bomb was dropped here at the end of World War II. Of Nagasaki's population of 212,000, 73,884 were killed and 76,796 injured, not counting the long-term victims of radiation.

Nagorno-Karabakh autonomous region of ◊Azerbaijan; population (1987) 180,000 (76% Armenian, 23% Azeri), the Christian Armenians forming an enclave within the predominantly Shi'ite Muslim Azerbaijan. An autonomous protectorate after the Russian Revolution 1917, Nagorno-Karabakh was annexed to Azerbaijan 1923 against the wishes of the largely Christian-Armenian population. Since the local, ethnic Armenian council declared its intention to transfer control of the region to Armenia 1989, the enclave has been racked by fighting between Armenian and Azeri troops, both attempting to assert control. By Feb 1992, the conflict had caused the loss of at least 1,000 lives (501 during 1991 alone) and the displacement of some 270,000 people, half of them Armenian and half Azeri.

Nagy Imre 1895–1958. Hungarian politician, prime minister 1953–55 and 1956. He led the Hungarian revolt against Soviet domination in 1956, for which he was executed.

Nahayan Sheik Sultan bin Zayed al-1918–   . Emir of Abu Dhabi from 1969, when he deposed his brother, Sheik Shakhbut. He was elected president of the supreme council of the United Arab Emirates 1971. In 1991 he was implicated, through his majority ownership, in the international financial scandals associated with the Bank of Commerce and Credit International.

Najibullah Ahmadzai 1947– . Afghan communist politician, state president 1986-92. A member of the Politburo from 1981, he was leader of the People's Democratic Party of Afghanistan (PDPA) from 1986. Although his government initially survived the withdrawal of Soviet troops Feb 1989, continuing pressure from the mujaheddin forces resulted in his eventual overthrow.

Nakasone Yasuhiro 1917– . Japanese conservative politician, leader of the Liberal Democratic Party (LDP) and prime minister 1982–87. He stepped up military spending and increased Japanese participation in international affairs, with closer ties to the USA. He was forced to resign his party post May 1989 as a result of having profited from insider trading in the ◊Recruit scandal. After serving a two-year period of atonement, he rejoined the LDP April 1991.

Namibia formerly (to 1968) *South West Africa* country in SW Africa, bounded N by Angola and Zambia, E by Botswana and South Africa, and W by the Atlantic Ocean. Walvis Bay, part of South Africa, forms an enclave in Namibia on the Atlantic coast.

chronology
1884 German and British colonies established.
1915 German colony seized by South Africa.
1920 Administered by South Africa, under League of Nations mandate, as British South Africa.
1946 Full incorporation in South Africa refused by United Nations (UN).
1958 South-West Africa People's Organization (◊SWAPO) set up to seek racial equality and full independence.
1966 South Africa's apartheid laws extended to the country.
1968 Redesignated Namibia by UN.
1978 UN Security Council Resolution 435 for the granting of full sovereignty accepted by South Africa and then rescinded.
1988 Peace talks between South Africa, Angola, and Cuba led to agreement on full independence for Namibia.
1989 Unexpected incursion by SWAPO guerrillas from Angola into

Namibia threatened agreed independence. Transitional constitution created by elected representatives; SWAPO dominant party.

1990 Liberal multiparty 'independence' constitution adopted; independence achieved. Sam Nujoma elected president.

1991 Agreement on joint administration of disputed port of Walvis Bay reached with South Africa, pending final settlement of dispute.

1992 Agreement on establishment of Walvis Bay Joint Administrative Body.

Narasimha Rao P(amulaparti) V(enkata) 1921– . Indian politician, prime minister of India from 1991 and Congress (I) leader. He governed the state of Andhra Pradesh as chief minister 1971-73, and served in the Congress (I) cabinets of Indira and Rajiv Gandhi as minister of external affairs 1980–85 and 1988–90 and of human resources 1985–88. He took over the party leadership after the assassination of Rajiv Gandhi. Elected prime minister the following month, he instituted a reform of the economy.

Narayan Jaya Prakash 1902–1979. Indian politician. A veteran socialist, he was an associate of Vinobha Bham in the Bhoodan movement for rural reforms that took place during the last years of the Raj. He was prominent in the protest movement against Indira Gandhi's emergency regime 1975–77, and acted as umpire in the ◊Janata party leadership contest that followed Indira Gandhi's defeat in 1977.

Nash Walter 1882–1968. New Zealand Labour politician. He was born in England, and emigrated to New Zealand 1909. He held ministerial posts 1935–49, was prime minister 1957–60, and leader of the Labour Party until 1963.

Nassau agreement treaty signed 18 Dec 1962 whereby the USA provided Britain with Polaris missiles, marking a strengthening in Anglo-American relations.

Nasser Gamal Abdel 1918–1970. Egyptian politician, prime minister 1954–56 and from 1956 president of Egypt (the United Arab Republic 1958–71). In 1952 he was the driving power behind the Neguib coup, which ended the monarchy. His nationalization of the Suez Canal 1956 led to an Anglo-French invasion and the ◊Suez Crisis, and his ambitions for an Egyptian-led union of Arab states led to disquiet in the Middle East (and in the West). Nasser was also an early and influential leader of the nonaligned movement.

National Association for the Advancement of Colored People
(NAACP) US civil-rights organization dedicated to ending inequality and
segregation for African-Americans through nonviolent protest. Founded
1910, its first aim was to eradicate lynching. The NAACP campaigned to
end segregation in state schools; it funded test cases that eventually led to
the Supreme Court decision 1954 outlawing school segregation, although it
was only through the ◊civil-rights movement of the 1960s that desegregation was achieved. In 1987 the NAACP had about 500,000 members, black
and white.

National Dock Labour Scheme in the UK, a scheme that guaranteed
continued employment and pay for dockworkers, even if there was no work
to be done; some 9,000 dockworkers were registered under the scheme,
which operated from 1947 until its abolition by the Thatcher government in
1989.

National Endowment for Democracy US political agency founded
1983 with government backing. It has funded a range of political organizations abroad, with over 95% of its $114 million annual income coming
from the US government after 1984.

National Guard ◊militia force recruited by each state of the USA. The
volunteer National Guard units are under federal orders in emergencies,
and under the control of the governor in peacetime, and are now an integral
part of the US Army. The National Guard has been used against demonstrators; in May 1970 at Kent State University, Ohio, they killed four students
who were protesting against the bombing of Cambodia by the USA.

National Insurance Act UK act of Parliament 1911, introduced by
Lloyd George, Liberal chancellor, which first provided insurance for workers against ill health and unemployment.

nationalization policy of bringing a country's essential services and
industries under public ownership. It was pursued, for example, by the UK
Labour government 1945–51. In recent years the trend towards nationalization has slowed and in many countries (the UK, France, and Japan) reversed
(◊privatization). Assets in the hands of foreign governments or companies
may also be nationalized; for example, Iran's oil industry (see ◊Abadan), the
◊Suez Canal, and US-owned fruit plantations in Guatemala, all in the 1950s.

National Party, Australian Australian political party representing the
interests of the farmers and people of the smaller towns. It developed from

about 1860 as the *National Country Party*, and holds the power balance between Liberals and Labor. It gained strength following the introduction of proportional representation 1918, and has been in coalition with the Liberals since 1949.

National Socialism official name for the ◊Nazi movement in Germany; see also ◊fascism.

NATO abbreviation for ◊*North Atlantic Treaty Organization*.

Nauru island country in Polynesia, SW Pacific, W of Kiribati.

chronology
1920 Administered by Australia, New Zealand, and UK until independence, except 1942–45, when it was occupied by Japan.
1968 Independence achieved from Australia, New Zealand, and UK with 'special member' Commonwealth status. Hammer ◊DeRoburt elected president.
1976 Bernard Dowiyogo elected president.
1978 DeRoburt re-elected.
1986 DeRoburt briefly replaced as president by Kennan Adeang.
1987 DeRoburt re-elected; Adeang established the Democratic Party of Nauru.
1989 DeRoburt replaced by Kensas Aroi, who was later succeeded by Dowiyogo.
1992 Dowiyogo re-elected.

Nazarbayev Nursultan 1940– . President of Kazakhstan from 1990. In the Soviet period he was prime minister of the republic 1984-89 and leader of the Kazakh Communist Party 1989-91, which established itself as the independent Socialist Party of Kazakhstan (SPK) Sept 1991. He advocates free-market policies, yet enjoys the support of the environmentalist lobby. He joined the Communist Party at 22 and left it after the failed Soviet coup 1991.

Nazism ideology based on racism, nationalism, and the supremacy of the state over the individual. The German Nazi party, the *Nationalsozialistische Deutsche Arbeiterpartei* (National Socialist German Workers' Party), was formed from the German Workers' Party (founded 1919) and led by Adolf ◊Hitler 1921–45.

Nazi-Soviet pact see ◊Hitler–Stalin pact.

Neave Airey (Middleton Sheffield) 1916–1979. British intelligence officer and Conservative member of Parliament 1953-79, a close adviser to Prime Minister Thatcher. During World War II he escaped from Colditz, a German high-security prison camp. As shadow undersecretary of state for Northern Ireland from 1975, he became a target for extremist groups and was assassinated by an Irish terrorist bomb.

Nehru Jawaharlal 1889–1964. Indian nationalist politician, prime minister from 1947. Before the partition (the division of British India into India and Pakistan), he led the socialist wing of the nationalist Congress Party, and was second in influence only to Mohandas Gandhi. He was imprisoned nine times by the British 1921–45 for political activities. As prime minister from the creation of the dominion (later republic) of India in Aug 1947, he originated the idea of nonalignment (neutrality towards major powers). His daughter was Prime Minister Indira Gandhi.

Nehru Report constitution drafted for India 1928. After Indian nationalists rejected the ◊Simon Commission 1927, an all-party committee was set up, chaired by Motilal ◊Nehru, to map out a constitution. Established to counter British charges that Indians could not find a constitutional consensus among themselves, it advocated that India be given dominion status of complete internal self-government. Many members of the Congress preferred complete independence to dominion status, and in 1929 announced a campaign of civil disobedience to support their demands.

NEP abbreviation for the Soviet leader Lenin's ◊*New Economic Policy*.

Nepal landlocked country in the Himalayan mountain range in Central Asia, bounded N by Tibet (an autonomous region of China), E, S, and W by India.

chronology
1923 Independence achieved from Britain.
1951 Monarchy restored.
1959 Constitution created elected legislature.
1960-61 Parliament dissolved by king; political parties banned.
1980 Constitutional referendum held following popular agitation.
1981 Direct elections held to national assembly.
1983 Overthrow of monarch-supported prime minister.
1986 New assembly elections returned a majority opposed to *panchayat* system of partyless government.

1988 Strict curbs placed on opposition activity; over 100 supporters of banned opposition party arrested; censorship imposed.

1989 Border blockade imposed by India in treaty dispute.

1990 *Panchayat* system collapsed after mass prodemocracy demonstrations; new constitution introduced; elections set for May 1991.

1991 Nepali Congress Party, led by Girija Prasad Koirala, won the general election.

1992 Communists led anti-government demonstrations in Katmandu and Pátan.

Neruda Pablo. Pen name of Neftalí Ricardo Reyes y Basualto 1904–1973. Chilean poet and diplomat. His work includes lyrics and the epic poem of the American continent *Canto General* 1950. He was awarded the Nobel Prize for Literature 1971. He served as consul and ambassador to many countries.

Netherlands, the country in W Europe on the North Sea, bounded E by Germany and S by Belgium.

chronology

1940–45 Occupied by Germany during World War II.

1947 Joined Benelux customs union.

1948 Queen Juliana succeeded Queen Wilhelmina to the throne.

1949 Became a founding member of North Atlantic Treaty Organization (NATO).

1953 Dykes breached by storm; nearly 2,000 people and tens of thousands of cattle died in flood.

1958 Joined European Economic Community.

1980 Queen Juliana abdicated in favour of her daughter Beatrix.

1981 Opposition to cruise missiles averted their being sited on Dutch soil.

1989 Prime Minister Ruud Lubbers resigned; new Lubbers-led coalition elected.

1991 Treaty on political and monetary union signed by European Community (EC) members at Maastricht.

1992 Maastricht Treaty ratified.

neutrality the legal status of a country that decides not to choose sides in a war. Certain states, notably Switzerland and Austria, have opted for permanent neutrality. Neutrality always has a legal connotation. In peacetime, neutrality towards the big power alliances is called *nonalignment* (see ◊nonaligned movement).

New Deal in US history, programme introduced by President F D Roosevelt 1933 to counter the Great Depression, including employment on public works, farm loans at low rates, and social reforms such as old-age and unemployment insurance, prevention of child labour, protection of employees against unfair practices by employers, and loans to local authorities for slum clearance.

New Economic Policy (NEP) economic policy of the USSR 1921–29 devised by the Soviet leader Lenin. Rather than requisitioning all agricultural produce above a stated subsistence allowance, the state requisitioned only a fixed proportion of the surplus; the rest could be traded freely by the peasant. The NEP thus reinstated a limited form of free-market trading, although the state retained complete control of major industries.

Ne Win adopted name of Maung Shu Maung 1911– . Myanmar (Burmese) politician, prime minister 1958–60, ruler from 1962 to 1974, president 1974–81, and chair until 1988 of the ruling Burma Socialist Programme Party (BSPP). His domestic 'Burmese Way to Socialism' policy programme brought the economy into serious decline.

New Ireland Forum meeting between politicians of the Irish Republic and Northern Ireland May 1983. It offered three potential solutions to the Northern Irish problem, but all were rejected by the UK the following year.

newly industrialized country (NIC) country that has in recent decades experienced a breakthrough into manufacturing and rapid export-led economic growth. The prime examples are Taiwan, Hong Kong, Singapore, and South Korea. Their economic development during the 1970s and 1980s was partly due to a rapid increase of manufactured goods in their exports.

New Socialist Destour Party former name (1988–89) of Tunisian political party Democratic Constitutional Rally (RCD).

New Zealand or *Aotearoa* country in the SW Pacific Ocean, SE of Australia, comprising two main islands, North Island and South Island, and other small islands.

chronology
1907 Created a dominion of the British Empire.
1931 Granted independence from Britain.
1947 Independence within the Commonwealth confirmed by the New Zealand parliament.

1972 National Party government replaced by Labour Party, with Norman ◊Kirk as prime minister.

1974 Kirk died; replaced by Wallace ◊Rowling.

1975 National Party returned, with Robert ◊Muldoon as prime minister.

1984 Labour Party returned under David ◊Lange.

1985 Non-nuclear military policy created disagreements with France and the USA.

1987 National Party declared support for the Labour government's non-nuclear policy. Lange re-elected. New Zealand officially classified as a 'friendly' rather than 'allied' country by the USA because of its non-nuclear military policy.

1988 Free-trade agreement with Australia signed.

1989 Lange resigned over economic differences with finance minister (he cited health reasons); replaced by Geoffrey ◊Palmer.

1990 Palmer replaced by Mike Moore. Labour Party defeated by National Party in general election; Jim ◊Bolger became prime minister.

1991 Formation of amalgamated Alliance Party set to challenge two-party system.

1992 Ban on visits by US warships lifted. Constitutional change agreed upon.

Nguyen Van Linh 1914–   . Vietnamese communist politician, member of the Politburo 1976–81 and from 1985; party leader 1986–91. He began economic liberalization and troop withdrawal from Cambodia and Laos.

Nicaragua country in Central America, between the Pacific Ocean and the Caribbean Sea, bounded N by Honduras and S by Costa Rica.

chronology

1926–1933 Occupied by US marines.

1936 General Anastasio ◊Somoza elected president; start of near-dictatorial rule by Somoza family.

1962 Sandinista National Liberation Front (FSLN) formed to fight Somoza regime.

1979 Somoza government ousted by FSLN.

1982 Subversive activity against the government promoted by the USA. State of emergency declared.

1984 The USA mined Nicaraguan harbours.

1985 Denunciation of Sandinista government by US president Reagan. FSLN won assembly elections.

1987 Central American peace agreement cosigned by Nicaraguan leaders.

1988 Peace agreement failed. Nicaragua held talks with ◊Contra rebel leaders. Hurricane left 180,000 people homeless.

1989 Demobilization of rebels and release of former Somozan supporters; cease-fire ended.

1990 FSLN defeated by UNO, a US-backed coalition; Violeta Barrios de Chamorro elected president. Antigovernment riots.

1991 First presidential state visit to USA for over fifty years.

1992 June: US aid suspended because of concern over role of Sandinista in Nicaraguan government. Sept: around 16,000 made homeless by earthquake.

Nicaraguan Revolution the revolt 1978–79 in Nicaragua, led by the socialist *Sandinistas* against the US-supported right-wing dictatorship established by Anastasio ◊Somoza. His son, President Anastasio (Debayle) Somoza (1925–1980), was forced into exile 1979 and assassinated in Paraguay. The Sandinista National Liberation Front (FSLN) was named after Augusto César Sandino, a guerrilla leader killed by the US-trained National Guard 1934.

Nicholas II 1868–1918. Tsar of Russia 1894–1917. He was dominated by his wife, Tsarina ◊Alexandra, who was under the influence of the religious charlatan ◊Rasputin. His mismanagement of the Russo-Japanese War and of internal affairs led to the revolution of 1905, which he suppressed, although he was forced to grant limited constitutional reforms. He took Russia into World War I in 1914, was forced to abdicate in 1917 after the ◊Russian Revolution and was executed with his family.

Niemöller Martin 1892–1984. German Christian Protestant pastor. He was imprisoned in a concentration camp 1938–45 for campaigning against Nazism in the German church. He was president of the World Council of Churches 1961–68.

Niger landlocked country in NW Africa, bounded N by Algeria and Libya, E by Chad, S by Nigeria and Benin, and W by Burkina Faso and Mali.

chronology

1960 Achieved full independence from France; Hamani Diori elected president.

1974 Diori ousted in army coup led by Seyni Kountché.

1977 Cooperation agreement signed with France.

1987 Kountché died; replaced by Col Ali Saibu.

1989 Ali Saibu elected president without opposition.

1990 Multiparty politics promised.

1991 Saibu stripped of executive powers; transitional government formed.

1992 Transitional government collapsed. Constitutional change allowing for multiparty politics approved in referendum.

Nigeria country in W Africa on the Gulf of Guinea, bounded N by Niger, E by Chad and Cameroon, and W by Benin.

chronology

1914 N Nigeria and S Nigeria united to become Britain's largest African colony.

1954 Nigeria became a federation.

1960 Independence achieved from Britain within the Commonwealth.

1963 Became a republic, with Nnamdi Azikiwe as president.

1966 Military coup, followed by a counter-coup led by General Yakubu ◊Gowon. Slaughter of many members of the Ibo tribe in north.

1967 Conflict over oil revenues led to declaration of an independent Ibo state of ◊Biafra and outbreak of civil war.

1970 Surrender of Biafra and end of civil war.

1975 Gowon ousted in military coup; second coup put General Olusegun Obasanjo in power.

1979 Shehu Shagari became civilian president.

1983 Shagari's government overthrown in coup by Maj-Gen Muhammadu Buhari.

1985 Buhari replaced in a bloodless coup led by Maj-General Ibrahim ◊Babangida.

1989 Two new political parties approved. Babangida promised a return to pluralist politics; date set for 1992.

1991 Nine new states created. Babangida confirmed his commitment to democratic rule for 1992.

1992 Multiparty elections won by Babangida's Social Democratic Party (SDP). Primary elections to be introduced; transition to civilian rule delayed.

Night of the Long Knives in World War II, a purge of the German Nazi party to root out possible opposition to Adolf Hitler. On the night of 29–30 June 1934 (and the following two days) the SS units under Heinrich ◊Himmler were used by Hitler to exterminate the Nazi private army

Sturm-Abteilung (SA or the Brownshirts) under Captain Ernst Roehm. Others were also executed for alleged conspiracy against Hitler (including Kurt von Schleicher). The Nazi purge enabled Hitler to gain the acceptance of the German officer corps and, when President Hindenburg died five weeks later, to become head of state.

Nimitz Chester William 1885–1966. US admiral, commander in chief of the US Pacific fleet. He reconquered the Solomon Islands 1942–43, Gilbert Islands 1943, the Marianas and Marshalls 1944, and signed the Japanese surrender 1945 as the US representative.

Nixon Richard (Milhous) 1913– . 37th president of the USA 1969–74, a Republican. He attracted attention as a member of the Un-American Activities Committee 1948, and was vice president to Eisenhower 1953–61. As president he was responsible for US withdrawal from Vietnam, and forged new links with China, but at home his culpability in the cover-up of the ◊Watergate scandal and the existence of a 'slush fund' for political machinations during his re-election campaign 1972 led to his resignation 1974 when threatened with impeachment.

Nkomati Accord nonaggression treaty between South Africa and Mozambique concluded 1984, under which they agreed not to give material aid to opposition movements in each other's countries, which in effect meant that South Africa pledged itself not to support the Mozambique National Resistance (Renamo), while Mozambique was committed not to help the then outlawed African National Congress (ANC).

Nkomo Joshua 1917– . Zimbabwean politician, vice-president from 1988. As president of ZAPU (Zimbabwe African People's Union) from 1961, he was a leader of the black nationalist movement against the white Rhodesian regime. He was a member of Robert ◊Mugabe's cabinet 1980–82 and from 1987.

Nkrumah Kwame 1909–1972. Ghanaian nationalist politician, prime minister of the Gold Coast (Ghana's former name) 1952–57 and of newly independent Ghana 1957–60. He became Ghana's first president 1960 but was overthrown in a coup 1966. His policy of 'African socialism' led to links with the communist bloc.

NKVD the Soviet secret police 1934–38, replaced by the ◊KGB. The NKVD was reponsible for Stalin's infamous purges.

Noel-Baker Philip John 1889–1982. British Labour politician. He was involved in drafting the charters of both the League of Nations and the United Nations. He published *The Arms Race* 1958, and was awarded the 1959 Nobel Peace Prize.

nonaligned movement countries adopting a strategic and political position of neutrality ('nonalignment') towards major powers, specifically the USA and former USSR. Although originally used by poorer states, the non-aligned position was later adopted by oil-producing nations. The 1989 summit in Belgrade was attended by 102 member states. With the ending of the Cold War, the movement's survival was in doubt.

non-cooperation movement or *satyagraha* in India, a large-scale civil disobedience campaign orchestrated by Mahatma ◊Gandhi 1920 following the ◊Amritsar massacre April 1919. Based on a policy of peaceful non-cooperation, the strategy was to bring the British administrative machine to a halt by the total withdrawal of Indian support. British-made goods were boycotted, as were schools, courts of law, and elective offices. The campaign made little impression on the British government, since they could ignore it when it was peaceful; when it became violent, Gandhi felt obliged to call off further demonstrations. Its most successful aspect was that it increased political awareness among the Indian people.

Noriega Manuel (Antonio Morena) 1940–   . Panamanian soldier and politician, effective ruler of Panama from 1982, as head of the National Guard, until deposed by the USA 1989. An informer for the US Central Intelligence Agency, he was known to be involved in drug trafficking as early as 1972. He enjoyed US support until 1987. In the 1989 US invasion of Panama, he was forcibly taken to the USA, tried, and convicted of trafficking in 1992.

Normandy landings alternative name for ◊D-Day.

North Oliver 1943–   . US Marine lieutenant colonel. In 1981 he was inducted into the National Security Council (NSC), where he supervised the mining of Nicaraguan harbours 1983, an air-force bombing raid on Libya 1986, and an arms-for-hostages deal with Iran 1985, which, when uncovered 1986 (◊Irangate), forced his dismissal and trial.

North Africa Campaign Allied military campaign 1940–42 during World War II. Shortly after Italy declared war on France and Britain June 1940, an Italian offensive was launched from Libya towards Egypt and the

Suez Canal. In Dec 1940 Britain launched a successful counter-offensive and captured Cyrenaica. Following agreement between Mussolini and Hitler, the German Afrikakorps was established under General Rommel. During 1941 and early 1942 the Axis powers advanced, recaptured Tobruk, and crossed the Egyptian border before halting at El ◊Alamein. The British 8th Army under General Montgomery won a decisive Allied victory against Rommel's forces at El Alamein on 4 Nov 1942, followed by advances across Libya from Tunisia. British and US troops advanced from French NW Africa and the Allied armies in N Africa converged on Tunis. After a last-ditch defence, the Axis forces surrendered in May 1943.

North Atlantic Treaty Organization (NATO) association set up 1949 to provide for the collective defence of the major W European and North American states against the perceived threat from the USSR. Its chief body is the Council of Foreign Ministers (who have representatives in permanent session), and there is an international secretariat in Brussels, Belgium, and also the Military Committee consisting of the Chiefs of Staff. The military headquarters SHAPE (Supreme Headquarters Allied Powers, Europe) is in Chièvres, near Mons, Belgium. After the E European ◊Warsaw Pact was disbanded 1991, an adjunct to NATO, the *North Atlantic Cooperation Council*, was established, including all the former Soviet republics, with the aim of building greater security in Europe.

North–South divide geographical division of the world that theoretically demarcates the rich from the poor. The South includes all of Asia except Japan, Australia, and New Zealand; all of Africa, the Middle East, Central and South America. The North includes Europe, the USA, Canada, and all republics of the former Soviet Union. Newly industrialized countries such as South Korea and Taiwan could, however, be said to have more in common with the industrialized North than with ◊Third World countries.

Norway country in NW Europe, on the Scandinavian peninsula, bounded E by Sweden, NE by Finland and Russia, S by the North Sea, W by the Atlantic Ocean, and N by the Arctic Ocean.

chronology
1905 Links with Sweden ended; full independence achieved.
1940-45 Occupied by Germany.
1949 Joined North Atlantic Treaty Organization (NATO).
1952 Joined Nordic Council.

1957 King Haakon VII succeeded by his son Olaf V.

1960 Joined European Free Trade Association (EFTA).

1972 Accepted into membership of European Economic Community; application withdrawn after a referendum.

1988 Gro Harlem ◊Brundtland awarded Third World Prize.

1989 Jan P Syse became prime minister.

1990 Brundtland returned to power.

1991 King Olaf V died; succeeded by his son Harald V.

1992 Defied whaling ban to resume whaling industry. Brundtland relinquished leadership of the Labour Party. Formal application made for EC membership.

Nott John 1932–   . British Conservative politician, minister for defence 1981–83 during the ◊Falkland Islands conflict with Argentina.

November criminals name given by right-wing nationalists in post-1918 Germany to the socialist politicians who had taken over the government after the abdication of Kaiser Wilhelm II and had signed the armistice with the Western Allies Nov 1918.

Nu U (Thakin) 1907–   . Myanmar politician, prime minister of Burma (now Myanmar) for most of the period from 1948 to the military coup of 1962. Exiled from 1966, U Nu returned to the country 1980 and, in 1988, helped found the National League for Democracy opposition movement.

nuclear warfare war involving the use of nuclear weapons. The worldwide total of nuclear weapons in 1990 was about 50,000, and the number of countries possessing nuclear weapons stood officially at five—USA, USSR, UK, France, and China—although some other nations were thought either to have a usable stockpile of these weapons (Israel) or the ability to produce them quickly (Brazil, India, Pakistan, South Africa). Nuclear-weapons research began in Britain 1940, but was transferred to the USA after it entered World War II. The research programme, known as the Manhattan Project, was directed by J Robert Oppenheimer.

atom bomb The original weapon relied on use of a chemical explosion to trigger a chain reaction. The first test explosion was at Alamogordo, New Mexico, 16 July 1945; the first use in war was by the USA against Japan 6 Aug 1945 over Hiroshima and three days later at Nagasaki.

hydrogen bomb A much more powerful weapon than the atom bomb, it relies on the release of thermonuclear energy by the condensation of hydrogen nuclei to helium nuclei (as happens in the Sun). The first detonation was at Eniwetok Atoll, Pacific Ocean, 1952 by the USA.

neutron bomb or *e*nhanced *r*adiation *w*eapon (ERW) A very small hydrogen bomb that has relatively high radiation but relatively low blast, designed to kill (in up to six days) by a brief neutron radiation that leaves buildings and weaponry intact.

nuclear methods of attack now include aircraft bombs, missiles (long-or short-range, surface to surface, air to surface, and surface to air), depth charges, and high-powered landmines ('atomic demolition munitions') to destroy bridges and roads.

Nujoma Sam 1929– . Namibian left-wing politician, president from 1990, founder and leader of ◊SWAPO (the South-West Africa People's Organization) from 1959. He was exiled in 1960 and controlled guerrillas from Angolan bases until the first free elections were held 1989, taking office early the following year.

Nuremberg rallies annual meetings 1933–38 of the German ◊Nazi Party. They were characterized by extensive torchlight parades, marches in party formations, and mass rallies addressed by Nazi leaders such as Hitler and Goebbels.

Nuremberg trials after World War II, the trials of the 24 chief ◊Nazi war criminals Nov 1945–Oct 1946 by an international military tribunal consisting of four judges and four prosecutors: one of each from the USA, UK, USSR, and France. An appendix accused the German cabinet, general staff, high command, Nazi leadership corps, ◊SS, ◊Sturmabteilung, and ◊Gestapo of criminal behaviour.

Nyerere Julius (Kambarage) 1922– . Tanzanian socialist politician, president 1964–85. He devoted himself from 1954 to the formation of the Tanganyika African National Union and subsequent campaigning for independence. He became chief minister 1960, was prime minister of Tanganyika 1961–62, president of the newly formed Tanganyika Republic 1962–64, and first president of Tanzania 1964–85.

Nyers Rezso 1923– . Hungarian socialist leader. A member of the politburo from 1966 and the architect of Hungary's liberalizing economic reforms in 1968, he was ousted from power by hardliners 1974. In 1988 he was brought back into the politburo, and became head of the newly formed Hungarian Socialist Party in 1989.

O

OAS abbreviation for ◊*Organization of American States*.

OAU abbreviation for ◊*Organization of African Unity*.

Obote (Apollo) Milton 1924– . Ugandan politician who led the independence movement from 1961. He became prime minister 1962 and was president 1966–71 and 1980–85, being overthrown by first Idi ◊Amin and then by Lt-Gen Tito Okello.

October Revolution second stage of the ◊Russian Revolution 1917, when, on 24 Oct (6 Nov in the Western calendar), the Bolshevik forces under Trotsky, and on orders from Lenin, seized the Winter Palace and arrested members of the Provisional Government. The following day the Second All-Russian Congress of Soviets handed over power to the Bolsheviks.

Octobrists group of Russian liberal constitutional politicians who accepted the reforming October Manifesto instituted by Tsar Nicholas II after the 1905 revolution and rejected more radical reforms.

Oder–Neisse Line border between Poland and East Germany agreed at the Potsdam Conference 1945 at the end of World War II, named after the two rivers that formed the frontier.

OGPU name 1923–34 of the Soviet secret police, later the ◊KGB.

Okuma Shigenobu 1838–1922. Japanese politician and prime minister 1898 and 1914–16. He presided over Japanese pressure for territorial concessions in China, before retiring 1916.

Olaf V 1903–1991. King of Norway from 1957, when he succeeded his father, Haakon VII.

Oman country at the SE end of the Arabian peninsula, bounded W by the United Arab Emirates, Saudi Arabia, and Yemen, SE by the Arabian Sea, and NE by the Gulf of Oman.

chronology
1951 The Sultanate of Muscat and Oman achieved full independence from Britain. Treaty of Friendship with Britain signed.
1970 After 38 years' rule, Sultan Said bin Taimur replaced in coup by his son Qaboos bin Said. Name changed to Sultanate of Oman.
1975 Left-wing rebels in south defeated.
1982 Memorandum of Understanding with UK signed, providing for regular consultation on international issues.
1985 Diplomatic ties established with USSR.
1991 Sent troops to Operation Desert Storm, as part of coalition opposing Iraq's occupation of Kuwait.

O'Neill Terence, Baron O'Neill of the Maine 1914–1990. Northern Irish Unionist politician. In the Ulster government he was minister of finance 1956–63, then prime minister 1963–69. He resigned when opposed by his party on measures to extend rights to Roman Catholics, including a universal franchise.

OPEC acronym for ◊*Organization of Petroleum-Exporting Countries*.

Orange, Project in South Africa, 1980 plan for a white 'homeland' (Projek Oranje) to be established on the border between Orange Free State and the Northern Cape. No black person would be allowed to live or work there.

Organisation de l'Armée Secrète (OAS) guerrilla organization formed 1961 by French settlers devoted to perpetuating their own rule in Algeria (Algérie Française). It collapsed on the imprisonment 1962–68 of its leader, General Raoul Salan.

Organization for Economic Cooperation and Development (OECD) international organization of 24 industrialized countries that provides a forum for discussion and coordination of member states' economic and social policies. Founded 1961, with its headquarters in Paris, the OECD superseded the Organization for European Economic Cooperation, which had been established 1948 to implement the ◊Marshall Plan.

Organization of African Unity (OAU) association established 1963 to eradicate colonialism and improve economic, cultural, and political cooperation in Africa. Its membership expanded to 51 countries when Namibia joined after independence 1990. The secretary general is Salim Ahmed Salim of Tanzania. Its headquarters are in Addis Ababa, Ethiopia.

Organization of American States (OAS) association founded 1948 by a charter signed by representatives of 30 North, Central, and South American states. It aims to maintain peace and solidarity within the hemisphere, and is also concerned with the social and economic development of Latin America.

Organization of Petroleum-Exporting Countries (OPEC) body established 1960 to coordinate price and supply policies of oil-producing states. Its concerted action in raising prices in the 1970s triggered worldwide recession but also lessened demand so that its influence was reduced by the mid-1980s. OPEC members in 1991 were: Algeria, Ecuador, Gabon, Indonesia, Iran, Iraq, Kuwait, Libya, Nigeria, Qatar, Saudi Arabia, the United Arab Emirates, and Venezuela.

Orlando Vittorio Emanuele 1860–1952. Italian politician, prime minister 1917–19. He attended the Paris Peace Conference after World War I, but dissatisfaction with his handling of the Adriatic settlement led to his resignation. He initially supported Mussolini but was in retirement 1925–46, when he returned to the assembly and then the senate.

Ortega Saavedra Daniel 1945– . Nicaraguan socialist politician, head of state 1981–90. He was a member of the Sandinista Liberation Front (FSLN), which overthrew the regime of Anastasio Somoza 1979. US-sponsored ◊Contra guerrillas opposed his government from 1982.

Osborne Judgement UK legal ruling of 1909 that prevented ◊trade unions from using membership subscriptions to finance the Labour Party. In 1913 the judgement was negated by the Trade Union Act, which permitted them to raise political levies and provide financial support to the Labour Party. Individual trade unionists could 'contract out' of the political levy by signing a form saying they did not wish to pay.

Oscar II 1829–1907. King of Sweden and Norway 1872–1905, King of Sweden till 1907. He tried hard to prevent the separation of his two kingdoms but relinquished the throne of Norway to ◊Haakon VII 1905.

Ottawa agreements trade agreements concluded at the Imperial Economic Conference, held in Ottawa 1932, between Britain and its dependent territories, lowering tariffs on British manufactured goods and increasing duties on non-Dominion produce.

Ottoman Empire Muslim empire of the Turks 1300–1920, the successor of the Seljuk Empire. At its greatest extent the Ottoman Empire's boundaries were Europe as far as Hungary, part of S Russia, Iran, the Palestinian coastline, Egypt, and N Africa. From the 17th century it was in decline. There was an attempted revival and reform under the ◊Young Turk party 1908, but the regime crumbled when Turkey sided with Germany in World War I. The sultanate was abolished by Kemal Atatürk 1922; the last sultan was Muhammad VI.

Overlord, Operation Allied invasion of Normandy 6 June 1944 (D-day) during World War II.

Owen David 1938– . British politician, Labour foreign secretary 1977–79. In 1981 he was one of the founders of the Social Democratic Party (SDP), and in 1983 became its leader. Opposed to the decision of the majority of the party to merge with the Liberals 1987, Owen stood down, but emerged 1988 as leader of a rump SDP, which was eventually disbanded 1990. In 1992 he was chosen to replace Lord Carrington as EC mediator in the peace talks on ◊Bosnia-Herzegovina. Together with UN mediator Cyrus Vance, he was responsible for devising a peace plan dividing the republic into 10 semi-autonomous provinces.

Oxford and Asquith, Earl of title of British Liberal politician Herbert Henry ◊Asquith.

Ozal Turgut 1927– . Turkish Islamic right-wing politician, prime minister 1983–89, president from 1989. He has been responsible for improving his country's relations with Greece, but his prime objective has been to strengthen Turkey's alliance with the USA.

P

pacifism belief that violence, even in self-defence, is unjustifiable under any conditions and that arbitration is preferable to war as a means of solving disputes. In the East, pacifism has roots in Buddhism, and non-violent action was used by Mahatma ◊Gandhi in the struggle for Indian independence.

Pacifist sentiment in Europe before and during World War I persuaded many to become conscientious objectors and refuse to fight, even when conscripted. They were imprisoned and in some cases executed. As a result of the carnage in the war, pacifism became more acceptable in the 1920s and 1930s, and organizations like the Peace Pledge Union in Britain were initiated. During World War II, conscientious objectors who refused to bear arms were often placed in noncombatant units such as the British Pioneer Corps, or in medical units.

pact of steel military alliance between Nazi Germany and Fascist Italy, instituted 1939.

Page Earle (Christmas Grafton) 1880–1961. Australian politician, leader of the Country Party 1920–39 and briefly prime minister in April 1939. He represented Australia in the British war cabinet 1941–42 and was minister of health 1949–55.

Pahlavi dynasty Iranian dynasty founded by Reza Khan (1877–1944), an army officer who seized control of the government 1921 and was proclaimed shah 1925. During World War II, Britain and the USSR were nervous about his German sympathies and occupied Iran 1941–46. They compelled him to abdicate 1941 in favour of his son Muhammad Reza Shah Pahlavi, who took office in 1956, with US support, and was deposed in the Islamic revolution of 1979.

Pakistan country in S Asia, stretching from the Himalayas to the Arabian Sea, bounded W by Iran, NW by Afghanistan, NE by China, and E by India.

chronology

1947 Independence achieved from Britain, Pakistan formed following partition of British India.

1956 Proclaimed a republic.

1958 Military rule imposed by General Ayub Khan.

1969 Power transferred to General Yahya Khan.

1971 Secession of East Pakistan (Bangladesh). After civil war, power transferred to Zulfiqar Alix Bhutto.

1977 Bhutto overthrown in military coup by General ◊Zia ul-Haq; martial law imposed.

1979 Bhutto executed.

1981 Opposition Movement for the Restoration of Democracy formed. Islamization process pushed forward.

1985 Nonparty elections held, amended constitution adopted, martial law and ban on political parties lifted.

1986 Agitation for free elections launched by Benazir ◊Bhutto.

1988 Zia introduced Islamic legal code, the *Shari'a*. He was killed in a military plane crash in Aug. Benazir Bhutto elected prime minister Nov.

1989 Pakistan rejoined the Commonwealth.

1990 Army mobilized in support of Muslim separatists in Indian Kashmir. Bhutto dismissed on charges of incompetence and corruption. Islamic Democratic Alliance (IDA), led by Nawaz Sharif, won Oct general election.

1991 *Shari'a* bill enacted; privatization and economic deregulation programme launched.

1992 Sept: Floods devastated north of country. Oct: Pakistan elected to UN Security Council 1993-95.

Palestine Liberation Organization (PLO) Arab organization founded 1964 to bring about an independent state of Palestine. It consists of several distinct groupings, the chief of which is al-◊Fatah, led by Yassir ◊Arafat, the president of the PLO from 1969. Originally seeking the destruction of the Israeli state, the PLO's main aim became the establishment of a Palestinian state alongside the Israeli one.

Palestine Wars another name for the ◊Arab-Israeli Wars.

Palme (Sven) Olof 1927–1986. Swedish social-democratic politician, prime minister 1969–76 and 1982–86. As prime minister he carried out constitutional reforms, turning the Riksdag into a single-chamber parliament and stripping the monarch of power, and was widely respected for his support of Third World Countries. He was assassinated Feb 1986.

Palmer A(lexander) Mitchell 1872–1936. US public official. He held office in the US House of Representatives 1909-15. A Quaker, he declined an appointment as secretary of war under President Wilson, and served instead as custodian of alien property during World War I. As US attorney general 1919-21, he led the controversial 'Palmer Raids' against alleged political radicals.

Palmer Geoffrey Winston Russell 1942–   . New Zealand Labour politician, prime minister 1989–90, deputy prime minister and attorney-general 1984–89.

Pan-Africanist Congress (PAC) militant black South African nationalist group, which broke away from the African National Congress (ANC) 1959. More radical than the ANC, the Pan-Africanist Congress has a black-only policy for Africa. PAC was outlawed from 1960 to 1990. Its military wing is called Poqo ('we alone').

Panama country in Central America, on a narrow isthmus between the Caribbean and the Pacific Ocean, bounded W by Costa Rica and E by Colombia.

chronology
1903 Full independence from Spain achieved on separation from the confederacy of Gran Colombia.
1974 Agreement to negotiate full transfer of the Panama Canal from the USA to Panama.
1977 USA–Panama treaties transferred the canal to Panama, effective from 1999, with the USA guaranteeing its protection and an annual payment.
1984 Nicolás Ardito Barletta elected president.
1985 Barletta resigned; replaced by Eric Arturo del Valle.
1987 General ¢Noriega (head of the National Guard and effective ruler) resisted calls for his removal, despite suspension of US military and economic aid.
1988 Del Valle replaced by Manuel Solis Palma. Noriega, charged with drug smuggling by the USA, declared a state of emergency.
1989 Opposition won election; Noriega declared results invalid; Francisco Rodríguez sworn in as president. Coup attempt against Noriega failed. Noriega declared head of government by assembly. 'State of war' with the

USA announced; US invasion deposed Noriega; Guillermo Endara installed as president. Noriega sought asylum in Vatican embassy; later surrendered and taken to US for trial.

1991 Attempted antigovernment coup foiled. Army abolished.

1992 Noriega found guilty of drug offences. Referendum voted down overwhelmingly government's constitutional changes, including abolition of a standing army.

Panama Canal canal across the Panama isthmus in Central America, connecting the Pacific and Atlantic oceans; length 80 km/50 mi, with 12 locks. Built by the USA 1904-14 after an unsuccessful attempt by the French, it was formally opened 1920. The *Panama Canal Zone* was acquired 'in perpetuity' by the USA 1903, comprising land extending about 5 km/3 mi on either side of the canal. The zone passed to Panama 1979, and control of the canal itself was ceded to Panama by the USA Jan 1990 under the terms of the Panama Canal Treaty 1977. The Canal Zone has several US military bases.

Pan-American Union former name (1910–48) of the ◊Organization of American States.

Pandit Vijaya Lakshmi 1900–1990. Indian politician, member of parliament 1964–68. She was involved, with her brother Jawaharlal ◊Nehru, in the struggle for India's independence and was imprisoned three times by the British. She was the first woman to serve as president of the United Nations General Assembly, 1953–54, and held a number of political and diplomatic posts until her retirement 1968.

Pankhurst Emmeline (born Goulden) 1858–1928. English suffragette. Founder of the Women's Social and Political Union 1903, she launched the militant suffragette campaign 1905. In 1926 she joined the Conservative Party and was a prospective Parliamentary candidate.

She was supported by her daughters *Christabel Pankhurst* (1880–1958), political leader of the movement, and *Sylvia Pankhurst* (1882–1960). The latter was imprisoned nine times under the ◊'Cat and Mouse Act', and was a pacifist in World War I.

Papandreou Andreas 1919–   . Greek socialist politician, founder of the Pan-Hellenic Socialist Movement (PASOK), and prime minister 1981–89, when he became implicated in the alleged embezzlement and diversion of funds to the Greek government of $200 million from the Bank of Crete, headed by George Koskotas, and as a result lost the election. In Jan 1992 a trial cleared Papandreou of all corruption charges.

Papen Franz von 1879–1969. German right-wing politician. As chancellor 1932, he negotiated the Nazi-Conservative alliance that made Hitler chancellor 1933. He was envoy to Austria 1934–38 and ambassador to Turkey 1939–44. Although acquitted at the ◊Nuremberg trials, he was imprisoned by a German denazification court for three years.

Papua New Guinea country in the SW Pacific, comprising the eastern part of the island of New Guinea, the Bismarck Archipelago, and part of the Solomon Islands.

chronology
1884 NE New Guinea annexed by Germany; SE claimed by Britain.
1914 NE New Guinea occupied by Australia.
1921–42 Held as a League of Nations mandate.
1942–45 Occupied by Japan.
1975 Independence achieved from Australia, within the Commonwealth, with Michael Somare as prime minister.
1980 Julius Chan became prime minister.
1982 Somare returned to power.
1985 Somare challenged by deputy prime minister, Paias Wingti, who later formed a five-party coalition government.
1988 Wingti defeated on no-confidence vote and replaced by Rabbie Namaliu, who established a six-party coalition government.
1989 State of emergency imposed on Bougainville in response to separatist violence.
1991 Peace accord signed with Bougainville secessionists. Economic boom as gold production doubled. Wiwa Korowi elected as new governor general. Deputy prime minister, Ted Diro, resigned, having been found guilty of corruption.
1992 April: killings by outlawed Bougainville secessionists reported. July: Wingti elected premier.

Paraguay landlocked country in South America, bounded NE by Brazil, S by Argentina, and NW by Bolivia.

chronology
1932–35 Territory won from Bolivia during the Chaco War.
1940–48 Presidency of General Higinio Morínigo.

1948–54 Political instability; six different presidents.
1954 General Alfredo Stroessner seized power.
1989 Stroessner ousted in coup led by General Andrés Rodríguez. Rodríguez elected president; Colorado Party won the congressional elections.
1991 Colorado Party successful in assembly elections.

Paris, Treaty of any of various peace treaties signed in Paris, including: *1763* ending the Seven Years' War; *1783* recognizing American independence; *1814* and *1815* following the abdication and final defeat of ◊Napoleon I; *1856* ending the Crimean War; *1898* ending the Spanish-American War; *1919-20* the conference preparing the Treaty of ◊Versailles at the end of World War I was held in Paris; *1946* after World War II, the peace treaties between the ◊Allies and Italy, Romania, Hungary, Bulgaria, and Finland; *1951* treaty signed by France, West Germany, Italy, Belgium, Netherlands and Luxembourg, embodying the Schuman Plan to set up a single coal and steel authority; *1973* ending US participation in the ◊Vietnam War.

Park Chung Hee 1917–1979. President of South Korea 1963–79. Under his rule South Korea had one of the world's fastest-growing economies, but recession and his increasing authoritarianism led to his assassination 1979.

Parkinson Cecil (Edward) 1931–   . British Conservative politician. He was chair of the party 1981–83, and became minister for trade and industry, but resigned Oct 1984 following disclosure of an affair with his secretary. In 1987 he rejoined the cabinet as secretary of state for energy, and in 1989 became transport secretary. He left the cabinet when John Major became prime minister 1990 and later announced his intention to retire from active politics.

partisan member of an armed group that operates behind enemy lines or in occupied territories during wars. The name 'partisans' was first given to armed bands of Russians who operated against Napoleon's army in Russia during 1812, but has since been used to describe Russian, Yugoslav, Italian, Greek, and Polish Resistance groups against the Germans during World War II. In Yugoslavia the communist partisans under their leader, Tito, played a major role in defeating the Germans.

Passchendaele village in W Flanders, Belgium, near Ypres. The Passchendaele ridge before Ypres was the object of a costly and unsuccessful

British offensive in World War I, between July and Nov 1917; British casualties numbered nearly 400,000.

pass laws South African laws that required the black population to carry passbooks (identity documents) at all times and severely restricted freedom of movement. The laws, a major cause of discontent, formed a central part of the policies of ◊apartheid. They were repealed 1986.

Patel Sardar Vallabhbhai 1875–1950. Indian political leader. A fervent follower of Mahatma ◊Gandhi and a leader of the Indian National Congress, he was deputy prime minister 1947–50, after independence.

Patten Christopher Francis 'Chris' 1944–   . British Conservative politician and governor of Hong Kong from 1992. A former director of the Conservative Party research department, he held junior ministerial posts under Margaret Thatcher and was later chairman of the party under John Major. He masterminded the successful 1992 Conservative election campaign but lost his own seat. He accepted the governorship of Hong Kong for the crucial five years prior to its transfer to China.

Patton George (Smith) 1885–1945. US general in World War II, known as 'Blood and Guts'. He was appointed to command the 2nd Armored Division 1940 and became commanding general of the First Armored Corps 1941. In 1942 he led the Western Task Force that landed at Casablanca, Morocco. After commanding the 7th Army, he led the 3rd Army across France and into Germany, and in 1945 took over the 15th Army.

Paul 1901–1964. King of the Hellenes (Greece) from 1947, when he succeeded his brother George II. He was the son of Constantine I. In 1938 he married Princess Frederika (1917–   ), daughter of the Duke of Brunswick.

Pauling Linus Carl 1901–   . US chemist, author of fundamental work on the nature of the chemical bond and on the helical structure of many proteins. Awarded the Nobel Prize for Chemistry 1954, he also received the Nobel Peace Prize 1962 for his outspoken opposition to nuclear testing.

Paulus Friedrich von 1890–1957. German field marshal in World War II, commander of the forces that besieged Stalingrad (now Volgograd) in the USSR 1942-43; he was captured and gave evidence at the Nuremberg trials before settling in East Germany.

Pavlov Valentin 1937– . Soviet communist politician, prime minister Jan–Aug 1991. He served in the Finance Ministry, the State Planning Committee (Gosplan), and the State Pricing Committee before becoming minister of finance 1989. In Jan 1991 he replaced Nikolai Ryzhkov as prime minister, with the brief of halting the gathering collapse of the Soviet economy. In Aug 1991 he was a member of the eight-man junta which led the abortive anti-Gorbachev coup. In the midst of the coup, he relinquished his position as premier, citing health reasons. He was arrested when the coup was finally thwarted.

Paz (Estenssoro) Victor 1907– . President of Bolivia 1952–56, 1960–64, and 1985–89. He founded and led the Movimiento Nacionalista Revolucionario (MNR) which seized power 1952. His regime extended the vote to Indians, nationalized the country's largest tin mines, embarked on a programme of agrarian reform, and brought inflation under control.

Peace Corps US organization of trained men and women, inspired by the British programme Voluntary Service Overseas (VSO) and established by President Kennedy 1961. The Peace Corps provides skilled volunteer workers for Third World countries, especially in the fields of teaching, agriculture, and health, for a period of two years.

peace movement collective opposition to war. The Western peace movements of the late 20th century can trace their origins to the pacifists of the 19th century and conscientious objectors during World War I. The campaigns after World War II have tended to concentrate on nuclear weapons, but there are numerous organizations devoted to peace, some wholly pacifist, some merely opposed to escalation.

Pearl Harbor US Pacific naval base in Oahu, Hawaii, USA, the scene of a Japanese aerial attack 7 Dec 1941, which brought the USA into World War II. The attack took place while Japanese envoys were holding so-called peace talks in Washington. More than 2,000 members of US armed forces were killed, and a large part of the US Pacific fleet was destroyed or damaged.

Pearse Patrick Henry 1879–1916. Irish poet prominent in the Gaelic revival, a leader of the ◊Easter Rising 1916. Proclaimed president of the provisional government, he was court-martialled and shot after its suppression.

Pearson Lester Bowles 1897–1972. Canadian politician, leader of the Liberal Party from 1958, prime minister 1963–68. As foreign minister

1948–57, he represented Canada at the United Nations, playing a key role in settling the ◊Suez Crisis 1956. Nobel Peace Prize 1957.

Pentagon Papers top-secret US Defense Department report on the history of US involvement in the Vietnam War that was leaked to the *New York Times* by Defence Department employee Daniel Ellsberg June 1971, fuelling the antiwar movement. President Nixon tried to stop publication, but the Supreme Court ruled in favour of the press.

People's Budget in UK history, the Liberal government's budget of 1909 to finance social reforms and naval rearmament. The chancellor of the Exchequer David Lloyd George proposed graded and increased income tax and a 'supertax' on high incomes. The budget aroused great debate and precipitated a constitutional crisis.

Peres Shimon 1923– . Israeli socialist politician, prime minister 1984–86. Peres was prime minister, then foreign minister, under a power-sharing agreement with the leader of the Consolidation Party (◊Likud), Yitzhak ◊Shamir. From 1989 to 1990 he was finance minister in a new Labour–Likud coalition.

Pérez de Cuéllar Javier 1920– . Peruvian diplomat, secretary general of the United Nations 1982–91. He raised the standing of the UN by his successful diplomacy in ending the Iran–Iraq War 1988 and securing the independence of Namibia 1989.

Pérez Jiménez Marcos 1914– . Venezuelan president 1952–58 who led the military junta which overthrew the Acción Democrática government of Rómulo Gallegos 1948. Pérez Jiménez was made provisional president 1952 and approved as constitutional president by Congress 1953. His regime had a reputation as the most repressive in Venezuelan history. It also encouraged European immigration and undertook massive public works in the capital Caracas.

Perkins Frances 1882–1965. US public official. She became the first female cabinet officer when she served as secretary of labour under F D Roosevelt 1933–45. Under Truman she was a member of the federal civil service commission 1946–53.

Perón Evita (María Eva) (born Duarte) 1919–1952. Argentine populist leader. A successful radio actress, she married Juan ◊Perón in 1945. When he became president the following year, she became his chief adviser and virtually ran the health and labour ministries, devoting herself to helping the poor, improving education, and achieving women's suffrage. She was politically astute and sought the vice-presidency 1951, but was opposed by the army and withdrew.

Perón (María Estela) Isabel (born Martínez) 1931– . President of Argentina 1974–76, and third wife of Juan Perón. She succeeded him after he died in office, but labour unrest, inflation, and political violence pushed the country to the brink of chaos. Accused of corruption, she was held under house arrest for five years. She went into exile in Spain.

Perón Juan (Domingo) 1895–1974. Argentine politician, dictator 1946–55 and from 1973 until his death. His populist appeal to the poor was enhanced by the charisma and political work of his second wife Eva (Evita) Perón. After her death in 1952 his popularity waned and he was deposed in a military coup 1955. He returned from exile to the presidency 1973, but died in office 1974, and was succeeded by his third wife Isabel Perón.

Pershing John Joseph 1860–1948. US general. He served in the Spanish War 1898, the Philippines 1899–1903, and Mexico 1916–17. He commanded the US Expeditionary Force sent to France 1917–18.

personality cult practice by which a leader is elevated to a pre-eminent status through a massive propaganda campaign. In the USSR, the cult of personality was developed by Joseph Stalin in the 1930s. More recently, both Mao Zedong in China and Kim-Il-Sung in North Korea have used similar techniques to reinforce their leadership and power.

Peru country in South America, on the Pacific, bounded N by Ecuador and Colombia, E by Brazil and Bolivia, and S by Chile.

chronology
1902 Boundary dispute with Bolivia settled.
1927 Boundary dispute with Colombia settled.
1942 Boundary dispute with Ecuador settled.
1948 Army coup, led by General Manuel Odría, installed a military government.
1963 Return to civilian rule, with Fernando ◊Belaúnde Terry as president.
1968 Return of military government in a bloodless coup by General Juan Velasco Alvarado.
1975 Velasco replaced, in a bloodless coup, by General Morales Bermúdez.
1980 Return to civilian rule, with Fernando Belaúnde as president.

1981 Boundary dispute with Ecuador renewed.

1985 Belaúnde succeeded by Social Democrat Alan ◊García Pérez.

1987 President García delayed the nationalization of Peru's banks after a vigorous campaign against the proposal.

1988 García pressured to seek help from the International Monetary Fund (IMF).

1989 ◊Mario Vargas Llosa entered presidential race; his Democratic Front won municipal elections Nov.

1990 Alberto Fujimori defeated Vargas Llosa in presidential elections. Assassination attempt on president failed.

1992 April: Fujimori sided with army to avert coup, announcing crackdown on rebels and drug traffickers. USA suspended humanitarian aid. Sendero Luminoso ('Shining Path') terrorists continued campaign of violence. May: Fujimori promised return to democracy. Sept: Sendero Luminoso leader, Abimael Guzman Reynoso, arrested; extremist attacks stepped up. Oct: Reynoso received life sentence. Nov: anti-government coup foiled; single-chamber legislature replaced two-chamber system.

Pétain Henri Philippe 1856–1951. French general and right-wing politician. His defence of Verdun 1916 during World War I made him a national hero. In World War II he became prime minister June 1940 and signed an armistice with Germany. Removing the seat of government to Vichy, a health resort in central France, he established an authoritarian regime. He was imprisoned after the war.

Peter I 1844–1921. King of Serbia from 1903. He was the son of Prince Alexander Karageorgevich and was elected king when the last Obrenovich king was murdered 1903. He took part in the retreat of the Serbian army 1915, and in 1918 was proclaimed first king of the Serbs, Croats, and Slovenes (renamed Yugoslavia in 1921).

Peter II 1923–1970. King of Yugoslavia 1934–45. He succeeded his father, Alexander I, and assumed the royal power after the overthrow of the regency 1941. He escaped to the UK after the German invasion, and married Princess Alexandra of Greece 1944. He was dethroned 1945 when Marshal Tito came to power and the Soviet-backed federal republic was formed.

Phalangist member of a Lebanese military organization (***Phalanges Libanaises***), since 1958 the political and military force of the Maronite

Church in Lebanon. The Phalangists' unbending right-wing policies and resistance to the introduction of democratic institutions helped contribute to the civil war in Lebanon.

Philby Kim (Harold) 1912–1988. British intelligence officer from 1940 and Soviet agent from 1933. He was liaison officer in Washington 1949–51, when he was confirmed to be a double agent and asked to resign. Named in 1963 as having warned Guy Burgess and Donald Maclean (similarly double agents) that their activities were known, he fled to the USSR and became a Soviet citizen and general in the KGB. A fourth member of the ring was Anthony Blunt.

Philippines country in SE Asia, on an archipelago of more than 7,000 islands W of the Pacific Ocean and S of the SE Asian mainland.

chronology

1898 Ceded to the USA by Spain after Spanish– American War.

1935 Granted internal self-government.

1942–45 Occupied by Japan.

1946 Independence achieved from USA.

1965 Ferdinand Marcos elected president.

1983 Opposition leader Benigno Aquino murdered by military guard.

1986 Marcos overthrown by Corazon Aquino's People's Power movement.

1987 'Freedom constitution' adopted, giving Aquino mandate to rule until June 1992; People's Power won majority in congressional elections. Attempted right-wing coup suppressed. Communist guerrillas active. Government in rightward swing.

1988 Land Reform Act gave favourable compensation to holders of large estates.

1989 Referendum on southern autonomy failed; ◊Marcos died in exile; Aquino refused his burial in Philippines. Sixth coup attempt suppressed with US aid; Aquino declared state of emergency.

1990 Seventh coup attempt survived by President ◊Aquino.

1991 June: eruption of Mount Pinatubo, hundreds killed. USA agreed to give up Clark Field airbase but keep Subic Bay naval base for ten more years. Sept: Philippines Senate voted to urge withdrawal of all US forces. US renewal of Subic Bay lease rejected. Nov: Imelda Marcos returned.

1992 Fidel Ramos elected to replace Aquino.

phoney war the period in World War II between Sept 1939, when the Germans had occupied Poland, and April 1940, when the invasions of Denmark and Norway took place. During this time there were few signs of hostilities in Western Europe; indeed, Hitler made some attempts to arrange a peace settlement with Britain and France.

Pieck Wilhelm 1876–1960. German communist politician. He was a leader of the 1919 ◊Spartacist revolt and a founder of the Socialist Unity Party 1946. He opposed both the Weimar Republic and Nazism. From 1949 he was president of East Germany; the office was abolished on his death.

Pilsudski Józef (Klemens) 1867–1935. Polish nationalist politician, dictator from 1926. Born in Russian Poland, he founded the Polish Socialist Party 1892 and was twice imprisoned for anti-Russian activities. During World War I he commanded a Polish force to fight for Germany but fell under suspicion of intriguing with the Allies and was imprisoned by the Germans 1917–18. When Poland became independent 1919, he was elected chief of state, and led an unsuccessful Polish attack on the USSR 1920. He retired 1923, but in 1926 led a military coup that established his dictatorship until his death.

Pindling Lynden (Oscar) 1930–   . Bahamian prime minister 1967–92. After studying law in London, he returned to the island to join the newly formed Progressive Liberal Party and then became the first black prime minister of the Bahamas.

Pinochet (Ugarte) Augusto 1915–   . Military ruler of Chile from 1973, when a coup backed by the US Central Intelligence Agency ousted and killed President Salvador Allende. Pinochet took over the presidency and governed ruthlessly, crushing all opposition. He was voted out of power when general elections were held in Dec 1989 but remains head of the armed forces until 1997.

Plaatje Solomon Tshekiso 1876–1932. Pioneer South African black community leader who was the first secretary general and founder of the ◊African National Congress 1912.

Plaid Cymru Welsh nationalist political party established 1925, dedicated to an independent Wales. In 1966 the first Plaid Cymru member of Parliament was elected.

Plekhanov Georgi Valentinovich 1857–1918. Russian Marxist revolutionary and theorist, founder of the ◊Menshevik party. He led the first populist demonstration in St Petersburg, became a Marxist and, with Lenin, edited the newspaper *Iskra* (spark). In 1903 his opposition to Lenin led to the Bolshevik-Menshevik split.

pogrom unprovoked violent attack on an ethnic group, particularly Jews, carried out with official sanction. The Russian pogroms against Jews began 1881, after the assassination of Tsar Alexander II, and again in 1903–06; persecution of the Jews remained constant until the Russian Revolution. Later there were pogroms in E Europe, especially in Poland after 1918, and in Germany under Hitler (see ◊Holocaust).

Poincaré Raymond Nicolas Landry 1860–1934. French politician, prime minister 1912–13, president 1913–20, and again prime minister 1922–24 (when he ordered the occupation of the Ruhr, Germany) and 1926–29.

Poindexter John Marlan 1936–   . US rear admiral and Republican government official. In 1981 he joined the Reagan administration's National Security Council (NSC) and became national security adviser 1985. As a result of the ◊Irangate scandal, Poindexter was forced to resign 1986, along with his assistant, Oliver North.

Poland country in E Europe, bounded N by the Baltic Sea, E by Lithuania, Belarus, and Ukraine, S by the Czech and Slovak Republics, and W by Germany.

chronology
1918 Poland revived as independent republic.
1939 German invasion and occupation.
1944 Germans driven out by Soviet forces.
1945 Polish boundaries redrawn at Potsdam Conference.
1947 Communist people's republic proclaimed.
1956 Poznań riots. Wladyslaw ◊Gomuľka installed as Polish United Workers' Party (PUWP) leader.
1970 Gomuľka replaced by Edward ◊Gierek after Gdańsk riots.
1980 ◊Solidarity emerged as a free trade union following Gdańssk disturbances.
1981 Martial law imposed by General Wojciech ◊Jaruzelski.
1983 Martial law ended.
1984 Amnesty for political prisoners.
1985 Zbigniew Messner became prime minister.
1987 Referendum on economic reform rejected.

1988 Solidarity-led strikes and demonstrations called off after pay increases. Messner resigned; replaced by the reformist Mieczysław F Rakowski.

1989 Solidarity relegalized. April: new 'socialist pluralist' constitution formed. June: widespread success for Solidarity in assembly elections, the first open elections in 40 years. July: Jaruzelski elected president. Sept: 'Grand coalition', first non-Communist government since World War II formed; economic restructuring undertaken on free-market lines; W Europe and US create $1 billion aid package.

1990 Jan: PUWP dissolved; replaced by Social Democratic Party and breakaway Union of Social Democrats. Lech ◊Wałesa elected president; Dec: prime minister Mazowiecki resigned.

1991 Oct: Multiparty general election produced inconclusive result. Five-party centre-right coalition formed under Jan Olszewski. Treaty signed agreeing to complete withdrawal of Soviet troops.

1992 June: Olszewski ousted on vote of no confidence; succeeded by Waldemar Pawlak. July: Hanna Suchocka replaced Pawlak as Poland's first woman prime minister.

1993 March: 14% of workforce (2.6 million) out of work.

Polish Corridor strip of land designated under the Treaty of ◊Versailles 1919 to give Poland access to the Baltic. It cut off East Prussia from the rest of Germany. When Poland took over the southern part of East Prussia 1945, it was absorbed.

Pol Pot (also known as *Saloth Sar*, *Tol Saut*, and *Pol Porth*) 1925–   . Cambodian politician and leader of the ◊Khmer Rouge communist movement that overthrew the government 1975. After widespread atrocities against the civilian population, his regime was deposed by a Vietnamese invasion 1979. Pol Pot continued to help lead the Khmer Rouge despite officially resigning from all positions in 1989.

Pompidou Georges 1911–1974. French conservative politician, president 1969–74. He negotiated a settlement with the Algerians 1961 and, as prime minister 1962–68, with the students in the revolt of May 1968.

popular front political alliance of liberals, socialists, communists, and other centre and left-wing parties. This policy was propounded by the Communist International 1935 against fascism and was adopted in France and Spain, where popular-front governments were elected 1936; that in France was overthrown 1938 and the one in Spain fell with the defeat of the Republic in the Spanish Civil War 1939.

Portugal country in SW Europe, on the Atlantic Ocean, bounded N and E by Spain.

chronology

1928–68 Military dictatorship under António de Oliveira ◊Salazar.

1968 Salazar succeeded by Marcello ◊Caetano.

1974 Caetano removed in military coup led by General Antonio Ribeiro de Spínola. Spínola replaced by General Francisco da Costa Gomes.

1975 African colonies became independent.

1976 New constitution, providing for return to civilian rule, adopted. Minority government appointed, led by Socialist Party leader Mario Soares.

1978 Soares resigned.

1980 Francisco Balsemão formed centre-party coalition after two years of political instability.

1982 Draft of new constitution approved, reducing powers of presidency.

1983 Centre-left coalition government formed.

1985 Aníbal Cavaco Silva became prime minister.

1986 Mario Soares elected first civilian president in 60 years. Portugal joined European Community.

1988 Portugal joined Western European Union.

1989 Constitution amended to allow major state enterprises to be denationalized.

1991 Mario Soares re-elected president; Social Democrat (PSD) majority slightly reduced in assembly elections.

Potsdam Conference conference held in Potsdam, Germany, 17 July–2 Aug 1945 between representatives of the USA, the UK, and the USSR. They established the political and economic principles governing the treatment of Germany in the initial period of Allied control at the end of World War II, and sent an ultimatum to Japan demanding unconditional surrender on pain of utter destruction.

poujadist member of an extreme right-wing political movement in France led by Pierre Poujade (1920–   ), which was prominent in French politics 1954–58. Known in France as the *Union de Défense des Commerçants et Artisants*, it won 52 seats in the national election of 1956. Its voting strength came mainly from the lower-middle-class and petit-bourgeois sections of society but the return of ◊de Gaulle to power 1958, and the foundation of the Fifth Republic led to a rapid decline in the movement's fortunes.

POUM acronym for *P*artido *O*brero de *U*nificación *M*arxista ('Workers' Marxist Union Party') a small Spanish anti-Stalinist communist party led by Andrés Nin and Joaquín Maurín, prominent during the Spanish Civil War. Since Republican Spain received most of its external help from the USSR, the Spanish communist party used this to force the suppression of POUM in 1937. POUM supporters included the English writer George Orwell, who chronicled events in his book *Homage to Catalonia*.

Pound (Alfred) Dudley Pickman Rogers 1877–1943. British admiral of the fleet. As First Sea Lord and chief of the British naval staff 1939–43, he was responsible for the effective measures taken against the German sub-marine U-boats in World War II.

Powell (John) Enoch 1912– . British Conservative politician. He was minister of health 1960–63, and contested the party leadership 1965. In 1968 he made a speech against immigration that led to his dismissal from the shadow cabinet. He resigned from the party 1974, and was Official Unionist Party member for South Down, Northern Ireland 1974–87.

Powell Adam Clayton, Jr 1908–1972. US political leader. A leader of New York's black community, he was elected to the city council 1941. He was appointed to the US Congress 1944, and later became chairman of the House Education and Labor Committee. Following charges of corruption, he was denied his seat in Congress 1967. Re-elected 1968, he won back his seniority by a 1969 decision of the US Supreme Court.

Powell Colin (Luther) 1937– . US general, chair of the Joint Chiefs of Staff from 1989 and, as such, responsible for the overall administration of the Allied forces in Saudi Arabia during the ◊Gulf War 1991. A Vietnam War veteran, he first worked in government 1972 and was national security adviser 1987–89.

Pozsgay Imre 1933– . Hungarian socialist politician, presidential candidate for the Hungarian Socialist Party from 1989. Influential in the democratization of Hungary 1988–89, he was rejected by the electorate in the parliamentary elections of March 1990, coming a poor third in his constituency.

Prague Spring the 1968 programme of liberalization, begun under a new Communist Party leader in Czechoslovakia. In Aug 1968 Soviet tanks invaded Czechoslovakia and entered the capital Prague to put down the liberalization movement initiated by the prime minister Alexander Dubček, who had earlier sought to assure the Soviets that his planned reforms would not threaten socialism. Dubček was arrested but released soon afterwards. Most of the Prague Spring reforms were reversed.

Prasad Rajendra 1884–1963. Indian politician. He was national president of the Indian National Congress several times between 1934 and 1948 and India's first president after independence 1950–62.

Premadasa Ranasinghe 1924– . Sri Lankan politician, a United National Party member of Parliament from 1960, prime minister from 1978, and president from 1988, having gained popularity through overseeing a major house-building and poverty-alleviation programme. He has sought peace talks with the Tamil Tiger guerrillas.

Prescott John Leslie 1938– . British Labour Party politician, a member of the shadow cabinet from 1983.

Primo de Rivera Miguel 1870–1930. Spanish soldier and politician, dictator from 1923 as well as premier from 1925. He was captain-general of Catalonia when he led a coup against the ineffective monarchy and became virtual dictator of Spain with the support of Alfonso XIII. He resigned 1930.

Prior James 1927– . British Conservative politician. He held ministerial posts from 1970. As employment secretary he curbed trade-union activity with the Employment Act 1980, and was Northern Ireland secretary 1981–84. After his resignation 1984 he became chair of the General Electric Company.

privatization policy or process of selling or transferring state-owned or public assets and services (notably nationalized industries) to private investors. Privatization of services involves the government contracting private firms to supply services previously supplied by public authorities. The policy has been pursued by the post-1979 Conservative administration in the UK, and by recent governments in France, Japan (Nippon Telegraph and Telephone Corporation 1985, Japan Railways 1987, Japan Air Lines 1987), Italy, New Zealand and elsewhere. By 1988 the practice had spread worldwide with communist countries such as China and Cuba selling off housing to private tenants.

Profumo John (Dennis) 1915– . British Conservative politician, secretary of state for war from 1960 to June 1963, when he resigned on the disclosure of his involvement with Christine Keeler, mistress also of a Soviet naval attaché. In 1982 Profumo became administrator of the social and educational settlement Toynbee Hall in London.

Prohibition in US history, the period 1920–33 when alcohol was illegal, representing the culmination of a long campaign by church and women's organizations, temperance societies, and the Anti-Saloon League. This led to bootlegging (the illegal distribution of liquor, often illicitly distilled), to the financial advantage of organized crime, and public opinion insisted on repeal 1933.

Pueblo US intelligence vessel captured by the North Koreans Jan 1968, allegedly within their territorial waters. The crew, but not the ship, were released Dec 1968. A naval court recommended no disciplinary action.

P'u-i (or *Pu-Yi*) Henry 1906–1967. Last emperor of China (as Hsuan Tung) from 1908 until his deposition 1912; he was restored for a week 1917. After his deposition he chose to be called Henry. He was president 1932–34 and emperor 1934–45 of the Japanese puppet state of ◊Manchukuo.

Punjab massacres in the violence occurring after the partition of India 1947, more than a million people died while relocating in the Punjab. The eastern section became an Indian state, while the western area, dominated by the Muslims, went to Pakistan. Violence occurred as Muslims fled from eastern Punjab, and Hindus and Sikhs moved from Pakistan to India.

putsch Swiss German term for a violent seizure of political power, such as Adolf Hitler and Erich von Ludendorff's abortive beer-hall putsch Nov 1923, which attempted to overthrow the Bavarian government.

Pu-Yi alternative transliteration of the name of the last Chinese emperor, Henry ◊P'u-i.

Pym Francis 1922–   . British Conservative politician. He was defence secretary 1979–81, and succeeded Lord Carrington as foreign minister 1982, but was dismissed in the post-election reshuffle 1983.

Q

Qaboos bin Saidq 1940– . Sultan of Oman, the 14th descendant of the Albusaid family. Opposed to the conservative views of his father, he overthrew him 1970 in a bloodless coup and assumed the sultanship. Since then he has followed more liberal and expansionist policies, while maintaining his country's position of international nonalignment.

Qaddafi alternative form of ◊Khaddhafi, Libyan leader.

Qatar country in the Middle East, occupying Qatar peninsula in the Arabian Gulf, bounded SW by Saudi Arabia and S by United Arab Emirates.

chronology
1916 Qatar became a British protectorate.
1970 Constitution adopted, confirming the emirate as an absolute monarchy.
1971 Independence achieved from Britain.
1972 Emir Sheik Ahmad replaced in bloodless coup by his cousin, Crown Prince Sheik Khalifa.
1991 Forces joined UN coalition in Gulf War against Iraq.

Quayle (J) Dan(forth) 1947– . US Republican politician, vice president 1989-93. A congressman for Indiana 1977–81, he became a senator 1981.

Quisling Vidkun 1887–1945. Norwegian politician. Leader from 1933 of the Norwegian Fascist Party, he aided the Nazi invasion of Norway 1940 by delaying mobilization and urging non-resistance. He was made premier by Hitler 1942, and was arrested and shot as a traitor by the Norwegians 1945. His name became a generic term for a traitor who aids an occupying force.

Quit India movement campaign against British rule in India led by Mahatma ◊Gandhi begun Aug 1942. In March 1942 Sir Stafford ◊Cripps tried unsuccessfully to persuade the Congress Party of the need for it to participate in the war effort against Japan. Instead, Gandhi called on the British to leave India and let Indians deal with the Japanese by non-violent means. Calls to 'Quit India' were met with the arrest of Gandhi and other Congress leaders, which led to bloodshed, violence, and suppression.

R

Rabin Yitzhak 1922– . Israeli Labour politician, prime minister 1974–77 and from 1992. Rabin was minister for defence under the conservative Likud coalition government 1984–90. His policy of favouring Palestinian self-government in the occupied territories contributed to the success of the centre-left party in the 1992 elections.

Rabuka Sitiveni 1948– . Fijian soldier and politician, prime minister from 1992. When the 1987 elections in Fiji produced an Indian-dominated government, Rabuka staged two successive coups (the first short-lived). Within months of the second, he stepped down, allowing a civilian government to take over. In May 1992 he was nominated as the new Fijian premier.

race-relations acts UK acts of Parliament 1965, 1968, and 1976 to combat discrimination. The Race Relations Act 1976 prohibits discrimination on the grounds of colour, race, nationality, or ethnic origin. Indirect as well as direct discrimination is prohibited in the provision of goods, services, facilities, employment, accommodation, and advertisements. The Commission for Racial Equality was set up under the act to investigate complaints of discrimination.

Radić Stjepan 1871–1928. Yugoslav nationalist politician, founder of the Croatian Peasant Party 1904. He led the Croat national movement within the Austro-Hungarian Empire and advocated a federal state with Croatian autonomy. His opposition to Serbian supremacy within Yugoslavia led to his assassination in parliament.

Rafsanjani Hojatoleslam Ali Akbar Hashemi 1934– . Iranian politician and cleric, president from 1989. When his former teacher Ayatollah ◊Khomeini returned after the revolution of 1979–80, Rafsanjani became the speaker of the Iranian parliament and, after Khomeini's death, state president and effective political leader.

Rahman Sheik Mujibur 1921–1975. Bangladeshi nationalist politician, president 1975. He was arrested several times for campaigning for the autonomy of East Pakistan. He won the elections 1970 as leader of the Awami League but was again arrested when negotiations with the Pakistan government broke down. After the civil war 1971, he became prime minister of the newly independent Bangladesh. He was presidential dictator Jan–Aug 1975, when he was assassinated.

Rahman Tunku Abdul 1903–1990. Malaysian politician, first prime minister of independent Malaya 1957–63 and of Malaysia 1963–70.

Ramos Fidel (Eddie) 1928– . Philippine politician and president from 1992. He was Corazon ◊Aquino's staunchest ally as defence secretary, and was later nominated her successor.

Ramphal Shridath Surendranath ('Sonny') 1928– . Guyanese politician. He was minister of foreign affairs and justice 1972–75 and secretary general of the British Commonwealth 1975–90.

Randolph Asa Philip 1889–1979. US labour and civil rights leader. Devoting himself to the cause of unionization, especially among black Americans, he was named a vice president of the American Federation of Labor and Congress of Industrial Organizations (AFL-CIO) 1957. He was one of the organizers of the 1963 civil rights march on Washington.

Rao P(amulaparti) V(enkata) Narasimha 1921– . Indian politician, see ◊Narasimah Rao.

Rapacki Plan plan put to the United Nations 2 Oct 1957 by Polish Foreign Minister Adam Rapacki, proposing a zone closed to the manufacture or deployment of nuclear weapons in Poland, Czechoslovakia, East and West Germany. The ban was to be enforced by NATO and Warsaw Pact observers. The USA and Britain rejected the plan as it gave the USSR advantages due to its superiority in conventional forces.

Rasputin (Russian 'dissolute') Grigory Efimovich 1871–1916. Siberian Eastern Orthodox mystic who acquired influence over the tsarina ◊Alexandra, wife of ◊Nicholas II, and was able to make political and ecclesiastical appointments. His abuse of power and notorious debauchery (reputedly including the tsarina) led to his murder by a group of nobles.

Rathenau Walther 1867–1922. German politician. He was a leading industrialist and was appointed economic director during World War I, developing a system of economic planning in combination with capitalism. After the war he founded the Democratic Party, and became foreign minister 1922. The same year he signed the Rapallo Treaty of Friendship with the USSR, cancelling German and Soviet counterclaims for indemnities for World War I, and soon after was assassinated by right-wing fanatics.

Rau Johannes 1931–   . German socialist politician. The son of a Protestant pastor, Rau became state premier of North Rhine–Westphalia 1978. In Jan 1987 he stood for chancellor of West Germany but was defeated by the incumbent conservative coalition.

Rayburn Samuel Taliaferro 1882–1961. US political leader. A Democrat, he was elected to the US Congress 1912. He supported President Roosevelt's New Deal programme 1933, and was elected majority leader 1937 and Speaker of the House 1940. With the exception of two terms, he served as Speaker until his death. His tenure in the House 1912-61 was the longest on record.

Reagan Ronald (Wilson) 1911–   . 40th president of the USA 1981–89, a Republican. He was governor of California 1966–74, and a former Hollywood actor. Reagan was a hawkish and popular president. He adopted an aggressive policy in Central America, attempting to overthrow the government of Nicaragua, and invading Grenada 1983. In 1987, ◊Irangate was investigated by the Tower Commission; Reagan admitted that USA–Iran negotiations had become an 'arms for hostages deal', but denied knowledge of resultant funds being illegally sent to the ◊Contras in Nicaragua. He increased military spending (sending the national budget deficit to record levels), cut social programmes, introduced deregulation of domestic markets, and cut taxes. His ◊Strategic Defense Initiative, announced 1983, proved controversial owing to the cost and unfeasibility. He was succeeded by George Bush.

Red Army name of the army of the USSR until 1946; later known as the *Soviet Army*. It developed from the Red Guards, volunteers who carried out the Bolshevik revolution, and received its name because it fought under the red flag. The Chinese revolutionary army was also called the Red Army.

Red Brigades (Italian *Brigate rosse*) extreme left-wing guerrilla groups active in Italy during the 1970s and early 1980s. They were implicated in many kidnappings and killings, some later attributed to right-wing *agents provocateurs*, including that of Christian Democrat leader Aldo Moro 1978.

Red Guard one of the school and college students, wearing red armbands, active in the ◊Cultural Revolution in China 1966–69. The armed workers who took part in the ◊Russian Revolution of 1917 were also called Red Guards.

Redmond John Edward 1856–1918. Irish politician, Parnell's successor as leader of the Nationalist Party 1890–1916. The 1910 elections saw him holding the balance of power in the House of Commons, and he secured the introduction of a ◊Home Rule bill, which was opposed by Protestant Ulster.

Red Scare in US history, campaign against radicals and dissenters which took place in the aftermath of World War I and the Russian Revolution, during a period of labour disorders in the USA. A wave of strikes in 1919 was seen as a prelude to revolution and violently suppressed. Thousands of people were arrested on suspicion, and communists were banned from entry to the country.

Rees-Mogg Lord William 1928– . British journalist, editor of *The Times* 1967–81, chair of the Arts Council 1982–89, and from 1988 chair of the Broadcasting Standards Council.

referendum procedure whereby a decision on proposed legislation is referred to the electorate for settlement by direct vote of all the people. It is most frequently employed in Switzerland, the first country to use it, but has become increasingly widespread. In 1992 several European countries (Ireland, Denmark, France) held referenda on whether or not to ratify the ◊Maastricht Treaty on closer European economic and political union.

refugee person fleeing from oppressive or dangerous conditions (such as political, religious, or military persecution) and seeking refuge in a foreign country. In 1991 there were an estimated 17 million refugees worldwide, whose resettlement and welfare were the responsibility of the United Nations High Commission for Refugees (UNHCR). Major refugee movements in 20th-century Europe include: Jews from the ◊pogroms of Russia 1881–1914 and again after the Revolution; White Russians from the USSR after 1917; Jews from Germany and other Nazi-dominated countries 1933–45; the displaced people of World War II; and from 1991 victims of the the civil wars in Croatia and Bosnia-Herzegovina.

Many Chinese fled the mainland after the communist revolution of 1949, especially to Taiwan and Hong Kong; many Latin Americans fled from Cuba, Colombia, Brazil, Chile, Argentina, and Central America when new governments took power; and many ◊boat people left Vietnam after the victory of the North over the South. Refugee movements created by natural disasters and famine have been widespread, most notably in Ethiopia and Sudan, where civil war has also contributed.

Regan Donald 1918–   . US Republican political adviser to Ronald ◊Reagan. He was secretary of the Treasury 1981–85, and chief of White House staff 1985–87, when he was forced to resign because of widespread belief in his complicity in the ◊Irangate scandal.

Rehnquist William 1924–   . Chief justice of the US Supreme Court from 1986. Under his leadership, the court has established a reputation for conservative rulings on such issues as abortion and capital punishment.

Reichstag Fire burning of the German parliament building in Berlin 27 Feb 1933, less than a month after the Nazi leader Hitler became chancellor. The fire was used as a justification for the suspension of many constitutional guarantees and also as an excuse to attack the communists. There is still debate over whether the Nazis were involved in this crime, of which they were the main beneficiaries.

René France-Albert 1935–   . Seychelles left-wing politician, the country's first prime minister after independence and president from 1977 after a coup. He has followed a non-nuclear policy of nonalignment.

reparation compensation paid by countries that start wars in which they are defeated, as by Germany in both world wars, and Iraq after its defeat in the Gulf War 1991.

Representation of the People Acts series of UK acts of Parliament from 1867 that extended voting rights, creating universal suffrage in 1928. The 1918 act gave the vote to men over the age of 21 and women over the age of 30, and the 1928 act extended the vote to women over the age of 21. Certain people had the right to more than one vote; this was abolished by the 1948 act. The 1969 act reduced the minimum age of voting to 18.

Republican Party one of the USA's two main political parties, formed 1854. It is considered more conservative than the Democratic Party, favouring capital and big business and opposing state subvention and federal controls. In the late 20th century most presidents have come from the Republican Party, but in Congress Republicans have been outnumbered.

resistance movement opposition movement in a country occupied by an enemy or colonial power, especially in the 20th century; for example, the French resistance to Nazism in World War II.

Reynaud Paul 1878–1966. French prime minister in World War II, who succeeded Edouard Daladier in March 1940 but resigned in June after the German breakthrough. He was imprisoned by the Germans until 1945, and again held government offices after the war.

Reynolds Albert 1933–   . Irish politician, prime minister from 1992. He joined Fianna Faíl 1977, and held various government posts including minister for industry and commerce 1987-88 and minister of finance 1989–92. He became prime minister when Charles ◊Haughey was forced to resign Jan 1992, but his government was defeated on a vote of confidence Nov 1992. Subsequent elections gave no party an overall majority but, after prolonged negotiations, Reynolds succeeded in forming a Fianna Faíl–Labour coalition.

Rhee Syngman 1875–1965. Korean right-wing politician. A rebel under Chinese and Japanese rule, he became president of South Korea from 1948 until riots forced him to resign and leave the country 1960.

Ribbentrop Joachim von 1893–1946. German Nazi politician and diplomat, foreign minister 1938–45, during which time he negotiated the Non-Aggression Pact between Germany and the USSR. He was tried at Nuremberg as a war criminal 1946 and hanged.

Ridley Nicholas 1929–   . British Conservative politician, cabinet minister 1983–90. After a period in industry he became active as a 'dry' right-winger in the Conservative Party: a 'Thatcherite' before Margaret ◊Thatcher had brought the term to public attention. He served under Harold Macmillan, Edward Heath, and Alec Douglas-Home, but did not become a member of the cabinet until 1983. His apparent disdain for public opinion caused his transfer, in 1989, from the politically sensitive Department of the Environment to that of Trade and Industry, and his resignation in July 1990 after criticisms of European colleagues and Germany.

Riom town on the river Ambène, in the Puy-de-Dôme *département* of central France. It was the scene in World War II of the 'war guilt' trials of several prominent Frenchmen by the ◊Vichy government Feb–April 1942. The accused included the former prime ministers ◊Blum and ◊Daladier, and General ◊Gamelin. The occasion turned into a wrangle over the reasons for

French unpreparedness for war, and, at the German dictator Hitler's instigation, the court was dissolved. The defendants remained in prison until
released by the Allies 1945.

Rivera Primo de. Spanish politician; see ◊Primo de Rivera.

Rivonia trial court proceedings begun Oct 1963 in South Africa against a
group of ten people, including Walter ◊Sisulu and Nelson ◊Mandela. They
were accused of sabotage and conspiracy to overthrow the South African
government, and nine were found guilty and sentenced to life imprisonment
June 1964.

Robinson Mary 1944– . Irish Labour politician, president from 1990.
She became a professor of law at 25. A strong supporter of women's rights,
she has campaigned for the liberalization of Ireland's laws prohibiting
divorce and abortion.

Rocard Michel 1930– . French socialist politician, prime minister
1988–91. A former radical, he joined the Socialist Party (PS) 1973, emerging as leader of its moderate social-democratic wing. He held ministerial
office under President François Mitterrand 1981–85.

Rockefeller John D(avison) 1839–1937. US millionaire, founder of Standard Oil 1870 (which achieved control of 90% of US refineries by 1882).
He founded the philanthropic *Rockefeller Foundation* 1913, to which his
son *John D(avison) Rockefeller Jr* (1874–1960) devoted his life.

Röhm Ernst 1887–1934. German leader of the Nazi Brownshirts, the SA
(◊Sturmabteilung). On the pretext of an intended SA *putsch* (uprising) by
the Brownshirts, the Nazis had some hundred of them, including Röhm,
killed 29–30 June 1934. The event is known as the ◊Night of the Long
Knives.

Roh Tae-woo 1932– . South Korean right-wing politician and general.
He held ministerial office from 1981 under President Chun, and became
chair of the ruling Democratic Justice Party 1985. He was elected president
1987, amid allegations of fraud and despite being connected with the massacre of about 2,000 anti-government demonstrators 1980.

Rohwedder Detler 1932–1991. German Social Democrat politician and
business executive. In Aug 1990 he became chief executive of Treuhand,
the body concerned with the privatization or liquidation of some 8,000 East
German businesses. His attempt to force market-oriented solutions on

Treuhand was controversial, many preferring a more interventionist stance. He was assassinated the following April.

Romania country in SE Europe, bounded N and E by Ukraine, E by Moldova, SE by the Black Sea, S by Bulgaria, SW by Yugoslavia, and NW by Hungary.

chronology

1944 Pro-Nazi ◊Antonescu government overthrown.

1945 Communist-dominated government appointed.

1947 Boundaries redrawn. King Michael abdicated and People's Republic proclaimed.

1949 New Soviet-style constitution adopted. Joined ◊Comecon.

1952 Second new Soviet-style constitution.

1955 Romania joined Warsaw Pact.

1958 Soviet occupation forces removed.

1965 New constitution adopted.

1974 ◊Ceauşescu created president.

1985–86 Winters of austerity and power cuts.

1987 Workers demonstrated against austerity programme.

1988–89 Relations with Hungary deteriorated over 'systematization programme'.

1989 Announcement that all foreign debt paid off. Razing of villages and building of monuments to Ceauşescu; Communist orthodoxy reaffirmed; demonstrations violently suppressed. Massacre in Timisoara. Army joined uprising; heavy fighting; bloody overthrow of Ceauşescu regime in 'Christmas Revolution'; Ceauşescu and wife tried and executed; estimated 10,000 dead in civil warfare. Power assumed by new military-dissident-reform communist National Salvation Front, headed by Ion ◊Iliescu.

1990 Securitate secret police replaced by new Romanian Intelligence Service (RIS); religious practices resumed; mounting strikes and protests against effects of market economy.

1991 April: treaty on cooperation and good neighbourliness signed with USSR. Aug: privatization law passed. Sept: prime minister Petre Roman resigned following riots, succeeded by Theodor Stolojan heading a new cross-party coalition government. Dec: new constitution endorsed by referendum.

1992 Iliescu re-elected in presidential runoff.

Rome–Berlin Axis another name for the ◊Axis.

Rome, Treaties of two international agreements signed 25 March 1957 by Belgium, France, West Germany, Italy, Luxembourg, and the Netherlands, which established the European Economic Community (◊European Community) and the European Atomic Energy Commission (EURATOM).

Rommel Erwin 1891–1944. German field marshal. He served in World War I, and in World War II he played an important part in the invasions of central Europe and France. He was commander of the N African offensive from 1941 (when he was nicknamed 'Desert Fox') until defeated in the Battles of El ◊Alamein.

Roosevelt (Anna) Eleanor 1884–1962. US social worker, lecturer, and First Lady; her newspaper column 'My Day' was widely syndicated. She influenced ◊New Deal policies, especially supporting desegregation. She was a delegate to the UN general assembly and chair of the UN commission on human rights 1946–51, and helped to draw up the Declaration of Human Rights at the UN 1945. She was married to President Franklin Roosevelt.

Roosevelt Franklin D(elano) 1882–1945. 32nd president of the USA 1933–45, a Democrat. He served as governor of New York 1929–33. Becoming president during the Great Depression, he launched the ◊*New Deal* economic and social reform programme, which made him popular with the people. After the outbreak of World War II he introduced ◊lend-lease for the supply of war materials and services to the Allies and drew up the ◊Atlantic Charter of solidarity. Once the USA had entered the war 1941, he spent much time in meetings with Allied leaders (see ◊Tehran, and ◊Yalta conferences).

Roosevelt Theodore 1858–1919. 26th president of the USA 1901–09, a Republican. After serving as governor of New York 1898–1900 he became vice president to ◊McKinley, whom he succeeded as president on McKinley's assassination 1901. He campaigned against the great trusts (associations of enterprises that reduce competition), while carrying on a jingoist foreign policy designed to enforce US supremacy over Latin America.

Rosebery Archibald Philip Primrose, 5th Earl of Rosebery 1847–1929. British Liberal politician. He was foreign secretary 1886 and 1892–94, when he succeeded Gladstone as prime minister, but his government survived less than a year. After 1896 his imperialist views gradually placed him further from the mainstream of the Liberal Party.

Rosenberg Alfred 1893–1946. German politician, born in Tallinn, Estonia. He became the chief Nazi ideologist and was minister for eastern occupied territories 1941–44. He was tried at ◊Nuremberg 1946 as a war criminal and hanged.

Rosenberg Julius 1918–53 and Ethel Greenglass 1915-53 US married couple, convicted of being leaders of a nuclear-espionage ring passing information from Ethel's brother via courier to the USSR. The Rosenbergs were executed after much public controversy and demonstration. They were the only Americans executed for espionage during peacetime.

Rowbotham Sheila 1943– . British socialist, feminist, historian, lecturer, and writer. Her pamphlet *Women's Liberation and the New Politics* 1970 laid down fundamental approaches and demands of the emerging women's movement.

Rowlatt Bills in India 1919, peacetime extensions of restrictions introduced during World War I to counter the perceived threat of revolution. The planned legislation would inhibit individual rights and allow the Indian administration to arrest and detain people without a warrant. The bills were vigorously opposed by Indian nationalists, and the young Congress Party leader Mohandas ◊Gandhi called for a nationwide campaign for their repeal. Only one of the two bills was enacted, but it was never used and was later repealed.

Rowling Wallace 'Bill' 1927– . New Zealand Labour politician, party leader 1969–75, prime minister 1974–75.

Rowntree Benjamin Seebohm 1871–1954. British entrepreneur and philanthropist. Much of the money he acquired as chair (1925–41) of the family firm of confectioners, H I Rowntree, he used to fund investigations into social conditions. His writings include *Poverty, A Study of Town Life* 1900. The three *Rowntree Trusts*, which were founded by his father *Joseph Rowntree* (1836–1925) in 1904, fund research into housing, social care, and social policy, support projects relating to social justice, and give grants to pressure groups working in these areas.

Roy Manabendra Nakh 1887–1954. Founder of the Indian Communist Party in exile in Tashkent 1920. Expelled from the Comintern 1929, he returned to India and was imprisoned for five years. A steadfast communist, he finally became disillusioned after World War II and developed his ideas on practical humanism.

Runciman Walter, 1st Viscount 1870–1949. British Liberal politician. He entered Parliament in 1899 and held various ministerial offices between 1908 and 1939. In Aug 1938 he undertook an abortive mission to Czechoslovakia to persuade the Czech government to make concessions to Nazi Germany.

Rundstedt Karl Rudolf Gerd von 1875–1953. German field marshal in World War II. Largely responsible for the German breakthrough in France 1940, he was defeated on the Ukrainian front 1941. As commander in chief in France from 1942, he resisted the Allied invasion 1944 and in Dec launched the temporarily successful Ardennes offensive.

Rusk Dean 1909–   . US Democrat politician. He was secretary of state to presidents J F Kennedy and L B Johnson 1961–69, and became unpopular through his involvement with the Vietnam War.

Russian civil war bitter conflict of nearly three years which followed Russian setbacks in World War I and the upheavals of the 1917 Revolution. In Dec 1917 counterrevolutionary armies, the 'Whites' began to organize resistance to the October Revolution of 1917. The Red Army (Bolsheviks), improvized by Leon Trotsky, opposed them and civil war resulted. Hostilities continued for nearly three years with the Bolsheviks being successful.

Russian Federation or *Russia* formerly, (until 1991) *Russian Soviet Federal Socialist Republic* (RSFSR) country in N Asia and E Europe, bounded N by the Arctic Ocean, E by the Bering Sea and the Sea of Okhotsk, W by Norway, Finland, the Baltic States, Belarus, and Ukraine, and S by China, Mongolia, Georgia, Azerbaijan, and Kazakhstan.

chronology
1945 Became a founding member of United Nations.
1988 Aug: Democratic Union formed in Moscow as political party opposed to totalitarianism. Oct: Russian-language demonstrations in Leningrad; Tsarist flag raised.
1989 March: Boris ◊Yeltsin elected to USSR Congress of People's Deputies. Sept: conservative-nationalist Russian United Workers' Front established in Sverdlovsk.
1990 May: anticommunist May Day protests in Red Square, Moscow; Yeltsin narrowly elected RSFSR president by Russian parliament. June: economic and political sovereignty declared; Ivan ◊Silaev became Russian prime minister. July: Yeltsin resigned his party membership. Aug:

Tatarstan declared sovereignty. Dec: rationing introduced in some cities; private land ownership allowed.

1991 March: Yeltsin secured the support of Congress of Peoples' Deputies for direct election of an executive president. June: Yeltsin elected president under a liberal-radical banner. July: Yeltsin issued a sweeping decree to remove Communist Party cells from workplaces; sovereignty of the Baltic republics recognized by the republic. Aug: Yeltsin stood out against abortive anti-Gorbachev coup, emerging as key power-broker within Soviet Union; national guard established and pre-revolutionary flag restored. Sept: Silaev resigned as Russian premier. Nov: Yeltsin also named as prime minister; Communist Party of the Soviet Union (CPSU) and Russian Communist Party banned; Yeltsin's goverment gained control of Russia's economic assets and armed forces. Oct: Checheno-Ingush declared its independence. Dec: Yeltsin negotiated formation of new confederal Commonwealth of Independent States (CIS); admitted into United Nations (UN); Russian independence recognized by USA and European Community (EC).

1992 Jan: admitted into Conference on Security and Cooperation in Europe (CSCE); assumed former USSR's permanent seat on UN Security Council; prices freed. Feb: demonstrations in Moscow and other cities as living standards plummeted. June: Yeltsin–Bush summit meeting; Yeltsin proposed further major reductions in strategic nuclear weapons. March: 18 out of 20 republics signed treaty agreeing to remain within loose Russian Federation; Tatarstan and Checheno-Ingush refused to sign. Aug: agreement with Ukraine on joint control of Black Sea fleet. Dec: Victor Chernomyrdin elected prime minister; new constitution agreed in referendum. START II arms-reduction agreement signed with USA.

1993 March: Congress of People's Deputies attempted to limit Yeltsin's powers to rule by decree and cancel referendum due 25 April. Yeltsin declared temporary presidential 'special rule' pending holding of referendum. Results of referendum showed Russians in favour of Yeltsin's reforms.

Russian Revolution two revolutions of Feb and Oct 1917 (Julian calendar) that began with the overthrow of the Romanov dynasty and ended with the establishment of a communist soviet (council) state, the Union of Soviet Socialist Republics (USSR).

Russian revolution, 1905 political upheaval centred in and around St Petersburg, Russia 1905–06, leading up to the February and October revolutions of 1917. On 22 Jan 1905 thousands of striking unarmed workers marched to Tsar Nicholas II's Winter Palace in St Petersburg, to ask for reforms. Government troops fired on the crowd, killing many people. After this 'Bloody Sunday' slaughter the revolution gained strength, culminating in a general strike which paralysed the whole country in Oct 1905. Revolutionaries in St Petersburg formed a 'soviet' (council) called the Soviet of Workers' Deputies. Nicholas II then granted the ⚭Duma (parliament) the power to pass or reject proposed laws. Although these measures satisfied the liberal element, the revolution continued to gain ground and came to a head when the army crushed a serious uprising in Dec 1905.

Russo-Japanese War war between Russia and Japan 1904–05, which arose from conflicting ambitions in Korea and Manchuria, specifically, the Russian occupation of Port Arthur (modern Dalian) 1896 and of the Amur province 1900. Japan successfully besieged Port Arthur May 1904–Jan 1905, took Mukden (modern Shenyang, see ⚭Mukden, Battle of) on 29 Feb–10 March, and on 27 May defeated the Russian Baltic fleet, which had sailed halfway around the world to Tsushima Strait. A peace was signed 23 Aug 1905. Russia surrendered its lease on Port Arthur, ceded S Sakhalin to Japan, evacuated Manchuria, and recognized Japan's interests in Korea.

Rutskoi Aleksander 1947–   . Russian politician, founder of the reformist Communists for Democracy group, and vice president of the Russian Federation from 1991. During the abortive Aug 1991 coup he led the Russian delegation to rescue Soviet leader Mikhail Gorbachev from his forced confinement in the Crimea.

Rwanda landlocked country in central Africa, bounded N by Uganda, E by Tanzania, S by Burundi, and W by Zaire.

chronology
1916 Belgian troops occupied Rwanda; League of Nations mandated Rwanda and Burundi to Belgium as Territory of Ruanda-Urundi.
1959 Interethnic warfare between Hutu and Tutsi.
1962 Independence from Belgium achieved, with Grégoire Kayibanda as president.
1972 Renewal of interethnic fighting.
1973 Kayibanda ousted in a military coup led by Maj-Gen Juvenal Habyarimana.

1978 New constitution approved; Rwanda remained a military-controlled state.

1980 Civilian rule adopted.

1988 Refugees from Burundi massacres streamed into Rwanda.

1990 Government attacked by Rwandan Patriotic Front (FPR), a Tutsi military-political organization based in Uganda. Constitutional reforms promised.

1992 Peace accord with FPR.

1993 Power-sharing agreement with government repudiated by FPR.

Ryzhkov Nikolai Ivanovich 1929–   . Soviet communist politician. He held governmental and party posts from 1975 before being brought into the Politburo and serving as prime minister 1985–90 under Gorbachev. A low-profile technocrat, Ryzhkov was the author of unpopular economic reforms.

S

Sabah Sheik Jabir al Ahmadal Jabir al-1928– . Emir of Kuwait from 1977. He suspended the national assembly 1986, after mounting parliamentary criticism, ruling in a feudal, paternalistic manner. On the invasion of Kuwait by Iraq 1990 he fled to Saudi Arabia, returning to Kuwait in March 1991.

Sacco-Vanzetti case murder trial in Massachusetts, USA, 1920–21. Italian immigrants Nicola Sacco (1891–1927) and Bartolomeo Vanzetti (1888–1927) were convicted of murder during an alleged robbery. The conviction was upheld on appeal, with application for retrial denied. Prolonged controversy delayed execution until 1927. In 1977 the verdict was declared unjust because of the judge's prejudice against the accuseds' anarchist views.

Sadat Anwar 1918–1981. Egyptian politician. Succeeding ◊Nasser as president 1970, he restored morale by his handling of the Egyptian campaign in the 1973 war against Israel. In 1974 his plan for economic, social, and political reform to transform Egypt was unanimously adopted in a referendum. In 1977 he visited Israel to reconcile the two countries, and shared the Nobel Peace Prize with Israeli prime minister Menachem Begin 1978. He was assassinated by Islamic fundamentalists.

Saigon, Battle of during the Vietnam War, battle 29 Jan–23 Feb 1968, when 5,000 Vietcong were expelled by South Vietnamese and US forces. The city was finally taken by North Vietnamese forces 30 April 1975, after South Vietnamese withdrawal from the central highlands.

St Christopher (St Kitts)–Nevis country in the West Indies, in the E Caribbean Sea, part of the Leeward Islands.

chronology
1958-62 Part of the Federation of the West Indies.
1967 St Christopher, Nevis, and Anguilla achieved internal self-government, within the British Commonwealth, with Robert Bradshaw, Labour Party leader, as prime minister.
1971 Anguilla returned to being a British dependency.

1978 Bradshaw died; succeeded by Paul Southwell.
1979 Southwell died; succeeded by Lee L Moore.
1980 Coalition government led by Kennedy Simmonds.
1983 Full independence achieved within the Commonwealth.
1984 Coalition government re-elected.
1989 Prime Minister Simmonds won a third successive term.

St Lucia country in the West Indies, in the E Caribbean Sea, one of the Windward Islands.

chronology
1967 Acquired internal self-government as a West Indies associated state.
1979 Independence achieved from Britain within the Commonwealth, with John Compton, leader of the United Workers' Party (UWP), as prime minister. Allan Louisy, leader of the St Lucia Labour Party (SLP), replaced Compton as prime minister.
1981 Louisy resigned; replaced by Winston Cenac.
1982 Compton returned to power at the head of a UWP government.
1987 Compton re-elected with reduced majority.
1991 Integration with Windward Islands proposed.
1992 UWP won general election.

St Valentine's Day Massacre the murder in Chicago, USA, of seven unarmed members of the 'Bugs' Moran gang on 14 Feb 1929 by members of Al Capone's gang disguised as police. The killings testified to the intensity of gangland warfare for the control of the trade in illicit liquor during ◊Prohibition.

St Vincent and the Grenadines country in the West Indies, in the E Caribbean Sea, part of the Windward Islands.

chronology
1958–62 Part of the West Indies Federation.
1969 Achieved internal self-government.
1979 Achieved full independence from Britain within the Commonwealth, with Milton Cato as prime minister.
1984 James Mitchell replaced Cato as prime minister.
1989 Mitchell decisively re-elected.
1991 Integration with Windward Islands proposed.

Salazar Antonio de Oliveira 1889–1970. Portuguese prime minister 1932–68 who exercised a virtual dictatorship. During World War II he maintained Portuguese neutrality but fought long colonial wars in Africa (Angola and Mozambique) that impeded his country's economic development as well as that of the colonies.

Salinas de Gortiari Carlos 1948–   . Mexican politician, president from 1988, a member of the dominant Institutional Revolutionary Party (PRI).

Salisbury Robert Arthur James Gascoyne-Cecil, 5th Marquess of Salisbury 1893–1972. British Conservative politician. He was Dominions secretary 1940-42 and 1943-45, colonial secretary 1942, Lord Privy Seal 1942-43 and 1951-52, and Lord President of the Council 1952-57.

Salt March demonstration 11 March–4 May 1930 during the period of Indian nationalist agitation against British rule, forming part of Mahatma Gandhi's campaign of civil disobedience.

samizdat in the USSR and eastern Europe before the 1989 uprisings, written material circulated underground to evade state censorship; for example, reviews of Solzhenitzyn's banned novel *August 1914* 1972.

Samoa, Western country in the SW Pacific Ocean, in ◊Polynesia, NE of Fiji.

chronology
1899-1914 German protectorate.
1920-61 Administered by New Zealand.
1959 Local government elected.
1961 Referendum favoured independence.
1962 Independence achieved within the Commonwealth, with Fiame Mata Afa Mulinu'u as prime minister.
1975 Mata Afa died.
1976 Tupuola Taisi Efi became first nonroyal prime minister.
1982 Va'ai Kolone became prime minister; replaced by Tupuola Efi. Assembly failed to approve budget; Tupuola Efi resigned; replaced by Tofilau Eti Alesana.
1985 Tofilau Eti resigned; head of state invited Va'ai Kolone to lead the government.
1988 Elections produced a hung parliament, with first Tupuola Efi as prime minister and then Tofilau Eti Alesana.
1990 Universal adult suffrage introduced.
1991 Tofilau Eti Alesana re-elected. Fiame Naome became first woman in cabinet.

sanction economic or military measure taken by a state or number of states to enforce international law. The first use of sanctions was the attempted economic boycott of Italy (1935–36) during the Abyssinian War by the League of Nations.

Sandys Duncan Edwin Sandys, Baron Duncan-Sandys 1908–1987. British Conservative politician. As minister for Commonwealth relations 1960-64, he negotiated the independence of Malaysia 1963. He was created a life peer in 1974.

San Francisco conference conference attended by representatives from 50 nations who had declared war on Germany before March 1945; held in San Francisco, California, USA. The conference drew up the United Nations Charter, which was signed 26 June 1945.

Sanger Margaret Higgins 1883–1966. US health reformer and crusader for birth control. In 1914 she founded the National Birth Control League. She founded and presided over the American Birth Control League 1921–28, the organization that later became the Planned Parenthood Federation of America, and the International Planned Parenthood Federation 1952.

San Marino small landlocked country within NE Italy.

chronology
1862 Treaty with Italy signed; independence recognized under Italy's protection.
1947-86 Governed by a series of left-wing and centre-left coalitions.
1986 Formation of Communist and Christian Democrat 'grand coalition'.
1992 Joined the United Nations.

San Yu 1919– . Myanmar (Burmese) politician. A member of the Revolutionary Council that came to power 1962, he became president 1981 and was re-elected 1985. He was forced to resign July 1988, along with Ne Win, after riots in Yangon (formerly Rangoon).

São Tomé e Príncipe country in the Gulf of Guinea, off the coast of W Africa.

chronology
1522–1973 A province of Portugal.
1973 Achieved internal self-government.
1975 Independence achieved from Portugal, with Manuel Pinto da Costa as president.

1984 Formally declared a nonaligned state.
1987 Constitution amended.
1988 Unsuccessful coup attempt against da Costa.
1990 New constitution approved.
1991 First multiparty elections held; Miguel Trovoada replaced Pinto da Costa.

Sarney (Costa) José 1930– . Brazilian politician, member of the centre-left Democratic Movement (PMDB), president 1985–90.

Sassau-Nguesso Denis 1943– . Congolese socialist politician, president 1979–92. He progressively consolidated his position within the ruling left-wing Congolese Labour Party (PCT), at the same time as improving relations with France and the USA. In 1990, in response to public pressure, he agreed that the PCT should abandon Marxism-Leninism and that a multiparty system should be introduced.

Satō Eisaku 1901–1975. Japanese conservative politician, prime minister 1964–72. He ran against Hayato Ikeda (1899–1965) for the Liberal Democratic Party leadership and succeeded him as prime minister, pledged to a more independent foreign policy. He shared a Nobel Prize for Peace in 1974 for his rejection of nuclear weapons. His brother *Nobosuke Kishi* (1896–1987) was prime minister of Japan 1957–60.

satyagraha nonviolent resistance to British rule in India, as employed by Mahatma ◊Gandhi from 1918 to press for political reform; the idea owes much to the Russian writer Leo Tolstoy.

Saudi Arabia country on the Arabian peninsula, stretching from the Red Sea in the W to the Arabian Gulf in the E, bounded N by Jordan, Iraq, and Kuwait; E by Qatar and United Arab Emirates; SE by Oman; and S by Yemen.

chronology
1926–32 Territories of Nejd and Hejaz united and kingdom established.
1953 King Ibn Saud died and was succeeded by his eldest son, Saud.
1964 King Saud forced to abdicate; succeeded by his brother, Faisal.
1975 King Faisal assassinated; succeeded by his half-brother, Khalid.
1982 King Khalid died; succeeded by his brother, Crown Prince Fahd.
1987 Rioting by Iranian pilgrims caused 400 deaths in Mecca; diplomatic relations with Iran severed.
1990 Iraqi troops invaded and annexed Kuwait and massed on Saudi Arabian border. King Fahd called for help from US and UK forces.

1991 King Fahd provided military and financial assistance in Gulf War. Calls from religious leaders for 'consultative assembly' to assist in government of kingdom. Saudi Arabia attended Middle East peace conference.

1992 Formation of a 'consultative council' seen as possible move towards representative government.

Savage Michael Joseph 1872–1940. New Zealand Labour politician. As prime minister 1935–40, he introduced much social-security legislation.

Savimbi Jonas 1934–   . Angolan soldier and right-wing revolutionary, founder and leader of the National Union for the Total Independence of Angola (UNITA). From 1975 UNITA under Savimbi's leadership tried to overthrow the government. An agreement between the two parties was reached May 1991, but fighting broke out again following elections Sept 1992.

Saw Maung 1929–   . Myanmar (Burmese) soldier and politician. Appointed head of the armed forces in 1985 by ◊Ne Win, he led a coup to remove Ne Win's successor, Maung Maung, in 1988 and became leader of a totalitarian 'emergency government', which remained in office despite being defeated in the May 1990 election. In April 1992 he was replaced as chair of the ruling military junta, prime minister, and commander of the armed forces by Than Shwe.

Scapa Flow expanse of sea in the Orkney Islands, Scotland, until 1957 a base of the Royal Navy. It was the main base of the Grand Fleet during World War I and in 1919 was the scene of the scuttling of 71 surrendered German warships.

Scargill Arthur 1938–   . British trade-union leader. Elected president of the National Union of Miners (NUM) 1981, he embarked on a collision course with the Conservative government of Margaret Thatcher. The damaging strike of 1984–85 split the miners' movement.

Scheer Reinhard 1863–1928. German admiral in World War I, commander of the High Sea Fleet in 1916 at the Battle of ◊Jutland.

Schlesinger Arthur Meier, Jr 1917–   . US historian. His first book, *The Age of Jackson*, won a Pulitzer Prize 1945. Becoming active in Democratic politics, he served as a speechwriter in the presidential campaigns of Adlai Stevenson 1956 and John Kennedy 1960.

Schlieffen Plan military plan produced Dec 1905 by German chief of general staff, General Count Alfred von Schlieffen (1833–1913), that formed the basis of German military planning before World War I, and inspired Hitler's plans for the conquest of Europe in World War II. It involved a simultaneous attack on Russia and France, the object being to defeat France quickly and then deploy all available resources against the Russians.

Schlüter Poul Holmskov 1929– . Danish right-wing politician, leader of the Conservative People's Party (KF) from 1974 and prime minister 1982–93. Having joined the KF in his youth, he trained as a lawyer and then entered the Danish parliament (Folketing) in 1964. His centre-right coalition survived the 1990 election and was reconstituted, with Liberal support. In Jan 1993 Schlüter resigned, accused of dishonesty regarding his role in an incident involving Tamil refugees.

Schmidt Helmut 1918– . German socialist politician, member of the Social Democratic Party (SPD), chancellor of West Germany 1974–83. As chancellor, Schmidt introduced social reforms and continued Brandt's policy of Ostpolitik. With the French president Giscard d'Estaing, he instigated annual world and European economic summits. He was a firm supporter of NATO and of the deployment of US nuclear missiles in West Germany during the early 1980s.

Schuman Robert 1886–1963. French politician. He was prime minister 1947–48, and as foreign minister 1948–53 he proposed in May 1950 a common market for coal and steel (the *Schuman Plan*), which was established as the European Coal and Steel Community 1952, the basis of the European Community.

Schumpeter Joseph A(lois) 1883–1950. US economist and sociologist. In *Capitalism, Socialism and Democracy* 1942 he contended that Western capitalism, impelled by its very success, was evolving into a form of socialism because firms would become increasingly large and their managements increasingly divorced from ownership, while social trends were undermining the traditional motives for entrepreneurial accumulation of wealth.

Schuschnigg Kurt von 1897–1977. Austrian chancellor 1934–38, in succession to ◊Dollfuss. He tried in vain to prevent Nazi annexation (*Anschluss*) but in Feb 1938 he was forced to accept a Nazi minister of the interior, and a month later Austria was occupied and annexed by Germany.

He was imprisoned in Germany until 1945, when he went to the USA; he returned to Austria 1967.

Schwarzkopf (H) Norman (nicknamed 'Stormin' Norman') 1934–   . US general who was supreme commander of the Allied forces in the ◊Gulf War 1991. He planned and executed a blitzkrieg campaign, 'Desert Storm', sustaining remarkably few casualties in the liberation of Kuwait. He was a battalion commander in the Vietnam War and deputy commander of the 1983 US invasion of Grenada.

SCLC abbreviation for US civil-rights organization ◊*Southern Christian Leadership Conference*.

Scopes monkey trial trial held in Dayton, Tennessee, USA, 1925. John T Scopes, a science teacher at the high school, was accused of teaching, contrary to a law of the state, Darwin's theory of evolution. He was fined $100, but this was waived on a technical point. The defence counsel was Clarence Darrow and the prosecutor William Jennings ◊Bryan.

Scullin James Henry 1876–1953. Australian Labor politician. He was leader of the Federal Parliamentary Labor Party 1928–35, and prime minister and minister of industry 1929–31.

Second Front in World War II, battle line opened against Germany on 6 June 1944 by the Allies (Britain and the USA). Following Germany's invasion of the USSR in June 1941 (the 'first front'), Soviet leader Joseph Stalin asked Britain to invade the European mainland, to relieve pressure on the ◊Red Army. An Anglo-American invasion fleet landed on the Normandy beaches and, after overcoming fierce German resistance, Paris was liberated by the Allied forces 25 Aug 1944.

Second World War alternative name for ◊World War II, 1939–45.

Seddon Richard John 1845–1906. New Zealand Liberal politician, prime minister 1893–1906.

Seebohm Frederick, Baron Seebohm of Hertford 1909–1990. English banker and philanthropist. Seebohm joined Barclays Bank at 20, progressing to become chair 1965–72. He was highly influential in the banking world, and chaired numerous governmental and quasi-governmental committees. A notable philanthropist, he was made a life peer 1972.

Selwyn Lloyd John, Baron 1904–1978. British Conservative politician. He was foreign secretary 1955–60 and chancellor of the Exchequer 1960–62.

Senanayake Don Stephen 1884–1952. First prime minister of independent Sri Lanka (formerly Ceylon) 1947–52. Active in politics from 1915, he became leader of the United National Party and negotiated independence from Britain 1947. A devout Buddhist, he promoted Sinhalese-Tamil racial harmony and rural development.

Senanayake Dudley 1911–1973. Prime minister of Sri Lanka 1952–53, 1960, and 1965–70; son of Don Senanayake, he sought to continue his father's policy of communal reconciliation.

Senegal country in W Africa, on the Atlantic Ocean, bounded N by Mauritania, E by Mali, S by Guinea and Guinea-Bissau, and enclosing the Gambia on three sides.

chronology
1902 Became a territory of French West Africa.
1959 Formed the Federation of Mali with French Sudan.
1960 Independence achieved from France, but withdrew from the federation. Léopold Sédar ◊Senghor, leader of the Senegalese Progressive Union (UPS), became president.
1966 UPS declared the only legal party.
1974 Pluralist system re-established.
1976 UPS reconstituted as Senegalese Socialist Party (PS). Prime Minister Abdou ◊Diouf nominated as Senghor's successor.
1980 Senghor resigned; succeeded by Diouf. Troops sent to defend Gambia.
1981 Military help again sent to Gambia.
1982 Confederation of Senegambia came into effect.
1983 Diouf re-elected. Post of prime minister abolished.
1988 Diouf decisively re-elected.
1989 Violent clashes between Senegalese and Mauritanians in Dakar and Nouakchott killed more than 450 people; over 50,000 people repatriated from both countries. Senegambia federation abandoned.
1991 Constitutional changes outlined.
1992 Diplomatic links with Mauritania re-established.

Senghor Léopold (Sédar) 1906–   . Senegalese politician and writer, first president of independent Senegal 1960–80. He was Senegalese deputy to the French National Assembly 1946–58, and founder of the Senegalese Progressive Union. He was also a well-known poet and a founder of *négritude*, a black literary and philosophical movement.

Serbia (Serbo-Croatian *Srbija*) constituent republic of Yugoslavia; population (1986) 9,660,000. Serbia's designs 1903–14 on Bosnia-Herzegovina, backed by Russia, led to friction with Austria, culminating in the outbreak of war 1914. Serbia was overrun 1915–16 and was occupied until 1918, when it became the nucleus of the new kingdom of the Serbs, Croats, and Slovenes, and subsequently ◊Yugoslavia. During World War II Serbia was under a puppet government set up by the Germans; after the war it became a constituent republic of the Yugoslav Federal Republic.   Following Croatia's secession from Yugoslavia 1991, the Serbian nationalist government, headed by President Slobodan ◊Milosević, attempted the forcible annexation of Serb-dominated regions in Croatia, making use of the largely Serbian federal army. In Oct 1991 Milosević renounced territorial claims on Croatia pressured by threats of European Community (EC) and United Nations (UN) sanctions, but the fighting continued until a cease-fire was agreed Jan 1992. EC recognition of Slovenia's and Croatia's independence in Jan 1992 and Bosnia-Herzegovina's in April left Serbia dominating a greatly reduced 'rump' Yugoslavia.

Servan-Schreiber Jean Jacques 1924–   . French Radical politician, and founder of the magazine *L'Express* 1953. His *Le Défi americain* 1967 maintained that US economic and technological dominance would be challenged only by a united left-wing Europe. He was president of the Radical Party 1971–75 and 1977–79.

Sèvres, Treaty of the last of the treaties that ended World War I. Negotiated between the Allied powers and the Ottoman Empire, it was finalized Aug 1920 but never ratified by the Turkish government.

Seychelles country in the Indian Ocean, off E Africa, N of Madagascar.

chronology
1903 Split away from Mauritius to become a separate British colony.
1975 Internal self-government agreed.
1976 Independence achieved from Britain as a republic within the Commonwealth, with James Mancham as president.
1977 France-Albert René ousted Mancham in an armed coup and took over presidency.
1979 New constitution adopted; Seychelles People's Progressive Front (SPPF) sole legal party.
1981 Attempted coup by South African mercenaries thwarted.

1984 René re-elected.
1987 Coup attempt foiled.
1989 René re-elected.
1991 Multiparty politics promised.
1992 Mancham returned from exile. Constitutional commission elected; referendum on constitutional reform received insufficient support.

Shamir Yitzhak 1915– . Polish-born Israeli right-wing politician; prime minister 1983–84 and 1986–92; leader of the ◊Likud (Consolidation Party). He was foreign minister under Menachem Begin 1980–83, and again foreign minister in the ◊Peres unity government 1984–86.

Sharpeville black township in South Africa, 65 km/40 mi S of Johannesburg and N of Vereeniging; 69 people were killed here when police fired on a crowd of anti-apartheid demonstrators 21 March 1960.

Shastri Lal Bahadur 1904–1966. Indian politician, prime minister 1964–66. He campaigned for national integration, and secured a declaration of peace with Pakistan at the Tashkent peace conference 1966.

Shevardnadze Edvard 1928– . Georgian politician, Soviet foreign minister 1985–91, head of state of Georgia from 1992. A supporter of ◊Gorbachev, he was first secretary of the Georgian Communist Party from 1972 and an advocate of economic reform. In 1985 he became a member of the Politburo, working for détente and disarmament. In July 1991, he resigned from the Communist Party (CPSU) and, along with other reformers and leading democrats, established the Democratic Reform Movement. In March 1992 he was chosen as chair of Georgia's ruling military council, and in Oct elected speaker of parliament.

Shidehara Kijuro 1872–1951. Japanese politician and diplomat, prime minister 1945–46. As foreign minister 1924–27 and 1929–31, he promoted conciliation with China, and economic rather than military expansion. After a brief period as prime minister 1945–46, he became speaker of the Japanese Diet (parliament) 1946–51.

show trial public and well-reported trial of people accused of crimes against the state. In the USSR in the 1930s and 1940s, Stalin carried out show trials against economic saboteurs, Communist Party members, army officers, and even members of the Bolshevik leadership.

Shultz George P 1920– . US Republican politician, economics adviser to President ◊Reagan 1980–82, and secretary of state 1982–89. Shultz taught as a labour economist at the University of Chicago before serving in the 1968–74 ◊Nixon administration, including secretary of labor 1969–70 and secretary of the Treasury 1972–74.

Shuskevich Stanislav 1934– . Byelorussian politician and scientist, president of Belarus from 1991. Renowned as a supporter of democratic change, he was at the forefront of the movement that established the ◊Commonwealth of Independent States.

shuttle diplomacy in international relations, the efforts of an independent mediator to achieve a compromise solution between belligerent parties, travelling back and forth from one to the other.

Siegfried Line in World War I, a defensive line established 1918 by the Germans in France; in World War II, the Allies' name for the West Wall, a German defensive line established along its western frontier, from the Netherlands to Switzerland.

Sierra Leone country in W Africa, on the Atlantic Ocean, bounded N and E by Guinea and SE by Liberia.

chronology

1961 Independence achieved from Britain within the Commonwealth, with Milton Margai, leader of Sierra Leone People's Party (SLPP), as prime minister.
1964 Milton succeeded by his half-brother, Albert Margai.
1967 Election results disputed by army, who set up a National Reformation Council and forced the governor general to leave.
1968 Army revolt made Siaka ◊Stevens, leader of the All People's Congress (APC), prime minister.
1971 New constitution adopted, making Sierra Leone a republic, with Stevens as president.
1978 APC declared only legal party. Stevens sworn in for another seven-year term.
1985 Stevens retired; succeeded by Maj-Gen Joseph ◊Momoh.
1989 Attempted coup against President Momoh foiled.
1991 Referendum endorsed multiparty politics.
1992 Military take-over; President Momoh fled. National Provisional Ruling Council (NPRC) established under Capt Valentine Strasser.

Sihanouk Norodom 1922– . Cambodian politician, king 1941–55, prime minister 1955–70, when his government was overthrown by a military coup led by Lon Nol. With Pol Pot's resistance front, he overthrew Lon Nol 1975 and again became prime minister 1975–76, when he was forced to resign by the ◊Khmer Rouge. He returned from exile Nov 1991 under the auspices of a United Nations-brokered peace settlement to head the Supreme National Council, a new coalition comprising all Cambodia's warring factions, including the Khmer Rouge.

Sikorski Wladyslaw 1881–1943. Polish general and politician; prime minister 1922–23, and 1939–43 of the Polish government in exile in London during World War II. He was killed in an aeroplane crash near Gibraltar in controversial circumstances.

Silayev Ivan Stepanovich 1930–   . Prime minister of the USSR Aug–Dec 1991, a founder member of the Democratic Reform Movement (with former foreign minister ◊Shevardnadze). A member of the Communist Party 1959–91 and of its Central Committee 1981–91, Silayev emerged as a reformer in 1990.

Simon John Allsebrook, Viscount Simon 1873–1954. British Liberal politician. He was home secretary 1915–16, but resigned over the issue of conscription. He was foreign secretary 1931–35, home secretary again 1935–37, chancellor of the Exchequer 1937–40, and lord chancellor 1940–45.

Simon Commission or *Indian Statutory Commission* all-party group set up Nov 1927 to examine the working of government in India and recommend future policy. Chaired by the Liberal Sir John Simon (1873-1954), it was entirely drawn from the British ruling classes. This exclusion of Indian representatives prompted an immediate boycott by the Indian National Congress and later the ◊Muslim League.

Sinai, Battle of battle 6–24 Oct 1973 during the Yom Kippur War between Israel and Egypt. It was one of the longest tank battles in history. Israeli troops crossed the Suez canal 16 Oct, cutting off the Egyptian 3rd Army.

Singapore country in SE Asia, off the tip of the Malay Peninsula.

chronology
1942 Invaded and occupied by Japan.
1945 Japanese removed by British forces.
1959 Independence achieved from Britain; ◊Lee Kuan Yew became prime minister.

1963 Joined new Federation of Malaysia.

1965 Left federation to become an independent republic.

1984 Opposition made advances in parliamentary elections.

1986 Opposition leader convicted of perjury and prohibited from standing for election.

1988 Ruling conservative party elected to all but one of available assembly seats; increasingly authoritarian rule.

1990 Lee Kuan Yew resigned as prime minister; replaced by ◊Goh Chok Tong.

1991 People's Action Party (PAP) and Goh Chok Tong re-elected.

Singh Vishwanath Pratap 1931– . Indian politician, prime minister 1989–90. As a member of the Congress (I) Party, he held ministerial posts under Indira Gandhi and Rajiv Gandhi, and from 1984 led an anti-corruption drive. When he unearthed an arms-sales scandal 1988, he was ousted from the government and party and formed a broad-based opposition alliance, the ◊*Janata Dal*, which won the Nov 1989 election. Mounting caste and communal conflict split the Janata Dal and forced him out of office Nov 1990.

Sinn Féin Irish nationalist party founded by Arthur Griffith (1872–1922) in 1905; in 1917 Eamon ◊de Valera became its president. It is the political wing of the Irish Republican Army, and is similarly split between comparative moderates and extremists. In 1985 it gained representation in 17 out of 26 district councils in Northern Ireland.

Sino-Japanese Wars two wars waged by Japan against China 1894–95 and 1931–45 to expand to the mainland. Territory gained in the First Sino-Japanese War (Korea) and in the 1930s (Manchuria, Shanghai) was returned at the end of World War II.

Sisulu Walter 1912– . South African civil-rights activist, one of the first full-time secretary generals of the African National Congress (ANC), in 1964, with Nelson Mandela. He was imprisoned following the 1964 Rivonia Trial for opposition to the apartheid system and released, at the age of 77, as a gesture of reform by President F W ◊De Klerk 1989. In 1991, when Mandela became ANC president, Sisulu became his deputy.

Six-Day War another name for the third ◊Arab-Israeli War.

Slim William Joseph, 1st Viscount 1891–1970. British field marshal in World War II. He commanded the 1st Burma Corps 1942–45, stemming the

Japanese invasion of India, and then forcing them out of Burma (now Myanmar). He was governor general of Australia 1953–60.

Slovak Republic landlocked country in E central Europe, bounded N by Poland, E by the Ukraine, S and SE by Hungary, SW by Austria, and W by the Czech Republic.

chronology
906–1918 Under Magyar domination.
1918 Independence achieved from Austro-Hungarian Empire; Slovaks joined Czechs in forming Czechoslovakia as independent nation.
1948 Communists assumed power in Czechoslovakia.
1968 Slovak Socialist Republic created under new federal constitution.
1989 Pro-democracy demonstrations in Prague and Bratislava; new political parties formed, including Slovak-based People Against Violence (PAV); Communist Party stripped of powers. Dec: new 'grand coalition' government formed, including former dissidents; political parties legalized; Václav ◊Havel appointed state president. Amnesty granted to 22,000 prisoners; calls for USSR to withdraw troops.
1990 July: Havel re-elected president in multiparty elections.
1991 Evidence of increasing Czech and Slovak separatism. March: PAV splinter group formed under Slovak premier Vladimir Meciar. April: Meciar dismissed, replaced by Jan Carnogursky; pro-Meciar rallies held in Bratislava. July: Soviet troops withdrawn. Oct: Public Against Violence renamed Civic Democratic Union–Public Against Violence (PAV).
1992 March: PAV renamed Civic Democratic Union (CDU). June: Havel resigned following Slovak gains in assembly elections. Aug: agreement on creation of separate Czech and Slovak states from Jan 1993.
1993 Jan: Slovak Republic became sovereign state, with Meciar, leader of the Movement for a Democratic Slovakia (MFDS), as prime minister. Feb: Michal Kovak became president.

Slovenia or *Slovenija* country in S central Europe, bounded N by Austria, E by Hungary, W by Italy, and S by Croatia.

chronology
1918 United with Serbia and Croatia.
1929 The kingdom of Serbs, Croats, and Slovenes took the name of Yugoslavia.
1945 Became a constituent republic of Yugoslav Socialist Federal Republic.

mid-1980s The Slovenian Communist Party liberalized itself and agreed to free elections. Yugoslav counterintelligence (KOV) began repression.
1989 Jan: Social Democratic Alliance of Slovenia launched as the first political organization independent of Communist Party. Sept: constitution changed to allow secession from federation.
1990 Feb: Slovene League of Communists, renamed as the Party of Democratic Reform, severed its links with the Yugoslav League of Communists. April: nationalist Democratic Opposition of Slovenia (DEMOS) coalition secured victory in first multiparty parliamentary elections; Milan Kucan became president. July: sovereignty declared. Dec: independence overwhelmingly approved in referendum.
1991 June: independence declared; 100 killed after federal army intervened; cease-fire brokered by the European Community (EC). July: cease-fire agreed between federal troops and nationalists. Oct: withdrawal of Yugoslav army completed. Dec: DEMOS coalition dissolved.
1992 Jan: EC recognized Slovenia's independence. April: Janez Drnovsek appointed prime minister designate; independence recognized by USA. May: admitted into United Nations (UN) and Conference for Security and Cooperation in Europe (CSCE). Dec: Liberal Democrats and Christian Democrats won assembly elections; Kucan re-elected president.
1993 Drnovsek re-elected prime minister.

Smith Al (Alfred Emanuel) 1873–1944. US political leader who served four terms as governor of New York but was unsuccessful as a candidate for the presidency. In 1928 he became the first Roman Catholic to receive a presidential nomination. In his lively, yet unsuccessful, campaign against Herbert Hoover he was called 'The Happy Warrior.'

Smith Ian Douglas 1919–   . Prime Minister of Rhodesia (now ◊Zimbabwe) 1964–79. He made a unilateral declaration of independence from Britain (UDI) 1965, maintaining it despite United Nations pressure and ◊sanctions.

   In 1979 he was succeeded as prime minister by Bishop Abel Muzorewa when the country was renamed Zimbabwe. He was suspended from parliament in 1987 and resigned as head of the white opposition party.

Smith John 1938–   . British Labour politician, party leader from 1992. He was secretary of state for trade 1978–79 and from 1979 held various shadow cabinet posts, culminating in shadow chancellor 1978–92.

Smuts Jan Christian 1870–1950. South African politician and soldier; prime minister 1919–24 and 1939–48. He supported the Allies in both world wars and was a member of the British imperial war cabinet 1917–18.

Snowden Philip, 1st Viscount Snowden 1864–1937. British right-wing Labour politician, chancellor of the Exchequer 1924 and 1929–31. He entered the coalition National Government in 1931 as Lord Privy Seal, but resigned in 1932.

Soames Christopher, Baron Soames 1920–1987. British Conservative politician. He held ministerial posts 1958–64, was vice president of the Commission of the European Communities 1973–77 and governor of (Southern) Rhodesia in the period of its transition to independence as Zimbabwe, Dec 1979–April 1980. He was created a life peer 1978.

Soares Mario 1924– . Portuguese socialist politician, president from 1986. Exiled 1970, he returned to Portugal 1974, and, as leader of the Portuguese Socialist Party, was prime minister 1976–78. He resigned as party leader 1980, but in 1986 he was elected Portugal's first socialist president.

Sobchak Anatoly 1937– . Soviet centrist politician, mayor of St Petersburg from 1990, cofounder of the Democratic Reform Movement (with former foreign minister ◊Shevardnadze), and member of the Soviet parliament 1989–91. He prominently resisted the abortive anti- Gorbachev coup of Aug 1991.

social credit theory, put forward by Canadian C H Douglas (1879–1952), that economic crises are caused by bank control of money, which leads to shortage of purchasing power. His remedy was payment of a 'social dividend'. There have been provincial social-credit governments in Canada, but the central government has always vetoed the plan.

socialism movement aiming to establish a classless society by substituting public for private ownership of the means of production, distribution, and exchange. The term has been used to describe positions as far apart as anarchism, communism, and social democracy. The late 19th and early 20th centuries saw a division between those who reacted against ◊Marxism, leading to the formation of social-democratic parties, and those who emphasized the original revolutionary significance of Marx's teachings. Weakened by these divisions, the second ◊International (founded in 1889) collapsed in 1914, right-wing socialists in all countries supporting participation in World War I while the left opposed it. The Russian Revolution took socialism from the sphere of theory to that of practice, and was followed in 1919 by the foundation of the Third International, which completed the division between right and left. This lack of unity, in spite of the temporary successes of the popular fronts in France and Spain in 1936–38, facilitated the rise of fascism and Nazism.

After World War II socialist and communist parties tended to formal union in Eastern Europe, although the rigid communist control that ensued was later modified in some respects in, for example, Poland, Romania, and Yugoslavia. In 1989, however, revolutionary change throughout Eastern Europe ended this rigid control; this was followed in 1991 by the disbanding of the Soviet Communist Party and the ensuing disintegration of the Soviet Union. Most countries in W Europe have a strong socialist party; for example, in Germany the Social Democratic Party and in Britain the ◊Labour Party.

'socialism in one country' concept proposed by ◊Stalin in 1924. In contrast to ◊Trotsky's theory of the permanent revolution, Stalin suggested that the emphasis be changed away from promoting revolutions abroad to the idea of building socialism, economically and politically, in the USSR without help from other countries.

Solidarity (Polish *Solidarność*) national confederation of independent trade unions in Poland, formed under the leadership of Lech ◊Wałesa Sept 1980. An illegal organization from 1981 to 1989, it was then elected to head the Polish government. Divisions soon emerged in the leadership. Solidarity had 2.8 million members in 1991.

Solomon Islands country in the SW Pacific Ocean, E of New Guinea, comprising many hundreds of islands, the largest of which is Guadalcanal.

chronology
1893 Solomon Islands placed under British protection.
1978 Independence achieved from Britain within the Commonwealth, with Peter Kenilorea as prime minister.
1981 Solomon Mamaloni of the People's Progressive Party replaced Kenilorea as prime minister.
1984 Kenilorea returned to power, heading a coalition government.
1986 Kenilorea resigned after allegations of corruption; replaced by his deputy, Ezekiel Alebua.

1988 Kenilorea elected deputy prime minister. Joined Vanuatu and Papua New Guinea to form the Spearhead Group, aiming to preserve Melanesian cultural traditions and secure independence for the French territory of New Caledonia.
1989 Solomon Mamaloni, now leader of the People's Alliance Party (PAP), was elected prime minister and formed a PAP-dominated coalition.
1990 Mamaloni resigned as PAP party leader, but continued as head of a government of national unity.

Somalia country in NE Africa (the Horn of Africa), on the Indian Ocean, bounded NW by Djibouti, W by Ethiopia, and SW by Kenya.

chronology
1884-87 British protectorate of Somaliland established.
1889 Italian protectorate of Somalia established.
1960 Independence achieved from Italy and Britain.
1963 Border dispute with Kenya; diplomatic relations broken with Britain.
1968 Diplomatic relations with Britain restored.
1969 Army coup led by Maj-Gen Mohamed Siad Barre; constitution suspended, Supreme Revolutionary Council set up; name changed to Somali Democratic Republic.
1978 Defeated in eight-month war with Ethiopia. Armed insurrection began in north.
1979 New constitution for socialist one-party state adopted.
1982 Antigovernment Somali National Movement formed. Oppressive countermeasures by government.
1987 Barre re-elected president.
1989 Dissatisfaction with government and increased guerrilla activity in north.
1990 Civil war intensified. Constitutional reforms promised.
1991 Mogadishu captured by rebels; Barre fled; Ali Mahdi Mohammed named president; free elections promised. Secession of NE Somalia, as the Somaliland Republic, announced. Cease-fire signed, but later collapsed. Thousands of casualties as a result of heavy fighting in capital.
1992 Relief efforts to ward off impending famine severely hindered by unstable political situation; relief convoys hijacked by 'war lords'. Dec: UN peacekeeping troops, mainly US Marines, drafted in to protect relief operations; dominant warlords agreed truce.
1993 March: leaders of armed factions agreed to federal system of government, based on 18 autonomous regions.

Somme, Battle of the Allied offensive in World War I July–Nov 1916 at Beaumont-Hamel-Chaulnes, on the river Somme in N France, during which severe losses were suffered by both sides. It was planned by the Marshal of France, Joseph Joffre, and UK commander in chief Douglas Haig; the Allies lost over 600,000 soldiers and advanced 32 km/20 mi. It was the first battle in which tanks were used. The German offensive around St Quentin March–April 1918 is sometimes called the Second Battle of the Somme.

Somoza Debayle Anastasio 1925–1980. Nicaraguan soldier and politician, president 1967–72 and 1974–79. The second son of Anastasio Somoza García, he succeeded his brother Luis Somoza Debayle (1922–1967; president 1956–63) as president of Nicaragua in 1967, to head an even more oppressive regime. He was removed by Sandinista guerrillas in 1979, and assassinated in Paraguay 1980.

Somoza García Anastasio 1896–1956. Nicaraguan soldier and politician, president 1937–47 and 1950–56. A protégé of the USA, who wanted a reliable ally to protect their interests in Central America, he was virtual dictator of Nicaragua from 1937 until his assassination in 1956. He exiled most of his political opponents and amassed a considerable fortune in land and businesses. Members of his family retained control of the country until 1979, when they were overthrown by popular forces.

Soong Ching-ling 1890–1981. Chinese politician, wife of the ◊Guomindang nationalist leader ◊Sun Yat-sen; she remained a prominent figure in Chinese politics after his death, being a vice chair of the People's Republic of China from 1959.

Souphanouvong Prince 1912– . Laotian politician, president 1975–86. After an abortive revolt against French rule in 1945, he led the guerrilla organization Pathet Lao, and in 1975 became the first president of the Republic of Laos.

South Africa country on the southern tip of Africa, bounded N by Namibia, Botswana, and Zimbabwe and NE by Mozambique and Swaziland.

chronology
1910 Union of South Africa formed from two British colonies and two Boer republics.

1912 ◊African National Congress (ANC) formed.

1948 Apartheid system of racial discrimination initiated by Daniel Malan, leader of National Party (NP).

1955 Freedom Charter adopted by ANC.

1958 Malan succeeded as prime minister by Hendrik ◊Verwoerd.

1960 ANC banned.

1961 South Africa withdrew from Commonwealth and became a republic.

1962 ANC leader Nelson ◊Mandela jailed.

1964 Mandela, Walter ◊Sisulu, Govan Mbeki, and five other ANC leaders sentenced to life imprisonment.

1966 Verwoerd assassinated; succeeded by B J ◊Vorster.

1976 Soweto uprising.

1977 Death in custody of Pan African Congress (PAC) activist Steve ◊Biko.

1978 Vorster resigned and was replaced by P W ◊Botha.

1984 New constitution adopted, giving segregated representation to Coloureds and Asians and making Botha president. Nonaggression pact with Mozambique signed but not observed.

1985 Growth of violence in black townships.

1986 Commonwealth agreed on limited sanctions. US Congress voted to impose sanctions. Some major multinational companies closed down their South African operations.

1987 Government formally acknowledged the presence of its military forces in Angola.

1988 Botha announced 'limited constitutional reforms'. South Africa agreed to withdraw from Angola and recognize Namibia's independence as part of regional peace accord.

1989 Botha gave up NP leadership and state presidency. F W ◊de Klerk became president. ANC activists released; beaches and public facilities desegregated. Elections held in Namibia to create independence government.

1990 ANC ban lifted; Nelson Mandela released from prison. NP membership opened to all races. ANC leader Oliver Tambo returned. Daily average of 35 murders and homicides recorded.

1991 Mandela and Zulu leader Chief Gatsha ◊Buthelezi urged end to fighting between ANC and ◊Inkatha. Mandela elected ANC president. Revelations of government support for Inkatha threatened ANC cooperation. De Klerk announced repeal of remaining apartheid laws. South Africa readmitted to international sport. USA lifted sanctions. PAC and Buthelezi withdrew from negotiations over new constitution.

1992 Constitution leading to all-races majority rule approved by whites-only referendum. Massacre of civilians at black township of Boipathong near Johannesburg by Inkatha, aided and abetted by police, threatened constitutional talks.

1993 Feb: de Klerk and Nelson Mandela agreed to formation of government of national unity after free elections late 1993/early 1994. Buthelezi not consulted; he opposed such an arrangement. April: ANC leader Chris Hani assassinated; Andries Treurnicht, leader of Conservative Party, and Oliver Tambo died.

Southeast Asia Treaty Organization (SEATO) collective military system 1954–77 established by Australia, France, New Zealand, Pakistan, the Philippines, Thailand, the UK, and the USA, with Vietnam, Cambodia, and Laos as protocol states. After the Vietnam War, SEATO was phased out.

Southern Christian Leadership Conference (SCLC) US civil-rights organization founded 1957 by Martin Luther ◊King, Jr, and led by him until his assassination 1968. It advocated nonviolence and passive resistance, and it sponsored the 1963 march on Washington DC that focused national attention on the civil-rights movement. Its nonviolent philosophy was increasingly challenged by militants, and it lost its central position in the movement.

soviet originally a strike committee elected by Russian workers in the 1905 revolution; in 1917 these were set up by peasants, soldiers, and factory workers. The soviets sent delegates to the All-Russian Congress of Soviets to represent their opinions to a future government. They were later taken over by the ◊Bolsheviks.

sovkhoz Soviet state-owned farm where the workers were state employees (such farms are still widespread in ex-Soviet republics). The sovkhoz differs from the *kolkhoz* where the farm is run by a collective (see ◊collective farm).

Spaak Paul-Henri 1899–1972. Belgian socialist politician. From 1936 to 1966 he held office almost continuously as foreign minister or prime minister. He was an ardent advocate of international peace.

Spain country in SW Europe, on the Iberian Peninsula between the Atlantic Ocean and the Mediterranean Sea, bounded N by France and W by Portugal.

chronology

1936–39 Civil war; General Francisco ◊Franco became head of state and government; fascist party Falange declared only legal political organization.

1947 General Franco announced restoration of the monarchy after his death, with Prince Juan Carlos as his successor.

1975 Franco died; succeeded as head of state by King Juan Carlos I.

1978 New constitution adopted with Adolfo ◊Suárez, leader of the Democratic Centre Party, as prime minister.

1981 Suárez resigned; succeeded by Leopoldo Calvo Sotelo. Attempted military coup thwarted.

1982 Socialist Workers' Party (PSOE), led by Felipe ◊González, won a sweeping electoral victory. Basque separatist organization (ETA) stepped up its guerrilla campaign.

1985 ETA's campaign spread to holiday resorts.

1986 Referendum confirmed NATO membership. Spain joined the European Economic Community.

1988 Spain joined the Western European Union.

1989 PSOE lost seats to hold only parity after general election. Talks between government and ETA collapsed and truce ended.

1992 ETA's 'armed struggle' resumed. Nov: Maastricht Treaty ratified by parliament.

Spanish Civil War 1936–39. See ◊Civil War, Spanish.

Spartacist member of a group of left-wing radicals in Germany at the end of World War I, founders of the *Spartacus League*, which became the German Communist Party in 1919. The league participated in the Berlin workers' revolt of Jan 1919, which was suppressed by the Freikorps on the orders of the socialist government. The agitation ended with the murder of Spartacist leaders Karl ◊Liebknecht and Rosa ◊Luxemburg.

Special Areas Acts UK acts of Parliament 1936 and 1937, aimed at dealing with high unemployment in some regions of Britain. These areas, designated 'special areas', attracted government assistance in the form of loans and subsidies to generate new employment. Other measures included setting up industrial and trading estates that could be leased at subsidized rates. The acts were an early example of regional aid.

special relationship belief that ties of common language, culture, and shared aims of the defence of democratic principles should sustain a political relationship between the USA and the UK, and that the same would not apply to relationships between the USA and other European states.

Spee Maximilian, Count von Spee 1861–1914. German admiral, born in Copenhagen. He went down with his flagship in the 1914 battle of the Falkland Islands, and the *Graf Spee* battleship was named after him.

Speer Albert 1905–1981. German architect and minister in the Nazi government during World War II. Commissioned by Hitler, Speer, like his counterparts in Fascist Italy, chose an overblown Classicism to glorify the state, as, for example, in his plan for the Berlin and Nuremberg Party Congress Grounds 1934.

Spring Richard 1950– . Irish Labour Party leader from 1982, who entered into coalition with ◊FitzGerald's Fine Gael 1982 as deputy prime minister (and minister for energy from 1983).

Sri Lanka (formerly, until 1972, *Ceylon*) island in the Indian Ocean, off the SE coast of India.

chronology
1948 Ceylon achieved independence from Britain within the Commonwealth.
1956 Sinhala established as the official language.
1959 Prime Minister Solomon ◊Bandaranaike assassinated.
1972 Socialist Republic of Sri Lanka proclaimed.
1978 Presidential constitution adopted by new government led by Junius Jayawardene of the United National Party (UNP).
1983 Tamil guerrilla violence escalated; state of emergency imposed.
1987 President Jayawardene and Indian prime minister Rajiv Gandhi signed Colombo Accord. Violence continued despite cease-fire policed by Indian troops.
1988 Left-wing guerrillas campaigned against Indo-Sri Lankan peace pact. Prime Minister Ranasinghe Premadasa elected president.
1989 Premadasa became president; D B Wijetunge, prime minister. Leaders of the Tamil United Liberation Front (TULF) and terrorist People's Liberation Front assassinated.
1990 Indian peacekeeping force withdrawn. Violence continued.
1991 March: defence minister, Ranjan Wijeratne, assassinated; Sri Lankan army killed 2,552 Tamil Tigers at Elephant Pass. October: impeachment motion against President Premadasa failed. Dec: new party, the Democratic United National Front, formed by former members of UNP.

SS Nazi elite corps (German *Schutz-Staffel* 'protective squadron') established 1925. Under ◊Himmler its 500,000 membership included the fulltime *Waffen-SS* (armed SS), which fought in World War II, and spare-time members. The SS performed state police duties and was brutal in its treatment of the Jews and others in the concentration camps and occupied territories. It was condemned at the Nuremberg Trials of war criminals.

Stahlhelm German paramilitary and ex-soldiers' organization prominent in the 1920s and 1930s and associated with the German National People's Party (DNVP) and German People's Party (DVP).

Stakhanov Aleksei 1906–1977. Soviet miner who exceeded production norms; he gave his name to the *Stakhanovite* movement of the 1930s, when workers were offered incentives to simplify and reorganize work processes in order to increase production.

Stalin Joseph. Adopted name (Russian 'steel') of Joseph Vissarionovich Djugashvili 1879–1953. Soviet politician. A member of the October Revolution Committee 1917, Stalin became general secretary of the Communist Party 1922. After ◊Lenin's death 1924, Stalin sought to create 'socialism in one country' and clashed with ◊Trotsky, who denied the possibility of socialism inside Russia until revolution had occurred in W Europe. Stalin won this ideological struggle by 1927, and a series of five-year plans was launched to collectivize industry and agriculture from 1928. All opposition was eliminated in the Great Purge 1936–38. During World War II, Stalin intervened in the military direction of the campaigns against Nazi Germany. His role was denounced after his death by Khrushchev and other members of the Soviet regime.

Stalingrad former name, 1925–61, of ◊Volgograd, a city in SW Russia.

Statute of Westminster in the history of the British Empire, legislation enacted 1931 which gave the dominions of the British Empire complete autonomy in their conduct of external affairs. It made them self-governing states whose only allegiance was to the British Crown.

Stauffenberg Claus von 1907–1944. German colonel in World War II who, in a conspiracy to assassinate Hitler, planted a bomb in the dictator's headquarters conference room in the Wolf's Lair at Rastenburg, East Prussia, 20 July 1944. Hitler was merely injured, and Stauffenberg and 200 others were later executed by the Nazi regime.

Steel David 1938– . British politician, leader of the Liberal Party 1976–88. He entered into a compact with the Labour government 1977–78, and into an alliance with the Social Democratic Party (SDP) 1983. Having supported the Liberal-SDP merger (forming the Social and Liberal Democrats), he resigned the leadership 1988, becoming the Party's foreign affairs spokesman.

Steinem Gloria 1934– . US journalist and liberal feminist who emerged as a leading figure in the US women's movement in the late 1960s. She was also involved in radical protest campaigns against racism and the Vietnam War. She cofounded the Women's Action Alliance 1970 and *Ms* magazine. In 1983 a collection of her articles was published as *Outrageous Acts and Everyday Rebellions*.

Stern Gang formal name *Fighters for the Freedom of Israel* Zionist guerrilla group founded 1940 by Abraham Stern (1907-1942). The group carried out anti-British attacks during the UK mandate rule in Palestine, both on individuals and on strategic targets. Stern was killed by British forces in 1942, but the group survived until 1948, when it was outlawed with the creation of the independent state of Israel.

Stevens Siaka Probin 1905–1988. Sierra Leone politician, president 1971–85. He was the leader of the moderate left-wing All People's Congress (APC), from 1978 the country's only legal political party.

Stevenson Adlai 1900–1965. US Democrat politician. As governor of Illinois 1949–53 he campaigned vigorously against corruption in public life, and as Democratic candidate for the presidency 1952 and 1956 was twice defeated by Eisenhower. In 1945 he was chief US delegate at the founding conference of the United Nations.

Stewart Michael, Baron Stewart of Fulham 1906–1990. English Labour politician, member of Parliament 1945–79. He held ministerial office in the governments of Clement Attlee and Harold Wilson, rising to foreign secretary 1968.

Stilwell Joseph Warren ('Vinegar Joe') 1883–1946. US general in World War II. In 1942 he became US military representative in China, when he commanded the Chinese forces cooperating with the British (with whom he quarrelled) in Burma (now Myanmar); he later commanded all US forces in China, Burma, and India until recalled to the USA 1944 after differences over nationalist policy with the ◊Guomindang (nationalist) leader Chiang

Kai-shek. Subsequently he commanded the US 10th Army on the Japanese island of Okinawa.

Stimson Henry Lewis 1867–1950. US politician. He was war secretary in Taft's cabinet 1911–13, Hoover's secretary of state 1929–33, and war secretary 1940–45.

Stonehouse John (Thompson) 1925–1988. British Labour Party politician. An active member of the Co-operative Movement, he entered Parliament in 1957 and held junior posts under Harold Wilson before joining his cabinet in 1967. In 1974 he disappeared in Florida in mysterious circumstances, surfacing in Australia, amid suspicions of fraudulent dealings. Extradited to Britain, he was tried and imprisoned for embezzlement. He was released in 1979, but was unable to resume a political career.

Strategic Arms Limitation Talks (SALT) series of US-Soviet discussions 1969–79 aimed at reducing the rate of nuclear-arms build-up (as opposed to disarmament, which would reduce the number of weapons, as discussed in ◊Strategic Arms Reduction Talks (START).

Strategic Arms Reduction Talks (START) phase in peace discussions dealing with ◊disarmament, initially involving the USA and the Soviet Union and from 1992 the USA and Russia. It began with talks in Geneva 1983, leading to the signing of the Intermediate Nuclear Forces (INF) Treaty 1987. Reductions of about 30% in strategic nuclear weapons systems were agreed 1991 (START) and more significant cuts Jan 1993 (START II).

Strategic Defense Initiative (SDI) also called *Star Wars*, attempt by the USA to develop a defence system against incoming nuclear missiles, based in part outside the Earth's atmosphere. It was announced by President Reagan in March 1983, and the research had by 1990 cost over $16.5 billion. In 1988, the joint Chiefs of Staff announced that they expected to be able to intercept no more than 30% of incoming missiles. Scientists maintained that the system is basically unworkable and it was phased out 1993.

Strauss Franz-Josef 1915–1988. German conservative politician, leader of the West German Bavarian Christian Social Union (CSU) party 1961–88, premier of Bavaria 1978–88.

Stresa Front summit meeting 11–14 April 1935 between the prime ministers of Britain, France, and Italy (Ramsay MacDonald, Pierre Flandin, and

Benito Mussolini) with the aim of forming a common front against Germany. This followed Adolf Hitler's announcement that Germany would not be bound by the limitations imposed upon its armaments by the Versailles Treaty of June 1919. The 'front' soon broke up: in Oct 1935 Italy was severely criticized for launching an Abyssinian War 1935–36 to establish an east African Italian empire, and on 2 Nov 1936 Benito Mussolini proclaimed the Rome–Berlin Axis, which brought Germany and Italy into close collaboration between 1936 and 1945.

Stresemann Gustav 1878–1929. German politician, chancellor in 1923 and foreign minister from 1923 to 1929 of the Weimar Republic. During World War I he was a strong nationalist but his views became more moderate under the Weimar Republic. His achievements included reducing the amount of war reparations paid by Germany after the Treaty of Versailles 1919; negotiating the Locarno Treaties 1925; and Germany's admission to the League of Nations. He shared the 1926 Nobel Peace Prize with Aristide Briand.

Stroessner Alfredo 1912– . Military leader and president of Paraguay 1954–89. As head of the armed forces from 1951, he seized power in a coup in 1954 sponsored by the right-wing ruling Colorado Party. Accused by his opponents of harsh repression, his regime spent heavily on the military to preserve his authority. Despite criticisms of his government's civil-rights record, he was re-elected seven times and remained in office until ousted in an army-led coup 1989.

Students for a Democratic Society (SDS) US student movement, founded 1962, which steered a middle line between Marxism and orthodox left-wing politics; its members opposed racism and imperialism. At its peak it had some 100,000 members. In 1968 they were split by the hardline Weatherman faction, which aimed for violent revolution and control from above.

Sturmabteilung (SA) German militia, also known as *Brownshirts*, of the ◊Nazi Party, established 1921 under the leadership of Ernst ◊Röhm, in charge of physical training and political indoctrination.

Suárez González Adolfo 1933– . Spanish politician, prime minister 1976–81. A friend of King Juan Carlos, he was appointed by the king to guide Spain into democracy after the death of the fascist dictator Franco.

Suchocka Hanna 1946–   . Polish politician, prime minister from 1992. She was chosen by President ◊Wałesa as a replacement for prime minister Waldemar Pawlak, who was unable to form a viable government.

Sudan country in NE Africa, bounded N by Egypt, NE by the Red Sea, E by Ethiopia, S by Kenya, Uganda, and Zaire, W by the Central African Republic and Chad, and NW by Libya. It is the largest country in Africa.

chronology
1899 Sudan administered as an Anglo-Egyptian condominium.
1955 Civil war between Muslim north and non-Muslim south broke out.
1956 Sudan achieved independence from Britain and Egypt as a republic.
1958 Military coup replaced civilian government with Supreme Council of the Armed Forces.
1964 Civilian rule reinstated.
1969 Coup led by Col Gaafar Mohammed Nimeri established Revolutionary Command Council (RCC); name changed to Democratic Republic of Sudan.
1970 Union with Egypt agreed in principle.
1971 New constitution adopted; Nimeri confirmed as president; Sudanese Socialist Union (SSU) declared only legal party.
1972 Proposed Federation of Arab Republics, comprising Sudan, Egypt, and Syria, abandoned. Addis Ababa conference proposed autonomy for southern provinces.
1974 National assembly established.
1983 Nimeri re-elected. *Shari'a* (Islamic law) introduced.
1985 Nimeri deposed in a bloodless coup led by General Swar al-Dahab; transitional military council set up. State of emergency declared.
1986 More than 40 political parties fought general election; coalition government formed.
1987 Virtual civil war with Sudan People's Liberation Army (SPLA).
1988 Al-Mahdi formed a new coalition. Another flare-up of civil war between north and south created tens of thousands of refugees. Floods made 1.5 million people homeless. Peace pact signed with SPLA.
1989 Sadiq al-Mahdi overthrown in coup led by General Omar Hassan Ahmed el-Bashir.
1990 Civil war continued with new SPLA offensive.
1991 Federal system introduced, with division of country into nine states.

1993 March: SPLA leaders John Garang and Riek Machar announced unilateral cease-fire in ten years' war with government in Khartoum.

Sudetenland mountainous region of N Czechoslovakia (now the Czech Republic), annexed by Germany under the ◊Munich Agreement 1938; it was returned to Czechoslovakia 1945.

Suez Crisis military confrontation Oct–Dec 1956 following the nationalization of the Suez Canal by President Nasser of Egypt. In an attempt to reassert international control of the canal, Israel launched an attack, after which British and French troops landed. Widespread international censure forced the withdrawal of the British and French. The crisis resulted in the resignation of British prime minister Eden.

suffragette or *suffragist* woman fighting for the right to vote. In the UK, women's suffrage bills were repeatedly introduced and defeated in Parliament between 1886 and 1911, and a militant campaign was launched 1906 by Emmeline ◊Pankhurst and her daughters. In 1918 women were granted limited franchise; in 1928 it was extended to all women over 21. In the USA the 19th amendment to the constitution 1920 gave women the vote in federal and state elections.

suffragist US term for ◊suffragette.

Suharto Raden 1921–   . Indonesian politician and general. He ousted Sukarno to become president 1967. He ended confrontation with Malaysia, invaded East Timor 1975, and reached a cooperation agreement with Papua New Guinea 1979. His authoritarian rule has met with domestic opposition from the left. He was re-elected 1973, 1978, 1983, and 1988.

Sukarno Achmed 1901–1970. Indonesian nationalist, president 1945–67. During World War II he cooperated in the local administration set up by the Japanese, replacing Dutch rule. After the war he became the first president of the new Indonesian republic, becoming president-for-life in 1966; he was ousted by ◊Suharto.

summit conference in international diplomacy, a personal meeting between heads of state to settle international crises and other matters of general concern. The term was first coined by Winston Churchill in 1950 although it could be applied to the meetings between himself, Roosevelt, and Stalin at ◊Tehran and ◊Yalta during World War II.

Sunningdale Agreement pact Dec 1973 between the UK and Irish governments, together with the Northern Ireland executive, drawn up in Sunningdale, England. The agreement included provisions for a power-sharing executive in Northern Ireland. However, the executive lasted only five weeks before the UK government was defeated in a general election, and a general strike May 1974 brought down the Northern Ireland government. The experiment has not been repeated.

Sun Yat-sen or *Sun Zhong Shan* 1867–1925. Chinese revolutionary leader, founder of the ◊Guomindang (nationalist party) 1894, and provisional president of the Republic of China 1912 after playing a vital part in deposing the emperor. He was president of a breakaway government from 1921.

Sun Zhong Shan Pinyin transliteration of ◊Sun Yat-sen.

superpower term used to describe the USA and the USSR from the end of World War II 1945, when they emerged as significantly stronger than all other countries.

Surinam country on the N coast of South America, bounded W by French Guiana, S by Brazil, E by Guyana, and N by the Atlantic Ocean.

chronology
1954 Achieved internal self-government as Dutch Guiana.
1975 Independence achieved from the Netherlands, with Dr Johan Ferrier as president and Henck Arron as prime minister; 40% of the population emigrated to the Netherlands.
1980 Arron's government overthrown in army coup; Ferrier refused to recognize military regime; appointed Dr Henk Chin A Sen to lead civilian administration. Army replaced Ferrier with Dr Chin A Sen.
1982 Army, led by Lt Col Desi Bouterse, seized power, setting up a Revolutionary People's Front.
1985 Ban on political activities lifted.
1986 Antigovernment rebels brought economic chaos to Surinam.
1987 New constitution approved.
1988 Ramsewak Shankar elected president.
1989 Bouterse rejected peace accord reached by President Shankar with guerrilla insurgents, vowed to continue fighting.
1990 Shankar deposed in army coup.
1991 Johan Kraag became interim president. New Front for Democracy won assembly majority. Ronald Venetiaan elected president.
1992 Peace accord with guerrilla groups.

Suu Kyi Aung San 1945– . Myanmar (Burmese) politician and human rights campaigner, leader of the National League for Democracy (NLD), the main opposition to the military junta. When the NLD won the 1990 elections, the junta refused to surrender power, and placed Suu Kyi under house arrest. She was awarded the Nobel Peace Prize 1991 in recognition of her 'non-violent struggle for democracy and human rights' in Myanmar. She is the daughter of former Burmese premier ◊Aung San.

Suzman Helen 1917– . South African politician and human-rights activist. A university lecturer concerned about the inhumanity of the apartheid system, she joined the white opposition to the ruling National Party and became a strong advocate of racial equality, respected by black communities inside and outside South Africa. In 1978 she received the United Nations Human Rights Award. She retired from active politics in 1989.

Suzuki Zenkō 1911– . Japanese politician. Originally a socialist member of the Diet in 1947, he became a conservative (Liberal Democrat) in 1949, and was prime minister 1980–82.

Swadeshi movement in India, a boycott of foreign-made goods orchestrated by Indian nationalists in response to the partition of Bengal 1905. Huge bonfires of imported cloth, especially Lancashire cotton, were lit throughout Bengal. Protesters vowed to use only domestic (Swadeshi) cottons, and other goods manufactured in India. The boycott spread throughout the subcontinent, providing a stimulus to indigenous Indian industry and nationalist protest.

Soweto (acronym for *South West Township*) racially segregated urban settlement in South Africa, SW of Johannesburg; population (1983) 915,872. It has experienced civil unrest because of the ◊apartheid regime.

Sudetenland mountainous region of N Czechoslovakia (now the Czech Republic), annexed by Germany under the ◊Munich Agreement 1938; it was returned to Czechoslovakia 1945.

SWAPO (*South West Africa People's Organization*) organization formed 1959 in South West Africa (now ◊Namibia) to oppose South African rule. SWAPO guerrillas, led by Sam Nujoma, began attacking with support from Angola. In 1966 SWAPO was recognized by the United Nations as the legitimate government of Namibia, and won the first independent election 1989.

Swarajiya or *Self-Government Party* political party established in India in 1922 as an attempt to reinforce the position of the Congress Party in the Indian legislature. In 1923, it became the largest party in the central assembly and also in some provincial assemblies, but its tactics of obstruction against British colonial rule were only partially successful. Recognized by the Congress Party in 1924, Swarajiya continued until 1929 and was revived to help the Congress Party to contest the 1934 elections.

Swaziland country in SE Africa, bounded E by Mozambique and SE, S, W, and N by South Africa.

chronology
1903 Swaziland became a special High Commission territory.
1967 Achieved internal self-government.
1968 Independence achieved from Britain, within the Commonwealth, as the Kingdom of Swaziland, with King Sobhuza II as head of state.
1973 The king suspended the constitution and assumed absolute powers.
1978 New constitution adopted.
1982 King Sobhuza died; his place was taken by one of his wives, Dzeliwe, until his son, Prince Makhosetive, reached the age of 21.
1983 Queen Dzeliwe ousted by another wife, Ntombi.
1984 After royal power struggle, it was announced that the crown prince would become king at 18.
1986 Crown prince formally invested as King Mswati III.
1987 Power struggle developed between advisory council Liqoqo and Queen Ntombi over accession of king. Mswati dissolved parliament; new government elected with Sotsha Dlamini as prime minister.
1991 Calls for democratic reform.
1992 Mswati dissolved parliament, assuming 'executive powers'.

Sweden country in N Europe, bounded W by Norway, NE by Finland and the Gulf of Bothnia, SE by the Baltic Sea, and SW by the Kattegat.

chronology
1914–45 Neutral in both world wars.
1951–76 Social Democratic Labour Party (SAP) in power.
1969 Olof ◊Palme became SAP leader and prime minister.
1971 Constitution amended, creating a single-chamber Riksdag, the governing body.
1975 Monarch's last constitutional powers removed.

1976 Thorbjörn Fälldin, leader of the Centre Party, became prime minister, heading centre-right coalition.

1982 SAP, led by Palme, returned to power.

1985 SAP formed minority government, with Communist support.

1986 Olof Palme murdered. Ingvar Carlsson became prime minister and SAP party leader.

1988 SAP re-elected with reduced majority; Green Party gained representation in Riksdag.

1990 SAP government resigned. Sweden to apply for European Community (EC) membership.

1991 Formal application for EC membership submitted. Election defeat for SAP; Carlsson resigned. Coalition government formed; Carl Bildt became new prime minister.

1992 Cross-party agreement to solve economic problems.

Switzerland landlocked country in W Europe, bounded N by Germany, E by Austria and Liechtenstein, S by Italy, and W by France.

chronology

1914–45 Neutral in both world wars.

1971 Women given the vote in federal elections.

1984 First female cabinet minister appointed.

1986 Referendum rejected proposal for membership of United Nations.

1989 Referendum supported abolition of citizen army and military service requirements.

1991 18-year-olds allowed to vote for first time in national elections. Four-party coalition remained in power.

1992 René Felber elected president with Adolf Ogi as vice president. Closer ties with European Community (EC) rejected in national referendum.

1993 Ogi replaced Felber as head of state.

Syria country in W Asia, on the Mediterranean Sea, bounded N by Turkey, E by Iraq, S by Jordan, and SW by Israel and Lebanon.

chronology

1946 Achieved full independence from France.

1958 Merged with Egypt to form the United Arab Republic (UAR).

1961 UAR disintegrated.

1967 Six-Day War resulted in the loss of territory to Israel.

1970–71 Syria supported Palestinian guerrillas against Jordanian troops.

1971 Following a bloodless coup, Hafez al-Assad became president.

1973 Israel consolidated its control of the Golan Heights after the Yom Kippur War.

1976 Substantial numbers of troops committed to the civil war in Lebanon.

1978 Assad re-elected.

1981-82 Further military engagements in Lebanon.

1982 Islamic militant uprising suppressed; 5,000 dead.

1984 Presidents Assad and Gemayel approved plans for government of national unity in Lebanon.

1985 Assad secured the release of 39 US hostages held in an aircraft hijacked by extremist Shi'ite group, Hezbollah. Assad re-elected.

1987 Improved relations with USA and attempts to secure the release of Western hostages in Lebanon.

1989 Diplomatic relations with Morocco restored. Continued fighting in Lebanon; Syrian forces reinforced in Lebanon; diplomatic relations with Egypt restored.

1990 Diplomatic relations with Britain restored.

1991 Syria fought against Iraq in Gulf War. President Assad agreed to US Middle East peace plan. Assad re-elected as president.

T

Tafawa Balewa Alhaji Abubakar 1912–1966. Nigerian politician, prime minister from 1957 to 1966, when he was assassinated in a coup d'état.

Taff Vale judgement 1901 decision by the British law lords that trade unions were liable for their members' actions, and could hence be sued for damages in the event of a strike, picketing, or boycotting an employer. It resulted in a rapid growth of union membership, and was replaced by the Trades Disputes Act 1906.

Taft Robert Alphonso 1889–1953. US right-wing Republican senator from 1939, and a candidate for the presidential nomination 1940, 1944, 1948, and 1952. He sponsored the Taft–Hartley Labor Act 1947, restricting union power. He was the son of President William Taft.

Taft William Howard 1857–1930. 27th president of the USA 1909–13, a Republican. He was secretary of war 1904–08 in Theodore Roosevelt's administration, but as president his conservatism provoked Roosevelt to stand against him in the 1912 election. Taft served as chief justice of the Supreme Court 1921–30.

Taiwan country in E Asia, officially the Republic of China, occupying the island of Taiwan between the E China Sea and the S China Sea, separated from the coast of China by the Formosa Strait.

chronology
1895 Ceded to Japan.
1945 Recovered by China.
1949 Flight of Nationalist government to Taiwan after Chinese communist revolution.
1954 US-Taiwanese mutual defence treaty.
1971 Expulsion from United Nations.
1972 Commencement of legislature elections.
1975 President Chiang Kai-shek died; replaced as Kuomintang leader by his son, Chiang Ching-kuo.

1979 USA severed diplomatic relations and annulled 1954 security treaty.

1986 Democratic Progressive Party (DPP) formed as opposition to the nationalist Kuomintang.

1987 Martial law lifted; opposition parties legalized; press restrictions lifted.

1988 President ◊Chiang Ching-kuo died; replaced by Taiwanese-born ◊Lee Teng-hui.

1989 Kuomintang won assembly elections.

1990 Formal move towards normalization of relations with China. Hau Pei-tsun became prime minister.

1991 President Lee Teng-hui declared end to state of civil war with China. Constitution amended. Kuomintang won landslide victory in assembly elections.

1992 Diplomatic relations with South Korea broken. Dec: in first fully democratic elections Kuomintang lost support to DPP but still secured a majority of seats.

1993 Lien Chan appointed prime minister.

Tajikistan (formerly until 1991 *Tadzhikistan*) country in central Asia, bounded N by Kyrgyzstan and Uzbekistan, E by China, and S by Afghanistan and Pakistan.

chronology

1921 Part of Turkestan Soviet Socialist Autonomous Republic.

1929 Became a constituent republic of USSR.

1990 Ethnic Tajik/Armenian conflict in Dushanbe resulted in rioting against Communist Party of Tajikistan (TCP); state of emergency and curfew imposed.

1991 Jan: curfew lifted in Dushanbe. March: maintenance of Union endorsed in referendum. Aug: President Makhkamov forced to resign after failed anti-Gorbachev coup; TCP broke links with Moscow. Sept: declared independence; Nabiyev elected president; TCP renamed Socialist Party of Tajikistan (SPT); state of emergency declared. Dec: joined new Commonwealth of Independent States (CIS).

1992 Jan: admitted into Conference for Security and Cooperation in Europe (CSCE). Nabiyev temporarily ousted; state of emergency lifted. Feb: joined the Muslim Economic Cooperation Organization (ECO). March: admitted into United Nations (UN); US diplomatic recognition achieved. May: coalition government formed. Sept: Nabiyev forced to resign; replaced by Akbasho Iskandrov; Abdumalik Abdulojonov became prime minister.

1993 Civil war between the forces of the country's communist former rulers and Islamic and pro-democracy groups continued to rage.

Takeshita Noboru 1924– . Japanese right-wing politician. Elected to parliament as a Libera Democratic Party (LDP) deputy 1958, he became president of the LDP and prime minister Oct 1987. He and members of his administration were shown in the Recruit scandal to have been involved in insider-trading and he resigned April 1989.

Tambo Oliver 1917–93. South African nationalist politician, in exile 1960–90, president of the African National Congress (ANC) 1977–91. Because of poor health, he was given the honorary post of national chair July 1991, and Nelson ♦Mandela resumed the ANC presidency.

Tanaka Kakuei 1918– . Japanese right-wing politician, leader of the dominant Liberal Democratic Party (LDP) and prime minister 1972–74. In 1976 he was charged with corruption and resigned from the LDP but remained a powerful faction leader.

Tanganyika African National Union (TANU) moderate socialist national party organized by Tanzanian politician Julius ♦Nyerere in the 1950s. TANU won electoral successes 1958 and 1960, ensuring that Nyerere was recognized as prime minister on 1 May 1961, when Tanganyika prepared for independence from Britain.

Tanzania country in E Africa, bounded N by Uganda and Kenya; S by Mozambique, Malawi, and Zambia; W by Zaire, Burundi, and Rwanda; and E by the Indian Ocean.

chronology
1890-1963 Zanzibar was a British protectorate.
1920-46 Tanganyika administered as a British League of Nations mandate.
1946-62 Tanganyika came under United Nations (UN) trusteeship.
1961 Tanganyika achieved independence from Britain, within the Commonwealth, with Julius Nyerere as prime minister.
1962 Tanganyika became a republic with Nyerere as president.
1964 Tanganyika and Zanzibar became the United Republic of Tanzania with Nyerere as president.
1967 East African Community (EAC) formed. Arusha Declaration.
1977 Revolutionary Party of Tanzania (CCM) proclaimed the only legal party. EAC dissolved.

1978 Ugandan forces repulsed after crossing into Tanzania.

1979 Tanzanian troops sent to Uganda to help overthrow the president, Idi Amin.

1985 Nyerere retired from presidency but stayed on as CCM leader; Ali Hassan Mwinyi became president.

1990 Nyerere surrendered CCM leadership; replaced by President Mwinyi.

1992 CCM agreed to abolish one-party rule. East African cooperation pact with Kenya and Uganda to be re-established.

Tariff Reform League organization set up 1903 as a vehicle for the ideas of the Liberal politician Joseph ◊Chamberlain on protective tariffs. It aimed to unify the British Empire by promoting imperial preference in trade.

Taylor Frederick Winslow 1856–1915. US engineer and management consultant, the founder of scientific management. His ideas, published in *Principles of Scientific Management* 1911, were based on the breakdown of work to the simplest tasks, the separation of planning from execution of tasks, and the introduction of time-and-motion studies. His methods were clearly expressed in assembly-line factories, but have been criticized for degrading and alienating workers and producing managerial dictatorship.

Teapot Dome Scandal US political scandal that revealed the corruption of President ◊Harding's administration. It centred on the leasing of naval oil reserves 1921 at Teapot Dome, Wyoming, without competitive bidding, as a result of bribing the secretary of the interior, Albert B Fall (1861–1944). Fall was tried and imprisoned 1929.

Tebbit Norman 1931–   . British Conservative politician. He was minister for employment 1981–83, minister for trade and industry 1983–85, chancellor of the Duchy of Lancaster 1985–87, and chair of the party 1985–87. As his relations with Margaret Thatcher cooled, he returned to the back benches 1987.

Tehran Conference conference held 1943 in Tehran, Iran, the first meeting of World War II Allied leaders Churchill, Roosevelt, and Stalin. The chief subject discussed was coordination of Allied strategy in W and E Europe.

Tennessee Valley Authority (TVA) US government corporation founded 1933 to develop the Tennessee river basin (an area of some 104,000 sq km/40,000 sq mi) by building hydroelectric power stations, producing and distributing fertilizers, and similar activities. The TVA was associated with President F D Roosevelt's ◊New Deal, promoting economic growth by government investment.

Test Ban Treaty agreement signed by the USA, the USSR, and the UK 5 Aug 1963 contracting to test nuclear weapons only underground. In the following two years 90 other nations signed the treaty, the only major nonsignatories being France and China, which continued underwater and ground-level tests.

Tet Offensive in the Vietnam War, a prolonged attack mounted by the ◊Vietcong against Saigon (now Ho Chi Minh City) and other South Vietnamese cities and hamlets, beginning 30 Jan 1968. Although the Vietcong were finally forced to withdraw, the Tet Offensive brought into question the ability of the South Vietnamese army and their US allies to win the war and added fuel to the antiwar movement in both the USA and Australia.

Thailand (formerly *Siam* to 1939 and 1945–49) country in SE Asia on the Gulf of Siam, bounded E by Laos and Cambodia, S by Malaysia, and W by Myanmar (Burma).

chronology

1896 Anglo-French agreement recognized Siam as independent buffer state.

1932 Constitutional monarchy established.

1939 Name of Thailand adopted.

1941-44 Japanese occupation.

1947 Military seized power in coup.

1972 Withdrawal of Thai troops from South Vietnam.

1973 Military government overthrown.

1976 Military reassumed control.

1980 General Prem Tinsulanonda assumed power.

1983 Civilian government formed; martial law maintained.

1988 Prime Minister Prem resigned; replaced by Chatichai Choonhavan.

1989 Thai pirates continued to murder, pillage, and kidnap Vietnamese 'boat people' at sea.

1991 Military seized power in coup. Interim civilian government formed under Anand Panyarachun. 50,000 demonstrated against new military-oriented constitution.

1992 March: general election produced five-party coalition; Narong Wongwan named premier but removed a month later. April: appointment of General Suchinda Kraprayoon as premier provoked widespread riots. May:

Suchinda forced to stand down. June: Anand made interim prime minister.
Sept: new coalition government led by Chuan Leekpai.

Thant, U 1909–1974. Burmese diplomat, secretary general of the United
Nations 1962–71. He helped to resolve the US-Soviet crisis over the Soviet
installation of missiles in Cuba, and he made the controversial decision to
withdraw the UN peacekeeping force from the Egypt–Israel border 1967
(see ◊Arab-Israeli Wars).

Thatcher Margaret Hilda (born Roberts), Baroness Thatcher of Kesteven
1925–   . British Conservative politician, prime minister 1979–90. She was
education minister 1970–74 and Conservative Party leader from 1975. In
1982 she sent British troops to recapture the Falkland Islands from
Argentina. She confronted trade-union power during the miners' strike
1984-85, sold off majority stakes in many public utilities to the private
sector, and reduced the influence of local government through such measures as the abolition of metropolitan councils, the control of expenditure
through 'rate-capping', and the introduction of the community charge, or
poll tax, from 1989. In 1990 splits in the cabinet over the issues of Europe
and consensus government forced her resignation. An astute Parliamentary
tactician, she tolerated little disagreement, either from the opposition or
from within her own party.

Thatcherism political outlook comprising a belief in the efficacy of
market forces, the need for strong central government, and a conviction that
self-help is preferable to reliance on the state, combined with a strong
element of nationalism. The ideology is associated with Margaret Thatcher
but stems from an individualist view found in Britain's 19th-century Liberal and 20th-century Conservative parties, and is no longer confined to
Britain.

Theodorakis Mikis 1925–   . Greek composer. He was imprisoned
1967–70 for attempting to overthrow the military regime of Greece.

Third Reich (Third Empire) term used by the Nazis to describe Germany
during the years of Hitler's dictatorship after 1933. The idea of the Third
Reich was based on the existence of two previous German empires, the
medieval Holy Roman Empire and the second empire 1871–1918.

Third World or *developing world* those countries that are less developed
than the industrialized free-market countries of the West (First World) and
the industrialized former Communist countries (Second World). Third

World countries are the poorest, as measured by their income per head of population, and are concentrated in Asia, Africa, and Latin America.

38th parallel demarcation line between North (People's Democratic Republic of) and South (Republic of) Korea, agreed at the ◊Yalta Conference 1945 and largely unaltered by the Korean War 1950–53.

Thomas Clarence 1948– . US Justice of the Supreme Court whose nomination to the Supreme Court 1991 by President Bush caused controversy. He is opposed to the policy of ◊affirmative action, which positively discriminates in favour of minority groups and from which he himself has benefited; and he is thought unlikely to uphold legislation that makes abortion freely available. At the public televised Senate confirmation hearings, Anita Hill, a former colleague, accused Thomas of sexually harassing her ten years earlier. He denied the allegations.

Thomas Norman Mattoon 1884–1968. US political leader, six times Socialist candidate for president 1928-48. One of the founders of the American Civil Liberties Union 1920, he also served as a director of the League for Industrial Democracy 1922–37. He was a brilliant speaker and published *A Socialist's Faith* 1951.

Thorpe Jeremy 1929– . British Liberal politician, leader of the Liberal Party 1967–76.

thousand days period of office of US president John F Kennedy from 20 Jan 1961 to his assassination on 22 Nov 1963.

three-day week in the UK, the policy adopted by Prime Minister Edward Heath Jan 1974 to combat an economic crisis and coal miners' strike. A shortage of electrical power led to the allocation of energy to industry for only three days each week. A general election was called Feb 1974, which the government lost.

Tiananmen Square paved open space in central Beijing (Peking), China, the largest public square in the world (area 0.4 sq km/0.14 sq mi). On 3–4 June 1989 more than 1,000 unarmed protesters were killed by government troops in a massacre that crushed China's emerging prodemocracy movement.

Tibet autonomous region of SW China. The independent kingdom of Tibet came under nominal Chinese rule about 1700. Independence was regained after a revolt 1912, but China regained control 1951 when the historic ruler and religious leader, the ◊Dalai Lama, was driven from the country and the monks (who formed 25% of the population) were forced out of the monasteries. Between 1951 and 1959 the Chinese People's Liberation Army (PLA) controlled Tibet, although the Dalai Lama returned as nominal spiritual and temporal head of state. A Tibetan uprising in 1959 was suppressed by the PLA, prompting the Dalai Lama and 9,000 Tibetans to flee to India. The Chinese proceeded to dissolve the Tibet local government, abolish serfdom, collectivize agriculture, and suppress Lamaism. In 1965 Tibet became an autonomous region of China. Chinese rule continued to be resented, however, and the economy languished. In 1989 many anti-China demonstrators were shot and all foreigners were expelled.

Tigré or *Tigray* region in the northern highlands of Ethiopia; area 65,900 sq km/25,444 sq mi. The region had an estimated population of 2.4 million in 1984, at a time when drought and famine were driving large numbers of people to fertile land in the S or into neighbouring Sudan. Since 1978 a guerrilla group known as the Tigré People's Liberation Front (TPLF) has been fighting for regional autonomy. In 1989 government troops were forced from the province, and the TPLF advanced towards Addis Ababa, playing a key role in the fall of the Ethiopian government May 1991.

Tikhonov Nikolai 1905–   . Soviet politician. He was a close associate of President Brezhnev, joining the Politburo 1979, and was prime minister (chair of the Council of Ministers) 1980–85. In April 1989 he was removed from the central committee.

Tirpitz Alfred von 1849–1930. German admiral. As secretary for the navy 1897–1916, he created the German navy and planned the World War I U-boat campaign.

Titanic British passenger liner, supposedly unsinkable, that struck an iceberg and sank off the Grand Banks of Newfoundland on its first voyage 14–15 April 1912; 1,513 lives were lost. In 1985 it was located by robot submarine 4 km/2.5 mi down in an ocean canyon, preserved by the cold environment. In 1987 salvage operations began.

Tito adopted name of Josip Broz 1892–1980. Yugoslav communist politician, in power from 1945. In World War II he organized the National Liberation Army to carry on guerrilla warfare against the German invasion 1941, and was created marshal 1943. As prime minister 1946–53 and president from 1953, he followed a foreign policy of 'positive neutralism'.

Tlatelolco, Treaty of international agreement signed 1967 in Tlatelolco, Mexico, prohibiting nuclear weapons in Latin America.

Tobruk Libyan port; population (1984) 94,000. Occupied by Italy 1911, it was taken by Britain 1941 during World War II, and unsuccessfully besieged by Axis forces April–Dec 1941. It was captured by Germany June 1942 after the retreat of the main British force to Egypt, and this precipitated the replacement of ◊Auchinleck by ◊Montgomery as British commander.

Todd Ron(ald) 1927– . British trade-union leader. He rose from shop steward to general secretary of Britain's largest trade union, the Transport and General Workers' (TGWU), a post he held 1985–92. Although a Labour Party supporter, he criticized its attitude toward nuclear disarmament.

Togliatti Palmiro 1893–1964. Italian politician who was a founding member of the Italian Communist Party 1921 and effectively its leader for almost 40 years from 1926 until his death. In exile 1926–44, he returned after the fall of the Fascist dictator Mussolini to become a member of Badoglio's government and held office until 1946.

Togo country in W Africa, on the Atlantic Ocean, bounded N by Burkina Faso, E by Benin, and W by Ghana.

chronology
1885–1914 Togoland was a German protectorate until captured by Anglo-French forces.
1922 Divided between Britain and France under League of Nations mandate.
1946 Continued under United Nations trusteeship.
1956 British Togoland integrated with Ghana.
1960 French Togoland achieved independence from France as the Republic of Togo with Sylvanus Olympio as head of state.
1963 Olympio killed in a military coup. Nicolas Grunitzky became president.
1967 Grunitzky replaced by Lt-Gen Etienne Gnassingbé Eyadéma in bloodless coup.
1973 Assembly of Togolese People (RPT) formed as sole legal political party.
1975 EEC Lomé convention signed in Lomé, establishing trade links with developing countries.

1979 Eyadéma returned in election. Further EEC Lomé convention signed.
1986 Attempted coup failed.
1991 Eyadéma legalized opposition parties. National conference elected Joseph Kokou Koffigoh head of interim government; troops loyal to Eyadéma failed to reinstate him.
1992 Overwhelming referendum support for multiparty politics.
1993 Feb: all-party talks to avoid civil war began in France but were suspended after disagreements among participants.

Tōgō Heihachirō 1846–1934. Japanese admiral who commanded the fleet at the battle of ◊Tsushima 1905, when Japan defeated the Russians and effectively ended the Russo-Japanese War of 1904–05.

Tōjō Hideki 1884–1948. Japanese general and premier 1941–44 during World War II. Promoted to Chief of Staff of Japan's Guangdong army in Manchuria 1937, he served as minister for war 1940–41. He was held responsible for defeats in the Pacific 1944 and forced to resign. After Japan's defeat, he was hanged as a war criminal.

Tokyo trials war-crimes trials 1946–48 of Japan's wartime leaders, held during the Allied occupation after World War II. Former prime minister Tōjō was among the seven sentenced to death by an international tribunal, while 16 were given life imprisonment. Political considerations allowed Emperor ◊Showa (Hirohito) to escape trial.

Tonga country in the SW Pacific Ocean, in ◊Polynesia.

chronology
1900 Became a British protectorate.
1965 Queen Salote died; succeeded by her son, King Taufa'ahau Tupou IV.
1970 Independence achieved from Britain within the Commonwealth.
1990 Three prodemocracy candidates elected. Calls for reform of absolutist power.

Tonkin Gulf Incident clash that triggered US entry into the Vietnam War in Aug 1964. Two US destroyers (USS *C Turner Joy* and USS *Maddox*) reported that they were fired on by North Vietnamese torpedo boats. It is unclear whether hostile shots were actually fired, but the reported attack was taken as a pretext for making air raids against North Vietnam. On 7 Aug the US Congress passed the *Tonkin Gulf Resolution*, which formed the basis for the considerable increase in US military involvement in the Vietnam War.

Tonton Macoute member of a private army of death squads on Haiti. The Tontons Macoutes were initially organized by François ◊Duvalier, president of Haiti 1957–71, and continued to terrorize the population under his successor J C Duvalier. It is alleged that the organization continued to operate after Duvalier's exile to France.

totalitarianism government control of all activities within a country, overtly political or otherwise, as in fascist or communist dictatorships. Examples of totalitarian regimes are Italy under Benito ◊Mussolini 1922–45; Germany under Adolph ◊Hitler 1933–45; the USSR under Joseph ◊Stalin from the 1930s until his death in 1953; more recently Romania under Nicolae ◊Ceauşescu 1974–89.

Totenkopfverbände the 'death's head' units of the Nazi ◊SS organization. Originally used to guard concentration camps after 1935, they became an elite fighting division attached to the Waffen-SS during World War II.

Tower John 1925–1991. US Republican politician, a senator from Texas 1961–83. Despite having been a paid arms-industry consultant, he was selected 1989 by President Bush to serve as defence secretary, but the Senate refused to approve the appointment because of Tower's previous heavy drinking.

trade union organization of employed workers formed to undertake collective bargaining with employers and to try to achieve improved working conditions for its members. Attitudes of government to unions and of unions to management vary greatly from country to country. Probably the most effective trade-union system is that of Sweden, and the most internationally known is the Polish ◊Solidarity.

Treurnicht Andries Petrus 1921–93. South African Conservative Party politician. A former minister of the Dutch Reformed Church, he was elected to the South African parliament as a National Party member 1971 but left it 1982 to form a new right-wing Conservative Party, opposed to any dilution of the ◊apartheid system.

Trinidad and Tobago country in the West Indies, off the coast of Venezuela.

chronology
1888 Trinidad and Tobago united as a British colony.
1956 People's National Movement (PNM) founded.

1959 Achieved internal self-government, with PNM leader Eric Williams as chief minister.

1962 Independence achieved from Britain, within the Commonwealth, with Williams as prime minister.

1976 Became a republic, with Ellis Clarke as president and Williams as prime minister.

1981 Williams died and was succeeded by George Chambers, with Arthur Robinson as opposition leader.

1986 National Alliance for Reconstruction (NAR), headed by Arthur Robinson, won general election.

1987 Noor Hassanali became president.

1990 Attempted antigovernment coup defeated.

1991 General election saw victory for PNM, with Patrick Manning as prime minister.

Triple Entente alliance of Britain, France, and Russia 1907–17. In 1911 this became a military alliance and formed the basis of the Allied powers in World War I against the Central Powers, Germany and Austria-Hungary.

Trotsky Leon. Adopted name of Lev Davidovitch Bronstein 1879–1940. Russian revolutionary. He joined the Bolshevik party and took a leading part in the seizure of power 1917 and raising the Red Army that fought the Civil War 1918–20. In the struggle for power that followed ◊Lenin's death 1924, ◊Stalin defeated Trotsky, and this and other differences with the Communist Party led to his exile 1929. He settled in Mexico, where he was assassinated with an ice pick at Stalin's instigation. Trotsky believed in world revolution and in permanent revolution, and was an uncompromising, if liberal, idealist.

Trotskyism form of Marxism advocated by Leon Trotsky. Its central concept is that of *permanent revolution*. In his view a proletarian revolution, leading to a socialist society, could not be achieved in isolation, so it would be necessary to spark off further revolutions throughout Europe and ultimately worldwide. This was in direct opposition to the Stalinist view that socialism should be built and consolidated within individual countries.

Trudeau Pierre (Elliott) 1919– . Canadian Liberal politician. He was prime minister 1968–79 and 1980–84. In 1980, having won again by a landslide on a platform opposing Québec separatism, he helped to defeat the Québec independence movement in a referendum. He repatriated the constitution from Britain 1982, but by 1984 had so lost support that he resigned.

Trujillo Molina Rafael (Leónidas) 1891–1961. Dictator of the Dominican Republic from 1930. As commander of the Dominican Guard, he seized power and established a ruthless dictatorship. He was assassinated.

Truman Harry S 1884–1972. 33rd president of the USA 1945–53, a Democrat. In Jan 1945 he became vice president to F D Roosevelt, and president when Roosevelt died in April that year. He used the atom bomb against Japan, launched the ◊Marshall Plan to restore W Europe's economy, and nurtured the European Community and NATO (including the rearmament of West Germany).

Truman Doctrine US president Harry Truman's 1947 dictum that the USA would 'support free peoples who are resisting attempted subjugation by armed minorities or by outside pressures'. It was used to justify sending a counterinsurgency military mission to Greece after World War II and sending US troops abroad (for example, to Korea).

Trust Territory country or area formerly held under the United Nations trusteeship system to be prepared for independence, either former ◊mandates, territories taken over by the Allies in World War II, or those voluntarily placed under the UN by the administering state.

Tubman William V S 1895–1971. Liberian politician. The descendant of US slaves, he was a lawyer in the USA. After his election to the presidency of Liberia 1944 he concentrated on uniting the various ethnic groups. Re-elected several times, he died in office of natural causes, despite frequent assassination attempts.

Tudjman Franjo 1922– . Croatian nationalist leader and historian, president from 1990. As leader of the centre-right Croatian Democratic Union (HDZ), he led the fight for Croatian independence. During the 1991–92 civil war his troops were hampered by lack of arms and the military superiority of the Serb-dominated federal army, but Croatia's independence was recognized following a successful UN-negotiated cease-fire Jan 1992. Tudjman was re-elected Aug 1992.

Tunisia country in N Africa, on the Mediterranean Sea, bounded SE by Libya and W by Algeria.

chronology
1883 Became a French protectorate.
1955 Granted internal self-government.

1956 Independence achieved from France as a monarchy, with Habib ◊Bourguiba as prime minister.

1957 Became a republic with Bourguiba as president.

1975 Bourguiba made president for life.

1985 Diplomatic relations with Libya severed.

1987 Bourguiba removed Prime Minister Rashed Sfar and appointed Zine el-Abidine ◊Ben Ali. Ben Ali declared Bourguiba incompetent and seized power.

1988 Constitutional changes towards democracy announced. Diplomatic relations with Libya restored.

1989 Government party, Constitutional Democratic Rally (RDC), won all assembly seats in general election.

1991 Opposition to US actions during the Gulf War. Crackdown on religious fundamentalists.

Tupamaros urban guerrilla movement operating in Uruguay, aimed at creating a Marxist revolution, largely active in the 1960s-70s, named after 18th-century revolutionary Túpac Amarú. It was founded by Raul Sendic (died 1989); he served more than 13 years in prison.

Turkey country between the Black Sea to the N and the Mediterranean Sea to the S, bounded E by Armenia, Georgia, and Iran, SE by Iraq and Syria, W by Greece and the Aegean Sea, and NW by Bulgaria.

chronology

1919–22 Turkish War of Independence provoked by Greek occupation of Izmir. Mustafa Kemal (◊Atatürk), leader of nationalist congress, defeated Italian, French, and Greek forces.

1923 Treaty of Lausanne established Turkey as independent republic under Kemal. Westernization began.

1950 First free elections; Adnan Menderes became prime minister.

1960 Menderes executed after military coup by General Cemal Gürsel.

1965 Suleyman ◊Demirel became prime minister.

1971 Army forced Demirel to resign.

1973 Civilian rule returned under Bulent Ecevit.

1974 Turkish troops sent to protect Turkish community in Cyprus.

1975 Demirel returned to head of a right-wing coalition.

1978 Ecevit returned, as head of coalition, in the face of economic difficulties and factional violence.

1979 Demeril returned. Violence grew.

1980 Army took over, and Bulent Ulusu became prime minister. Harsh repression of political activists attracted international criticism.

1982 New constitution adopted.

1983 Ban on political activity lifted. Turgut ♭Özal became prime minister.

1987 Özal maintained majority in general election.

1988 Improved relations and talks with Greece.

1989 Turgut Özal elected president; Yildirim Akbulut became prime minister. Application to join EC rejected.

1991 Mesut Yilmaz became prime minister. Turkey sided with UN coalition against Iraq in Gulf War. Conflict with Kurdish minority continued. Coalition government formed under Suleyman Demirel after inconclusive election result.

1992 Earthquake claimed thousands of lives.

1993 April: Turgut Özal died of heart attack.

Turkmenistan country in central Asia, bounded N by Kazakhstan and Uzbekistan, W by the Caspian Sea, and S by Iran and Afghanistan.

chronology

1921 Part of Turkestan Soviet Socialist Autonomous Republic.

1925 Became a constituent republic of USSR.

1990 Aug: economic and political sovereignty declared.

1991 Jan: Communist Party leader Niyazov became state president. March: endorsed maintenance of the Union in USSR referendum. Aug: President Niyazov initially supported attempted anti-Gorbachev. Oct: independence declared. Dec: joined new Commonwealth of Independent States (CIS).

1992 Jan: admitted into Conference for Security and Cooperation in Europe (CSCE). Feb: joined the Muslim Economic Cooperation Organization (ECO). March: admitted into United Nations (UN); US diplomatic recognition achieved. May: new constitution adopted. Nov–Dec: 60-member parliament popularly elected with Sakhat Muradov as prime minister.

Turner John Napier 1929–   . Canadian Liberal politician, prime minister 1984. He was elected to the House of Commons 1962 and served in the cabinet of Pierre Trudeau until resigning 1975. He succeeded Trudeau as party leader and prime minister 1984, but lost the 1984 and 1988 elections. Turner resigned as leader 1989, and returned to his law practice. He was replaced as Liberal Party chief by Herbert Gray in Feb 1990.

Tutu Desmond (Mpilo) 1931–   . South African priest, Anglican archbishop of Cape Town and general secretary of the South African Council of

Churches 1979–84. One of the leading figures in the struggle against apartheid in the Republic of South Africa, he was awarded the 1984 Nobel Prize for Peace.

Tuvalu country in the SW Pacific Ocean; formerly (until 1976) the Ellice Islands; part of ◊Polynesia.

chronology

1892 Became a British protectorate forming part of the Gilbert and Ellice Islands group.

1916 The islands acquired colonial status.

1975 The Ellice Islands were separated from the Gilbert Islands.

1978 Independence achieved from Britain within the Commonwealth with Toaripi Lauti as prime minister.

1981 Dr Tomasi Puapua replaced Lauti as premier.

1986 Islanders rejected proposal for republican status.

1989 Bikenibeu Paeniu elected new prime minister.

21 demands Japanese attempt 18 Jan 1915 to make China a virtual protectorate if 21 'outstanding questions' were not resolved. China's president ◊Yuan Shikai submitted to the extension of Japanese power in Manchuria, Shandong, the Chang Jiang valley, and the SE, but refused to appoint Japanese political and financial advisers to his government.

U

U-2 US military reconnaissance aeroplane, used in secret flights over the USSR from 1956 to photograph military installations. In 1960 a U-2 was shot down over the USSR and the pilot, Gary Powers, was captured and imprisoned. He was exchanged for a US-held Soviet agent two years later.

U-boat German submarine. The title was used in both world wars.

UDI acronym for ◊*unilateral declaration of independence*.

Uganda landlocked country in E Africa, bounded N by Sudan, E by Kenya, S by Tanzania and Rwanda, and W by Zaire.

chronology
1962 Independence achieved from Britain within the Commonwealth with Milton ◊Obote as prime minister.
1963 Proclaimed a federal republic with King Mutesa II as president.
1966 King Mutesa ousted in coup led by Obote, who ended the federal status and became executive president.
1969 All opposition parties banned after assassination attempt on Obote.
1971 Obote overthrown in army coup led by Maj-Gen Idi ◊Amin Dada; ruthlessly dictatorial regime established; nearly 49,000 Ugandan Asians expelled; over 300,000 opponents of regime killed.
1978 Amin forced to leave country by opponents backed by Tanzanian troops. Provisional government set up with Yusuf Lule as president. Lule replaced by Godfrey Binaisa.
1978-79 Fighting broke out against Tanzanian troops.
1980 Binaisa overthrown by army. Elections held and Milton Obote returned to power.
1985 After opposition by National Resistance Army (NRA), and indiscipline in army, Obote ousted by Brig Tito Okello; power-sharing agreement entered into with NRA leader Yoweri Museveni.
1986 Agreement ended; Museveni became president, heading broad-based coalition government.

1992 Announcement made that East African cooperation pact with Kenya and Tanzania would be revived.

UK abbreviation for the ◊*United Kingdom*.

Ukraine country in E central Europe, bounded E by Russia, N by Belarus, S by Moldova, Romania, and the Black Sea, and W by Poland, the Slovak Republic, and Hungary.

chronology

1918 Independent People's Republic proclaimed.

1920 Conquered by Soviet Red Army.

1921 Poland allotted charge of W Ukraine.

1932-33 Famine caused the deaths of more than 7.5 million people.

1939 W Ukraine occupied by Red Army.

1941–44 Under Nazi control; Jews massacred at Babi Yar; more than five million Ukrainians and Ukrainian Jews deported and exterminated.

1944 Soviet control re-established.

1945 Became a founder member of the United Nations.

1946 Ukrainian Uniate Church proscribed and forcibly merged with Russian Orthodox Church.

1986 April: Chernobyl nuclear disaster.

1989 Feb: Ukrainian People's Movement (Rukh) established. Ban on Ukrainian Uniate Church lifted.

1990 July: voted to proclaim sovereignty; Leonid ◊Kravchuk indirectly elected as president; sovereignty declared.

1991 Aug: demonstrations against the abortive anti-Gorbachev coup; independence declared, pending referendum; Communist Party (CP) activities suspended. Oct: voted to create independent army. Dec: Kravchuk popularly elected president; independence overwhelmingly endorsed in referendum; joined new Commonwealth of Independent States (CIS); independence acknowledged by USA and European Community (EC).

1992 Jan: admitted into Conference on Security and Cooperation in Europe (CSCE); pipeline deal with Iran to end dependence on Russian oil; prices freed. Feb: prices 'temporarily' re-regulated. March: agreed tactical arms-shipments to Russia suspended. May: Crimean sovereignty declared, but subsequently rescinded. Aug: joint control of Black Sea fleet agreed with Russia. Oct: Kuchma became prime minister. Production declined by 20% during 1992.

1993 Inflation at 35% a month in early part of year, budget deficit at 44% of GDP.

Ulbricht Walter 1893–1973. East German communist politician, in power 1960–71. He lived in exile in the USSR during Hitler's rule 1933–45. A Stalinist, he became first secretary of the Socialist Unity Party in East Germany 1950 and (as chair of the Council of State from 1960) was instrumental in the building of the Berlin Wall 1961. He established East Germany's economy and recognition outside the Eastern European bloc.

Umberto II 1904–1983. Last king of Italy 1946. On the abdication of his father, Victor Emmanuel III, he ruled 9 May–13 June 1946, when he had to abdicate since a referendum established a republic. He retired to Portugal.

UN abbreviation for the ◊*United Nations*.

Unilateral Declaration of Independence (UDI) unnegotiated severing of relations with a colonial power; especially, the declaration made by Ian Smith's Rhodesian Front government 11 Nov 1965, announcing the independence of Rhodesia (now Zimbabwe) from Britain.

Union Movement British political group. Founded as the *New Party* by Oswald ◊Mosley and a number of Labour members of Parliament 1931, it developed into the *British Union of Fascists* 1932. In 1940 the organization was declared illegal and its leaders interned, but it was revived as the Union Movement 1948, characterized by racist doctrines including anti-Semitism.

Union of Soviet Socialist Republics (USSR) former country in N Asia and E Europe that reverted to independent states following the resignation of Mikhail Gorbachev 1991; see ◊Armenia, ◊Azerbaijan, ◊Belarus, ◊Estonia, ◊Georgia, ◊Kazakhstan, ◊Kyrgyzstan, ◊Latvia, ◊Lithuania, ◊Moldova, ◊Russian Federation, ◊Tajikistan, ◊Turkmenistan, ◊Ukraine, and ◊Uzbekistan.

UNITA (acronym for *Uniao Nacional para a Independencia Total de Angola*/National Union for the Total Independence of Angola) Angolan nationalist movement backed by South Africa, which continued to wage guerrilla warfare against the ruling MPLA regime after the latter gained control of the country in 1976. The UNITA leader Jonas ◊Savimbi founded the movement 1966. A peace agreement ending the civil war between MPLA–PT and UNITA was signed May 1991, but fighting broke out again Sept 1992 after Savimbi disputed an election victory for the ruling party. UNITA forces rapidly took control of more than half the country, including northern diamond areas. Despite subsequently agreeing to participate in a new government of national unity, UNITA resumed fighting late 1992.

United Arab Emirates federation in SW Asia, on the Arabian Gulf, bounded NW by Qatar, SW by Saudi Arabia, and SE by Oman.

chronology
1952 Trucial Council established.
1971 Federation of Arab Emirates formed; later dissolved. Six Trucial States formed United Arab Emirates, with ruler of Abu Dhabi, Sheik Zayed, as president.
1972 The seventh state joined.
1976 Sheik Zayed threatened to relinquish presidency unless progress towards centralization became more rapid.
1985 Diplomatic and economic links with USSR and China established.
1987 Diplomatic relations with Egypt restored.
1990-91 Iraqi invasion of Kuwait opposed; UAE fights with UN coalition.
1991 Bank of Commerce and Credit International (BCCI), controlled by Abu Dhabi's ruler, collapsed.

United Australia Party Australian political party formed by Joseph ◊Lyons 1931 from the right-wing Nationalist Party. It was led by Robert Menzies after the death of Lyons. Considered to have become too dominated by financial interests, it lost heavily to the Labor Party 1943, and was reorganized as the Liberal Party 1944.

United Democratic Front moderate multiracial political organization in South Africa, founded 1983. It was an important focus of anti-apartheid action in South Africa until 1989, when the African National Congress and Pan-Africanist Congress were unbanned.

United Kingdom (UK) country in NW Europe off the coast of France, consisting of England, Scotland, Wales, and Northern Ireland.

chronology
1945 Labour government under Clement Attlee; welfare state established.
1951 Conservatives under Winston Churchill defeated Labour.
1956 Suez Crisis.
1964 Labour victory under Harold Wilson.
1970 Conservatives under Edward Heath defeated Labour.
1972 Parliament prorogued in Northern Ireland; direct rule from Westminster began.
1973 UK joined European Economic Community.
1974 Three-day week, coal strike; Wilson replaced Heath.

1976 James Callaghan replaced Wilson as prime minister.

1977 Liberal–Labour pact.

1979 Victory for Conservatives under Margaret Thatcher.

1981 Formation of Social Democratic Party (SDP). Riots occurred in inner cities.

1982 Unemployment over 3 million. Falklands War.

1983 Thatcher re-elected.

1984-85 Coal strike, the longest in British history.

1986 Abolition of metropolitan counties.

1987 Thatcher re-elected for third term.

1988 Liberals and most of SDP merged into the Social and Liberal Democrats, leaving a splinter SDP. Inflation and interest rates rose.

1989 The Green Party polled 2 million votes in the European elections.

1990 Riots as poll tax introduced in England. Troops sent to the Persian Gulf following Iraq's invasion of Kuwait. British hostages held in Iraq, later released. Britain joined European exchange rate mechanism (ERM). Thatcher replaced by John Major as Conservative leader and prime minister.

1991 British troops took part in US-led war against Iraq under United Nations umbrella. Support was given to the USSR during the dissolution of communism and the restoration of independence to the republics. John Major visited Beijing to sign agreement with China on new Hong Kong airport. At home, Britain suffered severe economic recession and rising unemployment.

1992 Economic recession continued. April: Conservative Party, led by John Major, won fourth consecutive general election, but with reduced majority. Neil Kinnock resigned. July: John Smith became new Labour leader. Sept: sterling devalued and UK withdrawn from ERM. Oct: drastic pit-closure programme encountered massive public opposition; subsequently reviewed. John Major's popularity at unprecedentedly low rating. Nov: government motion in favour of ratification of Maastricht Treaty narrowly passed. Revelations of past arms sales to Iraq implicated senior government figures, including the prime minister.

United Nations (UN) association of states for international peace, security, and cooperation, with its headquarters in New York. The UN was established 1945 as a successor to the ◊League of Nations, and has played a role in many areas, such as refugees, development assistance, disaster relief, and cultural cooperation. Its total proposed budget for 1992/93 was $2,006 million. Boutros Boutros-Ghali became secretary general 1992.

United States of America (USA) country in North America, extending from the Atlantic Ocean in the east to the Pacific Ocean in the west, bounded north by Canada and south by Mexico, and including the outlying states of Alaska and Hawaii.

chronology

1945 USA ended war in the Pacific by dropping A-bombs on Hiroshima and Nagasaki, Japan.

1950-53 US involvement in Korean War. McCarthy anticommunist investigations (HUAC) became a 'witch hunt'.

1954 Civil Rights legislation began with segregation ended in public schools.

1957 Civil Rights bill on voting.

1958 First US satellite in orbit.

1961 ◊Bay of Pigs abortive CIA-backed invasion of Cuba.

1963 President Kennedy assassinated; L B Johnson assumed the presidency.

1964-68 'Great Society' civil-rights and welfare measures in the Omnibus Civil Rights bill.

1964-75 US involvement in ◊Vietnam War.

1965 US intervention in Dominican Republic.

1969 US astronaut Neil Armstrong was the first human on the Moon.

1973 ◊OPEC oil embargo almost crippled US industry and consumers. Inflation began.

1973-74 ◊Watergate scandal began in effort to re-elect Nixon and ended just before impeachment; Nixon resigned as president; replaced by Ford, who 'pardoned' Nixon.

1975 Final US withdrawal from Vietnam.

1979 US–Chinese diplomatic relations normalized.

1979-80 Iranian hostage crisis; relieved by Reagan concessions and released on his inauguration day Jan 1981.

1981 Space shuttle mission was successful.

1983 US invasion of Grenada.

1986 ◊'Irangate' scandal over secret US government arms sales to Iran, with proceeds to antigovernment Contra guerrillas in Nicaragua.

1987 Reagan and Gorbachev (for USSR) signed intermediate-range nuclear forces treaty. Wall Street stock-market crash caused by programme trading.

1988 USA became world's largest debtor nation, owing $532 billion. George Bush elected president.

1989 Bush met Gorbachev at Malta, end to Cold War declared; high-level delegation sent to China amid severe criticism; large troop reductions and budget cuts announced for US military; USA invaded Panama; Noriega taken into custody.

1990 Bush and Gorbachev met again. Nelson Mandela freed in South Africa, toured USA. US troops sent to Middle East following Iraq's invasion of Kuwait.

1991 Jan-Feb: US-led assault drove Iraq from Kuwait in Gulf War. US support was given to the USSR during the dissolution of communism and the recognition of independence of the Baltic republics. July: Strategic Arms Reduction Treaty (START) signed at US–Soviet summit held in Moscow. Nov: Bush co-hosted Middle East peace conference in Spain.

1992 Bush's popularity slumped as economic recession continued. Widespread riots in Los Angeles. Nov: Bill Clinton won presidential elections for the Democrats; independent candidate Ross Perot won nearly 20% of votes.

1993 Jan: Clinton delayed executive order to suspend ban on homosexuality in the armed forces. Feb: medium-term economic plan proposed by Clinton to Congress to cut federal budget deficit.

Uno Sōsuke 1923– . Japanese conservative politician, member of the Liberal Democratic Party (LDP). Having held various cabinet posts since 1976, he was designated prime minister in June 1989 in an attempt to restore the image of the LDP after several scandals. He resigned after only a month in office when his affair with a prostitute became public knowledge.

Uruguay country in South America, on the Atlantic coast, bounded N by Brazil and W by Argentina.

chronology
1930 First constitution adopted.
1966 Blanco party in power, with Jorge Pacheco Areco as president.
1972 Colorado Party returned, with Juan Maria Bordaberry Arocena as president.
1976 Bordaberry deposed by army; Dr Méndez Manfredini became president.
1984 Violent antigovernment protests after ten years of repressive rule.

1985 Agreement reached between the army and political leaders for return to constitutional government. Colorado Party won general election; Dr Julio Maria Sanguinetti became president.

1986 Government of national accord established under President Sanguinetti's leadership.

1989 Luis Lacalle Herrera elected president.

USSR abbreviation for the former ◊*Union of Soviet Socialist Republics*.

Uštaše Croatian nationalist terrorist organization founded 1929 and led by Ante Pavelić against the Yugoslav state. It was responsible for the murder of King Alexander of Yugoslavia in France in 1934 but came to prominence during World War II through collaboration with the Italian and German forces occupying Yugoslavia. It achieved some success in establishing a puppet Croatian state led by Pavelić under German tutelage, but carried out widespread atrocities against ethnic minorities in its territories. The state was destroyed by the Axis defeat in 1945 and Pavelić fled to South America where he died. The organization persisted underground during the communist period and some of its members re-emerged to play a role in the formation of a separate Croatian state after the collapse of Yugoslavia 1990–92.

Ustashi Croatian militia that, during World War II, collaborated with the Nazis and killed thousands of Serbs, Romanies, and Jews.

U Thant Burmese diplomat; see ◊Thant, U.

Uzbekistan country in central Asia, bounded N by Kazakhstan and the Aral Sea, E by Kyrgyzstan and Tajikistan, S by Afghanistan, and W by Turkmenistan.

chronology

1921 Part of Turkestan Soviet Socialist Autonomous Republic.

1925 Became constituent republic of the USSR.

1944 Some 160,000 Meskhetian Turks forcibly transported from their native Georgia to Uzbekistan by Stalin.

1989 June: Tashlak, Yaipan, and Ferghana were the scenes of riots in which Meskhetian Turks were attacked; 70 killed and 850 wounded.

1990 June: economic and political sovereignty declared.

1991 March: Uzbek supported 'renewed federation' in USSR referendum. Aug: anti-Gorbachev coup in Moscow initially accepted by President Karimov; later, Karimov resigned from Soviet Communist Party (CPSU)

Politburo; Uzbek Communist Party (UCP) broke with CPSU; pro-democracy rallies dispersed by militia; independence declared. Dec: joined new Commonwealth of Independent States (CIS).
1992 Jan: admitted into Conference on Security and Cooperation in Europe (CSCE); violent food riots in Tashkent. March: joined the United Nations (UN); US diplomatic recognition achieved.

V1, V2 German flying bombs of World War II, launched against Britain in 1944 and 1945. The V1, also called the doodlebug and buzz bomb, was an uncrewed monoplane carrying a bomb, powered by a simple kind of jet engine called a pulse jet. The V2, a rocket bomb with a preset guidance system, was the first long-range ballistic missile. It was 14 m/47 ft long, carried a 1-tonne warhead, and hit its target at a speed of 5,000 kph/3,000 mph.

Valera éamon de. Irish politician; see ◊de Valera.

Vance Cyrus 1917– . US Democratic politician, secretary of state 1977–80. He resigned because he did not support President Carter's abortive mission to rescue the US hostages in Iran. In 1992 he was chosen as UN negotiator in the peace talks on ◊Bosnia-Herzegovina. Together with EC negotiator Lord Owen, he devised the Vance-Owen peace plan for dividing the republic into 10 semi-autonomous provinces.

Vandenberg Arthur Hendrick 1884–1951. US public official. A Republican, he was appointed to US Senate seat 1928 and remained in that office for the next 23 years. Although initially an isolationist, he supported F D Roosevelt's war policies and was a supporter of the United Nations 1945. He was chair of the Senate Foreign Relations Committee 1946–48.

Van Devanter Willis 1859–1941. US jurist. He was appointed as US Supreme Court justice 1910–37 by President Taft. Active in Republican politics, he served as assistant US attorney general 1897–1903 and federal circuit judge 1903–10. A staunch conservative, Van Devanter was a bitter opponent of the New Deal until his retirement.

Vansittart Robert Gilbert, 1st Baron Vansittart 1881–1957. British diplomat, noted for his anti-German polemic. He was permanent undersecretary of state for foreign affairs 1930–38 and chief diplomatic adviser to the foreign secretary 1938–41.

Vanuatu group of islands in the SW Pacific Ocean, part of ◊Melanesia.

chronology

1906 Islands jointly administered by France and Britain.

1975 Representative assembly established.

1978 Government of national unity formed, with Father Gerard Leymang as chief minister.

1980 Revolt on the island of Espíritu Santo delayed independence but it was achieved within the Commonwealth, with George Kalkoa (adopted name Sokomanu) as president and Father Walter Lini as prime minister.

1988 Dismissal of Lini by Sokomanu led to Sokomanu's arrest for treason. Lini reinstated.

1989 Sokomanu sentenced to six years' imprisonment; succeeded as president by Fred Timakata.

1991 Lini voted out by party members; replaced by Donald Kalpokas. General election produced Union of Moderate Parties–Vanuatu National Party coalition under Maxime Carlot.

Vargas Getúlio 1883–1954. President of Brazil 1930–45 and 1951–54. He overthrew the republic 1930 and in 1937 set up a totalitarian, pro-fascist state known as the *Estado Novo*. Ousted by a military coup 1945, he returned as president 1951 but, amid mounting opposition and political scandal, committed suicide 1954.

Vargas Llosa Mario 1937– . Peruvian novelist, author of *La ciudad y los perros/The Time of the Hero* 1963 and *La guerra del fin del mundo/The War at the End of the World* 1982. He ran for president but was defeated 1990.

Vassilou Georgios Vassos 1931– . Greek-Cypriot politician and entrepreneur, president of Cyprus from 1988. A self-made millionaire, he entered politics as an independent and in 1988 won the presidency, with Communist Party support. He has since, with United Nations help, tried unsuccessfully to heal the rift between the Greek and Turkish communities.

Vatican City State sovereign area within the city of Rome, Italy.

chronology

1929 Lateran Treaty recognized sovereignty of the pope.

1947 New Italian constitution confirmed the sovereignty of the Vatican City State.

1978 John Paul II became the first non-Italian pope for more than 400 years.

1985 New concordat signed under which Roman Catholicism ceased to be Italy's state religion.

Veil Simone 1927–   . French politician. A survivor of Hitler's concentration camps, she was minister of health 1974–79 and framed the French abortion bill. She was president of the European Parliament 1979–81.

Venezuela country in northern South America, on the Caribbean Sea, bounded E by Guyana, S by Brazil, and W by Colombia.

chronology
1961 New constitution adopted, with Rómulo Betancourt as president.
1964 Dr Raúl Leoni became president.
1969 Dr Rafael Caldera became president.
1974 Carlos Andrés Pérez became president.
1979 Dr Luis Herrera became president.
1984 Dr Jaime Lusinchi became president; social pact established between government, trade unions, and business; national debt rescheduled.
1987 Widespread social unrest triggered by inflation; student demonstrators shot by police.
1988 Carlos Andrés Pérez elected president. Payments suspended on foreign debts (increase due to drop in oil prices).
1989 Economic austerity programme enforced by $4.3 billion loan from International Monetary Fund. Price increases triggered riots; 300 people killed. Feb: martial law declared. May: General strike. Elections boycotted by opposition groups.
1991 Protests against austerity programme continued.
1992 Attempted anti-government coups failed. Pérez promised constitutional changes.

Venizelos Eleuthérios 1864–1936. Greek politician born in Crete, leader of the Cretan movement against Turkish rule until the union of the island with Greece in 1905. He later became prime minister of the Greek state on five occasions, 1910–15, 1917–20, 1924, 1928–32, and 1933, before being exiled to France in 1935.

Versailles, Treaty of peace treaty after World War I between the Allies and Germany, signed 28 June 1919. It established the League of Nations. Germany surrendered Alsace-Lorraine to France, and large areas in the east to Poland, and made smaller cessions to Czechoslovakia, Lithuania, Belgium, and Denmark. The Rhineland was demilitarized, German rearmament was restricted, and Germany agreed to pay reparations for war damage. The treaty was never ratified by the USA, which made a separate peace with Germany and Austria 1921.

Verwoerd Hendrik (Frensch) 1901–1966. South African right-wing Nationalist Party politician, prime minister 1958–66. As minister of native affairs 1950–58, he was the chief promoter of apartheid legislation (segregation by race). He made the country a republic 1961. He was assassinated 1966.

Vichy government in World War II, the right-wing government of unoccupied France after the country's defeat by the Germans June 1940, named after the spa town of Vichy, France, where the national assembly was based under Prime Minister Pétain until the liberation 1944. *Vichy France* was that part of France not occupied by German troops until Nov 1942. Authoritarian and collaborationist, the Vichy regime cooperated with the Germans even after they had moved to the unoccupied zone Nov 1942. It imprisoned some 135,000 people, interned another 70,000, deported some 76,000 Jews, and sent 650,000 French workers to Germany.

Victor Emmanuel III 1869–1947. King of Italy from the assassination of his father, Umberto I, 1900. He acquiesced in the Fascist regime of Mussolini from 1922 and, after the dictator's fall 1943, relinquished power to his son Umberto II, who cooperated with the Allies. Victor Emmanuel formally abdicated 1946.

Vietcong in the Vietnam War 1954–75, the members of the National Front for the Liberation of South Vietnam, founded 1960, who fought the South Vietnamese and US forces. The name was coined by the South Vietnamese government to differentiate these communist guerrillas from the ◊Vietminh.

Vietminh the Vietnam Independence League, founded 1941 to oppose the Japanese occupation of Indochina and later directed against the French colonial power. The Vietminh were instrumental in achieving Vietnamese independence through military victory at Dien Bien Phu 1954.

Vietnam country in SE Asia, on the South China Sea, bounded N by China and W by Cambodia and Laos.

chronology
1945 Japanese removed from Vietnam at end of World War II.
1946 Commencement of Vietminh war against French.
1954 France defeated at Dien Bien Phu. Vietnam divided along 17th parallel.
1964 US troops entered Vietnam War.
1973 Paris cease-fire agreement.

1975 Saigon captured by North Vietnam.
1976 Socialist Republic of Vietnam proclaimed.
1978 Admission into Comecon. Vietnamese invasion of Cambodia.
1979 Sino-Vietnamese border war.
1986 Retirement of 'old guard' leaders.
1987–88 Over 10,000 political prisoners released.
1988–89 Troop withdrawals from Cambodia continued.
1989 'Boat people' leaving Vietnam murdered and robbed at sea by Thai pirates. Troop withdrawal from Cambodia completed. Hong Kong forcibly repatriated some Vietnamese refugees.
1991 Vo Van Kiet replaced Do Muoi as prime minister. Cambodia peace agreement signed. Relations with China normalized.
1992 Sept: Le Duc Anh elected president. Dec: relations with South Korea normalized; USA eased 30-year-old trade embargo.

Vietnam War 1954–75. War between communist North Vietnam and US-backed South Vietnam. 200,000 South Vietnamese soldiers, 1 million North Vietnamese soldiers, and 500,000 civilians were killed. 56,555 US soldiers were killed 1961–75, a fifth of them by their own troops. The war destroyed 50% of the country's forest cover and 20% of agricultural land. Cambodia, a neutral neighbour, was bombed by the US 1969–75, with 1 million killed or wounded.

Vimy Ridge hill in N France, taken in World War I by Canadian troops during the battle of Arras, April 1917, at the cost of 11,285 lives. It is a spur of the ridge of Nôtre Dame de Lorette, 8 km/5 mi NE of Arras.

Vogel Hans-Jochen 1926–   . German socialist politician, chair of the Social Democratic Party (SPD) 1987–91. A former leader of the SPD in Bavaria and mayor of Munich, he served in the Brandt and Schmidt West German governments in the 1970s as housing and then justice minister and then, briefly, as mayor of West Berlin.

Volgograd formerly (until 1925) *Tsaritsyn* and (1925–61) *Stalingrad*, an industrial city in SW Russia, on the river Volga; population (1987) 988,000. Its successful defence 1942–43 against Germany was a turning point in World War II.

Voroshilov Klement Efremovich 1881–1969. Marshal of the USSR. He joined the Bolsheviks 1903 and was arrested many times and exiled, but escaped. He became a Red Army commander in the civil war 1918–20, a member of the central committee 1921, commissar for war 1925, member of the Politburo 1926, and marshal 1935. He was removed as war commissar 1940 after defeats on the Finland front and failing to raise the German siege of Leningrad. He was a member of the committee for defence 1941–44 and president of the Presidium of the USSR 1953–60.

Vorster Balthazar Johannes 1915–1983. South African Nationalist politician, prime minister 1966–78, and president 1978–79. During his term as prime minister some elements of apartheid were allowed to lapse, and attempts were made to improve relations with the outside world. He resigned the presidency because of a financial scandal.

Vranitzky Franz 1937– . Austrian socialist politician, federal chancellor from 1986. A banker, he entered the political arena through the moderate, left-of-centre Socialist Party of Austria (SPÖ), and became minister of finance 1984. He succeeded Fred Sinowatz as federal chancellor 1986, heading an SPÖ-ÖVP (Austrian People's Party) coalition.

Vyshinsky Andrei 1883–1954. Soviet politician. As commissar for justice, he acted as prosecutor at Stalin's treason trials 1936–38. He was foreign minister 1949–53 and often represented the USSR at the United Nations.

Wafd the main Egyptian nationalist party between World Wars I and II. Under Nahas Pasha it formed a number of governments in the 1920s and 1930s. Dismissed by King Farouk in 1938, it was reinstated by the British 1941. The party's pro-British stance weakened its claim to lead the nationalist movement, and the party was again dismissed by Farouk 1952, shortly before his own deposition. Wafd was banned in Jan 1953.

Wagner Robert 1910–1991. US politician, mayor of New York City 1954–65. He demolished slum areas, built public housing, and was instrumental in introducing members of ethnic minorities into City Hall.

Wagner Robert F(erdinand) 1877–1953. US Democratic senator 1927–49, a leading figure in the development of welfare provision in the USA, especially in the ◊New Deal era. He helped draft much new legislation, including the National Industrial Recovery Act 1933, the Social Security Act 1936, and the National Labor Relations Act 1935, known as the Wagner Act.

Waite Terry (Terence Hardy) 1939– . British religious adviser to the archbishop of Canterbury, then Dr Robert Runcie 1980–87. As the archbishop's special envoy, Waite disappeared 20 Jan 1987 while engaged in secret negotiations to free European hostages in Beirut, Lebanon. He had been taken hostage by an Islamic group and was released 18 Nov 1991.

Wald Lillian D 1867–1940. US public health administrator and founder of New York City's Henry Street Settlement House 1895. In 1912 she founded the National Organization for Public Health Nursing and was also active in union and antiwar activities.

Walden Brian (Alistair) 1932– . British journalist and, from 1977, television presenter. He was a Labour member of Parliament 1964–77.

Waldheim Kurt 1918– . Austrian politician and diplomat, president 1986–1992. He was secretary general of the United Nations 1972–81, having been Austria's representative there 1964–68 and 1970–71. He was elected president of Austria despite revelations that during World War II he had been an intelligence officer in an army unit responsible for transporting Jews to death camps. His election therefore led to some diplomatic isolation of Austria, and in 1991 he announced that he would not run for re-election.

Walesa Lech 1943– . Polish trade-union leader and president of Poland from 1990, founder of ◊Solidarity (Solidarność) in 1980, an organization, independent of the Communist Party, which forced substantial political and economic concessions from the Polish government 1980–81 until being outlawed. He was awarded the Nobel Prize for Peace 1983.

Walker Jimmy (James John) 1881–1946. US public official. In 1925 Walker was elected mayor of New York City and in that position became a popular personality, familiarly known to his constituents as 'Jimmy'. Although Walker made great improvements to the city's infrastructure, he was charged with graft and forced to resign 1932.

Walker Peter (Edward) 1932– . British Conservative politician, energy secretary 1983–87, secretary of state for Wales 1987–90.

Wallace George Corley 1919– . US politician who was opposed to integration; he was governor of Alabama 1963–67, 1971–79, and 1983–87. He contested the presidency in 1968 as an independent (the American Independent Party) and in 1972 campaigned for the Democratic nomination but was shot at a rally and became partly paralysed.

Wallace Henry Agard 1888–1965. US editor and public official. Appointed secretary of the treasury by Franklin Roosevelt 1933 he served as vice president during Roosevelt's third term 1941-45. He later broke with Truman and, after serving as editor of the *New Republic* 1946-47, was the unsuccessful Progressive Party candidate for president 1948.

Wallenberg Raoul 1912–1947. Swedish business executive who attempted to rescue several thousand Jews from German-occupied Budapest 1944, during World War II. He was taken prisoner by the Soviet army 1945 and was never heard from again.

Wall Street crash 1929 panic selling on the New York Stock Exchange following an artificial boom 1927–29 fed by speculation. On 24 Oct 1929, 13 million shares changed hands, with further heavy selling on 28 Oct and the disposal of 16 million shares on 29 Oct. Many shareholders were ruined, banks and businesses failed, and in the Depression that followed, unemployment rose to approximately 17 million.

Walters Alan (Arthur) 1926– . British economist and government adviser 1981–89. He became economics adviser to Prime Minister Thatcher, but his publicly stated differences with the policies of her chancellor Nigel ♢Lawson precipitated, in 1989, Lawson's resignation from the government as well as Walters's own departure.

war crime offence (such as murder of a civilian or a prisoner of war) that contravenes the internationally accepted laws governing the conduct of wars, particularly The Hague Convention 1907 and the Geneva Convention 1949. A key principle of the law relating to such crimes is that obedience to the orders of a superior is no defence. In practice, prosecutions are generally brought by the victorious side.

War Powers Act legislation passed 1973 enabling the US president to deploy US forces abroad for combat without prior Congressional approval. The president is nevertheless required to report to both Houses of Congress within 48 hours of having taken such action. Congress may restrict the continuation of troop deployment despite any presidential veto.

Warsaw capital of Poland, on the river Vistula; population (1990) 1,655,700. The city was taken by the Germans 27 Sept 1939, and 250,000 Poles were killed during two months of street fighting that started 1 Aug 1944. From 1940 about 500,000 Jews were confined to a section of the city called the *ghetto*; many were transported to concentration camps; virtually all died of hunger or disease or by execution. Warsaw was finally liberated 17 Jan 1945. The old city was virtually destroyed in World War II but has been reconstructed.

Warsaw Pact or *Eastern European Mutual Assistance Pact* military alliance 1955–91 between the USSR and East European communist states, originally established as a response to the admission of West Germany into NATO. Its military structures and agreements were dismantled early in 1991; a political organization remained until the alliance was officially dissolved July 1991.

Watergate US political scandal, named after the building in Washington DC that housed the Democrats' campaign headquarters in the 1972 presidential election. Five men, hired by the Republican Committee to Re-elect the President (CREEP), were caught after breaking into the Watergate with complex electronic surveillance equipment. Investigations revealed that the White House was implicated in the break-in, and that there was a 'slush fund', used to finance unethical activities. In Aug 1974, President ◊Nixon was forced by the Supreme Court to surrender to Congress tape recordings of conversations he had held with administration officials, which indicated his complicity in a cover-up. Nixon resigned rather than face impeachment for obstruction of justice and other crimes.

Wavell Archibald, 1st Earl 1883–1950. British field marshal in World War II. As commander in chief Middle East, he successfully defended Egypt against Italy July 1939. He was transferred as commander in chief India in July 1941, and was viceroy 1943–47.

Waverley John Anderson, 1st Viscount Waverley 1882–1958. British administrator. He organized civil defence for World War II, becoming home secretary and minister for home security in 1939 (the nationally distributed *Anderson shelters*, home outdoor air-raid shelters, were named after him). He was chancellor of the Exchequer 1943–45.

Wei Jingsheng 1951– . Chinese pro-democracy activist and essayist, imprisoned from 1979 for attacking the Chinese communist system. He is regarded as one of China's most important political prisoners.

Weimar town in the state of Thuringia, Federal Republic of Germany. It was the capital of the grand duchy of Saxe-Weimar 1815–1918. In 1919 the German National Assembly drew up the constitution of the new ◊Weimar Republic in Weimar.

Weimar Republic the constitutional republic in Germany 1919–33, which was crippled by the election of antidemocratic parties to the Reichstag (parliament), and then subverted by the Nazi leader Hitler after his appointment as chancellor 1933. It took its name from the city where in Feb 1919 a constituent assembly met to draw up a democratic constitution.

Weinberger Caspar (Willard) 1917– . US Republican politician. He served under presidents Nixon and Ford, and was Reagan's defence secretary 1981–87.

Weizmann Chaim 1874–1952. Zionist leader, the first president of Israel (1948–52), and a chemist. He conducted the negotiations leading up to the ◊Balfour Declaration, by which Britain declared its support for an independent Jewish state.

Weizsäcker Richard, Baron von 1920– . German Christian Democrat politician, president from 1984. He began his career as a lawyer and was also active in the German Protestant church and in Christian Democratic Union party politics. He was elected to the West German Bundestag (parliament) 1969 and served as mayor of West Berlin from 1981, before being elected federal president 1984.

Welch Robert H W, Jr 1899–1985. US anticommunist crusader and business executive. He founded the extreme right-wing John Birch Society 1958 in memory of the American Baptist missionary. A supporter of the losing Republican presidential candidate Barry Goldwater 1964, Welch later became increasingly venomous in his accusations against supposed communist agents and sympathizers.

Welensky Roy 1907–1991. Rhodesian politician. He was instrumental in the creation of a federation of Northern Rhodesia (now Zambia), Southern Rhodesia (now Zimbabwe), and Nyasaland (now Malawi) in 1953 and was prime minister 1956–63, when the federation was disbanded. His Southern Rhodesian Federal Party was defeated by Ian Smith's Rhodesian Front in 1964. In 1965, following Smith's Rhodesian unilateral declaration of Southern Rhodesian independence from Britain, Welensky left politics.

welfare state political system under which the state (rather than the individual or the private sector) has responsibility for the welfare of its citizens. Services such as unemployment and sickness benefits, family allowances and income supplements, pensions, medical care, and education may be provided and financed through state insurance schemes and taxation.

Wells Ida Bell 1862–1931. US journalist and political activist. She joined the staff of *New York Age* 1891 and embarked on extensive lecture tours. She served as secretary of the National Afro-American Council 1898–1902 and as a Chicago probation officer 1913–16.

West Bank area (5,879 sq km/2,270 sq mi) on the west bank of the river Jordan; population (1988) 866,000. The West Bank was taken by the Jordanian army 1948 at the end of the Arab-Israeli war that followed the creation of the state of Israel, and was captured by Israel during the Six-Day War 5–10 June 1967. The continuing Israeli occupation and settlement of the area has created tensions with the Arab population.

Western European Union (WEU) organization established 1955 as a consultative forum for military issues among the W European governments: Belgium, France, the Netherlands, Italy, Luxembourg, the UK, Germany, and (from 1988) Spain and Portugal.

Western Front battle zone in World War I between Germany and its enemies France and Britain, extending as lines of trenches from Nieuport on the Belgian coast through Ypres, Arras, Albert, Soissons, and Rheims to Verdun, constructed by both Germany and the Allies.

Western Sahara formerly *Spanish Sahara* disputed coastal territory in NW Africa bounded to the N by Morocco and to the W and S by Mauritania. The region was a Spanish possession until 1976, when two-thirds was taken over by Morocco and one-third by Mauritania (withdrew in 1979). Polisario (the Popular Front for the Liberation of Saguia al Hamra and Rio de Oro) rejected this partition, declared their own independent Saharan Arab Democratic Republic (SADR), and proceeded to wage a guerrilla war, securing indirect support from Algeria and, later, Libya. By 1979 they had succeeded in their struggle against Mauritania, which withdrew from their southern sector and concluded a peace agreement with Polisario, and in 1982 the SADR was accepted as a full member of the ◊Organization of African Unity. By the end of 1990, 70 countries had granted diplomatic recognition to the SADR.

Western Samoa see ◊Samoa, Western.

West Indies, Federation of the federal union 1958–62 comprising Antigua, Barbados, Dominica, Grenada, Jamaica, Montserrat, St Christopher (St Kitts)–Nevis and Anguilla, St Lucia, St Vincent, and Trinidad and Tobago. This federation came to an end when first Jamaica and then Trinidad and Tobago withdrew.

Westmoreland William (Childs) 1914– . US military leader who served as commander of US forces in Vietnam 1964–68. He was an aggressive advocate of expanded US military involvement there.

Weygand Maxime 1867–1965. French general. In 1940, as French commander in chief, he advised surrender to Germany, and was subsequently high commissioner of N Africa 1940–41. He was a prisoner in Germany 1942–45, and was arrested after his return to France; he was released 1946, and in 1949 the sentence of national infamy was quashed.

White Byron Raymond 1917– . US jurist. He worked to elect John F Kennedy to the presidency 1960 and was appointed by him as associate justice of the Supreme Court 1962– . He was a moderate conservative, usually dissenting on the rights of criminals, but upholding the right of accused citizens to trial by jury.

White Australia Policy Australian government policy of immigration restriction, mainly aimed at non-Europeans, which began in the 1850s in an attempt to limit the number of Chinese entering the Australian goldfields and was official until 1945.

Whitelaw William, Viscount Whitelaw 1918– . British Conservative politician. As secretary of state for Northern Ireland he introduced the concept of power sharing. He was chief Conservative whip 1964–70, and leader of the House of Commons 1970–72. He became secretary of state for employment 1973–74, but failed to conciliate the trade unions. He was chair of the Conservative Party 1974 and home secretary 1979–83, when he was made a peer. He resigned 1988.

White terror general term used by socialists and Marxists to describe a right-wing counterrevolution: for example, the attempts by the Chinese ◊Guomindang to massacre the communists 1927–31.

Whitlam Gough (Edward) 1916– . Australian politician, leader of the Labor Party 1967–78 and prime minister 1972–75. He cultivated closer relations with Asia, attempted redistribution of wealth, and raised loans to increase national ownership of industry and resources.

Wiesel Elie 1928– . US academic and human-rights campaigner, born in Romania. He was held in Buchenwald concentration camp during World War II, and has assiduously documented wartime atrocities against the Jews in an effort to alert the world to the dangers of racism and violence. Nobel Peace Prize 1986.

William II 1859–1941. Emperor of Germany from 1888, the son of Frederick III and Victoria, daughter of Queen Victoria of Britain. In 1890 he forced Chancellor Bismarck to resign and began to direct foreign policy himself, which proved disastrous. He encouraged warlike policies and built up the German navy. In 1914 he first approved Austria's ultimatum to Serbia and then, when he realized war was inevitable, tried in vain to prevent it. In 1918 he fled to Holland, after Germany's defeat and his abdication.

Williams Shirley 1930– . British Social Democrat Party politician. She was Labour minister for prices and consumer protection 1974–76, and education and science 1976–79. She became a founder member of the SDP (Social Democrat Party) 1981 and its president 1982. In 1983 she lost her parliamentary seat. She is the daughter of socialist writer Vera Brittain.

Willis Norman (David) 1933–   . British trade- union leader. A trade-union official since leaving school, he succeeded Len Murray as the general secretary of the Trades Union Congress (TUC) 1984.

Willkie Wendell Lewis 1892–1944. US politician who was the Republican presidential candidate 1940. After losing to F D Roosevelt, he continued as a leader of the liberal wing of the Republican Party. Becoming committed to the cause of international cooperation, he published *One World* 1942.

Wilson (James) Harold, Baron Wilson of Rievaulx 1916–   . British Labour politician, party leader from 1963, prime minister 1964–70 and 1974–76. His premiership was dominated by the issue of UK admission to membership of the European Community, the social contract (unofficial agreement with the trade unions), and economic difficulties.

Wilson (Thomas) Woodrow 1856–1924. 28th president of the USA 1913–21, a Democrat. He kept the USA out of World War I until 1917, and in Jan 1918 issued his ◊'Fourteen Points' as a basis for a just peace settlement. At the peace conference in Paris he secured the inclusion of the ◊League of Nations in individual peace treaties, but these were not ratified by Congress, so the USA did not join the League. Nobel Peace Prize 1919.

winter of discontent the winter of 1978–79 in Britain, marked by a series of strikes that contributed to the defeat of the Labour government in the general election of spring 1979. The phrase is from Shakespeare's *Richard III*: 'Now is the winter of our discontent/Made glorious summer by this sun of York.'

Winter War the USSR's invasion of Finland 30 Nov 1939–12 March 1940, also called the Russo-Finnish War.

Women's Land Army organization founded 1916 for the recruitment of women to work on farms during World War I. At its peak Sept 1918 it had 16,000 members. It re-formed June 1939, before the outbreak of World War II. Many 'Land Girls' joined up to help the war effort and, by Aug 1943, 87,000 were employed in farm work.

women's movement the campaign for the rights of women, including social, political, and economic equality with men. Early European campaigners of the 17th–19th centuries fought for women's right to own property, to have access to higher education, and to vote (see ◊suffragette). Once women's suffrage was achieved in the 20th century, the emphasis of the movement shifted to the goals of equal social and economic opportunities for women, including employment. A continuing area of concern in industrialized countries is the contradiction between the now generally accepted principle of equality and the demonstrable inequalities that remain between the sexes in state policies and in everyday life.

women's services the organized military use of women on a large scale, a 20th-century development. First, women replaced men in factories, on farms, and in noncombat tasks during wartime; they are now found in combat units in many countries, including the USA, Cuba, the UK, and Israel.

Women's Social and Political Union (WSPU) British political movement founded 1903 by Emmeline Pankhurst to organize a militant crusade for female suffrage.

Works Progress Administration (WPA, renamed *Works Projects Administration* 1939) in US history, a government initiative to reduce unemployment during the Depression (11 million in 1934). Formed 1935, it provided useful work for 8.5 million people during its eight-year existence, mainly in construction projects, at a total cost of $11 billion, and was discontinued only in 1943 when the change to a war economy eliminated unemployment. The WPA was an integral part of President Roosevelt's ◊New Deal.

World Bank popular name for the *International Bank for Reconstruction and Development* specialized agency of the United Nations that borrows in the commercial market and lends on commercial terms. It was established 1945 under the 1944 Bretton Woods agreement, which also created the International Monetary Fund. The *International Development Association* is an arm of the World Bank.

World War I 1914–1918. War between the Central European Powers (Germany, Austria-Hungary, and allies) on one side and the Triple Entente (Britain and the British Empire, France, and Russia) and their allies, including the USA (which entered 1917), on the other side. An estimated 10 million lives were lost and twice that number were wounded. It was fought on the eastern and western fronts, in the Middle East, Africa, and at sea. Towards the end of the war Russia withdrew because of the Russian Revolution 1917. The peace treaty of Versailles 1919 was the formal end to the war.

1914 outbreak On 28 June the heir to the Austrian throne was assassinated in Sarajevo, Serbia; on 28 July Austria declared war on Serbia; as Russia mobilized, Germany declared war on Russia and France, taking a short cut in the west by invading Belgium; on 4 Aug Britain declared war on Germany; dominions within the Empire, including Australia, were automatically involved.

Western Front The German advance reached within a few miles of Paris, but an Allied counterattack at the Marne drove them back to the Aisne River; the opposing lines then settled into trench warfare.

Eastern Front The German commander Hindenburg halted the Russian advance through the Ukraine and across Austria-Hungary at the Battle of Tannenberg in E Prussia.

Africa By Sept most of Germany's African colonies were in Allied hands; guerrilla warfare centred in Cameroon until 1916 and military operations in German East Africa until November 1918.

Middle East On 1 Nov Turkey entered the war on the side of the Central Powers and soon attacked Russia in the Caucasus Mountains.

1915 Western Front Several offensives on both sides resulted in insignificant gains. At Ypres, Belgium, the Germans used poison gas for the first time.

Eastern Front The German field marshals Mackensen and Hindenburg drove back the Russians and took Poland.

Middle East British attacks against Turkey in Mesopotamia (Iraq), the Dardanelles, and at Gallipoli (where 7,600 Anzacs were killed) were all unsuccessful.

Italy Italy declared war on Austria; Bulgaria joined the Central Powers.

war at sea Germany declared all-out U-boat war, but the sinking of the British ocean liner *Lusitania* (with Americans among the 1,198 lost) led to demands that the USA enter the war.

1916 Western Front The German attack at Verdun was countered by the Allies on the river Somme, where tanks were used for the first time.

Eastern Front Romania joined the Allies but was soon overrun by Germany.

Middle East Kut-al-Imara, Iraq, was taken from the British by the Turks.

war at sea The Battle of Jutland between England and Germany, although indecisive, put a stop to further German naval participation in the war.

1917 The USA entered the war in April. British and Empire troops launched the third battle at Ypres and by Nov had taken Passchendaele.

1918 Eastern Front On 3 March Soviet Russia signed the Treaty of Brest-Litovsk with Germany, ending Russian participation in the war (the Russian Revolution 1917 led into their civil war 1918-21).

Western Front Germany began a final offensive. In April the Allies appointed the French marshal Foch supreme commander, but by June (when the first US troops went into battle) the Allies had lost all gains since 1915, and the Germans were on the river Marne. The battle at Amiens marked the launch of the victorious Allied offensive.

Italy At Vittorio Veneto the British and Italians finally defeated the Austrians.

German capitulation This began with naval mutinies at Kiel, followed by uprisings in the major cities. Kaiser Wilhelm II abdicated, and on 11 Nov the armistice was signed.

1919 18 June, peace treaty of Versailles. (The USA signed a separate peace accord with Germany and Austria 1921.)

World War II 1939–1945. War between Germany, Italy, and Japan (the Axis powers) on one side, and Britain, the Commonwealth, France, the USA, the USSR, and China (the Allied powers) on the other. An estimated 55 million lives were lost, 20 million of them citizens of the USSR. The war was fought in the Atlantic and Pacific theatres. In 1945, Germany surrendered (May) but Japan fought on until the USA dropped atomic bombs on Hiroshima and Nagasaki (Aug).

Worner Manfred 1934–   . German politician, NATO secretary-general from 1988. He was elected for the Conservative Christian Democratic Union (CDU) to the West German Bundestag (parliament) 1965 and, as a specialist in strategic affairs, served as defence minister under Chancellor Kohl 1982–88. A proponent of closer European military collaboration, he succeeded the British politician Peter Carrington as secretary general of NATO July 1988.

Worrall Denis John 1935–   . South African politician, member of the white opposition to apartheid. A co-leader of the Democratic Party (DP), he was elected to parliament 1989.

Wrangel Peter Nicolaievich, Baron von 1878–1928. Russian general, born in St Petersburg. He commanded a division of Cossacks in World War I, and in 1920, after succeeding Anton Denikin as commander in chief of the White Army, defeated by the Bolsheviks in the Crimea.

Xian Incident kidnapping of the Chinese generalissimo and politician ◊Chiang Kai-shek in Xian 12 Dec 1936, by one of his own generals, to force his cooperation with the communists against the Japanese invaders.

Y

Yahya Khan Agha Muhammad 1917–1980. Pakistani president 1969–71. His mishandling of the Bangladesh separatist issue led to civil war, and he was forced to resign.

Yalta Conference in 1945, a meeting at which the Allied leaders Churchill (UK), Roosevelt (USA), and Stalin (USSR) completed plans for the defeat of Germany in World War II and the foundation of the United Nations. It took place in Yalta, a Soviet holiday resort in the Crimea.

Yamagata Aritomo 1838–1922. Japanese soldier, politician, and prime minister 1889–91 and 1898–1900. As war minister 1873 and chief of the imperial general staff 1878, he was largely responsible for the modernization of the military system. He returned as chief of staff during the Russo-Japanese War 1904–05 and remained an influential political figure until he was disgraced in 1921 for having meddled in the marriage arrangements of the crown prince.

Yamamoto Gombei 1852–1933. Japanese admiral and politician. As prime minister 1913–14, he began Japanese expansion into China and initiated political reforms. He became premier again 1923 but resigned the following year.

Yanayev Gennady 1937– . Soviet communist politician, leader of the failed Aug 1991 anti-Gorbachev coup, after which he was arrested and charged with treason. He was vice president of the USSR 1990–91.

Yang Shangkun 1907– . Chinese communist politician. He held a senior position in the party 1956–66 but was demoted during the Cultural Revolution. He was rehabilitated 1978, elected to the Politburo 1982, and to the position of state president 1988.

Yeltsin Boris Nikolayevich 1931– . Russian politician, president of the Russian Soviet Federative Socialist Republic (RSFSR) 1990–91, and president of the newly independent Russian Federation from 1991. He directed the Federation's secession from the USSR and the formation of a new, decentralized confederation, the ◊Commonwealth of Independent States (CIS), with himself as the most powerful leader. He established himself internationally as an advocate of nuclear disarmament and domestically as a proponent of price deregulation and accelerated privatization. Faced with severe economic problems, civil unrest, and threats of a communist backlash, he has consistently requested international aid to bring his country out of recession.

Yemen country in SW Asia, bounded N by Saudi Arabia, E by Oman, S by the Gulf of Aden, and W by the Red Sea.

chronology

1918 Yemen became independent.

1962 North Yemen declared the Yemen Arab Republic (YAR), with Abdullah al-Sallal as president. Civil war broke out between royalists and republicans.

1967 Civil war ended with the republicans victorious. Sallal deposed and replaced by Republican Council. The People's Republic of South Yemen was formed.

1970 People's Republic of South Yemen renamed People's Democratic Republic of Yemen.

1971-72 War between South Yemen and the YAR; union agreement signed but not kept.

1974 Ibrahim al-Hamadi seized power in North Yemen and Military Command Council set up.

1977 Hamadi assassinated and replaced by Ahmed ibn Hussein al-Ghashmi.

1978 Constituent People's Assembly appointed in North Yemen and Military Command Council dissolved. Ghashmi killed by envoy from South Yemen; succeeded by Ali Abdullah Saleh. War broke out again between the two Yemens. South Yemen president deposed and Yemen Socialist Party (YSP) formed with Abdul Fattah Ismail as secretary general, later succeeded by Ali Nasser Muhammad.

1979 Cease-fire agreed with commitment to future union.

1983 Saleh elected president of North Yemen for a further five-year term.

1984 Joint committee on foreign policy for the two Yemens met in Aden.

1985 Ali Nasser Muhammad re-elected secretary general of the YSP in South Yemen; removed his opponents. Three bureau members killed.

1986 Civil war in South Yemen; Ali Nasser dismissed. New administration under Haydar Abu Bakr al-Attas.

1988 President Saleh re-elected in North Yemen.
1989 Draft constitution for single Yemen state published.
1990 Border between two Yemens opened; countries formally united 22 May as Republic of Yemen.
1991 New constitution approved.
1992 Anti-government riots.
1993 Multiparty parliamentary elections set for April.

Yippie in the USA, a member of the *Youth International Party* (YIP), led by Abbie ◊Hoffmann and Jerry Rubin (1938-   ), who mocked the US political process during the 1960s.

Yom Kippur War the surprise attack on Israel October 1973 by Egypt and Syria; see ◊Arab-Israeli Wars. It is named after the Jewish national holiday on which it began, the holiest day of the Jewish year.

York Alvin Cullum 'Sergeant' 1887–1964. US war hero. At the Battle of the Argonne Forest 8 Oct 1918 during World War I, York led a charge against a German position in which he and his comrades captured 132 prisoners and 35 machine guns. A film biography, *Sergeant York*, appeared in 1940.

Yoshida Shigeru 1878–1967. Japanese conservative (Liberal Party) politician who served as prime minister of US-occupied Japan for most of the post-World War II period 1946–54. He was foreign minister 1945–46.

Young David Ivor (Baron Young of Graffham) 1932–   . British Conservative politician, chair of the Manpower Services Commission (MSC) 1982–84, secretary for employment from 1985, trade and industry secretary 1987–89, when he retired from politics. He was subsequently criticized by a House of Commons select committee over aspects of the privatization of the Rover car company.

Young Plan scheme devised by US entrepreneur Owen D Young to reschedule German payments of war reparations 1929.

Young Turk member of a reformist movement of young army officers in the Ottoman Empire founded 1889. The movement was instrumental in the constitutional changes of 1908 and the abdication of Sultan Abdul-Hamid II 1909. It gained prestige during the Balkan Wars 1912–13 and encouraged Turkish links with the German empire. Its influence diminished after 1918. The term is now used for a member of any radical or rebellious faction within a party or organization.

Ypres (Flemish *Ieper*) Belgian town in W Flanders, 40 km/25 mi S of Ostend, a site of three major battles 1914–1917 fought in World War I. The Menin Gate 1927 is a memorial to British soldiers lost in these battles.

Ypres, 1st Earl of title of Sir John ◊French, British field marshal.

Yuan Shikai 1859–1916. Chinese soldier and politician, leader of Republican China 1911–16. He assumed dictatorial powers 1912, dissolving parliament and suppressing Sun Yat-sen's ◊Guomindang. He died soon after proclaiming himself emperor.

Yugoslavia country in SE Europe, with a SW coastline on the Adriatic Sea, bounded W by Bosnia-Herzegovina, NW by Croatia, E by Romania and Bulgaria, and S by Greece and Albania.

chronology
1918 Creation of Kingdom of the Serbs, Croats, and Slovenes.
1929 Name of Yugoslavia adopted.
1941 Invaded by Germany.
1945 Yugoslav Federal Republic formed under leadership of Tito; communist constitution introduced.
1948 Split with USSR.
1953 Self-management principle enshrined in constitution.
1961 Nonaligned movement formed under Yugoslavia's leadership.
1974 New constitution adopted.
1980 Tito died; collective leadership assumed power.
1987 Threatened use of army to curb unrest.
1988 Economic difficulties: 1,800 strikes, 250% inflation, 20% unemployment. Ethnic unrest in Montenegro and Vojvodina; party reshuffled and government resigned.
1989 Reformist Croatian Ante Marković became prime minister. 29 died in ethnic riots in Kosovo province, protesting against Serbian attempt to end autonomous status of Kosovo and Vojvodina; state of emergency imposed. May: inflation rose to 490%; tensions with ethnic Albanians rose.
1990 Multiparty systems established in Serbia and Croatia.
1991 June: Slovenia and Croatia declared independence, resulting in clashes between federal and republican armies Slovenia accepted EC-sponsored peace pact. Fighting continued in Croatia; repeated calls for cease-fires failed. Dec: President Stipe Mesic and Prime Minister Ante Marković resigned.

1992 Jan: EC-brokered cease-fire established in Croatia; EC and USA recognized Slovenia's and Croatia's independence. Bosnia-Herzegovina and Macedonia declared independence. April: Bosnia-Herzegovina recognized as independent by EC and USA amid increasing ethnic hostility; bloody civil war ensued. New Federal Republic of Yugoslavia (FRY) proclaimed by Serbia and Montenegro but not recognized externally. May: Western ambassadors left Belgrade. International sanctions imposed against Serbia and Montenegro. Hostilities continued. Jun: Dobrica Cosic became president. Jul: Milan Panic became prime minister. Sept: UN membership suspended. Dec: Slobodan Milosevic re-elected Serbian president; Panic removed from office in vote of no confidence.
1993 Radoje Kontic became prime minister.

Z

Zahir Shah Mohammed 1914– . King of Afghanistan 1933–73. Zahir, educated in Kabul and Paris, served in the government 1932–33 before being crowned king. He was overthrown 1973 by a republican coup and went into exile. He became a symbol of national unity for the ⟩Mujaheddin Islamic fundamendalist resistance groups.

Zaire country in central Africa, bounded W by Congo, N by the Central African Republic and Sudan, E by Uganda, Rwanda, Burundi, and Tanzania, SE by Zambia, and SW by Angola. There is a short coastline on the Atlantic Ocean.

chronology
1908 Congo Free State annexed to Belgium.
1960 Independence achieved from Belgium as Republic of the Congo. Civil war broke out between central government and Katanga province.
1963 Katanga war ended.
1967 New constitution adopted.
1970 Col ⟩Mobutu elected president.
1971 Country became the Republic of Zaire.
1972 The Popular Movement of the Revolution (MPR) became the only legal political party. Katanga province renamed Shaba.
1974 Foreign-owned businesses and plantations seized by Mobutu and given in political patronage.
1977 Original owners of confiscated properties invited back. Mobutu re-elected; Zairians invaded Shaba province from Angola, repulsed by Belgian paratroopers.
1978 Second unsuccessful invasion from Angola.
1988 Potential rift with Belgium avoided.
1990 Mobutu announced end of ban on multiparty politics, following internal dissent.
1991 Multiparty elections promised. Sept: after antigovernment riots, Mobutu agreed to share power with opposition; Etienne Tshisekedi

appointed premier. Oct: Tshisekedi dismissed.

1992 Aug: Tshisekedi reinstated against Mobuto's wishes; interim opposition parliament formed. Oct: renewed rioting.

1993 Jan: French ambassador shot dead by loyalist troops during army mutiny; France and Belgium prepared to evacuate civilians. March: Tshisekedi dismissed by Mobuto, replaced by Faustin Birindwa, but Tshisekedi still considered himself in office.

Zambia landlocked country in S central Africa, bounded N by Zaire and Tanzania, E by Malawi, S by Mozambique, Zimbabwe, Botswana, and Namibia, and W by Angola.

chronology

1899–1924 As Northern Rhodesia, under administration of the British South Africa Company.

1924 Became a British protectorate.

1964 Independence achieved from Britain, within the Commonwealth, as the Republic of Zambia with Kenneth ◊Kaunda as president.

1972 United National Independence Party (UNIP) declared the only legal party.

1976 Support for the Patriotic Front in Rhodesia declared.

1980 Unsuccessful coup against President Kaunda.

1985 Kaunda elected chair of the African Front Line States.

1987 Kaunda elected chair of the Organization of African Unity (OAU).

1988 Kaunda re-elected unopposed for sixth term.

1990 Multiparty system announced for 1991.

1991 Movement for Multiparty Democracy won landslide election victory; Frederick Chiluba became president.

1992 Food and water shortages caused by severe drought.

ZANU (acronym for Zimbabwe African National Union) political organization founded in 1963 by the Reverend Ndabaningi Sithole and later led by Robert Mugabe. It was banned 1964 by Ian Smith's Rhodesian Front government, against which it conducted a guerrilla war from Zambia until the free elections of 1980, when the ZANU Patriotic Front party, led by Mugabe, won 63% of the vote. In 1987 it merged with ◊ZAPU in preparation for making Zimbabwe a one-party state.

Zapata Emiliano 1879–1919. Mexican Indian revolutionary leader. He led a revolt against dictator Porfirio Díaz (1830–1915) from 1911 under the slogan 'Land and Liberty', to repossess for the indigenous Mexicans the land taken by the Spanish. By 1915 he was driven into retreat, and was assassinated.

ZAPU (acronym *Z*imbabwe *A*frican *P*eople's *U*nion) political organization founded by Joshua Nkomo 1961 and banned 1962 by the Rhodesian government. It engaged in a guerrilla war in alliance with ◊ZANU against the Rhodesian regime until late 1979. In the 1980 elections ZAPU was defeated and was then persecuted by the ruling ZANU Patriotic Front party. In 1987 the two parties merged.

Zentrumspartei German name for the ◊Centre Party 1871–1933.

Zeppelin Ferdinand, Count von Zeppelin 1838–1917. German airship pioneer. On retiring from the army 1891, he devoted himself to the study of aeronautics, and his first airship was built and tested 1900. During World War I a number of Zeppelin airships bombed England. They were also used for luxury passenger transport but the construction of hydrogen-filled airships with rigid keels was abandoned after several disasters in the 1920s and 1930s. Zeppelin also helped to pioneer large multi-engine bomber planes.

Zhao Ziyang 1918– . Chinese politician, prime minister 1980–87 and secretary of the Chinese Communist Party 1987–89. His reforms included self-management and incentives for workers and factories. He lost his secretaryship and other posts after the Tiananmen Square massacre in Beijing June 1989.

Zhelev Zhelyu 1935– . Bulgarian politician, president from 1990. In 1989 he became head of the opposition Democratic Forces coalition. He is a proponent of market-centred economic reform and social peace.

Zhivkov Todor 1911– . Bulgarian Communist Party leader 1954–89, prime minister 1962–71, president 1971–89. His period in office was one of caution and conservatism. In 1991 he was tried for gross embezzlement.

Zhou Enlai or *Chou En-lai* 1898–1976. Chinese politician. Zhou, a member of the Chinese Communist Party (CCP) from the 1920s, was prime minister 1949–76 and foreign minister 1949–58. He was a moderate Maoist and weathered the Cultural Revolution. He played a key role in foreign affairs.

Zhu De or *Chu Teh* 1886–1976. Chinese Red Army leader from 1931. He devised the tactic of mobile guerrilla warfare and organized the ◊Long March to Shaanxi 1934–36. He was made a marshal 1955.

Zhukov Georgi Konstantinovich 1896–1974. Marshal of the USSR in World War II and minister of defence 1955–57. As chief of staff from 1941, he defended Moscow 1941, counterattacked at Stalingrad (now Volgograd) 1942, organized the relief of Leningrad (now St Petersburg) 1943, and led the offensive from the Ukraine March 1944 which ended in the fall of Berlin.

Zia ul-Haq Mohammad 1924–1988. Pakistani general, in power from 1977 until his death, probably an assassination, in an aircraft explosion. He became army chief of staff 1976, led the military coup against Zulfikar Ali ◊Bhutto 1977, and became president 1978. Zia introduced a fundamentalist Islamic regime and restricted political activity.

Zimbabwe extensive stone architectural ruins near Victoria in Mashonaland, Zimbabwe. The structure was probably the work of the Shona people who established their rule about AD 1000 and who mined minerals for trading. The word *zimbabwe* means 'house of stone' in Shona language. The new state of Zimbabwe took its name from these ruins.

chronology
1889–1923 As Southern Rhodesia, under administration of British South Africa Company.
1923 Became a self-governing British colony.
1961 Zimbabwe African People's Union (◊ZAPU) formed, with Joshua ◊Nkomo as leader.
1962 ZAPU declared illegal.
1963 Zimbabwe African National Union (◊ZANU) formed, with Robert ◊Mugabe as secretary general.
1964 Ian ◊Smith became prime minister. ZANU banned. Nkomo and Mugabe imprisoned.
1965 Smith declared unilateral independence.
1966-68 Abortive talks between Smith and UK prime minister Harold Wilson.
1974 Nkomo and Mugabe released.
1975 Geneva conference set date for constitutional independence.
1979 Smith produced new constitution and established a government with Bishop Abel Muzorewa as prime minister. New government denounced by

Nkomo and Mugabe. Conference in London agreed independence arrangements (Lancaster House Agreement).

1980 Independence achieved from Britain, with Robert Mugabe as prime minister.

1981 Rift between Mugabe and Nkomo.

1982 Nkomo dismissed from the cabinet, leaving the country temporarily.

1984 ZANU–Patriotic Front (PF) party congress agreed to create a one-party state in future.

1985 Relations between Mugabe and Nkomo improved. Troops sent to Matabeleland to suppress rumoured insurrection; 5,000 civilians killed.

1986 Joint ZANU–PF rally held amid plans for merger.

1987 White-roll seats in the assembly were abolished. President Banana retired; Mugabe combined posts of head of state and prime minister with the title executive president.

1988 Nkomo returned to the cabinet and was appointed vice president.

1989 Opposition party, the Zimbabwe Unity Movement, formed by Edgar Tekere; draft constitution drawn up, renouncing Marxism–Leninism; ZANU and ZAPU formally merged.

1990 ZANU–PF re-elected. State of emergency ended. Opposition to creation of one-party state.

1992 United Front formed to oppose ZANU–PF. March: Mugabe declared dire drought and famine situation a national disaster

Zimbabwe landlocked country in S central Africa, bounded N by Zambia, E by Mozambique, S by South Africa, and W by Botswana.

Zinoviev Grigory 1883–1936. Russian communist politician whose name was attached to a forgery, the *Zinoviev letter*, inciting Britain's communists to rise, which helped to topple the Labour government 1924.

Zionism political movement advocating the re-establishment of a Jewish homeland in Palestine, the 'promised land' of the Bible, with its capital Jerusalem, the 'city of Zion'.

Zog Ahmed Beg Zogu 1895–1961. King of Albania 1928–39. He became prime minister of Albania 1922, president of the republic 1925, and proclaimed himself king 1928. He was driven out by the Italians 1939 and settled in England.